THE AMERICAN JURY

THE AMERICAN JURY

Harry
KALVEN, Jr.

Hans
ZEISEL

with the collaboration of
THOMAS CALLAHAN and PHILIP ENNIS

THE UNIVERSITY OF CHICAGO PRESS
Chicago and London

Originally published in 1966 by Little, Brown & Company.
© 1966 by Harry Kalven, Jr., and Hans Zeisel.

International Standard Book Number: 0-226-42317-4
Library of Congress Catalog Card Number: 70-149361

The University of Chicago Press, Chicago 60637
The University of Chicago Press, Ltd., London

PREFACE TO PHOENIX EDITION

There have been two major responses to *The American Jury* in the five years since its initial publication: one from the official legal world of the United States Supreme Court and the British House of Commons; the other from reviewers and critics.

The book has been cited and used by the U.S. Supreme Court on some four occasions: Spencer v. Texas,[1] United States v. Jackson,[2] Williams v. Florida,[3] and Duncan v. Louisiana.[4] In two of the instances, it might be noted, the rule in question was held unconstitutional.

Spencer v. Texas involved the jury's reaction to the prior criminal record of the defendant. Under the Texas habitual criminal act, the record of the defendant was allowed to be disclosed to the jury prior to verdict. The disclosure was accompanied by a cautionary instruction from the trial judge that the record was not to be used as evidence in this case and that it had no bearing on guilt or innocence. Defendants challenged their convictions under the act arguing that this use of the record was certain to be prejudicial and indeed was "so egregiously unfair" as to violate the due process clause of the Fourteenth Amendment.

The Court, in a five to four decision, upheld the convictions. *The American Jury* was cited both in the majority opinion and in the dissent. Justice Harlan, writing for the Court, stated:

[1] 385 U.S. 554 (1967).
[2] 390 U.S. 570 (1968).
[3] 399 U.S. 78 (1970).
[4] 391 U.S. 145 (1968).

Indeed the most recent scholarly study of jury behavior does not sustain the premise that juries are especially prone to prejudice when prior-crime evidence is admitted as to credibility. Kalven & Zeisel, *The American Jury* (1966). The study contrasts the effect of such evidence on judges and juries and concludes that "Neither the one nor the other can be said to be distinctively gullible or skeptical." *Id.*, at 180.[5]

And here is Chief Justice Warren in dissent:

Of course it flouts human nature to suppose that a jury would not consider a defendant's previous trouble with the law in deciding whether he has committed the crime currently charged against him. As Mr. Justice Jackson put it in a famous phrase, "[t]he naive assumptions that prejudiced effects can be overcome by instructions to the jury . . . all practicing lawyers know to be unmitigated fiction. . . . Mr. Justice Jackson's assessment has received support from the most ambitious empirical study of jury behavior that has been attempted, see Kalven & Zeisel. *The American Jury,* pp. 127-130, 177-180."[6]

We note with mixed reaction that *The American Jury* has thus joined that distinctive group of books that can be quoted on both sides of the issue. In this particular instance, we would say that Justice Warren, who cites the technical passages, not just a sentence, had us right.

The three other instances involved in varying ways the right to jury trial itself. In U.S. v. Jackson, the Court held unconstitutional a provision of the Federal Kidnapping Act which allowed the death penalty if the victim had not been liberated unharmed, but only if the jury's verdict recommended it. The law thus put a price on the defendant's exercise of his right to jury trial since a jury, and only a jury, could return a verdict of death. The Court held this to be an impermissible burden upon the right to a trial by jury.

At issue, among other points, was the Government's claim "that trial judges have always agreed with jury recommenda-

---

[5] Spencer v. Texas, *supra* note 1; at 565, n. 8 (1967).
[6] *Idem.*, at 575.

tions of capital punishment under the statute...."[7] The Court
referring to data from *The American Jury* (pp. 436-44) found
this "an unrealistic assumption at best."[8]

The American Jury received a passing reference in Williams
v. Florida, in which the Court held that a defendant has no
constitutional right to a twelve-man jury, if a state prefers for
certain cases a somewhat smaller, here a six-man, jury. In
considering the claim that a twelve-man jury might be more
advantageous to the defendant, the Court cited our finding
"that jurors in the minority on the first ballot are likely to be
influenced by the proportional size of the majority aligned
against them. See H. Kalven & H. Zeisel, *The American Jury*,
462-463, 488-489 (1966)...."[9]

The most impressive references to the book came in the May
1968 decision in Duncan v. Louisiana. The defendant had
been convicted of a simple battery, an offense that under Louisiana law was punishable by up to two years imprisonment.
The Louisiana Constitution had restricted the right to jury
trial to major felonies, cases involving capital punishment or
imprisonment at hard labor. As a result, the Louisiana courts
had denied the defendant Duncan's request for trial by jury.
He now claimed that this denial violated his constitutional
rights.

The constitutional issue is somewhat technical and requires
a word of exposition. The Sixth Amendment of the Constitution provides for the right to trial by an impartial jury in all
criminal proceedings. The tradition has long been that the
provisions of the Bill of Rights, the first ten amendments, do
not apply directly to the states but only to the *federal* government. This tradition has been modified in an important way
by use of the "due process" clause of the Fourteenth Amendment which does apply directly to the states. Although the
matter remains a lively source of constitutional controversy,

---

[7] United States v. Jackson, *supra* note 2; also at 574.
[8] *Idem.,* at 574 and n. 8.
[9] Williams v. Florida, *supra* note 3; at 101, n. 49.

the Court in recent decades has been evolving an analysis whereby "fundamental rights" are incorporated into the concept of due process and thus made binding upon the states. The process has been one of moving only a step at a time, weighing carefully the significance of each right. In this fashion, in the past half century, federal standards have been extended over a good deal of important state law including, for example, freedom of speech, right to counsel, and freedom from unreasonable searches and seizures.

In a seven to two decision the Supreme Court held that Duncan's rights had been violated. The underlying premise was that jury trial as defined by the Sixth Amendment was another of those fundamental rights implied in the idea of due process of law. The occasion produced a sharp and interesting debate between Justice White writing for the majority and Justice Harlan writing this time for the dissent, a debate that in considerable part turned on their respective evaluations of the merits of trial by jury. The case thus served to add some pages to the long tradition of debate over the jury which we sketch in Chapter 1, but our immediate interest centers on the use the Court made of *The American Jury*.

The complex issue is captured with precision in the opening of Justice Harlan's dissent:

> Every American jurisdiction provides for trial by jury in criminal cases. The question before us is not whether jury trial is an ancient institution, which it is; nor whether it plays a significant role in the administration of criminal justice, which it does; nor whether it will endure, which it shall. The question in this case is whether the State of Louisiana which provides trial by jury for all felonies, is prohibited by the Constitution from trying charges of simple battery to the court alone. In my view, the answer to that question, mandated alike by our constitutional history and by the longer history of trial by jury, is clearly "no".[10]

The American Jury is cited six times in all, three times by

[10] Duncan v. Louisiana, *supra* note 4, at 171-2.

Justice White and three times by Justice Harlan.[11] The crucial reference is in the majority opinion after Justice White has reviewed various criticisms of the jury. "[A]t the heart of the dispute," he says, "have been express or implicit assertions that juries are incapable of adequately understanding evidence or determining issues of fact, and that they are unpredictable, quixotic, and little better than a roll of dice."[12] He meets the contention with the following passage:[13]

> Yet, the most recent and exhaustive study of the jury in criminal cases concluded that juries do understand the evidence and come to sound conclusions in most of the cases presented to them and that when juries differ with the result at which the judge would have arrived, it is usually because they are serving some of the very purposes for which they were created and for which they are now employed.[26]

Footnote 26 is to *The American Jury.*

The British use of *The American Jury* occurred in 1967 when the government proposed to abolish the unanimity requirement for criminal juries and to substitute 11 to 1 and 10 to 2 verdicts. In the ensuing debate both in the House of Commons[14] and in the Press,[15] the book was actively cited by opponents of the measure. They used it to support two lines of argument: (1) to predict that the change would not affect more than about two of every hundred trials; (2) to refute the popular notion that hung juries are the result of one lone "hanging juror" who is either eccentric or corrupt; rather hung juries reflect, as a rule, the serious doubts initially entertained by a sizable minority of the jury.[16] Although the measure

---

[11] *Idem.,* at 157, n. 24; 157, n. 26; 158, n. 29; 189, n. 37; 190, n. 42; 192, n. 51.

[12] *Idem.,* at 157.

[13] *Idem.*

[14] House of Commons Official Report (Hansard) v. 745, No. 188, cols. 1763–1784, 1847–1964. 27 April 1967.

[15] *The Times* (London) editorial page, 4 April 1967.

[16] *The American Jury,* p. 462.

was finally passed, observers were impressed with how close the vote became.[17]

This use of our data and opinions in the law-making process in the United States and Great Britain[18] reassures us that *The American Jury* achieved its purpose "simply to find out how in fact the jury is performing." We added, prophetically, "the study will have relevance for both the critics and the defenders of the jury system and will provide fresh material for the debate."

The second major response to our book has come of course from reviewers and critics. In the book we set out and succeeded, we feel, in three main objectives: we produced a systematic empirical study of a central legal institution; we produced a *book*, a coherent, consecutive essay despite the interlarding of over 100 statistical tables; finally and perhaps most important in the long run, we made clear the assumptions underlying each analytical step—not in an appendix but in the text itself—so that the reader if he wishes can follow the methodology and reach his own judgments about the weaknesses or strengths of particular lines of inquiry and proof.

A number of our lawyer reviewers—we had few others[19]—found this opportunity to assess method most attractive, and in good lawyer fashion, exploited it to the full. Many of them for the moment became social scientists, and some made even a good job of it.

[17] Cf. *Chicago Bar Record*, v. 48, pp. 195-201.

[18] *The American Jury* played also a significant role in the legal debates of a country outside the Anglo-American orbit. Austria, on its 1970 *Congress of Jurists,* discussed the possibility of reform of its jury system and the reporter, Professor Friedrich Nowakowski, and the discussants referred repeatedly to the findings of *The American Jury*.

[19] Which throws an interesting side light on the departmentalization of the social sciences in spite of efforts towards integration. Of the two leading American sociological journals only one reviewed the book and that one only briefly since the reviewer, a small-group expert, had expected to find an investigation of the jury deliberation process which, of course, was not the book's major topic.

Since we had carried out our intention to use to their limits the unique and valuable data we had obtained with difficulty, some critics felt these limits were set too generously. In varying degrees and with varying sophistication they noted and commented on the calculated risks we took in our key methodological choices: relying on the hypothetical decisions by the judge in what were real cases for the jury; relying too on the judge's perception of jury motivation, and on our hand-tailored method of analyzing the causes of the differences between judge and jury.

This is not the occasion to discuss at length points of methodological criticism. Our reviewers did not, we feel, add appreciably to our own explicit commentary on our methodology. Two observations may, however, be in order. First, the critics had the mistaken impression that questions of method can indeed be ultimately decided by reasoning alone. They did not perceive sufficiently that social-science research always evinces tension between the canons of ideal methodology and the opportunities for inquiry realistically available. They did not see that such research requires not only logic but also prudence.

Secondly, the critics did not perceive that in a research effort that covers many facets of a complex institution, not all claims are put forward with the same high level of confidence; some minor "findings" are not more than hypotheses suggested by marginal evidence. If and when new evidence is produced, many hypotheses of ours may have to be qualified or may indeed fall. But nothing less than new evidence can bring this about.[20]

On the whole we believe our lawyer critics learned more about social science methodology from us than we from them.

[20] A study of the role of Austrian lay-judges as members of criminal tribunals, now in progress, revealed impressive similarities with juror reactions here in the United States. A similar, more ambitious study of the role of lay-judges in the German Criminal Courts is being conducted by our colleague Professor Gerhard Casper.

Upon rereading *The American Jury* now with the benefit of five years hindsight, we are inclined on balance to make those same methodological choices again. We would not do the book differently if we had to do it all over again.

Finally, we would express our pleasure and our pride that five years after its publication the book is to have so attractive a second debut.

HARRY KALVEN, JR.
HANS ZEISEL

PREFACE TO FIRST EDITION

This book, like the prior volume, *Delay in the Court,* which appeared in 1959, is a result of the study of the American jury system undertaken at the University of Chicago Law School pursuant to a magnificent grant from the Ford Foundation.

The original program had a threefold thrust. It was to bring together into a working partnership the lawyer and the social scientist; in a phrase we have often used, the hope was to marry the research skills and fresh perspectives of the one to the socially significant problems of the other, and in the end to produce a new scholarship and literature for both. If it is tolerable to contrast sharply library research with field research, it was the intention that this be field research: that we do more than collate existing social science writings with a series of legal problems, that new data be collected about old legal institutions. And it was the intent that it be not a pilot effort but the real thing, the full gamble of money, energy, and time.

The venture turned out to be more ambitious than we originally anticipated. The collection of the data involved new problems of diplomacy and public relations; the analysis of it was rich in unexpected impasses; and, finally, the writing, the development of style to blend legal meaning with statistical measurement, proved extraordinarily difficult. In brief, it has taken a long time to get this far.

While, for reasons set forth in Chapters 38 and 39, we find the comparison between judge and jury decisions increasingly central to the study of the jury, we want to say that the present volume will be complemented by other lines of jury research.

One strength of the project was that it permitted multiple

lines of inquiry.   Aside from studying judge-jury differences by surveying the totality of the jury's business, we conducted experiments on sharply defined issues, such as the jury's handling of the defense of insanity, the impact of insurance, the response to the contributory negligence rule; conducted post-trial interviews, both in extended free-flowing conversations and with structured questionnaires; and examined jury selection procedures and voir dire strategies.   We also conducted opinion polls on the jury among judges, lawyers, and the community at large.   And we made the investigation of the costs of the jury system which led to *Delay in the Court*.

There will, therefore, be more books forthcoming.   We have begun work on the companion study of judge-jury differences in civil cases.   Since we never learn from experience, we are confident of readying it for publication within the next eighteen months.   One book-length study is now in the final stages of editing: Rita James Simon's examinations of the jury's handling of the defense of insanity, an experimental sequence testing the impact of varying instructions on the law of insanity.

As the work has proceeded, the project has published in law reviews and social science journals some sixty or so articles on various aspects of the jury.   Fred L. Strodtbeck, who worked out the intricate methodology for the mock experiments and who brought the insights of the social psychologist to the project, has published a number of papers on the jury deliberation process.   Dale Broeder, who at one time accompanied a federal district judge on circuit, has reported in detail on some of his interviews with the jurors.   These interim publications represent in themselves an important harvest; a bibliography is appended at the end of this study.

The jury study has had one special burden to bear along with all the customary difficulties of large-scale research.   At one point one of its research approaches generated a national scandal.   As one of several lines of approach, it was decided to obtain recordings of actual jury deliberations, partly to learn whether post-trial interviews with jurors permit reconstruc-

tion of the events of the jury room. The move was undertaken, with the consent of the trial judge and counsel, but
without the knowledge of the jurors, in five civil cases in the
federal district court in Wichita, Kansas. Although extensive
security measures were taken to insure the integrity of the effort, when the fact became public in the summer of 1955, there
followed public censure by the Attorney General of the United
States, a special hearing before the Sub-Committee on Internal
Security of the Senate Judiciary Committee, the enactment of
statutes in some thirty-odd jurisdictions prohibiting jury-
tapping, and for a brief, painful moment, widespread editorial and news coverage by the national press.

None of the Wichita data is included in this book, nor will
it be included in future books. We note the episode here simply to make clear to that man who would say, "That's all very
interesting, professors, but did you ever hear a real jury deliberate?" that the answer is Yes, and to point out that one of the
distinctions of the jury study is that it is a research project that
has a Purple Heart.

The roster of those who have worked on the Jury Project is
an extraordinary one, and it provides a ready index of the
scope of the work and the quality of the effort: Philip B.
Kurland and Bernard D. Meltzer, who served as directors of
the Project in what might be called its formative years, and
Fred Strodtbeck, Rita James Simon, Tom Callahan, Philip
Ennis, Dale Broeder, Allan Barton, Saul Mendlovitz, Joseph
Hamburger, Bernard Buchholz, Abner Mikva, Jean Allard,
Kathleen Beaufait, Ritchie Davis, Elaine Mohr Goodman,
George Kaufman, Jaro Mayda, Gerhard Mueller, and Victor
Stone.

The Project owes a distinctive debt to Edward H. Levi, now
Provost of the University of Chicago. He is the principal ar-
chitect of the whole venture; it was his energy and his insight
that sparked it and his enthusiasm that did much to sustain it.

We thank Francis A. Allen, who was kind enough to read
the manuscript. And we cannot leave without acknowledging
the continued generosity of the University of Chicago in as-

sisting with the financing, and without saluting Dean Phil C. Neal, who has been quickly supportive of our needs, patient with our pace, and generous with his personal interest in our materials.

A personal word of thanks, too, to our secretary, Mrs. Mildred Nash South, whose patience and skill in typing and re-typing the many drafts of this manuscript must rank high in the annals of secretarial heroism; to Mrs. Carole Simon of Little, Brown, who with love and care supervised the making of this book, and to her chief, Rodney Robertson, a great gentleman.

We are least adequate in acknowledging our great debt to the 555 trial judges throughout the United States who, with patience, literary verve, and great insight, filled out 3576 trial questionnaires. They, of course, are the true authors of the book.

The final word of gratitude goes, we suspect, to the jury itself. Over the long decade of this research we have been supported by many things, but most happily by the intellectual interest the jury materials continued to hold for us.

H.K.Jr.   H.Z.

Chicago
March 1966

CONTENTS

APPENDICES

THE AMERICAN JURY

*T*HE FIRST GROUP of chapters, moving from topic to methods to findings, provides an introduction to the study as a whole. The first two chapters complement each other. Chapter 1 outlines the history of the controversy over the jury system. It serves to remind that the study is one of a living institution which has a long intellectual tradition. From it we inherit a framework against which to place our fresh empirical findings. Chapter 2 places the jury in its present-day context. It sketches the universe of the contemporary criminal jury trial and the legal and behavioral factors which determine its extent.

Studies of social institutions necessarily proceed by way of inference; it is imperative to make accessible not only what we know but how we know it. The next two chapters thus open a discussion of methodology. Chapter 3 makes clear the merits and the shortcomings of the sample of 3576 cases, and Chapter 4 provides an exposition of the research design — a mail questionnaire completed by trial judges — on which this study is based.

Chapters 5 and 6 disclose basic findings. Chapter 5 discusses the core table on the magnitude and direction of judge-jury disagreement. Chapter 6 adds color and specificity to this data by presenting tables for forty-two crime categories, from Murder to Drunken Driving.

CHAPTER 1

The Problem and Its Tradition

The Anglo-American jury is a remarkable political institution. We have had it with us for so long that any sense of surprise over its main characteristics has perhaps somewhat dulled. It recruits a group of twelve laymen, chosen at random from the widest population; it convenes them for the purpose of the particular trial; it entrusts them with great official powers of decision; it permits them to carry on deliberations in secret and to report out their final judgment without giving reasons for it; and, after their momentary service to the state has been completed, it orders them to disband and return to private life. The jury thus represents a deep commitment to the use of laymen in the administration of justice, a commitment that finds its analogue in the widespread use of lay judges in the criminal courts of other countries.[1] It opposes the cadre of

[1] Lay judges have been a persistent part of the administration of criminal justice since antiquity. During the Middle Ages Europe developed two forms of lay participation in the criminal process, independently both of each other and of the Greco-Roman tradition: on the European continent, the scabini or Schöffen, and in England the jury. See Dawson, A History of Lay Judges (1960).

The Schöffen courts have survived in the mixed tribunals which today are the principal triers of criminal cases in Central, Eastern and Northern Europe. The jury migrated from its English home in two directions. The expanding orbit of the English law took it through what was then the British Empire. The French revolution and its aftermath brought it to Europe, where since Montesquieu's *Esprit des Lois* the jury had been looked at as democracy's way of administering criminal justice. From France the jury spread across Europe and further, first under the direct impact of the revolution and the Napoleonic conquest and, after 1848, more permanently when the second revolutionary wave

professional, experienced judges with this transient, ever-changing, ever-inexperienced group of amateurs. The jury is thus by definition an exciting experiment in the conduct of serious human affairs, and it is not surprising that, virtually from its inception, it has been the subject of deep controversy, attracting at once the most extravagant praise and the most harsh criticism.

The jury controversy has recruited some of the great names of political philosophy and the law: Alexander Hamilton, de Tocqueville, Blackstone, Montesquieu, Bentham, Spencer, Livingston, Holmes, Stephen, Corbin, Wigmore, Pound, Sunderland; and, more recently, Frank, Curtis, Green, Wyzanski, Bok, Glanville Williams, Denning, Devlin, and Griswold.[2]

Yet this long tradition of controversy over the jury system

---

carried democratic institutions eastward across the continent as far as Czarist Russia, which instituted jury trial in 1864.

On the whole, the European graft did not take well. See Ch. 2, note 3. But while the jury in recent decades has lost some ground, the principle of lay participation in the criminal process is more firmly established than ever. In the large, only the Near East and Japan and some of the Latin American countries have left the criminal trial exclusively to the learned judiciary. For a general bibliography of the jury in the United States and in other countries, see Pound, Seagle, Jury, in Encyc. Soc. Sci., v. 8, pp. 492-502 (1932).

[2] A complete bibliography on praise and blame of the jury would be formidable; we list a sampling: Livingston, A System of Penal Law for the State of Louisiana, pp. 10 et seq. (1833); Pound, Law in Books and Law in Action, Am. L. Rev., v. 44, p. 12 (1910); Sunderland, Verdicts, General and Special, Yale L.J., v. 29, p. 253 (1920); Wigmore, A Program for the Trial of a Jury Trial, J. Am. Jud. Soc., v. 12, p. 166 (1929); Green, Judge and Jury (1930); Frank, Law and the Modern Mind, Ch. XVI (1930); Frank, Courts on Trial (1949); Curtis, The Trial Judge and the Jury, Vand. L. Rev., v. 5, p. 150 (1952); Wyzanski, A Trial Judge's Freedom and Responsibility, Harv. L. Rev., v. 65, p. 1281 (1952); Devlin, Trial by Jury (1956); Williams, The Proof of Guilt (3d ed. 1963). See also, Broeder, The Functions of the Jury: Facts or Fictions, U. Chi. L. Rev., v. 21, p. 386 (1954). A reasonably complete bibliography on the jury debate was prepared by Professor Dale Broeder for the University of Chicago Jury Project as a staff memorandum; ironically it owes its publication to the Congressional hearings on jury tapping. See Hearing Before the Subcommittee to Investigate the Administration of the Internal Security Act of the Senate Committee on the Judiciary, 84th Cong., 1st Sess., pp. 63-81 (1955).

has produced unsatisfactory debate. Much of the criticism has stemmed from not more than the a priori guess that, since the jury was employing laymen amateurs in what must be a technical and serious business, it could not be a good idea. In comparable fashion, the enthusiasts of the jury have tended to lapse into sentimentality and to equate literally the jury with democracy. Not surprisingly, therefore, the very characteristics which the critics point to as defects, the jury's champions herald as assets.

The wide range of opinions about the jury is easily documented.[3] We begin with a very recent statement by one of the critics. The Dean of the Harvard Law School, in the course of his annual report for 1962-1963, made certain recommendations for improving the administration of justice, among them the abolition of the jury in civil cases. Dean Griswold argued:

> The jury trial at best is the apotheosis of the amateur. Why should anyone think that 12 persons brought in from the street, selected in various ways, for their lack of general ability, should have any special capacity for deciding controversies between persons?[4]

The more exasperated form of criticism is illustrated by the following excerpt from an article in the *American Bar Association Journal* in 1924:

> Too long has the effete and sterile jury system been permitted to tug at the throat of the nation's judiciary as it sinks under the smothering deluge of the obloquy of those it was designed to serve. Too long has ignorance been permitted to sit ensconced in the places of judicial administration where knowledge is so sorely needed. Too long has the lament of the Shakespearean character been echoed, "Justice has fled to brutish beasts and men have lost their reason."[5]

[3] The Jury Project has also conducted an opinion survey among the judiciary on the jury system, from which some findings are set forth in Chapter 37. The Jury Project will present at a future time a complete report of the data.

[4] 1962-1963 Harvard Law School Dean's Report, pp. 5-6.

[5] Sebille, Trial by Jury: An Ineffective Survival, A.B.A.J., v. 10, pp. 53, 55 (1924).

And to add still another unfriendly voice, the distinguished English scholar Glanville Williams, in the Seventh Series of Hamlyn Lectures in 1955 had, among other things, this to say of the jury:

> If one proceeds by the light of reason, there seems to be a formidable weight of argument against the jury system. To begin with, the twelve men and women are chosen haphazard. There is a slight property qualification — too slight to be used as an index of ability, if indeed the mere possession of property can ever be so used; on the other hand, exemption is given to some professional people who would seem to be among the best qualified to serve — clergymen, ministers of religion, lawyers, doctors, dentists, chemists, justices of the peace (as well as all ranks of the armed forces). The subtraction of relatively intelligent classes means that it is an understatement to describe a jury, with Herbert Spencer, as a group of twelve people of average ignorance. There is no guarantee that members of a particular jury may not be quite unusually ignorant, credulous, slow-witted, narrow-minded, biased or temperamental. The danger of this happening is not one that can be removed by some minor procedural adjustment; it is inherent in the English notion of a jury as a body chosen from the general population at random.[6]

The defenders of the jury are equally emphatic. Lord Justice Devlin, an experienced and greatly admired English judge, may speak here for them. In 1956, in the Eighth Hamlyn Lecture Series, he said of the jury:

> Each jury is a little parliament. The jury sense is the parliamentary sense. I cannot see the one dying and the other surviving. The first object of any tyrant in Whitehall would be to make Parliament utterly subservient to his will; and the next to overthrow or diminish trial by jury, for no tyrant could afford to leave a subject's freedom in the hands of twelve of his countrymen. So that trial by jury is more than an instrument of justice and more than one wheel of the constitution: it is the lamp that shows that freedom lives.[7]

[6] Williams, The Proof of Guilt, pp. 271-272 (3d ed. 1963).
[7] Devlin, Trial by Jury, p. 164 (1956).

Justice Devlin found it appropriate to conclude his lectures on the jury by quoting the famous passage from Blackstone, the words of which, he said, are still "after two centuries as fresh and meaningful as when they were written":

> So that the liberties of England cannot but subsist, so long as this *palladium* remains sacred and inviolate; not only from all open attacks, (which none will be so hardy as to make), but also from all secret machinations, which may sap and undermine it; by introducing new and arbitrary methods of trial, by justices of the peace, commissioners of the revenue, and courts of conscience. And however *convenient* these may appear at first, (as doubtless all arbitrary powers, well executed, are the most *convenient*) yet let it be again remembered, that delays, and little inconveniences in the forms of justice, are the price that all free nations must pay for their liberty in more substantial matters; that these inroads upon this sacred bulwark of the nation are fundamentally opposite to the spirit of our constitution; and that, though begun in trifles, the precedent may gradually increase and spread, to the utter disuse of juries in questions of the most momentous concern.[8]

Thus, after two hundred years, the debate over the jury system, with distinguished participants on both sides, is still going on apace.

This is not the occasion to review the debate systematically. It may be useful, however, to suggest its broad outline. The controversy centers around three large issues. First, there is a series of collateral advantages and disadvantages that are often charged against, or pointed to on behalf of, the jury as an institution. In this realm fall such positive points as that the jury provides an important civic experience for the citizen; that, because of popular participation, the jury makes tolerable the stringency of certain decisions; that, because of its transient personnel, the jury acts as a sort of lightning rod for animosity and suspicion which otherwise might center on the more permanent judge; and that the jury is a guarantor of integrity, since it is said to be more difficult to reach twelve men than

[8] Commentaries, v. IV, p. 350 (11th ed. 1791).

one. Against such affirmative claims, serious collateral disadvantages have been urged, chiefly that the jury is expensive; that it contributes to delay in civil litigation; that jury service imposes an unfair tax and social cost on those forced to serve; and that, in general, exposure to jury duty disenchants the citizen and causes him to lose confidence in the administration of justice.

Second, there is a group of issues that touch directly on the competence of the jury. Here the debate has been fascinating but bitter. On the one hand, it is urged that the judge, as a result of training, discipline, recurrent experience, and superior intelligence, will be better able to understand the law and analyze the facts than laymen, selected from a wide range of intelligence levels, who have no particular experience with matters of this sort, and who have no durable official responsibility. On the other hand, it is argued that twelve heads are inevitably better than one; that the jury as a group has wisdom and strength which need not characterize any of its individual members; that it makes up in common sense and common experience what it may lack in professional training, and that its very inexperience is an asset because it secures a fresh perception of each trial, avoiding the stereotypes said to infect the judicial eye.

The third group of issues about the jury goes to what is perhaps the most interesting point. The critics complain that the jury will not follow the law, either because it does not understand it or because it does not like it, and that thus only a very uneven and unequal administration of justice can result from reliance on the jury; indeed, it is said that the jury is likely to produce that government by man, and not by rule of law, against which Anglo-American political tradition is so steadfastly set.

This same flexibility of the jury is offered by its champions as its most endearing and most important characteristic. The jury, it is said, is a remarkable device for insuring that we are governed by the spirit of the law and not by its letter; for insuring that rigidity of any general rule of law can be shaped to justice in the particular case. One is tempted to say that what is one man's equity is another man's anarchy.

From even so brief a summary, it is apparent that there is little chance that the debate over the jury will soon be resolved; it is too threaded with difficult value judgments. For the special purposes of this book, however, three characteristics emerge as salient. First, most praise or blame of the jury can come only by way of the comparison of trial by jury with trial by a judge, the one serious and significant alternative to it.

Thus, throughout the jury controversy there is at least the implicit assumption on both sides that the decisions of the jury will sometimes and to some degree be different from those that would be given by the judge in the same case. Its critics point to these differences as evidence of the jury's fallibility and incompetence; its champions point to these differences as proof of the jury's distinctive function and its strength.

Second, most of the unrest over the jury today is limited to its use in civil trials.[9] It is agreed that the case for the jury in criminal trials is different and much stronger.

Third, while in no small part the jury controversy is clearly in the realm of value judgments and is but a variation on the age-old theme of rule versus equity, nevertheless much of the argument appears to rest on assumptions as to what the facts are — the facts, that is, as to how the jury actually performs. The present book reports an investigation into these facts. It is an effort to provide data on the actual decision-making by juries and judges. Its single purpose is to attempt to an-

[9] See generally, Kalven, The Dignity of the Civil Jury, Va. L. Rev., v. 50, p. 1055 (1964). See also Green, Juries and Justice — The Jury's Role in Personal Injury Cases, 1962 U. Ill. L. F., p. 152; Joiner, Civil Justice and the Jury (1962). The argument about the jury in civil cases has become much involved with the problem of court congestion. For a recent criticism by a distinguished New York judge, see Desmond, Should It Take 34 Months for a Jury Trial? N.Y. Times, Dec. 8, 1963 (Magazine), p. 29. For an estimate of the impact of the jury on delay, see Zeisel, Kalven, and Buchholz, Delay in the Court, Ch. 6 (1959).

swer the question when do trial by judge and trial by jury
lead to divergent results.

As a matter of both theoretical interest and methodological
convenience, we study the performance of the jury measured
against the performance of the judge as a baseline.   Our
material is a massive sample of actual criminal jury trials
conducted in the United States in recent years.   For each of
these trials we have the actual decision of the jury and a
communication from the trial judge, telling how he would
have disposed of that case had it been tried before him without
a jury.   In this sense, we have been able to execute the grand
experiment of having each case, over the wide universe of
contemporary jury business in the criminal law, tried by a
jury and also by a judge, thus obtaining matched verdicts
for study.   The result is a systematic view of how often the
jury disagrees with the judge, of the direction of such disagreement, and an assessment of the reasons for it.

From what has been said about the method it is not easy
to anticipate the full scope of the study.   Trial by judge and
trial by jury will emerge not simply as two different modes of
adjudication, but as different systems of law.   In that sense
this is a comparative study of two legal cultures, that of the
jury and that of the judge.

We would, however, emphasize that this research operation opens only a limited view on the behavior of the jury.
We can answer questions about the jury only in terms of a
comparison with the judge.   If, for example, we wish to
know whether a given factor, such as the defendant's being a
cripple, or the skill of counsel, or the commenting on evidence
by the judge, has any effect on the jury, we can answer only
by measuring what effect such factors have on the jury's propensity to agree or disagree with the judge.   But while as a
matter of clarity, it is important to emphasize this limitation,
it is also important not to make too much of it.   It will turn
out that through this special window one is able to observe a
very considerable amount of jury behavior.   For the most
part, the impact of a factor on the jury's propensity to agree

or disagree with the judge is a good, and perhaps the only practicable, index of its impact on the jury.

While this book then is essentially an empirical study of the jury in operation, we would pause to note its broader implications. It is a contribution to what has often been called realist jurisprudence; it is an effort to find out how the law in operation, as contrasted to the law on the books, is working. There are innumerable other instances of unwritten law in action besides those afforded by the jury, and the study may, therefore, be taken as some indication of what empirical efforts to map out the law in action can yield.[10]

Second, as will become more apparent as we proceed, the book links up with questions about legal decision-making generally, and especially with what the American law has found to be an endlessly fascinating topic: the decision-making of judges. Here again the book can be taken as some indication of what empirical study of the judicial process may yield.

In its concern with measuring jury against judge, the study is, of course, a contribution to the debate over the merits of the jury system. A word of qualification, however, is needed. It is not its purpose to decide whether the jury is a good institution. The purpose has been simply to find out how in fact the jury is performing. The study will have relevance for both the critics and the defenders of the jury system and will provide fresh material for the jury debate. It certainly will not terminate it.

[10] During recent years a number of rigorous empirical studies have made their appearance, among them, Conard *et al.,* Automobile Accident Costs and Payments (1964); La Fave, Arrest: The Decision to Take a Suspect into Custody (1965); Rosenberg, The Pretrial Conference and Effective Justice (1964). For its tremendous impact the bail bond experiment of the Vera Foundation deserves mention here: Ares, Rankin, and Sturz, The Manhattan Bail Project: In Interim Report on the Use of Pre-Trial Parole, N.Y.U.L. Rev., v. 38, p. 67 (1963). One might note also the emergence of centers attempting to apply social science inquiries to legal institutions at Columbia, Berkeley, and Wisconsin. For a general survey of these developments see Zeisel, The Law, in Uses of Sociology (Lazarsfeld ed. 1966).

CHAPTER 2

The Extent of the Criminal Jury
in the United States

Before turning directly to our data, it will be useful to look briefly at the nature and extent of the universe we are to study. It can be defined as criminal jury trials in the United States during the midfifties. The wretched state of judicial statistics permits only a rough approximation of its size. Our best estimate is that in the year 1955 approximately 60,000 criminal jury cases were tried through to a verdict.[1] Another 20,000 jury trials, or so, begin but do not terminate in a verdict, either because the defendant decides to plead guilty, or the prosecutor moves to dismiss, or the judge directs an acquittal or declares a mistrial because of some procedural violation or because the jury hangs. But there are hardly any data available on the frequency of these prematurely terminated trials.[2]

The United States emerges as the major home of the crimi-

---

[1] The estimated number of jury trials is derived from state-by-state reports, answers to special inquiries, and from special surveys made by the authors. The detailed results are presented in Appendix A. Apparently only nine of the fifty states and the federal system have a complete count of the annual number of criminal jury trials; thirteen states publish partial statistics; fourteen have no idea of how many jury trials occur in the jurisdiction, while the remaining states can offer approximations of varying precision. New York, for instance, estimates it has "about 3,000" criminal jury trials per year.

The reports that are issued on criminal proceedings vary immensely in format and items deemed significant. There is an acute need for adopting some minimum uniform statistical standards throughout the nation.

[2] See Appendix A.

nal jury trial; it probably accounts for not less than 80 per cent of all criminal jury trials in the world today.[3]

[3] Only rough estimates are possible. Outside the United States the largest number of criminal jury trials are held within the United Kingdom. For England and Wales, the number is about five or six thousand a year, Devlin, Trial by Jury, p. 130 (1956). Adding the rest of the British Commonwealth and the remainder of the world, we can probably double this figure.

On the whole, the scope of jury trial outside the ambit of Anglo-American countries, though not that of lay judges, has been steadily declining. See Chapter 1, note 1. Historically, wherever the jury was adopted it came as a symbol of democratic government, and any revival of absolutist forces became a threat to the existence of the jury. As time went on, the development of a democratic, independent judiciary tended to deprive the supporters of the jury of an important argument.

The inroads into the jury system were made through a variety of devices. One was simply for the government to remove certain critical crime categories from the jurisdiction of the jury to the ordinary courts. Prussia removed treason in 1850, only two years after jury trial had been instituted; the duchy of Nassau removed all political crimes in 1851; and almost a century later, Czechoslovakia, hard pressed by its ethnic irredenta, resorted to the same device; in 1923 it removed treason, and one year later libel, to the ordinary courts. Hungary suspended jury trial in 1919; it has never been restored there since.

A second method of emasculating the jury was to curtail its power even where it remained the trier of the case. This was done primarily by increasing the influence of the presiding learned judges, either by widening their power of instructing the jury, or by permitting them to be present at the jury's deliberation — as was the case in France — or by widening their power to set the jury verdict aside if they thought it to be in error. In Austria, under the present law, the three presiding judges, if they are unanimous, may set the jury verdict aside and order a new trial, but only once in each case.

Finally, some countries, such as Holland in 1813 and Luxembourg in 1814, and a century later Portugal in 1926, simply abolished jury trial altogether and transferred all trial power to the learned judges. Japan repealed its short-lived jury courts in 1943. Germany and France, while retaining the jury in name, replaced it by what is in fact a mixed tribunal. Germany replaced the jury in 1924 by the *Schwurgericht,* which consists of 6 jurors and 3 learned judges, and France under the Vichy regime replaced it by a court of 7 jurors and 3 judges. Such mixed tribunals, in a variety of numerical combinations, are the predominant mode of trial throughout central, eastern, and northern Europe.

Today, outside the Anglo-Saxon law orbit, only a few countries have

Standing by itself, however, this total number of jury trials does not mean very much. This chapter is devoted to placing the total in context. It will attempt to isolate the factors which go to determine the size of the jury trial universe, and will try to locate the position of the jury trial in the totality of the criminal process.

A fundamental fact about the jury trial is that it is the mode of final disposition for only a small fraction of all criminal prosecutions.[4] Taking, for the moment, the number of these prosecutions as given, there are three factors that determine the universe of jury trials. One of them is fixed by law; the other two are choices that, as a rule, the law leaves open to the defendant. The factors are (1) the availability of jury trial as a matter of right, (2) the decision to plead guilty rather than to stand trial, and (3) the choice as between jury trial and a trial before a judge without a jury.

The interplay of these factors is interesting and complex. We begin with the law. Contrary to widespread popular im-

---

retained the jury, defined as a group of ad hoc assembled lay judges who, without participation of the learned judges, decide at least the question of guilt. Austria, Belgium, Norway, Denmark, Greece, Geneva and some other Swiss cantons, and some of the Latin American countries are the hold-outs. See generally, Seagle, Jury: Other Countries (Ch. 1, note 1), and Gorphe, Reform of the Jury System in European Countries. J. of Crim. L. and Crimin., v. 27, pp. 17, 155 (Wigmore trans. 1936).

[4] The number of criminal prosecutions itself depends in the first instance on the frequency of crimes and the rate of apprehension. In addition, both the police and the prosecutor, and in some situations the grand jury, exercise a considerable amount of discretion in deciding whether or not to prosecute. Concerning the police, see La Fave, Arrest: The Decision to Take a Suspect into Custody (1965), a volume in the American Bar Foundation's series on Administration of Criminal Justice; Goldstein, Police Discretion Not to Invoke the Criminal Process: Low Visibility Decisions in the Administration of Justice, Yale L.J., v. 69, p. 543 (1960). Concerning the prosecutor, see Kaplan, The Prosecutorial Discretion, Nw. U.L. Rev., v. 60, p. 174 (1965), and Miller, Prosecution (to be published in the American Bar Foundation series, of which Professor Remington is the editor). One of the determinants of the decision whether to prosecute is the expected reaction of the jury. See also Skolnick, Justice Without Trial (1966).

pression, trial by jury is not available to the criminal defendant as a matter of law in all situations.   The right to trial by
jury, although enshrined in the Sixth Amendment of the Federal Constitution and in various specific provisions in state
constitutions, has generally been taken to mean the right as it
stood at common law at the time of the adoption of the Constitution.   But the common law, despite its veneration for the
jury, always recognized a wide range of petty offenses which
were tried summarily before a magistrate without the inter-
position of a jury.[5]

The American states, as might be expected, exhibit considerable variation in the way they have exercised their freedom

[5] This remains the principal architecture of the criminal law today.
Puttkammer, Administration of Criminal Law, pp. 87, 174-175 (1953).
The classic article by Frankfurter and Corcoran, Petty Federal Offenses
and the Constitutional Guarantee of Trial by Jury, Harv. L. Rev., v. 39,
p. 917 (1926), argued that even under the unqualified right to jury trial
granted by the Sixth Amendment in federal cases there is, as a constitutional matter, an implied exemption of petty offenses; but see Kaye,
Petty Offenders Have No Peers!   U. Chi. L. Rev., v. 26, p. 245 (1959).
It has never been decided whether the Constitution, as a matter of due
process, requires trial by jury for all criminal cases, largely because no
state has ventured to abolish jury trials for serious crimes.   There are
dicta suggesting that the jury is not an element of "ordered liberty"
and is, therefore, not mandatory upon the states.   Palko v. Connecticut,
302 U.S. 319, 324 (1937).

Mr. Justice Brennan, however, has recently expressed doubt whether
the Court would permit the states to abandon jury trials for serious
offenses.   See Brennan, The Bill of Rights and the States, Ch. IV in
The Great Rights (Cahn ed. 1963).

In England, the country of the jury's origin, the scope of the criminal
jury trial is limited to "indictable offenses," loosely the equivalent of
our felonies; the minor or summary offenses are tried before a lay magistrate without a jury.   There are an estimated 350 types of offenses
for which trial is in the exclusive jurisdiction of these magistrates.
See Frankfurter and Corcoran, above, at p. 934.   For all but the most
serious offenses, the defendant may waive the jury and elect to be tried
by a magistrate, thereby insuring a ceiling on the extent of the penalty
that can be imposed.   Approximately eight out of ten defendants
charged with indictable offenses do opt for such trial.   Devlin, Trial
by Jury, p. 130 (1956).   Thus, the great group of petty offenses, and
very much the larger part of the indictable offenses, are tried without
a jury.

within the constitutional framework to allow or disallow jury trials for minor crimes.

At one end are the states that allow jury trial only upon the charge of a major crime.[6] In these states, as would be expected, the number of jury trials is relatively small. Thus, Connecticut had in 1955 only 66 criminal jury trials, or 3 jury trials per 100,000 population, as against a national average of some 35 per 100,000 population.[7] At the other end are states, mostly southern ones, that allow jury trial on a much wider range of criminal charges.[8] As a result of this broad legal franchise, Georgia, for instance, in 1955 had 5300 criminal jury trials, or 144 trials per 100,000 population.[9]

Between these extremes, the states have fashioned their special rules. Our sample of jury trials accordingly reflects these regional variations in the law; we have reports on jury trials for some crimes that could be tried before a jury only in that particular state, but would have to be tried without a jury in other states.[10]

Speaking generally, denial of jury trial for such petty crimes as public drunkenness, disorderly conduct, prostitution, minor traffic violations, and petty gambling is unlikely to be held to violate the right to trial by jury under the law of most states.

The result is that the law has withdrawn from the universe

---

[6] E.g., Connecticut. See McGarty v. Deming, 51 Conn. 422 (1883), (no jury trial for drunkenness). For the history of the jury in Connecticut, see State v. Gannon, 75 Conn. 206 (1902).

[7] See Appendix A. In Connecticut the figure is particularly low because of the high jury waiver rate. See Table 3 below.

[8] Georgia is a good example, Haines v. State, 8 Ga. App. 627, 70 S.E. 84 (1910) (jury trial for drunkenness). For a review of the scope of the jury in Georgia, see Pearson v. Wimbish, 124 Ga. 701, 52 S.E. 751 (1905).

[9] See Appendix A. Here the figure is due to a higher crime rate, greater availability of the jury, and lower jury waiver rate.

[10] In one such case defendant was charged with installing a kitchen appliance without a license [II-1167], in another with the illegal possession of a mud turtle [I-4157]. For our convention as to these case citations, see Chapter 9, note 2.

of jury trials a wide range of matters which, although described as petty, may well involve the most frequent source of contact between the ordinary citizen and the law. As Professor Puttkammer has put it:

> Numerically these cases form a huge proportion of the total number of criminal charges, and from the standpoint of sociology they are unquestionably of great importance — indeed, they are conceivably of more social significance than the major crimes.[11]

Within the area where jury trial is available as a matter of right, the two choices open to the defendant — the guilty plea, or the waiver of the jury if he does want a trial — have an interesting and major impact on the kind of business the jury is asked to handle. Looking for the moment at both factors together, it is possible to give a statistical picture of the position of the jury trial within the framework of all prosecutions.

Table 1 shows that of the major crime controversies that reach the stage of formal prosecution and are not dismissed three fourths are disposed of without trial, and of those that do go to trial, 60 per cent or three out of every five are tried before a jury. Thus, about one seventh of all felony prosecutions end in jury trials. The corresponding figures for misdemeanors are quite different because the proportions of both guilty pleas and jury waivers are higher. And dropping still further down the scale to petty offenses for which

---

[11] Puttkammer, Administration of Criminal Law, pp. 87-88 (1953). Similarly: "[T]o ninety-seven per cent of the offenders against the law in the City of Hartford, the Police Court stands for all the law and justice they know. . . . This state of affairs may be, and frequently is, furthered by the exercise of a sound discretion by an intelligent prosecutor. The value of goods stolen may, by a conservative estimate, be reduced to a point where a minor court can take jurisdiction. . . . What might technically be a highway robbery may be charged on two counts as assault and battery and theft from the person," Day, Petty Magistrates' Courts in Connecticut, J. Crim. L. and Crimin., v. 17, pp. 343, 346-347 (1924).

TABLE 1

The Role of Jury Trial in Prosecutions for Major Crimes*

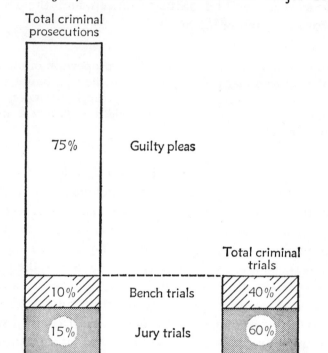

* Compiled from data in U. S. Bureau of the Census, Judicial Criminal Statistics (1945). Data from 24 states and the District of Columbia (only jurisdictions reporting) on 57,426 dispositions, in which 41,409 defendants pleaded guilty or were tried.

some states provide jury trial, the relative share of the jury trial is markedly smaller still.[12]

[12] Because of the state of judicial statistics only a suggestive view can be given on the high jury waiver rate in trials for misdemeanors, based on the few statistics available. Thus, in the Detroit Traffic Court about $2\frac{1}{2}$ per cent of all trials were before a jury; the corresponding percentage for the misdemeanor division of the Recorder's Court is about $\frac{1}{10}$ of 1 per cent. In the State of California about 3 per cent of all misdemeanor trials are conducted before juries. For Los Angeles County, in which this figure rises to over 10 per cent, we have even a finer breakdown by type of misdemeanor: of all trials for parking violations 1 per cent were jury trials; for other traffic violations 7 per cent; city ordinances, 11 per cent; all other misdemeanors, 19 per cent. Virtue, Survey of Metropolitan Courts Detroit Area, p. 126 (1950); Holbrook, A Survey of Metropolitan Trial Courts — Los Angeles Area, p. 121 (1956).

If one looks then at only the statistical share of the jury trial compared to the total number of criminal dispositions, it may appear startlingly small. However, before attempting a further assessment of the role and significance of jury trials today, it will be well to look more closely at the factors that determine the decision of the defendant to plead guilty or his decision to stand trial but to waive the jury.

Much is known, albeit in imprecise form, about the bargaining process that so often precedes a guilty plea;[13] functionally, it is the rough analogue of the settlement process in the civil case. The prosecutor will be moved by the twin advantages of removing the uncertainty of a conviction and saving the expense of trial. The defendant's calculus will be quite different: by pleading guilty he, of course, surrenders whatever chances he had for acquittal. But in exchange he often gains a reduction of the charge and in any event the prospect of a more lenient sentence than would have followed had he stood trial and been found guilty. In most cases there is thus at least the possibility of a bargain being struck between prosecution and defense. The ceremony of negotiation varies from state to state and courtroom to courtroom, and the judge himself is at times a broker in the process.

We can trace statistically some of the factors that influence the defendant's decision to enter a plea of guilty. That the decision is affected by the gravity of the expected punish-

---

For the State of California, which must repeatedly serve as an example because of its fine statistical record-keeping, we have this data:

Dispositions Before Trial

Traffic violations	99%
Other misdemeanors	95%
Felonies	76%

The large majority in each category are guilty pleas, Holbrook, Tables 37 and 38.

[13] See Note, Official Inducements to Plead Guilty: Suggested Morals for a Market Place, U. Chi. L. Rev., v. 32, p. 167 (1964). The prosecutor's control of the gravity of the charge often decides, as a technical matter, whether or not there can be a jury trial. See Day, Petty Magistrates' Courts in Connecticut, J. Crim. L., C. & P.S., v. 17, p. 341 (1924), and see generally Newman, Conviction (1966); Miller, Prosecution (volumes in the American Bar Foundation's Series).

ment is borne out by the data already noted,[14] showing that guilty pleas are far more frequent for misdemeanors than for felonies. Further, it can be documented that the defendant's decision to plead guilty is to some extent affected by the odds of being acquitted in case he chooses to go to trial. Table 2, based on the Bureau of the Census statistics for selected states, lists fifteen crimes ranked in order of the frequency of guilty pleas and also shows the incidence of acquittals for each crime category.

TABLE 2

Guilty Pleas and Acquittal Ratio for Major Crimes*

Crime	Proportion of Guilty Pleas		Trial Acquittal Ratio Bench and Jury Trials Combined	
	Per Cent	Rank	Per Cent	Rank
Murder	34	1	31	7
Manslaughter	52	2	46	14
Aggravated assault	56	3.5	37	12
Commercial vice	56	3.5	27	4.5
Rape	62	5.5	34	10
Robbery	62	5.5	31	7
Stolen property	63	7	31	7
Carrying weapons	71	8	38	13
Other sex offenses	73	9	36	11
Drug law violations	74	10	27	4.5
Embezzlement, fraud	80	11.5	51	15
Larceny	80	11.5	33	9
Burglary	82	13	22	2
Auto theft	89	14	23	3
Forgery	90	15	14	1

* Compiled from data in U. S. Bureau of the Census, Judicial Criminal Statistics (1945), New York eliminated here and in subsequent tables, because information incomplete.

We note first that the frequencies listed in the first column range from 34 per cent for murder, all the way up to 90 per cent where the crime is forgery, strongly suggesting that

[14] See note 12 above.

something about the nature of the crime influences the plea of guilty. The third column of Table 2 makes it possible to locate in part what that something is. It lists jointly for both jury and non-jury cases the proportion of acquittals for all defendants who went to trial. This acquittal ratio ranges from 51 per cent for embezzlement and fraud trials down to a mere 14 per cent for forgery trials. The fourth column in Table 2 then gives the rank order in terms of acquittal odds for the fifteen listed crimes. When the two rank orders are compared, it becomes apparent that there is a correlation between the frequency of guilty pleas and the odds on acquittal.

The correlation is inverse: the higher the chances for acquittal, the less likely the guilty plea, and vice versa.[15] Thus burglary, auto theft, and forgery, the three crimes that rank lowest in odds on acquittal, rank highest in percentage of guilty pleas. Similarly, manslaughter and assault, which rank low on guilty pleas, rank high in odds on acquittal.[16] Clearly, a variety of factors affects the defendant's decision to enter a guilty plea or to stand trial. Table 2 suggests that one major

[15] The impact of jury convictions on the rate of guilty pleas can be a very direct one; defendants scheduled for trial later in the day may watch the jury's first case. Following is a vivid description of this behavior from the Prohibition era: "It happens repeatedly at the beginning of a court term that defendants make up their minds whether or not to plead guilty only after the first case is tried. If the jury convicts, there is a rush to plead guilty. If they acquit, then other defendants will take a chance of a trial. The jury thus determines the degree of evidence which is sufficient to force defendants to plead guilty." National Commission on Law Observance and Enforcement, Prohibition Laws, Sen. Doc. 307, 71st Cong., 3d Sess., p. 61 (1931).

[16] The coefficient of correlation between the two rank orders in Table 2 is $\rho = -0.6$. The coefficient measures the relationship, first, in terms of its sign (plus or minus) and, second, in terms of its size, which varies between 0.0 and 1.0, or maximum correlation. The sign indicates whether the relationship is direct (+) or, as in Table 2, inverse (−): that is, the *more* acquittals, the *fewer* guilty pleas. The magnitude of the relationship is given by the square of the coefficient. Thus, in Table 2 the coefficient of −0.6 signifies that about one third of the variations ($-0.6^2 = 0.36$ or 36%) in guilty pleas is accounted for by the corresponding variation in the acquittal ratio; the remaining two thirds are caused by other considerations.

factor is simply the over-all likelihood of his being acquitted if he elects to stand trial.

We turn now to the third major determinant of the universe of jury trials. Once the defendant has decided to go to trial, he may waive his right to jury trial and elect to be tried by the judge alone. The law as a rule permits this choice, and the defendant often makes it.

We pause for a brief historical account of the law.[17] Jury waiver is an old institution; in two states, Maryland and Connecticut, its origin goes back to colonial times. As early as 1693 in Baltimore we find a waiver on a misdemeanor charge. In 1829 Maryland recorded the first jury waiver in a felony trial, and in 1852 a Maryland statute extended the right of waiver to all criminal cases, including capital cases. Several states soon followed the Maryland and Connecticut example, but other states rejected it.[18] Yet as late as 1930, whether a defendant in a federal criminal trial has the right to waive the jury was the subject of a major controversy in the United States Supreme Court in *Patton v. United States*.[19] The ques-

[17] For a detailed review of jury waiver, see Oppenheim, Waiver of Trial by Jury in Criminal Cases, Mich. L. Rev., v. 25, p. 695 (1927); Griswold, The Historical Development of Waiver of Jury Trial in Criminal Cases, Va. L. Rev. v. 20, p. 655 (1934). A careful and convenient summary of the history will be found in Singer v. U.S., 380 U.S. 24 (1965).

[18] New York, for example, was slow in coming to recognize jury waiver. It finally amended its constitution for this purpose. New York Const. Art. I, §2 (1894), as amended, 1935, 1937. But legislative enactment did not follow; it was not until 1957 that the constitutional provision was held to be self-executing. People v. Carroll, 7 Misc. 2d 581. 161 N.Y.S.2d 330 (Kings County Ct. 1957), 4 A.D.2d 537, 168 N.Y.S.2d 265 (2d Dept. 1957), aff'd, 3 N.Y.2d 686, 148 N.E.2d 875, 171 N.Y.S.2d 812 (1958).

[19] 281 U.S. 276 (1930). The question was a narrow one, involving the application of Article III §2, and the Sixth Amendment to the meaning and availability of jury waiver in the federal courts. While the decision was not direct authority for those states where waiver was limited or disallowed by local law, it was a prestigeful stimulus for the changes that were to follow.

tion was whether the constitutional provision for trial by jury was a privilege for the protection of the defendant or the pre-scribed mode of trial. On the first view, the defendant could waive this privilege; on the second view, jury trial would be compulsory.[20] It was further argued that since the defendant clearly had the power to waive trial by pleading guilty, he must have the lesser power to waive a given mode of trial.[21] The *Patton* case decided in favor of the power to waive the jury in federal cases and thus gave major impetus to the view that jury trial is a privilege of the defendant in state cases.

Although endorsing jury waiver as a privilege, the Supreme Court was full of cautions about its proper exercise.

> Not only must the right of the accused to a trial by a constitu-tional jury be jealously preserved, but the maintenance of the jury as a fact-finding body in criminal cases is of such impor-tance and has such a place in our traditions, that, before any waiver can become effective, the consent of government coun-sel and the sanction of the court must be had, in addition to the express and intelligent consent of the defendant. And the duty of the trial court in that regard is not to be discharged as a mere matter of rote, but with sound and advised discretion, with an eye to avoid unreasonable or undue departures from that mode of trial or from any of the essential elements thereof, and with a caution increasing in degree as the offenses dealt with increase in gravity.[22]

[20] This was the New York view: "[T]he right of trial by jury, both in England and here, is imbedded in the Constitution; and with us it is a right which in criminal cases cannot be waived." People v. Cosmo, 205 N.Y. 91, 97, 98 N.E. 408, 414 (1912).

[21] One traditional argument not stressed in Patton was the policy as to the possibility of error where the stakes are high. "We cannot believe that it is wise or expedient to place the life or liberty of any person accused of crime, even by his own consent, at the disposal of any one man . . . so long as man is a fallible being," State v. Worden, 46 Conn. 349, 367 (1878). See Hall, Has the State a Right to Trial by Jury in Criminal Cases? A.B.A.J., v. 18, p. 226 (1932).

[22] 281 U.S. 276, at 312-313. The holding of Patton was later in-corporated into Rule 23a, Fed. R. Crim. P. However, the warning not to give consent by rote seems to have been largely ignored. Note, Gov-ernment Consent to Waiver of Jury Trial under Rule 23a of the Federal Rules of Criminal Procedure, Yale L.J., v. 65, p. 1032 (1956). But see below note 25.

Today all states recognize jury waiver in one form or other.[23] While the majority of states and the Federal Rules today place qualifications on the defendant's unfettered freedom to waive a jury, these formal safeguards of the consent of court and prosecutor have become a matter of rote, due in part no doubt to the pressure of the court's workload.[24] In rare instances however, the court will insist that the public interest requires jury trial; and in at least a few cases, the prosecution has refused to consent to jury waiver possibly as a tactical move to disadvantage the defendant.[25] But as a rule the defendant can have his way.

Why then does a defendant choose to waive the jury? First Table 3 shows the extent of jury waiver by states. It carries a considerable surprise.

Table 3 suggests that a chief determinant in the decision whether or not to waive the jury in a criminal case is simply regional custom, and that the custom varies enormously from one part of the country to another. At one extreme are Wisconsin and Connecticut where, in felony cases, the jury is waived approximately three fourths of the time; at the other

[23] New York appears to have been the last to change. See above note 18.

[24] "The judges of our court by common agreement accept all jury waivers in both criminal and civil matters in the interest of saving the time of the court, although, of course, it adds considerably to their burden and responsibility." (Letter to the authors from Judge Ira W. Jayne of the Detroit Circuit Court, 1956.)

[25] In a recent case, the United States Supreme Court upheld the constitutionality of Rule 23a, which requires consent of the prosecutor as a condition to jury waiver. In that case the defendant, accused of mail fraud, wanted to waive the jury. The prosecutor objected and the defendant was found guilty in a jury trial. The Court was careful to allow for the possibility that the Government's insistence on jury trial might, under special circumstances, amount to a denial of impartial justice, but then the ignoble purpose of the prosecution's refusal to consent to the jury waiver would have to be claimed and substantiated, Singer v. United States, 380 U.S. 24 (1965). However, even in the federal courts such refusal by the prosecutor is an extremely rare event. The phenomenon that the jury convicts where the judge would have acquitted is treated in detail in Chapters 29-31.

TABLE 3

Jury Waiver for Major Crimes in Selected States*

State	Per Cent Jury Waiver (Bench Trials) of All Trials
Wisconsin	79
Connecticut	74
California	64
New Hampshire	58
New Jersey	57
Kansas	56
Ohio	50
North Dakota	50
Wyoming	45
Iowa	36
Pennsylvania	34
Massachusetts	33
South Dakota	24
Texas	18
Colorado	17
Oregon	15
New Mexico	13
Idaho	12
Washington	7
Minnesota	5
Utah	5
District of Columbia	3
Montana	0
Average all states	40%

* Compiled from data in U. S. Bureau of the Census, Judicial Criminal Statistics (1945).

extreme are Montana and the District of Columbia where in felony cases the jury is virtually never waived.

Although the use of waiver of the jury thus seems to depend largely on what other lawyers around are doing, on closer analysis it appears that a number of rational considerations are superimposed upon and intermingled with regional custom, as the defendant and the prosecutor each weigh their respective alternatives and odds.

Table 4 enables us to trace two such relationships: the relationship between waiver and type of crime, and between waiver and the frequency of guilty pleas.

TABLE 4

Jury Waiver and Guilty Pleas for Major Crimes*

Crime	Jury Waiver		Guilty Pleas	
	Per Cent	Rank	Per Cent	Rank
Murder	13	1	34	1
Manslaughter	25	2.5	52	2
Rape	25	2.5	62	5.5
Robbery	32	4	62	5.5
Stolen property	33	5	63	7
Embezzlement, Fraud	34	6	80	11.5
Burglary	35	7	82	13
Other sex offenses	41	8	73	9
Commercial vice	42	9	56	3.5
Aggravated assault	44	10	56	3.5
Forgery	50	11	90	15
Carrying weapons	52	12	71	8
Larceny	57	13	80	11.5
Auto theft	59	14	89	14
Drug law violations	70	15	74	10

* Compiled from data in U.S. Bureau of the Census, Judicial Criminal Statistics (1945). $\rho = 0.6$. See note 16 above.

Table 4 shows first of all a marked variation in jury waiver by crime categories, ranging from a low of 13 per cent for murder to 59 per cent for auto theft and 70 per cent for drug law violations. Our main interest centers on the relationship shown between the frequency of jury waiver and the frequency of guilty pleas for the various crimes. For this purpose the relevant comparison is between the second and fourth columns. Even cursory inspection reveals that the crimes that rank low in guilty pleas rank low in jury waivers, and conversely. This suggests that, to some extent, motivations leading to a guilty plea are similar to those leading to waiver. Paramount is the expectation of a lesser sentence if the conviction comes in a bench trial rather than from a jury, just as the plea of guilty carries a lesser sentence than the verdict of guilty. The defendant who does not want to wholly deprive himself of the possibility of an acquittal, but wants to assure a modicum of leniency in case of conviction, might be moved to waive the jury. There is some modest evidence that jury waiver may accomplish this.[26]

These relationships between region, or crime category, or guilty plea and jury waiver do not exhaust the rich variety of reasons that may move a defendant to forego jury trial. A useful profile of the defendant's calculus has been drawn by a distinguished judge:

> Every imaginable reason for thinking that a particular prisoner would stand a better chance of acquittal on the particular charge by the judge presiding than by the jury, must sometimes come into play. Small advantages in strategy, the personality and disposition of the judge, or the make-up of the jury panel — all such considerations must influence the choice . . . But there are more important reasons. Fear of the effect of popular prejudice upon a jury, either because of the nature of the charge, or because of something connected with the accused personally, is a very frequent ground of choice. It is common for defendants with known bad records to prefer trial before the court alone. And when the crime has aroused anger in the community from which the jury is chosen, trial before the court is frequently preferred. . . . Charges of a revolting nature, as of crimes against women and girls, seem to be tried more frequently before the court. Trial before the court, again, has been preferred in cases in which it has been feared that newspaper discussion might render the jury impatient of any defense, or of some particular defense. . . . Negro prisoners constitute a large proportion of the defendants in the criminal courts of Maryland, and they frequently prefer this method of trial to avoid any race prejudice in the jury box. Negro men charged with crimes against women commonly elect trial by the court alone. . . . Trial before the court alone is sometimes preferred when a defense is based mainly on a point of law. . . .[27]

[26] One of our judges reports: "I never suspend sentence if the defendant is found guilty by a jury." Such distinction, if established, might raise constitutional questions.

[27] Bond, The Maryland Practice of Trying Criminal Cases by Judges Alone, Without Juries, A.B.A.J., v. 11, pp. 699, 702 (1925). At one stage of the Jury Project we conducted a survey of lawyers to

In the end, the defendant must make an over-all estimate as to where he will fare better, before a judge or before a jury. If he goes to trial, he will presumably prefer to go to trial in the forum where he thinks his chances will be best.

In this sense, the defendant in deciding whether or not to waive the jury is putting to himself the very question which forms the central topic of this book: What difference will there be between jury and judge? We have, therefore, a welcome opportunity to confront the lore of the bar as to jury behavior, and we shall pause here for at least one such confrontation.

Since this study furnishes data on the varying levels of disagreement between judge and jury by specific crime categories, we anticipate the orderly reporting out of this material and use it here for purposes of comparison. For each of the fifteen crime categories Table 5 confronts the jury waiver ratio with the proportion of verdicts in which the defendant is treated more leniently by the jury than by the judge.[28]

The two lefthand columns present the percentages of jury waiver for the fifteen crimes and their rank order. We know

secure their reasons for waiving the jury. The reasons disclosed were very similar to the ones mentioned here; however, greater emphasis was placed on the cost factor.

Occasionally it is possible to trace a sharp decrease in waiver to a change in the law. For example, the Administrative Office of the Courts in California reports:

"The number of jury trials for traffic offenses in the municipal courts increased from 975 in 1953-54 to 3,663 in 1961-62. The 276 per cent increase, in large part, was caused by the Department of Motor Vehicles' initiation of a policy of mandatory license suspension in drunk driving cases and by the initiation by insurance companies of premium charges based on 'experience ratings.'" (Letter to the authors, 1964.)

[28] For the derivation of this leniency measure, see Chapter 6, note 4. In general, the measure is arrived at by subtracting the percentage of cases in which the judge is more lenient than the jury (cross-over) from the usually larger percentage of cases where the jury, in disagreeing, is more lenient than the judge (normal disagreement). The resulting percentage can be said to express in a rough sense the likelihood that the defendant charged with the particular crime will be treated more leniently by the jury than by the judge.

from Table 4 that they range from murder with the lowest waiver percentage to narcotics violations with the highest. The two righthand columns contain the new data on judge-jury disagreement as they come from our investigation.

TABLE 5

Jury Waiver and Jury Leniency for Major Crimes

Crime	Jury Waiver *		Jury Leniency †	
	Per Cent	Rank	Per Cent	Rank
Murder	13	1	29	1.5
Manslaughter	25	2.5	29	1.5
Rape	25	2.5	24	4
Robbery	32	4	18	8
Stolen property	33	5	24	5
Embezzlement, Fraud	34	6	8	13
Burglary	35	7	21	7
Other sex offenses	41	8	22	6
Commercial vice	42	9	8	13
Aggravated assault	44	10	27	3
Forgery	50	11	11	12
Carrying weapons	52	12	13	11
Larceny	57	13	18	8
Auto theft	59	14	15	10
Drug law violations	70	15	6	15

* Compiled from data in U. S. Bureau of the Census, Judicial Criminal Statistics (1945).

† The percentage of cases in which the jury is more lenient minus the percentage of cases in which the judge is more lenient, in the particular crime category. See Table 19.

The correlation is very marked in the expected direction. With narcotics violations, where the leniency advantage from the jury is slightest, the jury is waived most frequently; and, conversely, with murder and manslaughter, where the leniency advantage of the jury is greatest,[29] the jury is waived

[29] In Table 5 murder and manslaughter show the highest measure of net leniency, but this holds only for the 15 crimes covered by the selected data of the Bureau of the Census. Among all crimes, game law violations show the highest net leniency, namely 43 per cent. See Table 19 which gives the verdict patterns for all 42 crime categories.

least frequently. Thus, the defendant is more likely to waive the jury in those crime categories in which the net leniency expected from the jury is small.

Table 5 suggests a point of broad general interest. The defendant's decision to waive a jury trial is based on advice of counsel. What is of special interest here is that the lawyer could discern so accurately these regularities of jury net leniency which are here quantified for the first time; it would make a fascinating study to explore further just how the bar learns what it knows about judge and jury behavior.[30]

By now it has become clear how complicated a process it is by which the universe of jury trials is actually determined. The selection of jury cases is the result of an interplay of custom, economics, strategy, and game theory played by the defendant and the prosecutor. Thus, jury trials cannot possibly form a representative cross section of all criminal prosecutions; not only in number but also in quality they end up as a highly selected group of cases.

This process by which the universe of jury trials is determined has one special relevance for this study. The cases coming before a jury must, on the whole, be those in which the defendant has some chance, however remote, of acquittal, or at least of acquittal of the major charge.[31] If all controversies of criminal law were placed on a continuum from the weakest to the strongest in terms of the prosecution's case, the guilty plea, and to a lesser extent the jury waiver, would be likely to withdraw cases from the strong side of the continuum, leaving the weaker cases for jury trial.

---

[30] At several other points of our study the Jury Project encountered data that corroborated the lore and intuitive knowledge of the trial bar. In the selection of jurors, for instance, we found that the bar's notions as to which jurors tend to favor the prosecution and which the defense, are, on the whole, confirmed. Some data on this point will be found in Simon, The American Jury — The Defense of Insanity (1966).

[31] Further, the defendant may hope to receive a lighter penalty whenever setting the penalty is the jury's province. See Table 14.

The upshot is that, out of the great universe of criminal controversies, those surviving to jury trial, and therefore the subject of this study, are likely to be the more controversial cases where, in the nature of things, the chances of disagreement are increased. As we begin to measure and study the magnitude and direction of judge-jury disagreement, it is worth remembering that out of the whole realm of controversies in the criminal law, cases which come before the jury for decision are thus on the whole the more troublesome.[32]

The defendant's option under the waiver rules to determine whether there will be a jury trial has a further consequence for the nature of the cases that go to the jury. On the whole they will be more likely to involve pro-defendant sentiments than would the totality of all criminal trials.

Finally, we come back to the question of the significance of the jury in the criminal law, given the fact that, measured in percentages, the jury trial constitutes but a small fraction of all criminal dispositions. It has become something of a commonplace to read the statistics on the impact of guilty pleas and jury waivers as gravely reducing the significance of the jury and transferring its power largely to the prosecuting attorney in the bargaining over guilty pleas.[33] But we saw at every stage of this informal process of pre-trial dispositions that decisions are in part informed by expectations of what the jury will do. Thus, the jury is not controlling merely the imme-

---

[32] Still, as we shall see, the judge rates 57 per cent of the cases which come up for jury trial as clear on the evidence.

[33] In 1930 Raymond Moley wrote: "[T]here are many symptoms which suggest the decline, if not the utter dissolution, of trial by jury in criminal cases. . . . It may mean that we are witnessing in these days a legal evolution as epochal as that of centuries ago when the ordeal, the trial by fire, or battle, slowly yielded to the jury system. Or it may be the less portentous process of partial shift of power from jury to judge and prosecutor." Our Criminal Courts, p. 107. Similarly, Professor Jerome Hall, writing in 1935: "The influence of the jury [upon contemporary criminal law administration] is now relatively minor, due to perhaps the most important single change in criminal law administration, namely, the jury waiver. The decline of this ancient institution in the United States during the present century

diate case before it, but the host of cases not before it which are destined to be disposed of by the pre-trial process. The jury thus controls not only the formal resolution of controversies in the criminal case, but also the informal resolution of cases that never reach the trial stage.[34]   In a sense the jury, like the visible cap of an iceberg, exposes but a fraction of its true volume.

. . . has concentrated the administration of the criminal law in the courts and, even more, in the prosecuting attorneys." Theft, Law and Society, p. 112 (1st ed. 1935).

The same statistical fallacy pervades much thinking about the jury in civil cases.   There, too, it is said that the real law in tort cases is to be found in patterns of the settlement process; since such an overwhelming majority of cases are settled out of court, allegedly it hardly matters what the court and the jury do.   This was a main predicate of the famous Columbia Study in 1932.   The point is discussed in Blum and Kalven, Public Law Perspectives on a Private Law Problem: Auto Compensation Plans, pp. 17-21 (1965).

[34] There is a curious connection between this oddly shaped universe of jury trials and the current study.   We saw that this universe is in part determined by expectations as to the nature of judge-jury disagreement.   To the extent that the present study clarifies and makes known the sources and occasions of this disagreement, it may, through a feed-back process, modify the bar's expectations as to the judge-jury disagreement and thus conceivably affect, in turn, the decisions on guilty pleas and jury waivers.   The book, therefore, may in some degree, by this route modify the very phenomenon of its study and reshape the structure of the universe of future jury trials.

CHAPTER 3

Methodology: The Sample

With this chapter and the next we begin a consideration of certain problems of method. Such discussion is usually left to the appendix, but for two main reasons we have decided to bring our methodological problems out into the open. The investigation had to proceed along pathways somewhat removed from those of more routine surveys, and certain innovations in method have been required. More important, there has been concern for the legal audience and the general reader for whom social science methodology may be an alien field.

Social science more than natural science is forced to operate at a remove from the reality it studies. It must work, therefore, through a chain of inferences. In a formulation which should carry familiar overtones for the lawyer, social science works with quantified circumstantial evidence. We have, therefore, thought it profitable to mark the links of inference on which this study rests, to lay open the special logic of inquiry and proof.

This chapter focuses on a first major inference: the process by which we connect up the universe of actual jury trials, sketched in Chapter 2, with the sample collected for this study. The simple fact is that instead of having reports on all 60,000 or so criminal jury trials in the United States during any one year, we have reports on only 3576 trials.[1] We con-

---

[1] The trials on which these questionnaires report occurred mainly in 1954-1955 for Sample I and mainly in 1958 for Sample II. The actual period of time these questionnaires cover is a little over two years.

front at the outset the question of how we can be sure that what we discover about this small minority of cases is applicable to the larger universe which, in the end, is the true subject of this inquiry.

We are thus touching on what is by now a commonplace in modern social science work: the theory and practice of sampling. Through an authoritatively established theory, the details of which need not concern us here,[2] procedures have been designed for drawing a sample from a universe so that it is possible to state with precision the margin of error involved in matching the characteristics of the sample with the characteristics of the total universe.

The aim of sampling is to seek a cross section of the universe. While the techniques of sampling various kinds of universes differ in detail, their fundamental point is the same; in the end, they leave it to an impartial lottery process to decide which units of the universe are drawn for the sample. The logic is that if each unit of the universe has an equal chance of being selected, the sample will yield a representative cross section. If this lottery process of sampling can be carried out strictly, the predictive power of even a small sample is remarkable.

All samples are subject to two sources of error. The first, the "sampling error," results from the simple fact that a sample is taken instead of a count of the whole universe. In a properly drawn sample the magnitude of this error is known and, given the nature of the universe, it varies inversely with the size of the sample.

The second source of error, the "error in sampling," is a more serious and disturbing matter. It ensues when it is impossible for one reason or another to use the impartial lottery process; the result may be a bias in the construction of the

[2] For a book that discusses sampling with a minimum use of mathematics, see Wallis and Roberts, Statistics (1956); for a synopsis of the major mathematical techniques, see Yates, Sampling Methods for Censuses and Surveys (3d ed. 1960); for one of the many good standard works see Cochran, Sampling Techniques (2d ed. 1963).

sample itself which seldom can be known or measured in advance. And, increasing the sample size will only aggravate it.

For a number of reasons having a good deal to do with the exigencies of studying a living institution, we were unable to utilize the preferred sampling techniques in this study. The present chapter will describe precisely how the sample of jury trials was obtained and in what respects it falls short of the ideal. But we will also show why the sample finally emerges as quite reliable and merits in fact great confidence for the purposes of this study.

How might one have gone about selecting an ideal sample for this study? First, a list of all judges who were trying jury cases would be prepared; then by a random process, one tenth, say, would be selected. Finally, the procedure would have required that each of the selected judges report for the same specified period on all his jury trials.

We did none of these things. It was not possible to compile a complete list of judges engaged in jury trials throughout the United States, although we did our best to approximate such a list by using the latest directories. Nor did we send invitations to a random sample of judges from our list; instead we approached all judges. Finally, since these respondents were judges, there was of course no way of insisting that they cooperate; thus, the self-selection of the judges, and not a lottery design of ours, determined the composition of the sample. To be then, for the moment, but only for the moment, as harsh to ourselves as possible, our sample is simply the residue of self-selected judges, derived from a list imperfect to begin with.

The original list contained some 3500 judges[3] of whom we knew only that they *might* preside over criminal jury trials, since they were members of a court that had the necessary jurisdiction. Close to ten per cent of our letters were returned because the judge was deceased or was no longer a member of the court. To about forty per cent of the letters there was no

[3] We attempted a census, knowing that it would fail. The list included all state judges in courts listed as having criminal jurisdiction and all U.S. District Court Judges.

reply, and we do not know whether this was so because of an imperfect address or because the judge had no criminal jury trials or did not want to cooperate. The remaining judges, a little under half of those on the original list, answered with the following results:

No criminal jury trials		840
no jury trials	735	
only civil jury trials	105	
Refused to cooperate		68
Unable to cooperate		72
Agreed to cooperate but failed		111
sent no reports	71	
sent incomplete reports	40	
Cooperated effectively		**555**
		1646

It is the reports from these 555 judges that form the basic data for this study.

We deviated further from the ideal random process of selection by utilizing, wherever possible, extra help or contacts to secure cooperation from a particular state.[4] This tended to aggravate the problem of regional bias.

Table 6 shows the geographic distribution of cases by states and Census regions and compares it with the frequency of actual jury trials in each area. Although the sample has reports from every jurisdiction but one,[5] it shows marked regional deficiencies. The major shortcoming is that it under-represents the South. The three southern Census regions account for $(28.4 + 17.6 + 8.3 =)$ 54.3 per cent of all criminal jury trials, but only $(14.7 + 4.6 + 4.2 =)$ 23.5 per cent of the sample cases come from these regions.[6]

[4] See Preface. This was particularly true for California and New Jersey.

[5] In Rhode Island no judge cooperated. However, as shown in Table 6, Rhode Island accounts for only $\frac{1}{10}$ of 1 per cent of all criminal jury trials conducted in the United States.

[6] This is in part because cooperation from the South was generally low and partly because the southern states permit jury trial for a wide range of minor violations; practically no courts of limited jurisdiction reported cases for the second sample.

TABLE 6

Sample and Actual Distribution of Criminal Jury Trials by Regions and States

	Sample Per Cent	Actual Per Cent*
New England	**2.3**	**5.4**
Maine	.9	.4
New Hampshire	.3	.1
Vermont	.2	.2
Massachusetts	.4	4.5
Rhode Island	—	.1
Connecticut	.5	.1
Middle Atlantic	**19.1**	**11.4**
New York	1.6	4.9
New Jersey	11.2	1.5
Pennsylvania	6.3	5.0
East North Central	**10.7**	**5.5**
Ohio	3.0	1.0
Indiana	1.7	1.2
Illinois	3.3	1.3
Michigan	2.5	1.8
Wisconsin	.2	.4
West North Central	**9.8**	**4.6**
Minnesota	1.4	.2
Iowa	2.4	.5
Missouri	1.7	2.0
North Dakota	.6	.1
South Dakota	.5	.1
Nebraska	1.3	.4
Kansas	1.9	1.3
South Atlantic	**14.7**	**28.4**
Delaware	.2	.1
Maryland	.8	.8
District of Columbia	.1	.8
Virginia	2.0	3.5
West Virginia	1.6	1.9
North Carolina	2.2	7.1
South Carolina	1.1	1.0
Georgia	.9	9.5
Florida	5.8	3.7
East South Central	**4.6**	**17.6**
Kentucky	.9	2.1

* See Appendix A.

(*continued*)

	Sample *Per Cent*	Actual *Per Cent* *
Tennessee	1.4	5.7
Alabama	1.5	7.7
Mississippi	.8	2.1
West South Central	**4.2**	**8.3**
Arkansas	.3	.4
Louisiana	.4	.7
Oklahoma	1.2	.5
Texas	2.3	6.7
Mountain	**5.0**	**4.3**
Montana	.4	.1
Idaho	.2	.3
Utah	.6	.8
Wyoming	.3	.3
Colorado	1.3	1.8
New Mexico	.9	.3
Arizona	.9	.6
Nevada	.4	.1
Pacific	**19.9**	**10.4**
Washington	2.5	.6
Oregon	1.1	.9
California	16.3	8.9
Federal District Courts	**9.7**	**4.1**
Total	*100.0%*	*100%*
Number of Jury Trials	*3576*	*55,670*

* For the derivation of these per cent figures see Appendix A.

There is a second respect in which the sample deviates from the ideal. We were unable to control the exact period in which the cooperating judges did in fact cooperate. Some helped for a short while only and some for many months; some judges submitted but a few reports, others a large number. Table 7 sets forth the relevant data and indicates the variation among the judges in intensity of cooperation.

Even if we had been successful in imposing a uniform time limit on the judges, variation in their caseload would be expected. But the variations shown in Table 7 clearly go beyond this. Thus, 22 per cent of the cooperating judges submitted only one case each, constituting only 3 per cent of the total cases. At the other extreme, 9 per cent of the cases come from the 1 per cent of the judges who submitted over 50 cases. Further, while the vast majority of judges contributed anywhere from 2 to 25 cases, and thereby contributed the great bulk of the sample, nevertheless half of the cases come from the 15 per cent of the judges who submitted more than ten cases each.

TABLE 7

Number of Trials Reported per Judge

Number of Trials	Per Cent of All Judges	Per Cent of All Trials
1	22	3
2-5	41	21
6-10	22	26
11-25	12	29
26-50	2	12
Over 50	1	9
Total	100%	100%
Number	555	3576

We have deliberately elaborated on the shaky aspects of the sample so that its rehabilitation might illustrate and dramatize certain key points about the realistic and prudent practice of social science sampling operations.[7] There are perhaps three points to make. First, in new efforts it must be better to learn something, however imperfectly, than to withdraw from inquiry altogether when preferred methods are as a practical matter not available. Second, at times an apparently vulnerable sample will, on probing, turn out to be sounder than its design would lead us to believe. Third — and perhaps most important — the validity of a sample is meaningful only with respect to the specific purpose to which it is being put. The same sample may be wretched for the purpose of drawing one inference about its universe and yet be perfectly sound for drawing another.

It may perhaps be helpful to compare these difficulties in

[7] See Zeisel, Social Research on the Law: The Ideal and the Practical, in Law and Sociology, pp. 124-143 (Evan ed. 1962).

sampling with the celebrated difficulties encountered in the Kinsey studies. Indeed, our sample could be called a "Kinsey sample," — an extreme case of damning with faint praise. Dr. Kinsey too had to obtain his sample by voluntary cooperation and in the end fell far short of a cross section of the general population. His experience is illuminating. The difficulties arose not so much from a failure of technique on the part of the researcher, as from a stubbornness and intransigence in the matter under inquiry.[8] Given the unprecedented nature of the Kinsey inquiry, any sample was better than none,[9] and for some inferences the Kinsey sample was a good sample.

Fortunately the usefulness of our sample does not have to rest on the argument that half a loaf is better than none. The sample is a good deal more solid than we have thus far made it appear.

In Table 6, a regional bias was evident. We now proceed to trace what difference this regional bias might make. We begin with the distribution of jury trials by crime categories in Table 8.

It is immediately apparent that the Bureau of Census frequencies for jury trials for the fifteen crime categories are remarkably like the frequencies in the sample.[10] A moment's

---

[8] See Zeisel, Book Review of Kinsey, Sexual Behavior and the Human Female, U. Chi. L. Rev., v. 21, p. 517 (1954). Subsequently, though, ingenious suggestions were made as to how the Kinsey sample could have been verified. See Cochran, Mosteller, Tukey, Statistical Problems of the Kinsey Report (1954).

[9] The social scientist in these areas might be said to be with Darwin on his first voyage on H.M.S. *Beagle*. It will sometime have to suffice that some new insights were gained into life at the bottom of the sea, even if there can be no adequate assurance about representativeness.

[10] Table 8 offers only a raw comparison of the incidence of crimes in the Census and in the sample; it does not adjust for certain limitations of the Census reports. The major discrepancy is in drug law violations, possibly due to the time difference of ten years, which may entail a change in law enforcement; also, New York, with its high incidence of narcotics violations, is not included. The Census data cover state trials only; for this particular crime, more than one third of our cases stem from federal prosecutions.

reflection will show that there is no tension between Table 8 and Table 6 since the distribution of crimes is more or less the same in all regions.   Therefore, regional bias in a sample does not keep it from being a good sample of jury trials by crime categories.   And while we would have been delighted had it been possible to avoid the regional bias, for most purposes of the study it is more important that the sample be represent-ative of jury trials by crimes than that it be a good sample of jury trials by region.

TABLE 8

Frequency of Jury Trials for Major Crimes in Sample Compared With U.S. Census*

Crime	Sample Per Cent	Census Per Cent
Burglary	13	17
Aggravated assault	13	14
Robbery	10	13
Larceny	8	9
Other sex offenses	8	9
Rape	8	8
Murder	9	7
Stolen property	2	6
Manslaughter	4	4
Carrying weapons	1	3
Embezzlement, Fraud	6	3
Auto theft	5	3
Forgery	3	2
Commercial vice	2	1
Drug law violations	8	1
Total	100%	100%
Number of Cases	2232 †	

* Only those crimes in the sample are reported which are in-cluded in the referred to U.S. Bureau of the Census, Judicial Criminal Statistics (1945).

† These 2232 plus 1344 cases in the sample which were other felonies or minor crimes add up to the total sample of 3576 cases.

This line of analysis can be pursued one step further by testing another characteristic of the sample against the uni-verse.   Table 9, using the same set of census statistics, shows the frequency of jury acquittals for each of the specific crimes listed and confronts them with the comparable figures as derived from the sample. When the two sets of data are ranked in terms of the frequency of acquittals, a fair correlation between the two rank orders is apparent,[11] in spite of the fact that Stolen Property, the crime listed first, happens to be the major exception. Despite its regional bias, the sample seems to be reliable with respect to this second characteristic of central importance for this study, the frequency of jury acquittals.

TABLE 9

Jury Acquittal Rates* for Major Crimes, Sample and Census

Crime	Sample		Census†	
	Per Cent	Rank	Per Cent	Rank
Stolen property	47	1	27	11
Manslaughter	45	2	51	1
Rape	40	3	38	7
Carrying weapons	39	4	43	3
Embezzlement, Fraud	37	5	50	2
Aggravated assault	36	6	41	5
Larceny	35	7	42	4
Other sex offenses	34	8	40	6
Auto theft	32	9	29	9.5
Commercial vice	30	10	25	12.5
Robbery	24	11.5	29	9.5
Burglary	24	11.5	22	14
Forgery	22	13	14	15
Murder	19	14	32	8
Drug law violations	10	15	25	12.5
Number of Cases	2121**			

* Per cent acquittals of all jury verdicts.

† Compiled from data in U. S. Bureau of the Census, Judicial Criminal Statistics (1945).

** 2121 plus 1344 trials for crimes not reported in the Census, plus 111 hung juries in reported crimes add up to total sample of 3576.

Finally, we come to the most critical challenge to the validity of the sample, namely that it comprises only "cooperative"

[11] The rank order coefficient of correlation is $\rho = +0.6$.

judges. The challenge is that there might be a significant difference between the judges who cooperated and those who did not, and that this difference might be related to the judge's propensity to agree or disagree with the jury. There is danger that this self-selection influences the data at the very heart of this study, the data on agreement and disagreement between judge and jury.

Various techniques have been developed for testing whether there is likely to be a relevant difference between cooperators and non-cooperators in a survey.[12] The problem is not an easy one to solve, since one cannot make a direct comparison of the non-cooperators, who by definition have deprived us of data about themselves. One can, however, as is so often the case in social science, "take the second ship." In this case, the next best thing involves comparing judges who cooperated for only a very short time and sent in only a few reports (see Table 7 above) with judges who cooperated for a long time and sent in many reports. If, so the argument runs, there is no difference between the highly cooperative and the minimally cooperative judges, it is then a fair inference that the judges who did not cooperate at all would not be too different from those who cooperated to only a minimal degree. Table 10 makes this comparison.

TABLE 10

Judge-Jury Disagreement for Judges with Few and
with Many Cases

	Number of cases per judge					
	1	2-5	6-10	11-25	26-50	51+
Per cent *jury* acquittals	31	34	34	29	27	40
Per cent *judge* acquittals	14	17	16	15	14	19

The pattern of judge-jury agreement is not related to the degree of cooperation of the judge, except in the last category

[12] It has been shown that persons who give minimal cooperation in mail surveys are highly comparable to those who do not cooperate at all. See Ford and Zeisel, Bias in Mail Surveys Cannot Be Controlled by One Mailing, Pub. Opinion Q., v. 13, p. 495 (1949).

where the judges sent in over fifty reports.[13] We are thus reasonably satisfied that in essential respects judicial self-selection has not distorted the sample.[14]

In the end, our conclusions about the sample come down to this: modern social science research on vital problems and living institutions will always be confronted with large practical difficulties; the pure canons of methodology can seldom be followed. In these situations it is important that the researcher into the problems of society be prudent, by being prepared to make some concessions to reality and some compromises with ideal methodology.

Throughout the remainder of the analysis we shall proceed on the proposition that what is true for the sample of 3576 criminal jury trials is true for the universe of criminal jury trials in the United States.

[13] For this category the explanation resides in an extrinsic factor: these were judges who because of local law had a large number of jury misdemeanor cases.

[14] In addition, there are two details tending further to buttress confidence that judicial self-selection has not been a distorting factor. First, we insisted that the judges submit reports on *consecutive* trials only. This avoided the difficulties that would have arisen had the judges been permitted to report on cases selected according to some private notion of what was interesting or significant. Second, a sustained effort was made to contact noncooperating judges and secure reasons for their refusal to help. In the very great majority of cases the reasons were highly impersonal, such as illness, change of assignment, over-burdened schedule, etc., and did not relate to any attitudes about the study itself and, therefore, possibly about the jury.

CHAPTER 4

Methodology: The Research Design

In the prior chapters we discussed the nature of the phenomena in the real world that we wish to study, the universe of jury trials in the United States, and we discussed why statements which are true for the sample of 3576 jury trials can be projected as true for the full universe of trials. This chapter now takes up the kinds of information obtained and the way the information was obtained. In brief, the topic is that of research design which, like sampling technique, is a major building block in any research.

In broad outline, the design was a simple one and has already been touched on.[1] By mail questionnaire trial judges were asked to report, for cases tried before them, how the jury decided the case, and how they would have decided it, had it been tried before them without a jury. In addition, the judge was asked to give some descriptive and evaluative material about the case, the parties, and counsel.

We might reflect for a moment on the reasons that led to this particular research design. Even in theory, alternative approaches to the special problem of jury-judge disagreement are severely limited. The ideal method for exploring it — trying each case twice, once to a judge and once to a jury — is grossly impractical. The easiest and most practical method would be simply to compare cases actually tried to a judge with cases actually tried to a jury, but such a comparison would not be very helpful. As we have seen, criminal cases before a judge differ in significant ways from those that go to

[1] Chapter 1, page 10.

a jury.[2]   It is of small interest to learn how judge and jury decide *different* cases; the question is how judge and jury would decide the *same* case.

Again one might have stepped back from the particularity of the case, and essayed a general opinion poll of the bar and the judiciary on when and why they thought judge and jury would differ.   Given the undeniable expertise of lawyers and judges, whose business it is to try cases with and without juries, such a study would have had some value, but it would necessarily have been bland and lacking secure foundation.[3] In the light then of available alternatives, the design of matching a real jury verdict and a hypothetical judge verdict[4] for a great number of actual cases emerges as the most rigorous practicable approach.

The use of the mail questionnaire requires perhaps an additional word of explanation, since the mail questionnaire is not often the preferred instrument of research.[5]   It makes it difficult to achieve a sufficient level of cooperation and creates the problem of self-selection.   Moreover, the reporting is usually done by an inexpert respondent without assistance from a trained interviewer.   It requires further that the questions be rigidly framed once and for all in advance.

For this study, however, the mail questionnaire proved to be the most efficient approach.   It would have been extrav-

---

[2] See Table 5.

[3] At one point we place considerable reliance on a nationwide opinion poll of judges conducted by the Jury Project.   The questions in this poll, however, relate to the judges' views of the jury *as an institution*.   The results of the poll will be analyzed in a separate study, but some of its data are used in Chapter 37.

[4] The judge was asked for the jury trial he was conducting and reporting on: "How would *you* have decided the case had you tried it *without* a jury?"   As a matter of convenience we shall call the judge's hypothetical decision "the judge's verdict," in contrast to the jury's verdict, although in strict legal terminology a judge sitting without a jury renders not a verdict but a "judgment."

[5] For a list of the manifold problems in the use of the mail questionnaire, see Wales and Ferber, A Basic Bibliography on Marketing Research §7.3 (2d ed. Chicago 1963).

agant to arrange for a staff of interviewers throughout the United States to personally interview a judge each time he finished a jury trial.   And our respondents were anything but inexpert; they were judges being asked about a matter in which they had the greatest interest and the greatest professional competence.

In the end, the mail questionnaire had a decisive advantage for a study that made great demands on confidential information.   The elimination of the personal interviewer made it possible for the judge to report to the Jury Project, in confidence, information about his disagreements with the jury in particular cases which he might understandably have been reluctant to disclose face to face.

A distinctive feature of the research design is that it was able to use two questionnaire forms, building a second on experience with the first.   The original form, the Sample I questionnaire, was a relatively open, unstructured effort.   After considerable experience with its analysis, a second version more tightly controlled and more detailed, was designed and put into the field.   The total sample is distributed between the two questionnaires as follows:

	Trials	Per Cent
Sample I	2385	67
Sample II	1191	33
Total	3576	100%

Many questions were identical on both questionnaires, and for such items the two samples can be treated as one.   At times, however, Sample II recruited special information, and thus for some points we rely on it exclusively.

Although we had the rare chance of designing a second questionnaire after long experience with a first one, now after experience with the second version, we readily see changes we would make were there to be a third.[6]   The difficulties in

[6] For example, we would ask whether defendant's counsel was privately retained, a public defender, or assigned; whether the defendant was hurt in the commission of the crime; further questions about the

drafting these two questionnaires provide a vivid instance of the commonplace in survey research that there is a genuine tension between the researcher's desire to obtain as much detailed information as possible, and the need, on the other hand, not to so burden the respondent as to cause him to give up cooperation altogether. In this study the problem was particularly acute, since respondents were busy judges and the research venture was imposing an important social cost on them.[7]

Questionnaire I, as we said, had a simple structure.[8] After certain routine questions it called for a brief description of the case in the judge's own words. Further, it asked in check-list fashion for such details as whether the defendant had taken the witness stand; whether he had a criminal record; whether, if he had a record, the jury learned of it; the defendant's sex, age, and race; the relative quality of counsel on both sides; and whether the jury, once deliberations had begun, ever returned to the court with a request for information or assistance. At the core of the questionnaire, however, were just three items: the actual verdict of the jury, the hypothetical decision of the judge, and the judge's explanation of the disagreement when his decision differed from that of the jury. This questionnaire version invited the judge to write freely in his own words about the case.

Two basic considerations led to the development of Questionnaire II. First, from experience with Questionnaire I we had the benefit of hindsight as to certain additional items of information it would be helpful to have. Second, and more important, it became evident that the judge would describe

---

defendant's appearance and his family; a variety of more specific questions designed to capture jury sentiments on the law, e.g., whether counsel tried to minimize the crime in his handling of the case; and finally whether the judge interviewed the jury after the case, and whether he had special information about the case which might have influenced, but was kept from, the jury.

[7] See generally, Blum and Kalven, The Art of Opinion Research: A Lawyer's Appraisal of an Emerging Science, U. Chi. L. Rev., v. 24, p. 1 (1956).

[8] Both questionnaire forms will be found in Appendix E.

the cases of disagreement in much greater detail than he described the cases of agreement. For the purposes of statistical analysis this was a disadvantage, because the aim was to find out how the *agreement* cases differed from the *disagreement* cases. To achieve this, what was needed was an equally complete set of descriptive data for *all* cases, and not just for the cases of disagreement.

Questionnaire II was developed primarily to meet this need and met it by employing some forty specific questions. Some were of the same flat descriptive type used in Questionnaire I. However, several new topics were added, such as the type of evidence at the trial, the personal characteristics of the victim, and further details about the person of the defendant.

But beyond this, we asked a series of new descriptive questions that involved a summary, a *gestalt* evaluation by the judge.[9] Illustrative is the question in which the judge is asked to state whether the defendant "as a person, was sympathetic, average, or unattractive"; or where he is asked to tell whether the case "was easy to comprehend, somewhat difficult, or very difficult"; or where he is asked to say whether on all the evidence the defendant's guilt or innocence was "very clear or a close question;" or, again, where he is asked in cases of disagreement to state how he feels about the jury's verdict: Is it "without any merit," "a tenable position for a jury though not for a judge," or, "one a judge might also come to"?[10]

Although Questionnaire II was quite different in format and much more elaborate than Questionnaire I, the core information sought was again threefold: the jury's actual verdict, the judge's hypothetical verdict, and his reasons for any disagreements.

So much for a description of the design. What questions can be raised about it? There is always the problem of sheer oversight, and too, there are some sources of disagreement, too

[9] For discussion of the utility of summary terms, see the use of the concept "tolerance" in Stouffer, Communism, Conformity, and Civil Liberties: A Cross-section of the Nation Speaks Its Mind (1955). See also Blum and Kalven, note 7 above.

[10] These are respectively questions 20(a), 11, 12, and 5.

subtle and too varied to be captured by a questionnaire.[11]
What remains to be examined, however, are not shortcomings
of this kind, but the possibility that the very method by
which the data was reported has introduced certain impurities
or inaccuracies which warp our conclusions. We look here at
a second major link in the chain of inferences.[12] The concern
for the remainder of the chapter is with the reliability of the
trial judge as reporter.

It may be helpful at the start to recall four types of information requested from the trial judge, each of which raises
a different problem in reliability:

1. Reports on such routine objective facts as the nature of
the case, the types of evidence presented, the demographic
characteristics of the defendant and the victim, etc. Here
there can be no problem about the reliability of the judge's reporting, except for an occasional lapse in accuracy that could
befall any reporter.

2. Facts about the trial which require some judgment or
evaluation on the part of the judge. He was asked, as we
saw, to report whether the case was difficult to comprehend,
whether defense counsel was superior, and whether the defendant was sympathetic. The issue here is whether the
judge's subjective judgment corresponds to some reality. Can
we be sure, in other words, that one counsel *is* better than his
adversary if the judge has rated him so?

The important safeguard is the special experience and competence of the reporter. If anyone can make a meaningful
judgment on a question such as the quality of counsel, the trial
judge can. In fact, because he is likely to have seen many
jury trials in his career, he is in a position far superior to any
independent staff member in making such a judgment. Thus,
it is reasonable to rely on the judge on points like these,
which are peculiarly within his special experience.[13]

[11] See for instance the discussion of credibility in Chapter 13.

[12] For the first link, see Chapter 3, Methodology: The Sample.

[13] The operational theory can be put this way: If it had been
possible to assign these tasks of classification to more than one judge
in each case, they would have come to the same result in the great

3. The reasons the judge gives for his disagreement with the jury. Two points are here involved: whether the judge was candid in telling why he thinks the disagreement arose, and whether the judge's explanation is likely to be correct. For the moment, we confront only the issue of whether there is reason to doubt the judge's candor.[14] The issue need not detain us: a judge interested enough and serious enough to cooperate in the survey, and trusting the research venture enough to supply it with confidential information, would not dissemble on this point.

4. Lastly, we come to the judge's statement of how he would have decided the case had it been tried before him without a jury. Since the judge's verdict is hypothetical, justification is needed for relying on it. Several considerations suggest that this "verdict" represents a sober act of judgment on the part of the judge. The matter lies somewhat differently for agreements and disagreements. Presumably the judge, in general, would find it more comfortable to report agreement. If, therefore, he nevertheless reports disagreement, it seems only reasonable to accept his statement. In addition, when he states a disagreement he corroborates it in a variety of important ways. In cases where he would have convicted, he states the sentence he would have imposed. He also gives reasons for his disagreement, and, as will be seen, he exercises the opportunity afforded to show the intensity of his disagreement by grading the merits of the jury verdict.[15]

---

majority of the cases and, not unexpectedly, would have disagreed in some borderline cases. Such borderline disagreement does not derive from any unreliability of the reporter but from an inherent ambiguity in all questions that contain broad gradations. Fortunately, ambiguities at the borderline do little harm; it is the extreme cases that produce significant differences, not the borderline cases which fall now to this side and now to that. Hence we conclude that the margin of error in these evaluative items is self-correcting. See Kendall, Conflict and Mood: Factors Affecting Stability of Response (1954).

[14] The second question involves a major step in the study and will be discussed in detail in Chapter 7, which deals with the logic of explanation.

[15] Question 5, Sample II, Appendix E. The data from this question are reported in Chapter 34, The Judge as Critic.

Most important, the judge, in the course of an ordinary jury trial, comes to some conclusion in his own mind as he listens to the case. Therefore, when the research operation intrudes into the trial process, it is not really asking the judge to make a decision he otherwise would not have made, but rather simply to report a judgment he probably has made anyway. Hence, again it seems certain that the disagreements reported by the judges indicate real differences.

The possibility of distortion in his report of *agreements* is not so easily dismissed. The judge might claim agreement when in fact he disagreed, or when, instead of making an independent judgment, he simply accepted the jury's verdict.

This particular source of bias was anticipated in the original design. To guard against it, the judge was requested to write down his verdict before the jury returned. Insofar as the judge followed this instruction, the problem is, of course, solved. There is no way of knowing to what extent the instruction was followed, but in some cases there is evidence that the judge did put down his verdict while the jury was out; and in some other cases, although he wrote in the verdict after the jury's return, he is clearly reporting a verdict he had reached earlier.[16]

More important, the majority of judges in the sample reported disagreements with the jury in at least some of their cases:[17] It is unlikely that they were disposed to state agreement as a matter of principle in order to maintain outward appearances of harmony with the jury.

Nevertheless, there perhaps is a residuum of cases where, if the judge had reported prior to the rendering of the jury's verdict, he might have disagreed, but, where, reporting later, he was willing to conform his judgment to that of the jury. In such cases, however, the disagreement thus glossed over must have been one of low intensity. In fact, the judge

[16] E.g., "I felt positive the jury was going to disagree with me." [I-3308] See also Chapter 16, note 9. [I-1880]

[17] Out of the 205 judges who submitted over 5 cases, only 18 reported no disagreement.

would be indicating that he had no firm opinion about the case, and that since the jury had decided it that way, he might as well go along. The upshot is that some minor disagreements may have been lost, but that the disagreement which the judge does report must have been serious enough to be declared. For our study, it is precisely these disagreements that are most relevant.

Finally, there remains to be considered one other possible objection to the judge's hypothetical verdict which, arguably, introduces another bias. One of the judges reported to us in conversation that he had wondered if he would have decided a given case as he did, had he been exposed to the responsibilities and full pressures of the actual decision. The implication was that he might be more legalistic on paper than he would have been in a real trial.

Despite a number of reassuring considerations,[18] this re-

[18] There is much corroboration in support of the argument that the judge is not more "legalistic" in the hypothetical verdict than where the verdict is his real responsibility. (a) The judge is asked to report on the intensity of his disagreement. See Chapter 34. (b) There are two universes of disagreement: those in which the judge is more severe than the jury (normals) and those in which he is less severe (cross-overs). The verdict patterns for individual judges show both types of disagreement by the same judge. (c) The judge for the vast majority of cases in which he disagrees offers an explanation, often in considerable detail. (d) The logic of the explanation, when it is not purely evidential, is sufficiently "extra-legal" to constitute quite a leap for a judge to have to make, were he to agree with the jury's point; his stand in these cases is not mere legalism but is at the heart of the law as seen by judges. (e) The judge further objectifies his decision in the normal disagreement by recording the penalty he would have given. Finally, in any event, one might as well argue the contrary point that the judge would be likely to oversentimentalize in the hypothetical situation as argue that he would tend to legalism.

Beyond these specific items, there are two general points to consider, bearing on the over-all thrust of this study. Our principal interest is not the mere size of disagreement between the two deciders, although that has importance; our main concern is the *reason* for their disagreement. And as to the magnitude of disagreement, assuming that legalism would tend to increase it beyond its true measure, we find most impressive not the extent of disagreement, but its modesty.

mains a valid point of criticism. There is no way of completely ensuring that a hypothetical decision will have all the characteristics of a real one, and no way, in a study of living institutions such as ours, to avoid its use.

However, we are secure that the force of such criticism, theoretically impressive though it may be at this point, will diminish considerably, if not disappear altogether, as the study unfolds, and a more intimate acquaintance with the material becomes possible. Experience with these disagreements themselves and the vividness with which the judge reports them is the best test of their reality. In the end we conclude, as we must, that there are sufficient reasons for taking the hypothetical judge verdicts as reliable.

One other aspect deserves attention. This inquiry has tested importantly the possibilities of studying living institutions. The cooperation required of the trial judges would appear to have levied a formidable tax on their time and sense of propriety. The fact that so many trial judges spent the time, and gave their trust, may carry a welcome suggestion about not unduly exaggerating the practical barriers to social research.

CHAPTER 5

The Basic Pattern of Disagreement
Between Jury and Judge

This study seeks to answer two basic questions: First, what is the magnitude and direction of the disagreement between judge and jury? And, second, what are the sources and explanations of such disagreement? It is the business of this chapter to give the over-all answers to the first question. The remainder of the book is fundamentally devoted to analyzing ·and explaining the differences between judge and jury which this chapter reports.

Although any distinctive function of the jury must be found in the possibility of disagreement between judge and jury, there is something curious in the question how much judge and jury agree and disagree. No prior expectations exist either among the legal profession or in legal tradition as to what a proper amount of disagreement between judge and jury should be. We lack a pre-existing context in which to place the measurements. You may find it amusing to make your own private guess and to see whether it overestimates or underestimates the amount of actual disagreement.

Table 11 reports for the full sample of 3576 cases the actual verdict of the jury and the matching hypothetical verdict of the judge. Since the jury may acquit, convict, or hang, where realistically the judge may only acquit or convict, the verdicts distribute in six cells.[1]

---

[1] Though to be precise Table 11 is a sixfold table (2 x 3), it can serve to introduce its simpler prototype, the fourfold (2 x 2) contingency

TABLE 11
Verdict of Jury and Judge
(In Per Cent of All 3576 Trials)

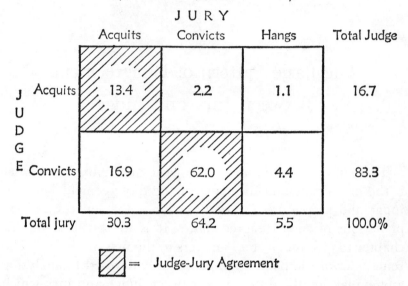

JURY

		Acquits	Convicts	Hangs	Total Judge
J U D G E	Acquits	13.4	2.2	1.1	16.7
	Convicts	16.9	62.0	4.4	83.3
Total jury		30.3	64.2	5.5	100.0%

▨ = Judge-Jury Agreement

Table 11 thus furnishes the basic measure of the magnitude of judge-jury disagreement. Reading the two shaded cells first, we obtain the percentage of cases in which judge and jury agree. They agree to acquit in 13.4 per cent of all cases and to convict in 62.0 per cent of all cases, thus yielding a total agreement rate of 75.4 per cent.

Looking next at the four unshaded cells, we see that the total disagreement, 24.6 per cent of all cases, consists of (16.9 + 2.2 =) 19.1 per cent of cases in which judge and jury disagree

---

table (see Table 12 below). It matches the verdicts of jury and judge by confronting two dichotomies: *jury acquits* or *convicts* with *judge acquits* or *convicts*. Such a matrix is a remarkably economic expositive device. It enables us to see not only what juries and judges do independently (this is reflected in the pair of marginal percentages outside the quadrangle), but simultaneously, what they decide as against each other. See Zeisel, Say It With Figures, Chs. VIII and IX (4th ed. 1957). Table 11 has, of course, no provision for judges who "hang," but not surprisingly we had two cases (excluded from the sample) in which the judges stated that they simply could not make up their minds.

on guilt, and $(1.1 + 4.4 =)$ 5.5 per cent of cases in which the jury hangs.[2]

It is not easy to know what to make of these figures. To some, no doubt, the fact that judge and jury agree some 75 per cent of the time will be read as a reassuring sign of the competence and stability of the jury system; to others the fact that they disagree 25 per cent of the time will be viewed as a disturbing sign of the anarchy and eccentricity of the jury. We would suggest that the significance of these figures for any judgment about the jury must depend on the reasons for these disagreements and must wait upon the detailed examination of those reasons.

The inclusion of hung juries makes Table 11 somewhat awkward to handle. At times it will prove useful to employ the following convention in the counting of hung juries: a hung jury will be considered as in effect half an acquittal.[3] Accordingly in Table 12, Table 11 is rewritten by redistributing the hung juries half to the acquittals and half to the convictions and rounding off to integers.[4]

---

[2] The figure of 5.5 per cent hung juries conceivably understates somewhat the true frequency of hung juries. Since our instructions to the judges as to what constitutes a reportable jury trial were perhaps imprecise on the point, it is possible that some felt no need to report on what is technically a mistrial. However, the total lack of more reliable data on this point moved us to accept our figure. See Appendix A.

[3] Before the hung juries are redistributed, it is worth noting that the judge's ratio of acquittals to convictions is roughly the same for cases where the jury reaches a verdict as for cases where the jury does not:

	Jury hangs	Jury decides
Judge acquits	1.1	15.6
Judge convicts	4.4	78.9
	5.5	94.5

Further points on the hung jury are examined in Chapter 36.

[4] This distribution is predicated on the experience that, as a practical matter, roughly half the hung jury cases end up having the same consequences for the defendant as an acquittal, either because his prosecution is dropped or because he is acquitted in a

TABLE 12

Verdict of Jury and Judge — Consolidated
(Per Cent of All 3576 Trials)

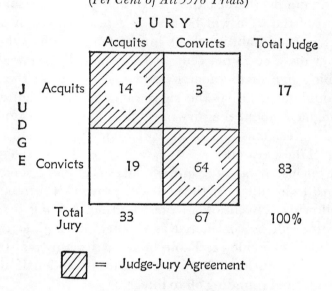

J U R Y

		Acquits	Convicts	Total Judge
J	Acquits	14	3	17
U				
D				
G				
E	Convicts	19	64	83
	Total Jury	33	67	100%

▨ = Judge-Jury Agreement

It is immediately apparent in Table 12 that the jury's disagreement with the judge is massively in one direction, and the direction is the expected one. The jury has long been regarded as a bulwark of protection for the criminal defendant, and Table 12 can be taken to retell this story. There is some

---

subsequent trial. This is based on an estimate we were given by an experienced prosecutor. We were unable to obtain reliable statistics on the final disposition of the hung juries. The practice varies according to jurisdiction. The Los Angeles Municipal Court, for instance, considers the final vote, and if a clear majority found the defendant guilty the case is retried. For data on that court, see generally, Holbrook, A Survey of Metropolitan Trial Courts — Los Angeles Area (1956). And, of course, some of the retried cases end in acquittal, if not in a second hung jury.

Compare also the English practice: "There is . . . no compulsion upon the Crown to re-indict a man, after a disagreement of the jury, but it is the usual practice to re-indict once, and then, if the jury disagree a second time, to enter a *nolle prosequi* or consent to a directed acquittal. Sometimes, for special reasons, the Crown abandons a case after a single disagreement of the jury." Williams, the Proof of Guilt, p. 283, London (1955).

puzzle, however, as to how best to state the extent of this imbalance in favor of the defendant. After considerable deliberation over the point, we now conclude that the most meaningful statement is the simplest. The jury is less lenient than the judge in 3 per cent of the cases and more lenient than the judge in 19 per cent of the cases. Thus, the jury trials show on balance a net leniency of 16 per cent. This means that in the cases which the defendant decides to bring before the jury, on balance, he fares better 16 per cent of the time than he would have in a bench trial.[5]

But this figure must not be made the basis for a general probability calculus by *any* defendant, because the cases to which this 16 per cent applies have been selected for jury trial *because* they are expected to evoke pro-defendant sentiments.[6]

Tables 11 and 12 summarize the most important area of disagreement between judge and jury, namely disagreement on acquittal and conviction. There are, however, further ways in which judge and jury can disagree in criminal cases, and, to round out the picture, we look now at the possibilities of disagreements on charge and on penalty. Such subsidiary disagreements arise from special characteristics of the case and from special provisions of the law which vary from one jurisdiction to another.

In a fair number of cases more than one charge is pre-

---

[5] Another way of stating this is by comparing the marginal figures in Table 12. The jury acquits in 33 per cent, the judge in only 17 per cent of all trials. Thus, if all these cases had been tried without a jury, the acquittal ratio would be cut in half.

[6] This marked balance of leniency toward the defendant should not, however, be read as rendering unimportant the 3 per cent of the cases in which the jury reverses itself and is less lenient than the judge. Chapters 29 and 32 analyze in detail these "cross-over" cases which must form a major component of any over-all theory about the performance of the jury.

Essentially, we suspect the jury is non-rule minded. The fact that the jury's pro-prosecution sentiments do not come into play more often is due primarily to the selection of cases that come before it. See pages 30-31 and 495.

sented to the jury; hence, judge and jury can agree to convict but may disagree as to the charge.[7] Again, in some jurisdictions the jury is given the power to set the penalty, as in many southern states with respect to all crimes, and in almost all states with respect to the death penalty. Here, judge and jury may agree to convict and even agree on the charge (if there is more than one) but still disagree as to the level of penalty. In Tables 11 and 12 both these subsidiary disagreements are concealed as agreements to convict.

Table 13 provides the relevant data for disagreements on charge.

TABLE 13

Jury and Judge Agree to Convict, May Disagree on Charge

(Per Cent of All 3576 Trials)

Verdict	Single Charge Cases	Multiple Charge Cases	Total
Judge more lenient *	—	.7	.7
Both agree	38.2	18.6	56.8
Jury more lenient†	—	4.5	4.5
Total	38.2	23.8	62.0**

* Judge, in disagreement with the jury, would have found for lesser charge.
† Jury, in disagreement with the judge, finds for lesser charge.
** This 62.0 per cent appears in Table 11 and represents the trials in which judge and jury agree to convict.

While the picture is somewhat complicated by the circumstance that almost forty per cent of the cases offer no possibility of disagreement on charge, nevertheless in these disagreements the jury once again shows a marked imbalance (4.5 per cent to 0.7 per cent) in favor of the defendant.

[7] The multiple charge may either be concurrent, such as assault and carrying a concealed weapon, where the defendant may be convicted or acquitted on either or both of the charges; or the multiple charge may arise from a doubt as to whether the defendant committed only a "lesser included offense," such as manslaughter instead of murder. Here the defendant can be found guilty of only one of these crimes, not of both. Lesser offenses are included most frequently where a specific intent is at issue, e.g., intention to kill as against intention only to harm.

In an important sense, the 5.2 per cent enlarges the amount of disagreement between jury and judge and hence will be added to the universe of disagreement cases which it is the central objective of this study to analyze. For almost all purposes hereafter disagreements on charge will be considered as full units of disagreement.

The final opportunity for disagreement between judge and jury arises in those cases where the law allows the jury to set the penalty. To trace disagreements on penalty we need carry forward from Table 13 only the 56.8 per cent of all cases in which there was agreement on charge as well as on guilt; it is only in these cases that an independent disagreement on penalty can arise. Table 14 provides the relevant data. While the directionality is the same, the ratio of jury leniency to severity is more evenly balanced for disagreements on penalty than for those on guilt or charge.[8]

TABLE 14

Jury and Judge Agree on Conviction and Charge, May Disagree on Penalty

(Per Cent of All 3576 Trials)

	Per Cent
Judge gives more lenient penalty	1.5
Jury and Judge agree on penalty	5.4
Jury gives more lenient penalty	2.5
Total	9.4*

* In 47.4 per cent of all trials, judge and jury convict on the same charge, but since the judge sets the penalty no penalty disagreement can occur. Adding to these 47.4 per cent the 9.4 per cent penalty disagreement and the 5.2 per cent charge disagreement, we obtain the 62.0 per cent of all trials in which judge and jury agree to convict. See Table 11.

[8] The disagreement ratios for the four types of issues are as follows:

Area of Disagreement	Jury more lenient Per Cent	Judge more lenient Per Cent	Approximate Ratio
Guilt	16.9	2.2	(8:1)
Charge	4.5	.7	(6:1)
Hung jury	4.4	1.1	(4:1)
Penalty	2.5	1.5	(2:1)

The disagreements on penalty will not be included in the later analysis of disagreements,[9] although we devote a separate chapter to the death penalty.[10] Table 15 gives one last view of the full range of disagreement between judge and jury. Beginning with the disagreements on guilt and hung juries, it separates out from the agreements to convict the disagreements on charge, and finally from the agreements to convict on the same charge, the disagreements on penalty.

TABLE 15

Summary View of Judge-Jury Disagreement

(Per Cent of All 3576 Trials)

Disagreement on *guilt*		**19.1**
Judge acquits	2.2	
Jury acquits	16.9	
Jury *hangs* while judge —		**5.5**
would have acquitted	1.1	
would have convicted	4.4	
Disagreement on *charge* only		**5.2**
Judge for lesser offense	.7	
Jury for lesser offense	4.5	
Disagreement on *penalty* only		**4.0**
Judge more lenient	1.5	
Jury more lenient	2.5	
Total disagreement		**33.8%** *
Judge more lenient	**5.5%**	
Jury more lenient	**28.3%**	

* The figures for disagreements on guilt and for the hung juries are taken from Table 11. The figures for disagreements on charge from Table 13 and those on penalty from Table 14. The figure which complements the 33.8 per cent disagreement for 100.0 per cent is 66.2 per cent; it represents the number of trials in which there is no disagreement between jury and judge, neither on guilt nor on charge nor on penalty.

[9] The reason is twofold: first, these disagreements are limited to that small group of states in which the jury may set the penalty; second, and mainly, this study was not designed to catch the subtleties that motivate disagreements on the size of penalty. The problem of differential sentencing for comparable offenses deserves to be studied in a wider context that includes differences between judges.

[10] Chapter 35.

This then is the summary report on the magnitude and direction of judge-jury disagreement in criminal cases, in all its dimensions. Table 15 shows that even when hung juries, disagreements on charge, and disagreements on penalty are included, the general impression left by Table 11, is not substantially altered.

It may be illuminating to set the data on the criminal jury in another perspective by placing it into a complementary context.

We can compare the results in criminal cases with the parallel data from the study of civil jury trials.[11]

TABLE 16

Judge-Jury Disagreement in Civil Cases

(In Per Cent of All Trials)

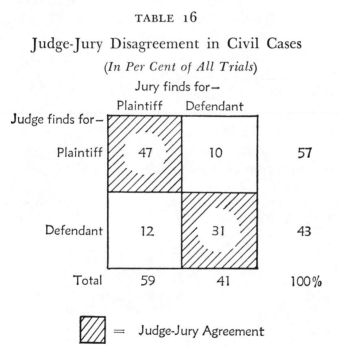

Jury finds for —

	Plaintiff	Defendant	
Judge finds for —			
Plaintiff	47	10	57
Defendant	12	31	43
Total	59	41	100%

▨ = Judge-Jury Agreement

Once again, reading the diagonal of agreement, one notes that the over-all magnitude of agreement of 78 per cent is exactly the same as the 78 per cent for the criminal cases in Table 12.

---

[11] These data come from a companion volume, now in the manuscript stage. It is based on a comparable sample of some four thousand *civil* jury cases.

In some 47 per cent of all cases judge and jury find in favor of the plaintiff on liability, and in some 31 per cent find for the defendant, producing the over-all agreement on liability of 78 per cent. It is quite striking then that the over-all level of agreement between jury and judge is roughly the same whether the business is criminal or civil.

In one important respect, however, the disagreement patterns in criminal and in civil cases are in sharp contrast. In civil cases the disagreement is distributed evenly in the two directions. In 12 per cent of the cases it is the jury that will be more favorable to the plaintiff, and in 10 per cent of the cases it is the judge who would be more favorable to the plaintiff. This finding is in the teeth of the popular expectation that the jury in personal injury cases favors the plaintiff,[12] at least if that expectation is taken to mean that the jury is more likely to favor the plaintiff than is the judge.[13]

Undoubtedly this contrast indicates something profound about the values, attitudes, and functions of the jury in its criminal and civil spheres, a matter which will be explored in depth in the volume reporting out the civil jury cases. There is, however, a line of explanation suggested by our study of

[12] Table 16 includes all civil cases. The pattern for personal injury cases alone is practically the same, partly because these cases form the bulk of all civil jury trials.

Jury Disagreement in Personal Injury Cases

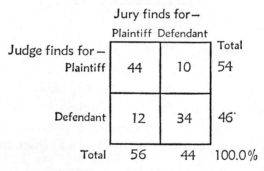

Judge finds for —	Jury finds for—		
	Plaintiff	Defendant	Total
Plaintiff	44	10	54
Defendant	12	34	46
Total	56	44	100.0%

[13] To be sure, once liability has been found and it comes to the handling of the issue of damages, the jury's award is on the average about twenty per cent higher than that of the judge.

jury waiver in criminal cases which should be noted here.   To some degree the difference in the directionality of the disagreements must be a function of the difference in the waiver practice in civil and criminal cases.   As we have seen, the defendant in a criminal case in law and in practice tends to have the option between jury and bench trial.   He therefore chooses the jury in cases where he thinks it will be favorable to him and waives the jury in cases where he thinks it will be unfavorable.   If the defendant were completely knowledgeable there would be only normal disagreements and no cross-overs, since he would have withdrawn the cross-over possibilities from the jury trial universe by waiving the jury.[14]

In the civil case the matter stands differently.   The jury cannot be waived unless both parties consent, and wherever there is an expectation that jury trial may favor one side, that side is going to insist on a jury trial.   Thus in civil cases the waiver rules do not operate to screen out any one class of disagreements.   The marked lack of directionality in judge-jury disagreement in civil cases must at least in part be the result of this situation.

This brief comparison of the criminal and civil jury has been made simply to underscore the directionality of the disagreement of the criminal jury and will have to suffice here.[15]

Chapter 6 will take one more step in measuring the magnitude of judge-jury disagreement by tracing it through for specific crime categories.   After that brief interlude, the remainder of the book, in a very real sense, is but an elaborate gloss on this chapter, as we seek to locate the sources and explanations for the disagreements found to exist in criminal jury trials.

[14] See Chapter 29, note 4, for data comparing waiver rate and the incidence of cross-overs.

[15] We are able to offer one further interesting basis of comparison for the figures presented in this chapter.   The Lord Chief Justice of England, Lord Parker, has been kind enough to furnish us with his informed impressions of what a parallel study of judge-jury disagreement would show in England.   His communication is reproduced in Appendix C.

C H A P T E R   6

The Pattern of Disagreement
for Specific Crimes

The legal mind is accustomed to thinking about the criminal law in terms of specific crime categories. Hence, the lawyer may not feel quite at home until he has seen this additional dimension. By distributing the 3576 cases among forty-two crime categories,[1] we can now redraw the profile of judge-jury disagreement and, in effect, give forty-two specific versions of the basic disagreement pattern.

This set of data has the virtue of bringing us a step closer to the full flavor of the materials the jury deals with, since one of the more striking characteristics of the jury in criminal cases is the extraordinary variety of business which it gets. It ranges, as the sample discloses, from first degree murder all the way down to a prosecution for the illegal keeping of

[1] Reducing the crimes to 42 categories must be to some extent arbitrary, and it is clear at a glance that an occasional catch-all category is used, viz., Other Sex Crimes, Other Traffic Offenses, and the other miscellaneous groupings. There is, however, no convention for establishing a categorization for all crimes. In any event, the breakdown by crime categories will be used only rarely after this chapter. One category deserves perhaps special comment: Forgery here includes some cases of passing a check without sufficient funds.

Generally speaking, there is no one optimal solution for this classification problem, since each effort to classify requires a frame of reference and there are many such frames. One might classify crimes, for instance, by whether or not they have a personal victim, by the severity of the penalty, by the chances of recidivism, and so forth. Sellin and Wolfgang, The Measurement of Delinquency (1964), is a heroic effort to provide what could be called pure categories. But the problem is intrinsically insoluble: what is a good classification for one purpose is an inefficient one for all other purposes.

a mud turtle.[2] Table 17 shows how the sample of 3576 cases is distributed among the forty-two crime categories.

TABLE 17

The Range of Jury Business
(By Crimes)

Person		Property	
Murder	210	Robbery	229
Manslaughter	80	Burglary, breaking and	
Negligent homicide	94	entering	298
Aggravated assault	292	Auto theft	111
Simple assault	78	Mail theft	12
Kidnaping	13	Other grand larceny	128
Prohibited and concealed		Petit larceny	42
weapon	23	Receiving stolen goods	51
		Embezzlement	42
Sex		Fraud	89
Forcible rape	106	Forgery, bad check	112
Statutory rape	70	Extortion	11
Incest	48	Arson	31
Sodomy	46		
Molestation of a minor	38	*Regulatory*	
Indecent exposure	31	Gambling	49
Commercial vice	42	Game laws	21
Other sex offenses	31	Liquor (tax)	51
		Other liquor offenses	82
Traffic		Other regulatory offenses	25
Drunken driving	455		
Other traffic offenses	105	*Misc. Felonies*	
		Narcotics	192
Misc. Misdemeanors		Perjury	19
Miscellaneous public disorder	49	Tax evasion	22
Malicious mischief	18	Escape	14
Non-support and other fam-		Bribery, official misconduct	39
ily offenses	77	Total	3576

The real interest, of course, is in seeing the verdict patterns for each of these crimes. To facilitate the comparison of one verdict pattern with another, certain alterations are made in the structure of the basic fourfold table. Rewritten, the basic table for all cases[3] would appear as follows:[4]

---

[2] One reason for the breadth of this range is the uneven allocation of the right to jury trial below the felony level. See Chapter 2 at page 16.

[3] See Tables 11 and 12.

[4] The format is changed with respect to the following details. Dis-

TABLE 18

Basic Verdict Pattern

(Per Cent of 3576 Trials)

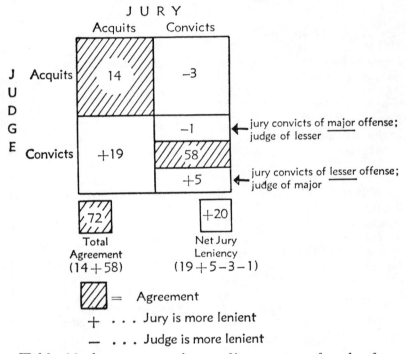

Table 19 then reports the verdict patterns for the forty-two crimes.

---

agreements on charge are added by using three figures rather than just one for the convict-convict cell. The *minus* figure indicates cases where the judge is more lenient than the jury on charge, the middle figure (without a sign) indicates the cases which had only a single charge and those cases of multiple charge where judge and jury agreed on the handling of the charges, and the *plus* figure indicates disagreements on charge where the jury is the more lenient. Two indices of the over-all disagreement are added. In the lower lefthand square the percentage of cases is shown where there is agreement on guilt as well as on charge; in the righthand square we show what we call the measure of *net leniency,* the difference between the disagreements in which the jury is *more lenient* than the judge (normal) and the disagreements in which the jury is *more severe* than the judge (cross-overs).

TABLE 19

Verdict Pattern for Various Crimes

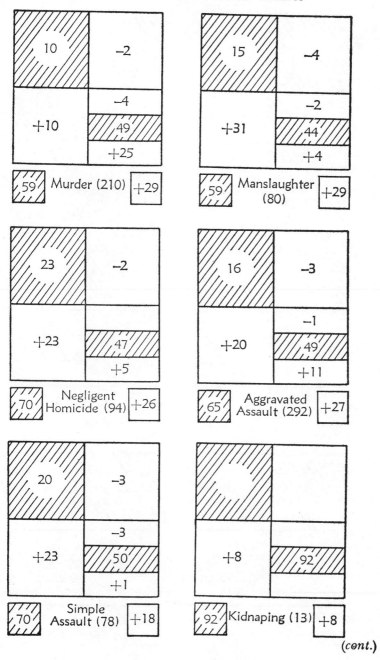

(*cont.*)

TABLE 19 (continued)

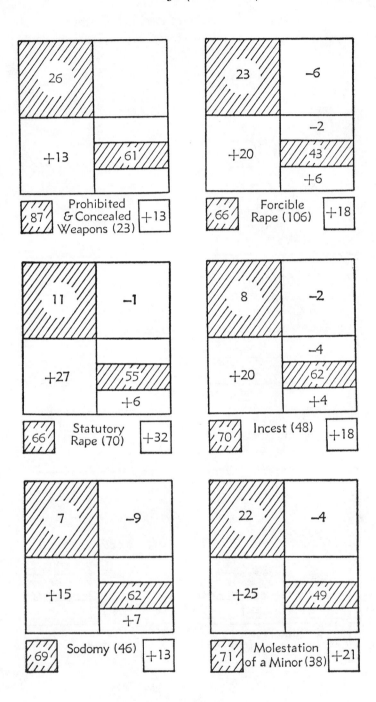

TABLE 19 (continued)

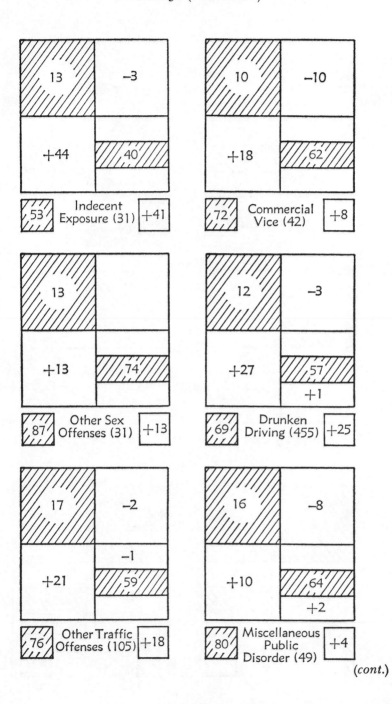

(cont.)

TABLE 19 (continued)

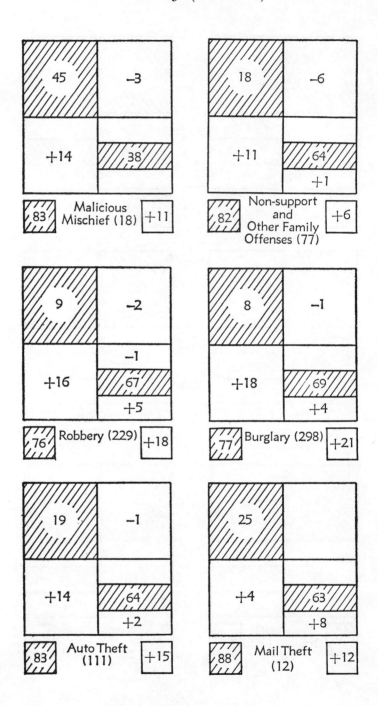

TABLE 19 (continued)

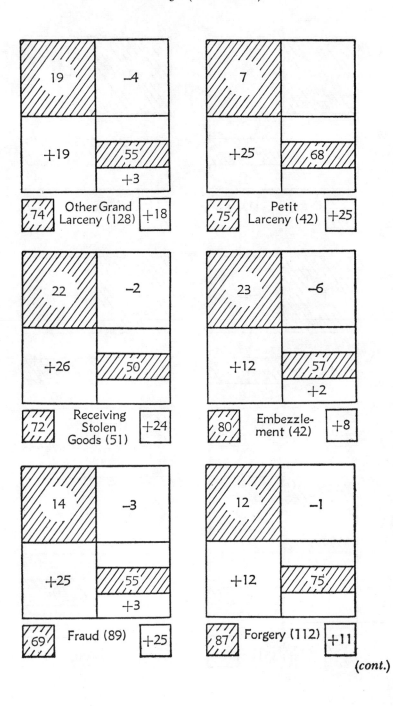

(cont.)

TABLE 19 (continued)

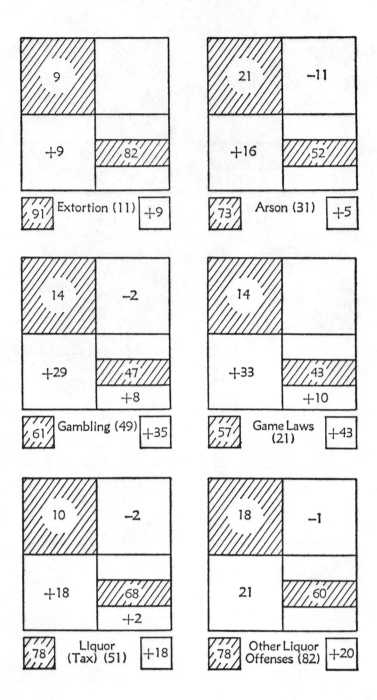

TABLE 19 (continued)

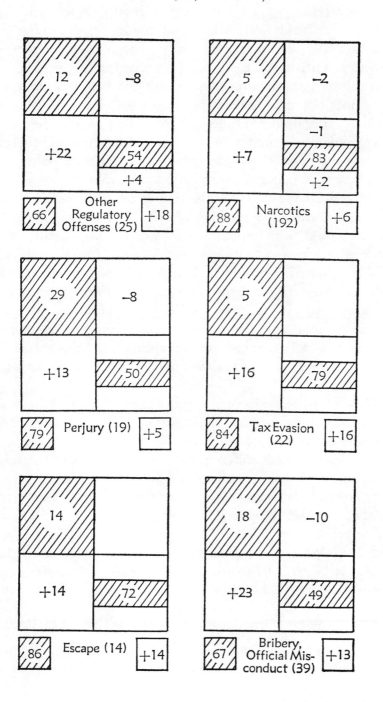

Table 19 invites an important observation.   There is no crime category in which the jury is totally at war with the law, as it probably was in the twenties with respect to the prohibition laws, and as it is said to have been in the eighteenth century with respect to prosecutions for seditious libel. Therefore, what disagreement exists today between judge and jury does not arise because of the impact of one or two particularly unpopular crime categories.[5]   Rather, the jury's disagreement is distributed widely and diffusely over all crime categories.   The jury's war with the law is now a polite one.

There is a common-sense expectation that the sources of disagreement must have something to do with the particular crime, and that an inspection of the disagreements crime-by-crime should bring us halfway toward the final explanation. Indeed, the great variation in net leniency for the crimes in Table 19 seems rich in analytic promise.   Net leniency varies from 43 per cent for game law violations down to 5 per cent for arson and 4 per cent for miscellaneous public disorder.   Or, again, the total agreement between judge and jury shows such extremes as 92 per cent for kidnaping and 88 per cent for narcotics violations as against only 53 per cent for indecent exposure.

The promise, however, is short-lived.   If the crimes are grouped more systematically, according to total disagreement or to net leniency, we reach an analytical impasse.   High on either list are such different crimes as game law violations, indecent exposure, gambling, and murder, and at the bottom are non-support, narcotics, disorderly conduct, and arson. Clearly, to find the common denominators for crimes so diverse requires more than an inspection of the disagreement pattern.   What is required is the inspection of the individual case.   It is part of the odd autobiography of this study that we were a long time arriving at this crucial insight.[6]   After

[5] What remains of this reaction is discussed in Chapter 19, Unpopular Laws.

[6] Approaching the crimes themselves as an explanation, while it failed in its overt purpose, provided an excellent warm-up for the

a procession of frustrating failures we concluded that the approach by way of analyzing crime categories, as such, was a mistake. To borrow a legal metaphor, only as we came to "pierce the veil" of the crime entity and went on to the individual cases did we begin to make headway with the formidable task of locating the sources of judge-jury disagreement. The reasons for disagreement are on the whole not crime specific; the same reason may appear in several or all crimes; in the end the crime categories differ only in the mix.

It may, however, be useful at this point to go a step further and anticipate explanations, reported later, and illustrate the kind of bridge that leads from the individual case to the different verdict patterns for the crime categories. This additional material is intended primarily as a descriptive footnote to this chapter.

Table 20 is based on a question in the Sample II questionnaire that rates each case as to whether the evidence presented with respect to the defendant's guilt was very clear or a close question. For each of the crime categories it gives the percent of all trials in which the judge rated the cases as close on the evidence.

The table reveals, not unexpectedly, that the various crime categories differ considerably with respect to the degree of clarity with which the presented evidence tends to convict, or as the case may be, absolve the defendant. The crimes in Table 20 are ranked in descending order, beginning with arson, where the evidence in the great majority of trials was close, and ending with kidnaping, where the evidence in all trials was clear.[7] Why the various crime categories recruit

---

framing of the eventual reason code. The disagreements were broken down into specific crimes, and for each crime the reasons were tallied and a memorandum prepared therefrom. This operation helped to sensitize us to the problems of the reason code and served as an important first step in the coding methodology discussed in Chapter 7.

[7] To be sure, all the percentages in Table 20 are, like all such data, subject to sampling error, which is the greater, the smaller the number of cases on which the percentage is based. And for some of the crimes the number of cases is very small indeed.

TABLE 20

Closeness of the Evidence for Various Crimes

Crime	Per Cent "Close" of All Trials	Number of Cases *
Arson	86	14
Game law violation	71	7
Commercial vice	70	10
Negligent Homicide	68	31
Misc. public disorder	67	3
Perjury	67	6
Manslaughter	66	38
Receiving stolen goods	64	31
Molestation of a minor	63	16
Petit larceny	62	8
Grand larceny	55	40
Forcible rape	52	44
Malicious mischief	50	2
Incest	50	18
Aggravated assault	48	97
Liquor violations	47	13
Traffic offenses	46	24
Murder	46	70
Drunken driving	44	112
Family offenses	43	21
Forgery, bad check	43	42
Gambling	43	14
Regulatory offenses	40	5
Fraud	40	37
Indecent exposure	40	10
Auto theft	39	46
Narcotics	38	68
Robbery	37	91
Sodomy	36	14
Embezzlement	33	12
Extortion	33	3
Burglary, breaking & entering	31	130
Statutory rape	28	28
Bribery, official misconduct	25	12
Liquor (tax)	24	25
Tax evasion	20	5

* Sample II only.

Crime	Per Cent "Close" of All Trials	Number of Cases*
Prohibited and concealed weapons	20	10
Escape	17	6
Mail theft	17	6
Other sex offenses	14	7
Simple assault	10	10
Kidnaping	0	5

* Sample II only.

evidence so differentially is an interesting question for inquiry and not an easy one to answer. It need not, however, concern us in this study.

In Table 21 we present another, and in this context, last characteristic of jury trials in terms of individual crime categories: the type of defendant that is recruited by these crimes, in terms of a simple but important characteristic, namely whether or not the defendant had a record. Again, we find, as expected, wide variations by crime. Why some crimes are more likely than others to recruit defendants who have no criminal record is another intriguing question this study must forego.

TABLE 21

Proportion of First Offenders for Various Crimes

Crime	Per Cent First Offenders of All Defendants	Number of Cases*
Tax evasion	89	22
Negligent homicide	86	94
Other sex crimes	85	31
Extortion	82	11
Family offenses	80	77
Perjury	79	19
Malicious mischief	77	18
Arson	76	31
Embezzlement	75	42
Statutory rape	74	70
Bribery, official misconduct	74	39
Manslaughter	73	80

* Samples I and II.

Crime	Per Cent First Offenders of All Defendants	Number of Cases*
Fraud	72	89
Traffic offenses	71	105
Liquor violations	68	82
Molestation of a minor	67	38
Game laws	65	21
Regulatory offenses	65	25
Sodomy	65	46
Murder	64	210
Incest	64	48
Receiving stolen goods	61	51
Forcible rape	61	106
Simple assault	61	78
Indecent exposure	58	31
Aggravated assault	58	292
Drunken driving	57	455
Kidnaping	54	13
Prohibited and concealed weapons	48	23
Gambling	44	49
Misc. public disorder	44	49
Robbery	39	229
Liquor (tax)	38	51
Grand larceny	37	128
Mail theft	36	12
Forgery	35	112
Auto theft	32	111
Narcotics	31	192
Petit larceny	23	42
Burglary	22	298
Escape	21	14
Commercial vice	17	42

* Samples I and II.

We might add that both these factors, closeness of the evidence and the frequency of defendants with prior records, show some correlation with the disagreement between jury and judge, but these correlations rather obscure than illuminate the points which will emerge with greater clarity later on.[8]

[8] The rank order correlations of the percentages in Tables 20 and 21 with judge-jury disagreement are of the magnitude of only about +.03.

However interesting these data on the individual crime categories may be in themselves, this closer look at them remains a side trip not materially advancing our search for the reasons for disagreement. The answer begins with the analysis of the reasons for disagreement in each individual case, and once these reasons are found, it is a simple matter and ironically no longer one of great interest to explain why the verdict patterns for the specific crimes are as they are.

W E SEEK to do more than measure the magnitude and direction of judge-jury disagreement. The quest is to establish explanations for this disagreement.

Chapter 7 covers the crucial methodological step in the study; it exposes critically the methods — reason assessment in the individual cases, and cross-tabulation — by which the particular sources of disagreement are located.

Chapter 8 offers an overview of the sources of disagreement. It organizes and summarizes the disagreements into five grand categories, which then serve as an architecture for the rest of the book.

CHAPTER 7

Methodology: The Logic
of Explanation

What does it mean to *explain* why A decides a case as he
does? Or, to put the question more precisely, what does it
mean to explain why A decides a case differently from the
way B decides it? The philosophy of science is heavy with
discussions on the nature of explanation[1] but such a formidable
issue need not detain us long. Our aspirations are modest, and
this essay on the logic of explanation can be brief.

An example or two will help. If we go back for a moment to
a basic table on judge-jury verdict differences and say that the

---

[1] It will suffice here to cite three general references, each representing
a different level of complexity: Nagel, The Structure of Science, especially Ch. 2, Patterns of Scientific Explanation, and Ch. 14, Explanation
and Understanding in the Social Sciences (1961); on a less rigorous level,
Brown, Explanation in Social Science (1963); and finally, from the perspective of the research analyst, Zeisel, Tools of Causal Analysis, Part II
of Say It With Figures (4th ed. 1957).

There is of course a vast traditional literature on the judicial process,
explaining why appellate judges decide the way they do. Among the
major efforts are Levi, An Introduction to Legal Reasoning (1949);
Llewellyn, The Common Law Tradition, Deciding Appeals (1960); and
Hart, The Concept of Law (1961). The legal realist movement had as a
principal concern the reasons that lie beyond the stated opinions.
Recently this interest has been revived by a group of political scientists stressing quanitative analysis. See Judicial Decision Making
(Schubert ed. 1963). To some extent the analysis of judicial behavior
has been an ideological battle between those who emphasize the logical
aspects of decision making and those who emphasize its behavioral
aspects.

20 per cent net leniency difference[2] is explained by the jury's being more favorable to the criminal defendant than is the judge, we will in effect have said nothing and explained nothing. We will simply have repeated in a slightly different and less precise form the fact shown by the table that the over-all net leniency of the jury is 20 per cent.

But suppose we now move on and consider the differences in the disagreement patterns for different crimes. We confront the sharp contrast between the 41 per cent jury leniency in indecent exposure cases and the 6 per cent leniency in narcotics trials.[3] To say that this difference is explained by the difference between narcotics violations and indecent exposure cases will again not have advanced matters very far. Once more, we will have simply repeated in words the numerical results shown in the table.

If now we anticipate a later finding and state that the jury distinguishes in indecent exposure cases between those involving an adult victim and those involving a child victim,[4] and that its disagreement with the judge arises primarily in cases involving an adult victim, we are moving toward what we regard as a significant explanation. Further, we can move from this single explanation to a more general one. If we perceive that in the case of exposure to the adult female, at least where she is already sexually experienced, the crime takes on a marked *de minimis* aspect, and if moreover, we find other instances in which the jury, in disagreeing with the judge, expresses a *de minimis* sentiment, we have arrived at a more rounded explanation of judge-jury disagreement.

The judge presumably does not draw the jury's distinction between adult and child victims in these cases because the formal law does not draw it, and he is bound by tradition and role to stay within the sentiments of the formal law. The jury, on the other hand, does not have a comparable tradition, discipline, or role; it, in fact, necessarily retains a certain

2 Table 18.
3 Table 19, pages 71 and 75, respectively.
4 Table 76.

degree of discretion and autonomy no matter what the judge tells it about the law. Therefore, within its irrepressible discretion, the jury finds room to respond to the *de minimis* sentiment that such indecent exposure cases present.

This, in general, is what we mean by explanation, and there is nothing mysterious about it. In retrospect it appears to involve two special steps: First, pinpointing an isolated, highly specific source of disagreement so as to reduce the possibility that other intervening variables are still operating; and, second, finding by way of corroboration some larger reason-category under which the specific reason can be subsumed.

There are two additional observations to be made. Necessarily there is a self-imposed limit on how far back to go in a string of causes. The present analysis does not go beyond the observation that the institution of the jury, by its very architecture, permits a kind of response to common-sense equities which the institution of the judge does not equally permit.[5]

A specific hypothesis as to the source of judge-jury disagreement, such as in indecent exposure cases, does not assert that the jury is always conscious of this explanation and that all jurors would necessarily give this reason if interviewed as to why they acquitted these defendants. The decision-maker may not be fully aware of his motivation; nevertheless, it makes sense to talk of this or that as the cause of his choice. Moreover, when, as with the jury, it is a group that is making the decision, it will frequently be true that not all members of the group will have reached the joint decision for the same reason.[6]

---

[5] At times the limit for pursuing further a string of causes is imposed by technical obstacles, such as are met in inquiries into unconscious motivations, or simply by interviewing costs. Frequently, however, the exploration ends because there simply is no further need for it. A stone falls to the ground because of gravitation; a husband gives flowers to his wife because it is her birthday. In both situations, there is no obvious need to go further. See Zeisel, Say It With Figures, pp. 158, 212 (4th ed. 1957).

[6] We know from other parts of the Jury Project in which the jury deliberation process is investigated that the jurors often agree on a verdict without necessarily agreeing on all the premises thereto. For

If this then is what is meant by an explanation, what are the methods by which explanations can be discovered? The customary method for survey data is cross-tabulation, a technique designed to approximate a controlled experiment. It may be helpful to compare, for a specific instance, the way an experiment works with the way cross-tabulation works.[7]

Assume that it is our purpose, as in fact it will be later, to ascertain the extent to which the lawyer is the cause of judge-jury disagreement, testing the hypothesis that the jury in fact tries the lawyer and not the case. If one were to explore this point by way of experiment and could waive the practical difficulties, the model would look somewhat as follows. One would arrange for two sets of paired counsel: one set in which defense counsel was always superior to the prosecutor and one set in which counsel on both sides were always evenly matched. Assuming again that practicality proved no obstacle, cases would be drawn at random for trial, alternately with equal and with unequal counsel. Having repeated this process sufficiently often,[8] it would be possible to read off the results and to know whether superiority of defense counsel had any impact

---

a classic example of one of the more unusual ways in which such agreements can be reached, see Kalven, The Jury the Law and the Personal Injury Damage Award, Ohio St. L.J., v. 19, pp. 158, 177 (1958). This is, of course, also true for collegial decisions by judges. For example, in Kingsley Pictures Corp. v. Bd. of Regents, 360 U.S. 684 (1959), the decision was based on sharply divergent opinions; for a discussion of the various opinions in the Kingsley case, see Kalven, Metaphysics of the Law of Obscenity, 1960. Supreme Ct. Rev., p. 1.

[7] For a standard discussion of this comparison, consult Kendall and Lazarsfeld, Problems of Survey Analysis, in Continuities in Social Research, p. 133 (Merton and Lazarsfeld eds. 1950).

[8] The frequency is related to the confidence one may have in the result of the experiment. It is the same problem that arises with the drawing of a sample from a finite population: the larger the sample, the greater the certainty that the measurements of the sample will be close to the measurements that would have been obtained from a census. In the case of an experiment one samples an *infinite* population, namely the universe of all possible repetitions of the experiment. The mathematical relationship between the sample size and the degree of confidence in its findings is almost the same for both situations.

on the amount of judge-jury disagreement. If one found that the jury disagreed with the judge more often in the group of cases where defense counsel was superior, one would conclude that disparity of counsel was a cause of judge-jury disagreement. One would be able to conclude this because the logic of the controlled experiment requires that everything be held constant and comparable — except the experimental variable itself. If, all other things being equal, there is a difference in result, the difference is inescapably attributable to the variation introduced by the experimental variable, in this case the difference in the quality of counsel. This is the logic of the controlled experiment in its simplest form, and within its limits it is, of course, unbeatable.

In large part the problem of contemporary social science is that, on serious issues, the controlled experiment under natural field conditions is unavailable, as much for reasons of propriety as for reasons of expense.[9] In survey research, however, the powerful substitute technique, cross-tabulation, has been developed, and it can often be made reasonably to approximate the rigor of the experiment. It can be viewed as simply a retrospective controlled experiment. The cases are grouped *after the fact* by the critical variable to see if the variable has produced a difference. In terms of our example, we would collect in one group the cases in which counsel were equal and in another group the cases in which defense

[9] Ordinarily, controlled experiments with human beings can be performed only with captive audiences: school children, members of the armed forces, and, of course, inmates of jails and other institutions. The efficiency of different teaching methods has been thus tested in schools where different classes were assigned different teaching procedures at random. Similarly, the effectiveness of certain indoctrination procedures has been tested by random assignment to different companies of the same regiment; finally, the effect of differential treatment of convicts has been tested in this way to measure effects on future recidivism. Concerning the specific difficulty of experimentation with legal institutions, see The Case for the Official Experiment, in Zeisel, Kalven, Buchholz, Delay in the Court, Ch. 21 (1959); Zeisel, The Law, in Uses of Sociology (Lazarsfeld ed. 1966). For a recent sophisticated application of the official controlled experiment, see Rosenberg, The Pretrial Conference and Effective Justice (1964).

counsel was superior, and compare the resulting verdicts. The logic is precisely the same as for the experiment, except for one important and in the end ineradicable difficulty; one can never be sure that the groups of cases to be compared are comparable in all respects other than the critical variable. To be specific, the cases in which defense counsel was superior may, and probably will, differ in other respects as well from the cases in which defense counsel was not superior. They may be more serious cases; they may be more difficult cases; they may involve less attractive, or more wealthy defendants; and so forth. In the language of statistics the aim is to avoid spurious correlations, where for example, what appears on the surface to be a jury response to superior defense counsel may in fact be a response to a more sympathetic defendant who in turn was more likely to recruit superior counsel. There is also the problem of a spurious noncorrelation, that is, of an existing difference being concealed by the noncomparability of the two sets of cases. This would be the result if, for example, defendants with long criminal records tended to have superior counsel. In such cases the jury's lack of sympathy for these defendants might offset and hence conceal its response to the superior lawyer.[10]

There is a standard technique designed to reduce the dangers of noncomparability. By dividing the sample into subgroups, one can progressively increase the homogeneity of these groups. In the counsel example one might divide by the nature of the crime, the type of defendant, the closeness of the evidence, etc. Thus, in much survey work today, the problem of noncomparability admits of a tolerable solution and a fair approximation to an experiment can be made.

The original strategy of our survey looked to a major use

[10] A study of milk consumption showed a surprising lack of correlation between the amount of milk purchased and income. But when the number of children per family was held constant, a correlation appeared. The explanation of course was that the richer families bought more milk per child but had fewer children. See Zeisel, Say It With Figures, p. 203 (4th ed. 1957).

of cross-tabulation, especially since we had the rare opportunity of using two questionnaires.[11] However the most surprising fact about the evolution of the methodology of this study is that these apparently secure expectations of relying on cross-tabulation were largely, although not entirely, defeated.

The reason is flattering to the law. The variety of circumstances that affect the verdicts in criminal cases turn out, as the lawyer would suspect, to be so great as to hobble the use of cross-tabulation. In spite of elaborate efforts, our analytic network of questions will have failed to pick up some of the significant variables. Even with so old and so well known an institution as the jury, one is not likely to have sufficient foresight in design to insure maximum use of cross-tabulation.

Yet in another sense we were equally embarrassed by the number of factors we did have. Here the difficulty was that the necessity of cross-tabulating by relevant subgroups, to insure some homogeneity, very soon exhausted our sample; after using a matrix of just a few factors, we would encounter cells that had hardly any or even no cases. Perhaps a sample ten times the size of ours might have enabled us to succeed; as it was, we reached the limits of utility of cross-tabulation at an early stage.[12]

While it is thus true that we were unable to make cross-tabulation the primary method of establishing explanations, nevertheless, as will become apparent as the study proceeds, cross-tabulation retains a critical, if limited role.

[11] See Chapter 4, page 47.

[12] Even resorting to statistical sign tests (which count the number of times a paired comparison favors one alternative over another) and other so-called non-parametric techniques one may fall back on when one has many cells and the number of cases in the cells becomes small could not be applied because of the sparsity of the data. The truth is that we underestimated the number of relevant variables, although we should have been forewarned by Stouffer's experience in Communism, Conformity and Civil Liberties (1955). There, in a much less complex situation, he soon ran out of cases. On the use of the sign test, see Brownlee, Statistical Theory and Methodology in Science and Engineering, Ch. 7 (rev. ed. 1965).

With, then, experiment out of the question and cross-tabulation often unemployable, a different method was required to locate the needed explanations.

The method turned out to be what for convenience we call *reason assessment,* the assessment by a third party on an individual case-by-case basis. It was the trial judge who was the third party assessor as he gave his reasons for the causes of disagreement with the jury in the case before him. In addition, from time to time, based on the information he supplied, we ourselves acted as assessors and made the estimate of the cause of disagreement in the individual case.

In an important way this use of the judge as a third party assessor was a unique, custom-made method with little precedent. There are however at least two methods that are analogous: the assessment of causes in studies of traffic accidents and motivational research interviewing.

While a variety of methods are being used in an effort to discover the causes of auto accidents, a particularly vigorous one today is that of having an expert assess the causes of the accident from post-accident clues.[13] Since the principal actors will in many cases be dead or unhelpful because they are unaware of critical circumstances, the assessment of causes by a third party becomes indispensable. His expertise with the performance of automobiles, roads, and drivers, and the special configuration of post-accident clues, yields distinctive insights into the particular case. The effectiveness of the method in part depends on the circumstance that it concerns itself only with the exceptional, the deviant case.

The second analogous method, motivational research, seeks to establish reasons for individual acts by eliciting and analyzing the actor's motives as spelled out in his own utterances. For relatively simple decisions, such as are often found in marketing research, this has proved a powerful research tool. It is similar to our judge reason assessment in two respects: it

[13] See Baker, A Framework for Assessment of Causes of Automobile Accidents, reprinted in The Language of Social Research, pp. 438-488 (Lazarsfeld ed. 1955).

pursues reasons or motives for decisions, and it does it in the individual case. An example may help. Suppose we wanted to learn why somebody who for years has been using one grocery store has now switched to another. Obviously one way to find out would be to ask him why he changed. And, although both such asking and answering are more complicated than it would seem, this is clearly the best research approach.[14] The utility of the method depends on the actor's knowledge of his own motivations and on his willingness to disclose them. It is, therefore, best suited for surface, everyday decisions. When the decision is a complex one, the method quickly reaches its limits. One need only contemplate the question "Why did you marry Barbara?" to realize that there are many problems for which this method is likely to be ineffective.[15]

In a way, then, the novelty of our approach is that we combine these two methods. The accident assessment method is not used to explain a physical event, but to unearth human motivations. It is perhaps worth a few words to explain why the direct interviewing of motivational research did not prove feasible. Unlike the customary problem in such research,

---

[14] The method was orginally outlined in a paper by Lazarsfeld, The Art of Asking Why, National Marketing Review, v. 1 (Summer 1935), and has since become an established technique in the search for motivations. The technique is described in Zeisel, Say It With Figures, Chs. VI and VII (4th ed. 1957). A comprehensive presentation will appear in the article Motivation Research (Kadushin) in the forthcoming edition of the International Encyclopedia of Social Sciences.

[15] The problem here is that the exploration of motives of which the actor is unconscious is at best a job for the psychoanalytic method. Some minor forays into the area of unconscious motivation can be made in ordinary social science investigations by using projective techniques, such as showing an ambiguous picture and asking for the respondent's interpretation. In the area of market research such problems assume major importance when actual product differences are small and therefore the product "image" becomes vital. Thus, studies on cigarette smoking revealed that certain personality types are attracted to particular brands of cigarettes because of a feeling of compatibility with, or emulation for, the "image" that the brand's advertising projects. (From unpublished studies by Herta Herzog.)

ours was complicated by the fact that the aim was not to find out why A or B decided the way he did, but why A decided *differently* from B.   The full use of motivational research techniques would have required interviewing both judge and jury.   In effect we interviewed only the judge, although he in many cases had interviewed the jury.[16]

In the end, under reason assessment, what the judge was asked to do was to make a *gestalt* judgment encompassing all the many facets of the case and finally pinpointing the circumstances that accounted for any difference between the jury's decision and his own.

General considerations of method apart, there are some strong reasons why the trial judge can be relied upon to locate the sources of judge-jury disagreement, beyond the simple circumstance that he often established them by talking to the jurors after they had rendered their verdict.[17]

First, the judge has the advantage of continuous exposure to jury behavior.   There is the reassuring fact that he was reacting to a particular case rather than giving his opinions of

[16] To interview each jury would have proved a task of impossible magnitude.   We know the magnitude because in another part of the Jury Project we undertook the job.   With permission of the courts, jurors were extensively interviewed in one federal and one state court. A subsequent volume of the Project will deal with the findings that emerged from these interviews.   Since it is never known in advance when the jury will begin and end its deliberations, such interviewing requires a prolonged waiting time for the interviewers.   Moreover, at the end of the trial the jurors are anxious to go home, and it is necessary to keep at least six interviewers in readiness so that no juror need be detained overlong.   Since in the case of the present study these arrangements would have been necessary for several hundred courts over a period of years, the magnitude of such a task is clearly prohibitive.

In any event, the data from such interviews are involved and ambiguous.   A jury verdict is a group decision often reached for a number of individual reasons.   At best, a substantial job would have been left for third party assessment as to why the verdicts of judge and jury differed.

[17] It is not improbable that the judges talked to jurors more often than normally because they were confronted with the task of answering our questionnaire.

jury performance in general. He had just heard the case and he was fully sensitized to the difficulties of deciding it. He was thus a very special observer.

Secondly, the judge's task was purposely narrowed at the outset by the fact that he was directed to give reasons only for the cases where he and the jury disagreed. The inquiry thus gains a helpful directionality. The search is for something in the case which moved the jury away from the law and the facts as the judge saw them. One may expect in these cases a higher visibility of the jury's motives.

But the major arguments for trusting the judge's perceptiveness are not a priori based but come from a study of the reasons he in fact gave. In some cases the given explanation was totally obvious on the face of the questionnaire itself and was perfectly captured by the trial judge. To cite but one instance, in a case where the defendant is charged with serving liquor to a minor and where the facts are not really disputed, the jury nevertheless acquits. The distinctive circumstance is that the minor in question was a sailor in uniform. The judge nails down the explanation with the remark:

> The jury seemed to feel that if a boy can be taken and forced to fight, he can buy and consume a bottle of beer. [I-0140] [18]

Moreover, the judge has little difficulty in empathizing with the jury. He must be tempted by the same considerations, which not only tempt, but move the jury. As Lord Bramwell is said to have remarked: "One third of the judge is a common law juror, if you get beneath the ermine." [19] Thus, while the judge for good reasons might not yield to his juror-impulses, he will perceive them all the same. And one of the most remarkable aspects of his reporting has been his sensitivity to reasons which did not move him.

Rarely are the judge's explanations given in terms of general stereotypes such as that the defendant was a beautiful

[18] The numerical case citations used throughout the book are explained in Chapter 9, note 2.

[19] Quoted in Cohen, Robson and Bates, Parental Authority: The Community and the Law, p. 5 (8th ed. 1958).

woman, or that the jury was too stupid to understand the case, or something of that sort. As the many excerpts from judge's comments given in the remainder of the book will show, the trial judge reports, as a rule, with flavor, intensity, and literary skill and with that degree of particularity that is the mark of saying something fresh about *this* case.[20]

One further reason for trusting the judge's explanation in the individual case is difficult to perceive until one has read the study through. It turns on the fact that his highly individualized explanations for particular cases tend to fall into larger categories of explanation. Thus the recurring pattern from different cases, from different judges, and from different jurisdictions strengthens the explanation in the individual case.[21]

One might also consider it support for the judge's ability to suggest the true explanations that at times he was unable to find one. The fact that such cases occurred can be read as a comforting sign that there was some special shock of recognition in the cases for which the explanation emerged. As we will see, for roughly ten per cent of the cases, no explanation could be found.[22]

The judge's ability to assess reasons has, to be sure, its limitations. Not only may he at times err, but his very focus on the individual case may prevent him from seeing causes for disagreement that emerge only from a broader analysis. For example, only rarely does the judge refer to the possibility of there being a different threshold of reasonable doubt for the jury and for the judge,[23] or to the possibility that defendants without a criminal record, testifying on their own

[20] There are, however, two points in the study where the judge's comments do tend to generality. The explanations are flat and do not reflect so much the immediate case as they do a broader and somewhat too convenient theorizing about disagreement in cases of that particular kind. In such instances we require corroboration. For the treatment of these cases, see Chapter 14, A Different Threshold of Reasonable Doubt, and Chapter 26, A Note on Crime in a Subculture.

[21] The few cases which escape classification are reviewed in Chapter 27, An Anthology of Non-Recurring Sentiments.

[22] Table 25.

[23] This is discussed in Chapter 14.

behalf, may evoke a higher degree of credibility from the jury than from the judge.[24]

It remains to say a further word about *our* role in making assessments. In about 10 per cent of the cases some reasons for disagreement were assessed by us and not by the judge. This variant on reason assessment recommended itself at several points. In many instances little more was involved than a matter of form. The judge would leave blank the space provided for the explanation, but would mention elsewhere on the questionnaire, simply by way of describing the case, factors which clearly implied an explanation. Thus he might describe in sensitive detail characteristics which made the defendant sympathetic to the jury, without explicitly offering this as an explanation of jury leniency. In other cases, the judge, although again offering distinctive and helpful facts in briefing the case, might announce that he was mystified by the jury's disagreement and had no explanation for it. Occasionally a judge would give one reason and we would add another based on the implications of his description.

In the end there are two things to emphasize about our intrusion into the assessment process. First, the clues always came from something the judge himself had said and considered worth reporting. Second, in view of our training and intense experience with the questionnaires in the study, we acquired some degree of expertise for the very special problem at hand.[25]

As a final comment on the method of reason assessment we come back to cross-tabulation. We indicated earlier that cross-tabulation plays a limited but critical role in this study. We can now state precisely what the role is. First, at a few points cross-tabulation was the prime source of establishing the explanation, especially with respect to some evidence problems.[26]

[24] The effect of this is examined in Chapter 13.
[25] Chapter 17, which deals with behavior of the victim contributory to the crime, affords a good illustration of our role.
[26] Cf. Tables 56-57 (record-stand), Table 76 (exhibitionism), and Table 52 (evidence map).

Its chief role, however, arose in cases where the two methods overlapped, in the sense that each furnished evidence of the same explanation. Where the two methods led essentially to the same finding, they served to corroborate each other;[27] where they failed to reveal such convergence, we hesitate to draw a conclusion.[28]

In theory cross-tabulation and reason assessment, it should be stressed, must lead to the same result. The influence of the lawyer may again serve as example. Assume that in some twenty cases we find as the reason for disagreement the fact that the defense counsel was superior. A cross-tabulation then comparing all cases in which defense counsel was superior to all cases in which counsel were equal should, ideally, mirror this situation. The cases with superior counsel should show a higher rate of disagreement, and it should be higher by the same twenty cases, as shown in Table 22.

Table 22 illustrates the implications of the hypothesis that there will be a higher rate of jury disagreement in favor of the defendant in the cases in which defense counsel is superior to his adversary. The disagreement there is assumed to be 60 per cent, as against 40 per cent in the cases where the defense is not superior. The implication is that a 40-per-cent level is being reached without superior counsel, hence only $(60 - 40 =)$ 20 per cent of the disagreement cases above the 40 per cent level can be attributed to the presence of superior counsel.

[27] For points in this study where we take the unusual step of confronting cross-tabulation and reason assessment, and thus test empirically the relationship that is shown to exist between the two, see Table 92 on the effect of superior counsel and Table 68 on the effect of sympathy. There is also an occasional confrontation of negative results, such as on the question whether the jury understands the case, see Chapter 11, Table 50, and note 15, and on the effect of the repudiated confession, Table 54.

[28] One instance in which cross-tabulation failed to bear out reason assessment is the case of the accomplice testifying for the prosecution; the judge occasionally blames the jury's refusal to accept such testimony as a reason for a disagreement. See Chapter 13 at Table 55. But see Tables 56 and 57 for an important exception.

TABLE 22

Schematic Relationship Between Cross-tabulation and Reason Assessment

Effect of Superior Counsel on Disagreement between Jury and Judge

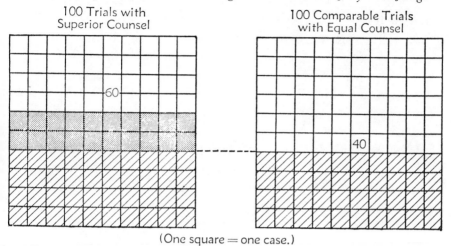

100 Trials with Superior Counsel

100 Comparable Trials with Equal Counsel

(One square = one case.)

 = Agreements

☒ = Number of disagreements in which reason assessment should reveal superiority of counsel as cause

▨ = Number of disagreements due to factors other than superiority of counsel

We have now finished outlining the basic logic of the study. What remains is to deal with two marginal problems, each of which involves a special methodological stance: multiple explanations for the single case and the fact that neither all juries nor all judges are alike.

The multiplicity of reasons raises the question of whether the disagreements were overdetermined; were all reasons needed to produce the disagreement, or did any one of the reasons suffice to bring it about? [29]

[29] The problem of overdetermination poses logical as well as practical problems. The more specific a process is, the more difficult it is to assign weights to the various elements of causation. This is why psychoanalytic theory admits quite frankly an overdetermination in the individual case history. In theory, confrontation between cross-

Overdetermination raised a profound issue which we had no way of handling directly. We therefore "solved" it by establishing two conventions. First, all cases were to be treated the same way. And since we had no means of detecting when a disagreement was overdetermined, we assumed that each reason was essential. The convention therefore was that *all* factors were required to produce the disagreement and that each of the multiple reasons was to be accorded the same weight. Thus in a case with only one reason, that reason received a full unit of weight; in a case with two reasons, each reason received a half unit of weight, and so forth.[30]

The matter of nonhomogeneity is somewhat more troublesome. As everyone knows, and especially the trial lawyer, no two juries are alike nor are any two judges. To sharpen the point, some juries will be more rule-minded than the average judge, and many a judge will be more accessible to sentiment than is the average jury.

Since such differences have direct effects on verdicts, how does this nonhomogeneity complicate the basic analysis of judge-jury differences? For purposes of this study we can treat all juries as if they were the same and all judges as if they too were the same; this simplification does not distort the findings.

The precise purpose of the study is to compare the institution of the jury to the institution of the judge. Any difference between the two, if one exists, must transcend the indi-

---

tabulation and reason assessment could provide clues concerning the weight of reasons. In fact, the confrontation process is too crude to allow such refined instances. The law recognizes the existence of overdetermined events in its doctrine of concurrent causation; for example, damage done by two converging fires, see Kingston v. Chicago and N.W. Ry., 191 Wis. 610, 211 N.W. 913 (1927).

[30] Reasons in both their unweighted and weighted forms are relevant. The unweighted form permits the statement that "in x% of the cases this particular reason is operative," whereas the weighted form signifies that the particular reason is responsible for x% of the disagreements. Compare Table 26 and Table 29.

vidual variations there are within each.   A homely example might clarify what it means to compare two heterogeneous groups.   There is no difficulty at all in understanding the statement that American soldiers are taller than Japanese soldiers, even though there will be great variations in height in each group and many Japanese soldiers will be taller than some Americans.[31]   To bring the example one step closer to the judge-jury situation, assume that an American is paired with each Japanese soldier and the number of times one or the other group has the taller representative in the pair is counted. If the average height of the Americans is higher and the matching is random, once again the Americans will emerge as taller.   It is in this sense that we assert that the *jury* is different from the *judge*.

It is true that our 3576 cases in one sense involve an accidental matching of one particular judge and one particular jury, accidental in the sense that it might easily have been a different judge or a different jury.   In the aggregate this accidental matching has no significance, because the very method of matching is part of the institution of judge and jury and remains essentially a random process.   As long as the method continues to be used, it will continue to reflect the differences between judge and jury just as it did the differences in height in our example.   Thus, if the study were done again — assuming no historic changes in the interim — the results of any new set of matchings would reproduce the present findings.[32]

As a consequence of what has been said, the findings of the

[31] The use of such averages, true or imagined, probably can be seen as the rational foundation of prejudice. By generalizing from the average one forecloses the individual case for which the average may in fact be invalid. As for our example of the Japanese soldier's height, this might not be true a few years hence. The average height of the Japanese is growing inordinately due to dietary changes and allegedly also because of the gradual giving up of their traditional sitting posture.

[32] Clearly, whether or not there will be disagreement between jury and judge in the individual case must depend on the accidental matching of the particular judge with that particular jury. But the nature of randomness insures a certain over-all stability of this matching pattern for the total sample of cases.

study are of necessity probabilistic. Almost none of the reasons for disagreement can be taken to mean that under the given circumstances a jury will always disagree with the judge. The best we can say is that there is a distinctive probability that the jury will disagree, although it is one of the limitations of the study that for the most part we cannot measure this probability.[33] For example, in the instance of the indecent exposure cases we have a sentiment that must be felt very differently by different parts of the community. There will be some people who completely share the law's view that indecent exposure is a crime irrespective of the maturity of the victim; there will be some people who think it a ridiculous crime under all circumstances; and, finally, there will be a considerable number who see an important difference between exposure to adults and to children. Since the juries are drawn from this population, they will reflect in various combinations these differing sentiments.

As so much opinion research makes clear today, it is possible to relate individual opinions to background characteristics of those who hold them. And indeed it is the assumption of such relationships which guides the lawyer in his selection of jurors. Had we money enough and time, we might well have attempted to add this dimension to our scheme of explanations. As it was, we decided not to pursue it.[34] We terminate the search for explanations at the point where we

---

[33] In some cases though, whenever cross-tabulation can be put to use, such an attempted quantification is made. Generally speaking, the probability of disagreement due to a specific factor depends on both the frequency with which that factor occurs and its power in the cases in which it occurs. For example, how often the superior defense lawyer will cause disagreement depends not only on the power of this factor in given cases but also on the sheer frequency of its incidence. See discussion at Table 92. The reason this quantification cannot be attempted for most law sentiment factors is the absence of information on the frequency with which the particular factor occurs *in agreement* cases. See Chapter 38.

[34] To some extent we depart from this decision in Chapter 37, where we consider briefly the effect of nonhomogeneity among judges and juries.

locate a specific sentiment in the jury. We do not investigate whether it arises, as it well may, because the jurors in
question were Italians, or women, or farmers. The important
point is that even if we knew this last link, while it would
clearly add to our knowledge, it would not qualify or impeach any prior findings. It would still be true that the jury
differs from the judge because of the prevalence of a given
sentiment in the population from which the jury is drawn.

CHAPTER 8

Reasons for Judge-Jury Disagreement—
A Summary View

This chapter gives some idea of the content of the reason code and, more important, gives an over-all summary of the reasons found for disagreements. In a sense it complements in summary form the report on the magnitude and direction of disagreement,[1] so as to bring us to the answer to our two major questions: how much disagreement is there between judge and jury in criminal cases? And, what are the reasons or sources of this disagreement?

We begin with the content of the reason code. It may be recalled that the coding operation involved assigning highly specific reasons to the individual instances of disagreement. As the coding developed, it became possible to group the individual reasons into narrow sub-categories and those into larger categories. In the final stage of the coding process the reasons were subsumed into five generic categories.

It may prove helpful to run quickly through the evolution of this over-all framework. We will begin with excerpts from the raw, detailed reason code, in the hope that they will give some preliminary sense of the variety of the items that move the jury. In its original form the coding resulted in 227 specific items,[2] which resolved themselves into the five ultimate

[1] See Chapter 5.

[2] Something of the specificity of the code is suggested by the fact that about one third of the code items explained a single case only. On the average each code item subsumed seven cases.

Coding, we might note in passing, is the term used in the social sciences for classifying individual characteristics or events for purposes of grouping them and of eventually counting their frequency. The group-categories. We list below, as illustrations, two sub-groups of the code: that for the *individual defendant,* with thirty items, and that for the sentiment the *defendant has been punished enough,* which has nine items. We would emphasize again that the development of the code was an evolutionary process. We perfected it as we coded, and we refined it further as we wrote up the materials.[3] Coding was in no way a mere clerical operation, but rather it was close to the very heart of the study.

Sentiments About the Individual Defendant

• Personal Character-istics of Defendant

Youth
Old age
Woman
Attractive woman
Mother
War widow
Cripple, ill health
Sympathy in general

• Social Status

Poor, underprivi-
leged
From influential
family

• Family

Wife in court
Family in court
Children in court
Pregnant wife in
court
Large family re-
sponsibility

**• Special
Circumstances**

Model prisoner
Rendered valuable
service to the gov-
ernment
Kind to victim
In no position to re-
peat crime
Long interval since
last conviction

• Court Appearance

Favorable impres-
sion
Repentant
Crying, collapsed
— defendant
— witness for de-
fendant

**• Occupational
Record**

Soldier, veteran
Policeman, sheriff
Clergy
Student, football
player
Long employment
record
Prosecutor, political
office

---

ing may occur on several levels, so that specific codes are subsumed under more general classifications, and so forth. If the relevant group-ings are known in advance, the range of answers may be pre-coded on the questionnaire, as it was done on our Questionnaire II. This time-saving operation is predicated on prior free-answer questioning as was done in this study through Questionnaire I. The lawyer will recog-nize the logical affinity between coding and the operation of the West Digest key number system which classifies topics of legal decisions.

[3] The coding process continued as we wrote. Some sense of this evo-lution can be gained by comparing the basic codes presented here with their final exposition in Chapter 15, Sentiments About the Individual Defendant, and Chapter 20, Defendant Has Been Punished Enough.

Defendant Sufficiently Punished

• **Directly Through His Act**

Had been in jail awaiting trial long enough

Only defendant was hurt

Loses parole anyway

Spouse already fined for same act

• **Indirectly Through His Act**

Relative or friend killed or hurt

Punished by conscience

Defendant afterwards beaten

• **Independently**

Financial misfortunes

Other misfortunes

So much for illustrations of the individual reason items. At the end of the coding process they seemed to fall into these categories:

- Evidence factors
- Facts only the judge knew
- Disparity of counsel
- Jury sentiments about the individual defendant
- Jury sentiments about the law

Since these labels are not self-explanatory, a brief description of each is provided. It should be stressed that, in each instance, the category locates a generic source of disagreement, without regard to whether it is the judge or the jury who is the more lenient.[4]

Evidence factors. Although the traditional view of the jury is that it is largely concerned with issues of fact, it turns out to be surprisingly difficult to give a thumbnail sketch of evidence as a category of judge-jury disagreement. At times the jury may evaluate specific items of evidence differently; at other times the jury might simply require a higher degree of proof. Frequently evidentiary disagreement, in our usage, refers simply to the closeness of the case, which liberated the jury to respond to non-evidentiary factors. Under these special circumstances, issues of evidence, as we were able to handle them, are

---

[4] The illustrations have been taken from the code for normal disagreements. A detailed analysis of reasons for cross-over disagreements is given in Chapters 29-32. The relation of the rationales for the two kinds of disagreement is treated explicitly in Chapter 29.

properly speaking not so much a cause for disagreement as a condition for it.[5]

Facts only the judge knew.   Here the concern is with the occasional circumstance that, during or prior to the trial, an important fact will become available to the judge but not to the jury, such as whether the defendant had a prior specific criminal record or not.   Whenever the judge notes such special knowledge on his part in a disagreement case, it has been taken as a reason for his disagreement.   The rationale is that judge and jury were, in fact, trying different cases, and had the jury known what the judge knew, it would have agreed with him.[6]

Disparity of counsel.   It was possible to collect data systematically on how evenly counsel for prosecution and for defense were matched.   This category covers the instances in which the superiority of either defense or prosecution counsel was given as one of the reasons for the jury's disagreement with the judge.

Jury sentiments about the individual defendant.   The type of defendant involved in a criminal case can vary across the entire spectrum of human personality and background, from the crippled war veteran who evokes intense sympathy to the loud mouth who alienates the jury.   In this category are included all reasons for judge-jury disagreement attributable to the personal characteristics of the defendant.

Jury sentiments about the law.   This category includes particular instances of "jury equity," reasons for disagreement that imply criticism of either the law or the legal result.   For

---

[5] There is something awkward about the classification of evidence itself as a source of disagreement where it serves as *the condition* for the jury's response to a sentiment, but, as will become apparent, in the close case where there is a sentiment both evidence and sentiment are assigned equal weight in producing the disagreement.   Thus we resolve the problem of distinguishing the necessary condition from what is perhaps the sufficient condition somewhat arbitrarily.   The liberation hypothesis is discussed in Chapter 12.

[6] Logically this category would include cases where the jury had information not possessed by the judge, but such an occurrence would seem to be extremely rare.

example, the jury may regard a particular set of facts inappropriately classified as rape, because it perceives what might be called contributory negligence on the part of the victim. A similar notion may operate in fraud cases in which the victim first hoped for an improper gain. Thus, a broader concept, contributory fault of the victim, evolves as a defense to a crime. This general category of jury sentiments about the law includes roughly a dozen sub-categories of such jury sentiments.[7]

There must remain, of course, a certain blandness and ambiguity about the major categories for the present. Since the purpose here is only to provide an over-all summary view of the explanations for judge-jury disagreement, these sketches will have to suffice. At this point the categories simply provide a handy device for summarizing the data.

But in the end they will provide the basic framework for the organization of the book. Subsequent chapters will discuss the five reason categories in detail, and will disclose the idiosyncratic features of the individual cases. To say that the reason code fell into these five major categories is to make more than a point about coding technique. It is to state a theory. In its most general and also its least exciting form, the theory is that all disagreement between judge and jury arises because of disparity of counsel, facts that only the judge knew, jury sentiments about the defendant, jury sentiments about the law, and evidentiary factors, operating alone or in combination with each other; and as a corollary, that the judge is less likely to be influenced by these factors than is the

---

[7] It may be of interest at this point to preview the elements of the Sentiments on the Law category. The four major sentiments are: The Boundaries of Self-Defense, Contributory Fault of the Victim, De Minimis, and Unpopular Laws, followed by seven lesser sentiments: Defendant Has Been Punished Enough, Punishment Threatened Is Too Severe, Preferential Treatment, Improper Police Methods, Inadvertent Conduct, Insanity and Intoxication, and Crime in a Subculture. A separate chapter has been devoted to each of these eleven themes; see Chapters 16 through 26, and also Chapter 27.

jury.[8] There is some gain in emphasis if we invert the statement: unless at least one of these factors is present in a case, the jury and the judge will not disagree.

We are now ready to quantify the explanations for judge-jury disagreement. We begin with a revised version of the basic table of disagreement.[9]

TABLE 23

Judge-Jury Disagreements in the 3576 Trials

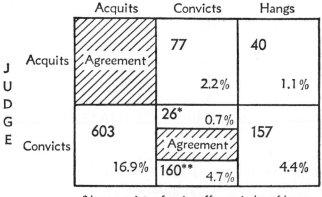

J U R Y

		Acquits	Convicts	Hangs
JUDGE	Acquits	Agreement	77 2.2%	40 1.1%
	Convicts	603 16.9%	26* 0.7% Agreement 160** 4.7%	157 4.4%

*Jury convicts of <u>major</u> offense; judge of lesser.
**Jury convicts of <u>lesser</u> offense; judge of major.

The universe of disagreement can now be defined with precision. It comprises the disagreements on guilt, disagreements on charge, and the cases in which the jury hangs.[10] Reading off the relevant figures from Table 23, it can be seen that this total universe of disagreement consists of 1063 instances that fall conveniently into six groups as follows. With Table 24 we establish a usage already adverted to which it will be con-

[8] This is not to say that the factors have no effect on the judge, but only that they have a differential impact on the two deciders.
[9] This table has not appeared previously in quite this form. It is a composite of Table 11 and Table 13.
[10] As noted earlier in Chapter 5, note 9, we are excluding disagreements on penalty.

venient to follow henceforth. Cases of disagreement where *the jury is more lenient* than the judge will be called *normal* disagreements; cases where, in the less frequent situation, *the judge is more lenient* will be called *cross-over* disagreements.

TABLE 24

Type and Direction of Disagreement

	Per Cent	Number
Normal disagreements on —		
Guilt	57	603
Charge	15	160
Hung Jury	15	157
Cross-over disagreements on —		
Guilt	7	77
Charge	2	26
Hung Jury	4	40
Total disagreements	100%	1063

The precise quest of this study then is to explain what caused the disagreements in these 1063 instances, constituting 30 per cent of all trials.

We must adjust now for the circumstance that it was not possible to find an explanation for every case of disagreement. Table 25 presents the basic tabulation of success and failure in obtaining explanations.

TABLE 25

Percentage of Unexplained Disagreements

Normal disagreements on			Cross-overs on			Total
Guilt	Charge	Hung	Guilt	Charge	Hung	Disagreements
7%	11%	19%	3%	4%	15%	10%

No explanation was forthcoming in 101 out of 1063 cases, or about 10 per cent of all disagreements. The percentage is smallest for the disagreements on guilt and largest, as might be expected, for hung juries. The percentage of failures is, on the average, smaller for the cross-over cases than it is for the normal disagreements, suggesting that the reversal of the jury's normal response is so exceptional that explanations for it are easier to see.[11] Subtracting 101 from 1063 leaves 962 instances, or 90 per cent of all disagreement for which we have an explanation.

An exhaustive comparison of the 101 unexplained cases with the 962 explained cases revealed no marked differences between the two groups such as would suggest any peculiarities in the unexplained cases. We will therefore disregard these cases in future discussion, on the assumption that even if we knew the answers, they would not represent new sources of disagreement but would have satisfied some one of the established categories of explanation without changing their relative frequency.[12]

In the future discussion, then, the relevant universe will be the 962 disagreements for which it proved possible to find an explanation. Table 26 reports the basic data for these cases in terms of the five basic reason categories.

TABLE 26

Summary Explanation of Disagreement

	Normal disagreements on			Cross-overs on			Total disagreements
	Guilt	Charge	Hung	Guilt	Charge	Hung	
	%	%	%	%	%	%	%
Sentiments on the law	53	59	32	49	72	26	50
Sentiments on the defendant	23	27	17	28	20	3	22
Evidence factors	78	62	84	93	100	100	79
Facts only the judge knew	7	3	3	4	4	—	5
Disparity of counsel	9	6	9	5	4	—	8
Average number of reasons per case *	1.7	1.6	1.5	1.8	2.0	1.3	1.6
Number of cases	*559*	*142*	*127*	*75*	*25*	*34*	*962*

* Percentages add to more than 100 because, as indicated in the Average line, some cases have more than one reason, e.g., column one adds to 170 per cent or 1.7 reasons per case.

[11] Arguably the cross-over is not exceptional; see the discussion of the impact on it of waiver practice in Chapter 5, p. 65.

[12] Zeisel, Say It With Figures, Ch. III, How to Handle the "Don't Knows" and "No Answers," (4th ed. 1957).

The last column of Table 26 yields the first over-all measure of the relative roles of the five major reason categories in explaining the judge-jury disagreement. As might more or less be expected, in 79 per cent of all cases, or in four out of every five cases, the disagreement in whole or in part derives from evidence problems. At the other extreme, the over-all roles of disparity of counsel and of differential knowledge to which the judge is privy are low (8 per cent and 5 per cent), a result which in the case of disparity of counsel may cause surprise. A second result that may be unexpected is that in 50 per cent of the cases there is found a jury sentiment at odds with the law.

By way of gaining a preliminary perspective on the broader sources of disagreement, we see that, apart from evidence difficulties, the primary sources of disagreement are the jury sentiments about the law and about the defendant. Thus, the data in Table 26 give focus to a general theory of judge-jury disagreement.

The data permit another basic observation. The rank order of reasons which we obtained for the Total column, representing all cases of disagreement, remains the same for all six types of disagreements, whether it concerns guilt, charge, or the hung jury, and whether it is in the direction of greater or of lesser jury leniency. But although the rank order remains the same, there is a difference in emphasis: sentiments on the law are most important in respect to disagreements on charge and least important to hung juries; hung juries show a higher level of evidence issues than do the other disagreements on guilt and charge.

Thus far we have counted each reason as one. It is helpful, however, to adjust for multiple reasons and reach a more precise estimate of the roles of the five categories. This is the function of Tables 27, 28, and 29.

Table 27 shows that for roughly half the disagreements there is more than one reason, but in no case were all five reason categories required, and in only 1 per cent of the cases were there four reasons.

TABLE 27

Frequency of Multiple Reasons

Number of reasons* per case	Per Cent	Number of cases
1	47	456
2	41	395
3	11	105
4	1	6
5	—	—
Total disagreements	100%	962

* The term "reason" refers here only to the five major categories. The multiplicity of reasons *within* one of these categories is ignored. One reason is treated as sufficient to bring the category into play. For example, the defendant may be a mother in one case, and a mother, a widow, and poor in a second case. Yet in each case *Sentiments on the Defendant* would be counted only once as a reason for disagreement.

Next we explore whether the five basic reason categories differ from each other in the degree to which they combine with other reasons as sources of explanation. Table 28 shows how dependent each of the five basic categories is.

TABLE 28

Frequency with which Major Reasons Appear Alone or with Other Reasons

	Sentiment on Law	Sentiment on Defendant	Issues of Evidence	Facts Only Judge Knew	Disparity of Counsel
	%	%	%	%	%
Appears — alone	22	8	43	2	8
with other reasons	78	92	57	98	92
Total	100%	100%	100%	100%	100%
Number of cases*	484	213	758	52	78

* The number of cases adds to 1585 although there are actually 962 cases because the same case may appear again in two or more of the five columns.

Each of the reason categories appears more frequently in combination with other reasons than it does alone. Interest.

ingly enough, it is the evidence category that appears alone most frequently, a point on which more will be said later.

The sharing of reasons is particularly interesting with respect to disparity of counsel and jury sentiments about the defendant, both of which combine with other reasons over 90 per cent of the time they operate.[13] This fact has broad implications. Disparity of counsel, for the most part, will not make a difference by itself but will require materials which superior counsel can exploit; the implication is that the cases do not present such material evenly. Again, sentiments about the individual defendant are seldom powerful enough to cause disagreement by themselves; rather, they gain their effectiveness only in partnership with some other factor in the case. The implication again is that for the defendant to be poor and crippled or beautiful and blonde is by itself rarely a sufficient stimulus for the jury to disagree with the judge.

Putting together the sheer frequency with which the reason categories appear in Table 26 and the perspective on multiple reasons gained in Tables 27 and 28, it is possible to show the *power* of each reason category in explaining disagreement. We have adverted earlier to the process by which multiple reasons would be weighed; they are valued inversely to their frequency in the particular case.[14] Making these weighting computations, one obtains the profile presented in Table 29.[15]

---

[13] Table 28 shows that the differential knowledge category has, as expected, the highest ratio of interdependence, 98 per cent. Here, almost by definition, the reason depends on another category.

[14] Chapter 7, p. 99 ff.

[15] An example of the weighting process may prove helpful. It will be recalled from Table 28 that the over-all frequency of Counsel as a reason is 8 per cent, but that in 92 per cent of the cases Counsel appears with one or more other reasons. The breakdown is as follows.

(a) alone	8
(b) plus one other reason	49
(c) plus two other reasons	37
(d) plus three other reasons	6
	100%

The weighting process assigns to Counsel all of (a), half of (b), one third of (c) and one fourth of (d), totaling about 46 per cent of its over-

TABLE 29

Summary of Weighted Reasons

	Per Cent
Sentiments on the law	29
Sentiments on the defendant	11
Issues of evidence	54
Facts only the judge knew	2
Disparity of counsel	4
Total	100%
Number of cases	962

Table 29 permits a major conclusion for a theory of judge-jury disagreement.[16] By giving weights to each of the major reason categories, it states in the large, but with precision, the answer to the question: what causes jury and judge to disagree? Slightly over half the job of explanation falls to the evidence category. Apart from evidence factors, the explanation for disagreements resides principally in jury sentiments on the law or jury sentiments about the defendant. Perhaps the most interesting aspect of Table 29 is the salient role played by jury sentiments on the law in causing disagreements; jury equity looms as a significant factor.

The reason data can be arranged into one further profile. Reducing the categories to two, as in Table 30, by simply placing the evidence category on one side and the other four categories on the other, one gets a crucial image of the jury's per-

---

all frequency. Since the over-all frequency is 8 per cent (Table 26), 46 per cent of it is roughly 4 per cent.

[16] Table 29 gives the distribution for the five reason categories in terms of total disagreement. The breakdown as to direction is as follows.

	Normal (%)	Cross-over (%)
Sentiments on the Law	30	24
Sentiments on the Defendant	11	9
Issues of Evidence	53	64
Facts Only the Judge Knew	2	1
Disparity of Counsel	4	2
Total	100%	100%
Number of cases	828	134

formance in terms of *facts* on one hand and *values* on the other.[17]

TABLE 30

Values and Facts as Causes of Disagreement

Disagree on —	*Per Cent*	
Facts alone	34	} Total facts, 79%
Values and Facts	45	} Total values, 66%
Values alone	21	
Total	100%	
Number of cases	*962*	

The conventional and official role of the jury, although it is not clear that anyone believes this, is that it is the trier of the facts and nothing else. Table 30 tells us that in only one third of the cases is the jury's fact-finding the sole source of judge-jury disagreement; in the remaining two thirds of the cases the sources of disagreement are to be seen fully only by looking beyond the official role of the jury. On the other hand, only 21 per cent of the disagreements arise from a source having nothing to do with the facts, but purely with values or sentiments. Thus, Table 30 serves to spotlight the peculiar difficulty that attends any effort to isolate the causes of judge-jury disagreement. The difficulty arises because to a considerable extent, or in exactly 45 per cent of the cases, the jury in disagreeing with the judge is neither simply deciding a question of fact nor simply yielding to a sentiment or a value; it is doing both. It is giving expression to values and sentiments under the guise of answering questions of fact. If the factual leeway is not present, the sentiments or values will as a rule have to be particularly strong to move the jury to disagree. Conversely, if only ambiguity in the facts is present, and the directionality

[17] To treat everything that is not *Evidence* as *Value* is somewhat arbitrary, particularly with respect to the "Facts Only the Judge Knew" category where in one sense what the judge knows is a fact. By definition, however, it is not an evidentiary fact. Since this category is small and in only one instance appears as the sole basis for disagreement, whichever way it is classified would make no appreciable difference.

of the sentiment is absent, the jury will be less likely to disagree with the judge. The decision-making patterns we are pursuing are subtle ones.

In one sense the basic task of this inquiry is now completed. Answers have been given to the question of how often judge and jury disagree and to the question of why they disagree. In another sense, of course, these first chapters have served simply as an extended preface. There is an inescapable blandness about any discussion of jury behavior at such a level of abstraction and generality. The remainder of the book will be devoted to the task of giving precise content to these general findings. The significant statement of our theory of jury behavior, therefore, is yet to come.

*A*T THIS POINT we begin the detailed examination of the reasons for the normal disagreement, a task which will occupy us through Chapter 28. By tracing the components of the reason categories in detail, the discussion illumines and gives full meaning to each category.

The first group of chapters embraces two of the five basic categories, the smallest and the largest. Chapter 9 discusses an anomalous and rare kind of disagreement, that caused by the judge's occasionally having information that is withheld from the jury. The consequence is that judge and jury are not deciding quite the same case.

The largest and most obvious reason category covers the handling of evidentiary matters by judge and jury. This story is complex and requires Chapters 10 through 14 to tell.

CHAPTER 9

Facts That Only the Judge Knew

It has been, of course, a key assumption of this study that the judge and the jury are deciding *the same case*. On occasion, however, judge and jury, even though they are present together in the same courtroom at the same trial, may not be dealing with exactly the same case. The institutional arrangement under which jury cases are tried, or some other factor, will from time to time keep from the jury some information about the case which is available to the judge. In these situations the jury is deciding a case which has n facts and the judge is deciding a case which has $n + 1$ facts, and the disagreement may turn on this difference. In a sense this is the most neutral of the categories of explanation, since the disagreement of jury and judge does not turn on any sentiments or values or differences in competence, but rather on the procedures for communicating information about the case.

This chapter thus opens a window on a small source of friction in the administration of justice in criminal cases.[1] The ideal of the legal system is a trial record which contains all of the relevant information about the case, which has been fully exposed to the adversaries, and which puts finite limits to the controversy. In theory, this is a necessary condition for the rational solution of controversy. In practice, as we have long known in terms of the exclusionary rules of evidence and as this chapter confirms, the trial record does not always achieve this ideal.

[1] This reason accounts for only 2 per cent of the normal disagreements, or for 48 cases. See Table 29.

We begin with an instance where the judge's image of the case and the image of the case in the eye of the jury are startlingly different. The judge's description underscores the point.

> Defendant was a young Negress. She was charged with entering the right front seat of an auto while her male companion entered the left side, slugged and robbed the driver, an old man, of the $117 he had in his billfold. Her defense was that she did not know her companion intended to rob the victim. They did not want to send the girl to jail when there was some doubt that she knew her companion was going to rob the victim. The jury did not know that she had a record of murder with parole from a manslaughter conviction. The jury also did not know that the victim had previously implicated her physically and actively in the commission of the robbery, but refused to do so at the trial. [I-0126] [2]

The defendant, through the strategy of not taking the stand, is successful in keeping her record from the jury, a tactic we shall meet frequently in this chapter. Of special interest, however, is the fact that the complainant, out of some sense of equity of his own, refuses to fully implicate the girl at the time of trial, so that at the worst she appears to the jury, as only passively involved in the crime. Quite apart from its contribution to the particular theme of this chapter, the case indicates that the rigor of the criminal law may be tempered not only by prosecution and jury discretion, but by complainant discretion as well. In any event, there can be little doubt that the difference in what judge and jury knew about the defendant is the major source of their disagreement.

The bulk of the cases are more routine. There is the occa-

---

[2] The numerical designation of the case, as above, is intended as a sort of proper name. The form of the citation establishes a convention which will be followed throughout. The Roman numeral "I" or "II" indicates whether the case belongs to samples one or two; the four-digit number following is the unique designation for the case. In trials of more than one defendant, a fifth number indicates the specific defendant. Because of the phenomenon of multiple reasons some cases are quoted in more than one place, according to the relevance of the judge's comment to the problem under discussion.

sional case in which the judge has acquired his special information by some route not directly connected with the trial process. An easy illustration of this is an attempted rape case in which the judge tells us he knew the complaining witness personally and was thereby influenced in his judgment of credibility.

> The jury did not know these people and if I had been in the same position the jury was in, I possibly would have arrived at the same conclusion they did. The case depended largely on whether you believed the man or the woman, as most of these cases do. [I-0984]

Or again, in a neighborhood brawl the issue is whether the defendant was the aggressor, and when the jury acquits, the judge observes:

> Jury did not realize as I did from past experience with defendant that he was a dangerous man when drinking. [I-0704]

As a rule the judge's extra knowledge appears to be gained not so much through personal acquaintance as through his tenure as a judge. Thus, in a case of bootlegging where the jury acquits, the judge simply notes:

> Difficult generally to convict bootleggers and perhaps difficult for the judge to dismiss from his mind previous knowledge of defendant. [I-0808]

In the same vein the judge sometimes makes explicit that he somehow has an impression that the reputation of the defendant was unknown to the jury. Thus in an auto theft case, even though the defendant takes the stand and the jury thereby learns of his prior record, the judge appears to have known something over and beyond the record which was influential enough to cause him to disagree with the jury. He puts it this way:

> Court was perhaps influenced in judgment here by its knowledge of the general reputation of defendant which was not completely shown to the jury by the evidence. [I-1888]

One last example will show another way in which the judge may acquire extra information. In a prosecution under a state law against moonshining, the item of distinctive information is that the defendants were caught again at the same still on the night before the case was being tried. The jury, not allowed in on this interesting piece of information, brings in an acquittal. [I-1326-1 & 2]

More often the judge's extra information comes through official channels, and, as a matter of legal policy, is kept from the jury. And although the system allows the judge this knowledge, it is not intended that he should consider it in reaching his decision. It would appear, however, that the judge is sometimes not able to keep from being influenced.

The cases often center on such legal circumstances as the administration of blood tests, the withdrawal of guilty pleas, prior arrests for the same offense, acquittal for the same offense, and finally, as the most frequent circumstance, a prior record, usually for a similar crime.

Sometimes a blood test, damning to the defendant, will be ruled inadmissible because of failure to comply with requirements that blood tests be voluntary.[3] Under such circumstances the judge, but not the jury, will know the results of the test.[4] Other cases turn on the fact that the defendant's refusal to take a test is kept from the jury.[5]

[3] The law on the admissibility of blood tests is surprisingly complex. It has constitutional overtones and varies with the jurisdiction. In all jurisdictions strictest compliance with the statutory procedure must be shown. Generally the matter turns on consent. If the defendant agrees to the test he cannot later object to presentation of the results at the trial. If he refuses the test, jurisdictions vary on whether to permit comment on the refusal. Finally, there is variation in the rule in the special situation where the defendant is unconscious when the test is administered. See generally Wigmore on Evidence §§2264 and 2265 (McNaughton ed. 1961). See also Ladd and Gibson, Medico-Legal Aspects of the Blood Test to Determine Intoxication, Iowa L. Rev., v. 24, p. 191 (1939), and Sullivan, Driving Under the Influence of Intoxicating Liquor — Proof, Prosecution and Defense, 1958 Wis. L. Rev., p. 195.

[4] In one case of manslaughter second degree due to alleged drunken driving, the judge comments: "State relied on blood test but I suppressed evidence thereof as there was no evidence that defendant consented to his blood being taken. Patrolman took defendant to hospital

Somewhat similar are cases where the defendant has withdrawn a guilty plea. Here again the fact cannot escape the judge, but is advisedly kept from the jury. One example will suffice. Two young boys, charged with burglary, make a sympathetic appearance before the jury. The judge not only knows something detrimental about the boys' reputations but also tells us that "one of the defendants offered to plead guilty but the other insisted on taking his chances with the jury. As a result both were acquitted." [I-0610-1 & 2][6]

These last cases suggest the larger point, appropriately noted here, that the jury may in a special way provide an important safeguard for the criminal process. Given the realities of that process, it appears important that negotiations for guilty pleas be accommodated. If all criminal cases were to be tried to the judge alone, the process of bargaining over a guilty plea might impair the trial. The jury system provides an institution allowing for a trial which is insulated against the knowledge of such prior negotiations. Much the same point can be made about the administration of blood tests. It is a basic policy that blood tests be admissible only if voluntary. Again, the jury system provides an institution for trial insulated from the knowledge that the defendant exercised his option to refuse a blood test.

---

without securing consent." [I-1645] In a similar manslaughter case, where the defendant submitted to the test and then thought better of it, the judge explains: "Inability of the state to get to the jury evidence of a very high blood test, because of technicality arising from law requiring accident reports for statistical purposes. [II-0439]

[5] In the event of a refusal to submit to a test in a "no-comment" jurisdiction, the explanation is routine. In one such case the judge is succinct: "Defendant refused to take a blood test. This refusal cannot be introduced into evidence." [I-1745]

[6] See a comparable case (I-0938-2) in Chapter 22, at note 3. The defendant may plead guilty and then make a motion for withdrawal of the plea. The decisions are conflicting as to the admissibility of such a plea in the trial that follows. The rule in favor of exclusion is based on the rationale that the reasons which induced the judge to allow the withdrawal are sufficient to render it inadmissible. United States v. Adelman, 107 F.2d 497 (2d Cir. 1939). See the cases in Note A.L.R., v. 124, p. 1527 (1939).

Returning now to the cases, we find the judge's role is more troublesome when his extra knowledge is simply that the defendant has been previously arrested for the same offense. In one case the jury acquits a mother of several children of the charge of defrauding a finance company by selling mortgaged property. The judge, in disagreeing, notes that he alone knew that she had "previously been charged with the same crime and had been acquitted." [I-0448]

Perhaps a bit more colorful is the case where the owner of a corner grocery store is charged with operating a numbers game. The judge tells us of the additional information that he had.

> This particular defendant had been in court time and again through the years and on most occasions has gone out of court a free man because of the shrewd, careful way in which he operates. [I-3118]

It would, of course, be quite disturbing to entertain the suspicion that the judge, as a rule, draws a negative inference from a previous arrest.[7] Actually, it seems that he does this only in exceptional cases where the particular history of arrests generates a common-sense inference against the defendant, as in the two examples just mentioned. Perhaps an even more striking instance of this is a third illustration, involving a rape charge. The judge knows the defendant has been arrested twice before for rape, and, further, he knows of the odd circumstance that the defendant has another rape charge pending in the adjoining county, "arising out of the instant trans-

---

[7] This case reveals a certain ambiguity in the rationale of this category of explanation. Ideally, the situation should be symmetrical: if the judge had known only what the jury knew, he would have agreed with the jury, and, conversely, if the jury had known what the judge knew it would have agreed with the judge. In the large majority of cases the extra factor is bound to work both ways and leaves no mystery as to the cause of disagreement. In some cases, however, we cannot be sure whether the extra information would work both ways. As a matter of convenience we consider it sufficient if either the judge would have come *down* to the jury or the jury come *up* to the judge. But most often the implication is that the jury would have acted differently had it known the special fact, e.g., case II-0654 in note 16 below, where the judge explains not why he convicted, but why the jury failed to.

action and involving another woman on that same night."
[I-0488]

The materials just reviewed suggest that, in addition to his wide experience with the likelihood that the defendant before him is guilty, the judge is exposed to prejudicial information which the law, in its regard for the right of the defendant, aims to screen out of the evaluation of his guilt or innocence. The law's ideal in these situations may be something of a libertarian luxury. Our only point is that the law cannot easily achieve it without the jury.

The extra information most frequently available to the judge is the defendant's criminal record.[8] The law has a complex set of rules which determine when such a record may be disclosed. Ordinarily, it may be shown only to impeach the defendant's veracity and consequently is brought into the case only if the defendant chooses to take the stand.[9] Prosecutor and defense counsel often play a complex game in which the

[8] Cf. Table 44.

[9] The broad outlines of this difficult area of law will suffice. The prosecution may introduce the defendant's record even when he refuses to testify, if, in the light of the facts in the case, the record tends to prove that the defendant committed the crime charged by revealing a pattern of similar facts, an idiosyncratic *modus operandi,* motive, or intent. Again, if the charge is under a habitual criminal statute, the prosecution, of course, must prove the record to secure a conviction, whether or not the defendant testifies.

Where the defendant does take the stand the prosecution may as a rule introduce the record to impeach the defendant's credibility. The states vary, however, in regard to the type of conviction they allow for impeachment purposes; they range from the broad view that a conviction for certain misdemeanors and any felony may be introduced, to the stricter jurisdictions which require that the record pertain to a *crimen falsi* (forgery, perjury, etc.) which may be evidence of untruthfulness. If the defendant, or his witnesses or counsel, put the defendant's character in issue, the judge in his discretion may permit the prosecutor to offer proof with a wider latitude to discredit the defendant, even allowing evidence of acts of moral turpitude which are not strictly criminal offenses. The judge retains discretion to exclude the record on the grounds of remoteness and relevancy. For a good general summary, see McCormick, Evidence, especially §§45 and 157 (1954).

defense must weigh the disadvantages of exposing the defendant to a negative inference by keeping him from the witness stand against the disadvantages of exposing the defendant's record by having him testify. And it is not without interest that when the defendant does take the stand and the record is disclosed to the jury, the law resorts to one of its most heroic instructions, cautioning the jury to disregard the record as evidence of guilt and to consider it only as it may affect credibility. We deal elsewhere with details of the jury's reaction to this intricate situation.[10] Our concern here is simply with the case where the record is known to the judge but not to the jury.

From the many cases that involve differential knowledge of the defendant's record, we have selected a few as illustrations. Perhaps the most vivid examples involve forgery cases where, unknown to the jury, the defendant has a record for forgery. Since forgery is a highly specialized crime, there is in fact a considerable common-sense inference against the defendant from the prior record.[11]

In one case the defendant allegedly purchases a camera with a forged check. The case is unusual in that although the defendant takes the stand, nevertheless the jury does not learn of his prior record. He is rated as having good demeanor throughout the trial and as making a sympathetic impression. The judge explains:

> Prosecutor did not know defendant's prior conviction for similar offense [and therefore failed to bring it out] and the jury concluded the defendant had no previous record and decided to acquit him. [II-0193]

The information gap between judge and jury is lessened when the defendant does not take the stand, insofar as the jury

[10] See Chapter 13, p. 179 ff.

[11] The inference is good, of course, only so long as a subsequent arrest is independent of the prior record. However, it is a well-known difficulty in the administration of the criminal law that those most likely to be arrested as suspects in a new crime are those who have a record for that crime. See La Fave, Arrest: The Decision to Take a Suspect into Custody, pp. 287-288 (1965).

might at least suspect that one of his reasons for not taking the stand is to hide a record. In contrast, the judge knows with certainty whether such a record exists, and also whether it is a record tied closely to the instant trial.[12] Thus, where a defendant charged with forging a government check mistakenly delivered to his address appears sympathetic and the jury acquits, the jury does not learn of the defendant's prior record because he did not take the stand. [II-1003] In still another forgery case the defendant appears to the jury as a sympathetic elderly man. He does not take the stand, and once again only the judge knows of his record. To him the defendant is "an old offender." [I-1998]

In another case an elderly man is charged with giving a bad check in payment for merchandise; the defendant does not take the stand but makes a sympathetic impression. The jury resolves doubts in his favor, but the judge knows that "he had been previously convicted for a like situation." [I-1737]

Thus far, we have dealt with offenses which, because of their specialized nature, would indeed justify a common-sense inference based on a prior similar record. The remaining instances involve crimes of violence, where one might expect the inference to be less powerful. On closer examination, however, the special circumstances of these cases make the jury's disagreement with the judge understandable. Thus, in a homicide case the defendant, a mild appearing middle-aged man, kills another man in a domestic triangle situation. There are various other complicating factors in the case: the wife had been unfaithful and the parties were intoxicated. And the jury's disagreement is merely to reduce the judge's first degree murder conviction to manslaughter. There is little doubt, however, that the crucial factor is that the defendant was able to keep his record from the jury by not taking the stand. The jury's image of the defendant as a put-upon husband, finally aggravated to the point of violence, might well have suffered had the jury known what the judge knew. As he puts it:

[12] Or in some cases, a very long one.

The defendant was a very meek appearing man; had killed a man previously in Kentucky and been in prison therefore. This did not (could not) come out in evidence. After a verdict, questioning showed jury did not know this was second offense but would have brought in a different, more severe verdict, had they known. [I-0681]

A second case of violence presents an equally dramatic contrast between the jury's image of the case and the judge's. The defendant is charged with shooting a bartender in the leg during a tavern brawl. The judge would have convicted of assault with attempt to murder; the jury hangs. The defendant does not take the stand, and again his record is kept from the jury. The judge states sharply the impact of this non-disclosure on the case.

The complaining witness was an ex-convict (24 years of age). This was brought out on direct examination. The other state's witness (23 years of age) was also an ex-convict and this was brought out in direct examination. The defendant was also an ex-convict (murderer) but did not take the stand. So jury was not informed as to his past record. [I-0632]

Finally, in a weird and complex homicide case in which the defendant agrees to play "Russian roulette" with the victim, who as a result is killed, the jury convicts of manslaughter, whereas the judge considers it second degree murder. Since the defendant does not take the stand, the jury does not learn of his record. The judge is explicit about the impact of this.

If defendant's prior criminal record could have been brought out, the jury might have found defendant guilty of second degree murder. [II-0108]

It is convenient at this point to summarize the various types of extra knowledge on the part of the judge which we have been inventorying and to give their frequency in Table 31.

We must also consider the interesting complementary question of whether judge-jury disagreement ever results from the jury's knowing something that the judge does not know. The sample contains one case in which this situation is approximated. In a drunken driving prosecution where the judge

TABLE 31

Facts Only the Judge Knew

Judge alone knew:

Complainant changed testimony	1
Defendant personally	2
Of other brushes with the law	2
Other charges were pending	3
Blood test refused or suppressed	9
Guilty plea withdrawn	6
Prior arrest for same offense	4
Prior acquittal for same offense.	2
Prior record	23
Other data	2
Total	54*

* There are 48 such cases; some cases had more than one item.

would have convicted, one of the jurors surreptitiously takes into the jury room a medical book containing estimates of the critical levels of alcohol in the blood which differed from those given by medical experts at the trial. As the judge completes the story:

> This juror was chosen foreman and persuaded the entire jury to agree with the thesis contained in the book which required a blood alcohol level of .222 instead of .150 to constitute a person as an unsafe driver. [II-0537] [13]

To be sure, the jury often has extra knowledge of a different sort. Interviews with jurors and access to experimental jury deliberations abundantly show that jurors bring to their deliberations much extra knowledge — some of which certainly

[13] The recommendations of a joint committee of the National Safety Council and the AMA have been generally adopted. Where there is less than 0.05 per cent alcohol in the blood (or other body fluids or breath), the subject is presumed *not* to be under the influence of alcohol. If tests show 0.15 per cent or more, the contrary presumption results. Findings between these two limits are evidence to be viewed along with other evidence on the question of intoxication. J.A.M.A. v. 112, p. 2164 (1939). See Ladd and Gibson, Medico-Legal Aspects of the Blood Test to Determine Intoxication, Iowa L. Rev. v. 24, p. 191 (1939). All states now permit the use of chemical tests; see National Safety Council, Report of Committee on Tests for Intoxication (1956).

would not be known to the judge. The jury's extra information tends to be some item of personal experience not part of
the trial,[14] or some generalization about human nature, such
as "people drink a good deal at Polish weddings" or "the very
inability of the doctor to find anything wrong with a person's
back is really good evidence that there is something seriously
wrong," to take two vivid examples from our files for other
parts of the jury study.

Bringing knowledge such as this to bear on its deliberations
is, of course, one of the jury's most engaging and flavorsome
characteristics. It raises the interesting problem of how the
legal system expects the jurors to confine their deliberations to
the trial record on the one hand, and yet on the other to bring
into their deliberations their common experience with life.
In any case, to the extent that the jury utilizes in its deliberations things it knows about life in general or about human
nature, it is using a kind of knowledge which the judge, as a
human being, must also have, although twelve jurors coming
from many strata of the society may well produce more such
knowledge than one judge.

It has been a repeated theme that the jury system makes exclusionary rules possible by providing a trier of fact which can
be effectively insulated from the forbidden knowledge. The
disagreements that are the subject of this chapter offer an in-
interesting commentary on the merits of the exclusionary rules.

---

[14] This refers to data from other parts of the Jury Project. In a
wrongful death case where expert testimony had been in conflict as
to which way a tractor would swerve when a certain rod slipped, one
of the jurors during the deliberation offered "testimony" that when the
same thing happened to his friend's tractor, the tractor had swerved to
the right. This resolved the issue.

The jury's use of extra-record experience bearing on the issue of insanity is reported in Simon, The American Jury — The Defense of
Insanity, (1966). See also Kalven, The Jury, the Law, and the Personal Injury Damage Award, Ohio St. L.J., v. 19, p. 158 (1958). Our
richest examples of the extra-record knowledge of the jury have come
from the research of Professor Dale Broeder, which is in the process of
publication. See, for instance, Broeder, Previous Jury Trial Service
Affecting Jury Behavior, Insur. Law J., v. 506, p. 138 (1965).

Some of these cases represent the price — in "unjustified" acquittals — which the system is willing to pay for avoiding prejudice in other cases, where the shared information could lead to an unjust conviction.[15]

The category of disagreement we have been tracing differs in several respects from the explanations for disagreement we offer elsewhere. It has little scope; as a source of disagreement it emerges as surprisingly limited. And it reveals nothing distinctive about the jury's view of things, for if the jury knew fully what the judge knew, it would have agreed with him.[16] This discussion of differential knowledge has almost been a digression; in the chapters that follow we return to the instances of disagreement that arise when judge and jury are deciding the *same* case.

[15] Of course, sometimes the purpose of an exclusionary rule is to further other legal policies, such as the protection of privacy or the prevention of illegal search and seizure.

[16] In a sense differential knowledge is not so much a cause for disagreement as a condition; it enables factors to influence the jury which a shared knowledge of the special fact known to the judge would have foreclosed. The category, therefore, almost by definition, cannot be independent but must combine with other reasons to explain disagreement. Such indeed is the case; this reason shares the role of explanation 98 per cent of the time, which is to say in all but one case. And this by the way is a case of incest between a father and his 15-year-old daughter in which the judge comments tersely: "Pertinent data not introduced because of Supreme Court rulings in this state. Would have changed jury's verdict." [II-0654]

CHAPTER 10

The Anatomy of the Evidence

We pause here to present descriptive data on the composition of the evidence in the variety of criminal trials. This survey offers a unique opportunity for a systematic inventory of the patterns of evidence.

The data are of two kinds: first, specific details as to the number of witnesses, the types of witnesses, the presence or absence of a criminal record, with other details; and, second, an over-all view of the evidence in terms of a single simple question put to the judge as to whether the case on all the evidence was clear or close.

We begin in Table 32 with the over-all view. In a rough form, the judge's answer to the clear-close question serves to provide a map of the evidence in the cases that come before a jury.

TABLE 32

Frequency of Clear and Close Cases

	Per Cent
Clear for acquittal	5
Close	43
Clear for conviction	52
Total	100%
Number of cases	*1191**

* Sample II only.

Table 32 gives an important first impression of the range of doubt in the criminal trial. Only 43 per cent of all cases are rated by the judge as close to the reasonable doubt threshold [1] or, in our terms, as presenting evidence problems of any substance. The majority of cases are rated as clear, and of these the majority are clear in the direction of conviction.[2] We can see at the outset that insofar as the jury is having trouble with issues of fact in criminal cases and may thus be moved to disagree with the judge, the trouble is confined to this 43 per cent of the cases.

From the over-all view we turn to the details of the evidence and begin with the number of witnesses in the criminal case. Table 33 shows the number of witnesses testifying for the prosecution and for the defense. As might be expected, these numbers vary widely, ranging from cases with one witness to one extraordinary case in which there were 131 witnesses.[3]

[1] There is perhaps an apparent paradox, when the legal test is whether the evidence places the defendant's guilt beyond a reasonable doubt, in referring to a case as "close," particularly if the term suggests an even chance either way. What is meant by "close" in a criminal case is "close to the borderline of reasonable doubt," which might be, if it were measurable, 80 per cent sure or 95 per cent sure, etc., depending on one's sense of the test. In any event "close" does not refer to the mere preponderance of the evidence, the test for a close case in civil negligence actions.

[2] There may be some interest at this point in a preview of a companion variable relating to evidence, critical use of which is made in the next chapter. The Sample II questionnaire asked (Q. 11) "Was the evidence as a whole easy to comprehend, somewhat difficult [or] very difficult to comprehend?" The distribution of comprehensibility is as follows.

	%
Easy	86
Somewhat Difficult	12
Very Difficult	2
	100%
	1191

For our immediate purposes, the interesting fact is that over fifty per cent of all cases are both clear and easy. See Table 50, also the discussion of agreement cases in Chapter 38.

[3] Where the defendant was accused of participating in a scheme to defraud an insurance company by presenting false fire insurance

Table 33 makes a major point about the posture of proof in the criminal jury trial. There is a striking imbalance between the number of witnesses for the prosecution and the number of witnesses for the defense. In $(10 + 25 =)$ 35 per cent of all cases the defense has one witness or less, whereas in only

TABLE 33

Number of Witnesses for Prosecution and Defense

Number of Witnesses	For Prosecution	For Defense
	(Per Cent of All Cases)	
0	—	10
1	2	25
2-5	56	49
6-10	28	11
11 or more	14	5
	100%	100%
Average number of witnesses per case	5	2
Number of cases	1191 *	

* The total size of Sample II is 1191 cases. This figure is used in this and the following tables for purposes of identification, the actual number differs slightly from table to table because of some "no answers;" the actual figures vary between 1155 and 1055.

$(0 + 2 =)$ 2 per cent of the cases does the prosecution have so few witnesses. Again, in $(28 + 14 =)$ 42 per cent of all cases the prosecution has six or more witnesses, whereas in only $(11 + 5 =)$ 16 per cent does the defense have so many. On the average, the prosecution has five witnesses against two for the defense. A sheer head count of witnesses is, to be sure, not an accurate index of the strength of a case, but, as the chapter unfolds, the basic imbalance suggested here between defense and prosecution is met again.[4]

---

claims, the prosecution mustered 120 witnesses against the defendant's 11, for the sample's high of 131. Judge and jury agreed to convict. [II-1128]

[4] In the end, this imbalance may simply reflect the fact that the prosecution has the burden of proof. Since there will be repeated occasion to refer to imbalance, it is perhaps important to emphasize that we use the word "imbalance" as a descriptive term, referring to quantity only.

There are also data on the kinds of witnesses presented by each side. Table 34 gives the relevant information for the prosecution, Table 35, for the defense.

TABLE 34
Evidence for the Prosecution

	Per Cent of All Cases *
Police	78
Complainant as witness	57
Eyewitness	25
Expert	25
Alleged confession	19
Family and friends of complainant	18
Accomplice turned state's evidence	9
Other witnesses	7

* Sample II only. Percentages add up to more than 100 because in most trials more than one kind of prosecution evidence is presented.

TABLE 35
Evidence for the Defense

	Per Cent of All Cases *
Defendant takes stand	82
Family and friends of defendant	47
Character witness	25
Eyewitness	11
Expert	6
Accomplice	3
Other witnesses	4

* See footnote to Table 34.

The two tables taken together underscore once again the imbalance in the evidence marshalled by defense and prosecution. Apart from the two more cogent categories, eyewitnesses and experts, which appear in but 11 and 6 per cent respectively of the defense cases, the defense evidence is seen to consist overwhelmingly of the defendant himself, his family and friends, and his character witnesses.

Tables 34 and 35 also answer two questions of great interest to the administration of the criminal law. Table 35 shows how often a defendant in a criminal trial elects to exercise his privilege of not testifying on his own behalf.   He testifies in 82 per cent of the cases, thus claiming his privilege not to testify in only 18 per cent.   Again, Table 34 shows how often the prosecution introduces into evidence an alleged confession: it does so in 19 per cent of the cases.

One may focus more closely on the distribution of particular categories of witnesses.   The eyewitness, as we know from Tables 34 and 35, appears in 25 per cent of the prosecution cases and in 11 per cent of the defense cases.   Table 36 completes the pattern.

TABLE 36

Eyewitnesses

Per Cent

Neither side	69
Defense only	6 } Total defense, 11%
Both sides	5 } Total prosecution, 25%
Prosecution only	20
Total*	100%

* Sample II only.

It is a commentary on the difficulties of proof in the ordinary criminal case that in some 69 per cent of all trials neither side has an eyewitness.[5]   In only one out of five cases in which the prosecution has an eyewitness does the defendant have one too, but in half the cases in which the defendant has an eyewitness

---

[5] The absence of relationship between the incidence of eyewitnesses and the closeness of the evidence is indicated by the following fourfold table:

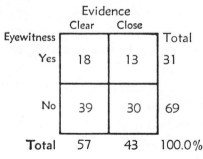

Eyewitness	Evidence Clear	Close	Total
Yes	18	13	31
No	39	30	69
Total	57	43	100.0%

the prosecution has one to oppose him. In only 5 per cent of all cases do both sides have eyewitnesses, making possible the confrontation of conflicting eyewitness' testimony.

The analogous statistics on the expert witness read very much the same. The expert witness, it will be recalled, appeared in 25 per cent of the prosecution cases and in 6 per cent of the defense cases. Table 37 sets out the data.

TABLE 37

Expert Witnesses

	Per Cent	
Neither side	72	
Defense only	3	} Total defense, 6%
Both sides	3	}
Prosecution only	22	} Total prosecution, 25%
Total*	100%	

* Sample II only.

Again, the imbalance between prosecution and defense appears. In 22 per cent of the cases the prosecution has the only expert witness, whereas in only 3 per cent of the cases does the defense have such an advantage. And while in 69 per cent of the trials there are, as we saw, no eyewitnesses, it appears that in 72 per cent there are no experts. Finally, Table 37 puts into focus the celebrated "battle of experts." In only 3 per cent of the cases do both sides present experts, and even this figure must overstate the frequency of the battle, since in some of these cases the experts are in different fields and are testifying on different issues.

It may not be without interest to carry the description of expert testimony one step further and show in Table 38 the variety of experts.

A medical expert appears in little less than half the cases in which there are experts, or in 12 per cent of all cases. In view of the widespread contemporary interest in the role of psychiatry in criminal law, it may be somewhat surprising to see how infrequently the psychiatrist makes an appearance in court. As we can infer from Table 38, a psychiatrist appears in less than 2 per cent of all cases, and slightly more often for the defense than for the prosecution.[6]

TABLE 38

Type of Expert Witnesses

(In per cent of the 291 cases with experts)

	Prosecution (Per Cent)	Defense (Per Cent)
Medical, general **	43	9
Medical, psychiatric	4	5
Chemical	22	*
Intoxication	5	*
Handwriting	10	1
Firearms	9	*
Misc. Laboratory Technicians	4	—
Accountants, appraisers	11	1
Narcotics	2	—
Misc. other sciences (fire engineers, opticians, etc.)	6	4
Misc. police, FBI	6	—
Other	2	4

* Less than one half of 1 per cent.
** Not all categories in Table 38 are mutually exclusive. Experts on "Intoxication," for example, might also be "Laboratory Technicians"; occasionally it was impossible to clarify the function further.

A somewhat different perspective on the evidence is obtained by observing how this profile of evidence changes for different types of crimes. Six crime categories have been se-

[6] In addition to the various items reported in the text, the judge was asked to indicate whether witnesses on either side involved themselves in contradictions at any point. See Appendix E, Sample II, Q. 10. The question is perhaps somewhat spoiled in that it is indeterminable from this answers whether one witness contradicted himself or two witnesses on the same side contradicted each other. The distribution of contradictions is as follows:

	Prosecution Witnesses	Defense Witnesses
	%	%
Contradictions:		
Major	6	13
Minor	29	26
None	65	61
	100%	100%

TABLE 39

Number of Witnesses for Selected Crimes

Number of Witnesses	Homicide Prosecution %	Homicide Defense %	Assault Prosecution %	Assault Defense %	Rape Prosecution %	Rape Defense %	Burglary Prosecution %	Burglary Defense %	Drunken driving Prosecution %	Drunken driving Defense %	Narcotics Prosecution %	Narcotics Defense %
0	—	6	—	2	—	9	—	17	—	4	—	16
1	—	17	1	26	—	19	—	31	3	21	—	37
2-5	21	39	58	52	51	45	56	44	82	60	54	46
6-10	41	24	31	15	39	18	28	8	14	11	45	1
11 or more	38	14	10	5	10	9	16	—	1	4	1	—
Total	100%	100%	100%	100%	100%	100%	100%	100%	100%	100%	100%	100%
Average number of witnesses per case	11.3	5.7	6.4	3.7	6.3	2.2	6.5	2.4	4.1	3.5	6.1	1.9
Number of cases	108		107		72		79		112		68	

lected for this comparison: homicide, simple and aggravated assault, rape, burglary, drunken driving, and narcotics.[7]

By retracing the various descriptive steps one can see how each item varies over these six crimes. Table 39 begins with the number of witnesses presented by both sides.

The variation is perhaps less than might have been expected, but the total number of witnesses is clearly larger for murder cases than, for example, for narcotics cases. Further, the imbalance of witnesses between prosecution and defense varies by crime from a 3 to 1 ratio in narcotics to a 1 to 1 ratio in drunken driving.

Table 40 sets forth the details of the various types of evidence offered by the prosecution in the six crime categories.

TABLE 40

Prosecution Evidence for Selected Crimes

Number indicates the percentage of trials for the particular crime in which this kind of evidence is presented.

	Homicide	Assault	Rape	Burglary	Drunken Driving	Narcotics
	%	%	%	%	%	%
Police	90	72	60	91	98	86
Complainant	3	94	97	68	27	17
Eyewitness	44	29	4	20	22	8
Expert	58	18	28	5	5	77
Confession	43	16	27	30	1	3
Family or friends of victim	35	34	46	6	5	2
Accomplice	5	—	4	24	—	11
Other witnesses	5	2	3	3	4	11
Number of Cases *	*108*	*107*	*72*	*131*	*112*	*68*

* Sample II only.

[7] These six crimes constitute 46 per cent of all cases as follows: homicide 8 per cent, assault 10 per cent, rape 5 per cent, burglary 5 per cent, drunken driving 13 per cent, narcotics 5 per cent. The over-all number of cases varies slightly as between Tables 39, 40, and 41, because of occasional "don't knows." For the fourfold tables on these six crimes, see Table 19.

Several points are worthy of comment. First, the frequency of confession, 19 per cent over-all, varies considerably by crime; there is one in almost half the homicide cases (43 per cent) but virtually none in drunken driving and narcotics cases (1 per cent and 3 per cent). Again, the expert witness, present in 77 per cent of the narcotics cases and in 58 per cent of the homicide cases, is found in only 5 per cent of the burglary cases. Finally, as would be expected, a dominant witness group in each crime category is the police.

Table 41 gives a comparable breakdown for the kinds of evidence presented by the defense.

TABLE 41

Defense Evidence for Selected Crimes

Numbers indicate the percentage of trials for the particular crime in which this kind of evidence is presented.

	Homicide	Assault	Rape	Burglary	Drunken Driving	Narcotics
	%	%	%	%	%	%
Defendant himself	79	96	85	70	90	85
Family or friends of defendant	57	55	39	39	59	24
Character witness	34	28	34	15	23	11
Eyewitness	16	18	16	4	12	3
Expert	25	1	—	—	5	3
Accomplice	1	2	—	5	—	3
Other witnesses	15	7	13	35	7	16
*Number of Cases**	*108*	*107*	*72*	*131*	*112*	*68*

* Sample II only.

In concluding this description of the lay of the evidence in the criminal trial, we turn to an item of special interest and complexity: the defendant himself as a witness. Whether or not he testifies depends on several factors. It is a characteristic of American law that it allows the defendant to decide for himself whether he will testify and gives him the privilege of not testifying if he so wishes. This privilege, a variant of the constitutional privilege against self-incrimination, has been a celebrated point of legal controversy since the days of Jeremy Bentham. In recent years it has become the focus of public controversy as witnesses before Congressional committees have claimed the privilege.[8] In general, the legal rule not only protects the defendant from testifying, but also says that no inference may be drawn from his failure to do so.[9] Critics of the rule have stressed that this is quixotic and self-defeating, since the trier of fact cannot avoid drawing a negative inference when the defendant refuses to testify, no matter what the formal rule is. The defendant, it is argued, must know more about his alleged innocence than anyone else, and if he decides to withhold evidence, he must be doing so for a reason.

The data cannot decide the policy controversy. However, considerable light is thrown on the strategic game the defendant in the criminal trial often plays in deciding whether or not to testify. To begin with, it has been seen that the defendant testifies in 82 per cent of all cases and elects not to testify in only 18 per cent. Thus, in the large majority of cases, the defendant clearly prefers the balance of advantages and disadvantages that come from testifying. The strategic considerations may be complex.[10] There is the possibility that the

[8] For a sampling of the controversy, see Meltzer, Invoking the Fifth Amendment — Some Legal and Practical Considerations. Bulletin of the Atomic Scientists, v. 9, p. 176 (1953); Kalven, Invoking the Fifth Amendment — Some Legal and Impractical Considerations, ibid., p. 181; Meltzer, Invoking the Fifth Amendment: A Rejoinder, ibid., p. 185; Griswold, The Fifth Amendment Today (1955); Hook, Common Sense and the Fifth Amendment (1957); Packer, Ex-Communist Witnesses (1962).

[9] The Supreme Court has recently held that the self-incrimination clause of the Fifth Amendment, binding on the states by reason of the Fourteenth Amendment, forbids comment or instruction that a defendant's failure to testify is evidence of guilt. Griffin v. California 380 U.S. 609 (1965); Malloy v. Hogan, 378 U.S. 1 (1963).

[10] Table 41, above, suggests that one possible determinant is the kind of crime with which the defendant is charged. Thus in burglary and murder cases the stand is refused 30 per cent and 21 per cent of the time, whereas in assault cases the defendant testifies 96 per cent of the time. Since the decision to testify has a high correlation to the absence

defendant by his demeanor will make a poor witness and thus
defense counsel prefers his silence as a better risk. The defense may want to underscore that the prosecution has the
burden of proof and not complicate the jury's appraisal of the
prosecution evidence by efforts at rebuttal. Finally, there is
the important legal rule[11] that once the defendant takes the
stand it will be possible under some circumstances to disclose
to the jury his prior criminal record, for the purpose of im-
peaching his credibility as a witness. Against these three potential advantages to be gained by the defendant's silence is to
be weighed the common-sense inference of the defendant's
guilt, if he chooses not to talk.

Table 42 shows the frequency of criminal records for defendants in all criminal cases.[12]

TABLE 42

Frequency of Criminal Record

	Per Cent
Defendant has —	
No record	53
Record for similar crime	22
Record for different crime	25
Total	100%
Number of Cases *	*1143*

* Sample II only; 48 no answers.

---

of a record, and since defendants with records are not distributed ran-
domly among the crime categories, it is likely that this variation by
crime reflects in part variations in the incidence of records. See Table
21.

[11] As noted, the rule is complicated; see Chapter 9, note 9.

[12] Table 42 is limited to data for Sample II; there the distinction between record for a similar or different crime is preserved. The distribution in Sample I is as follows.

	%
No Record	53
Record	47
Total	100%
Cases	2385

Table 43 gives a first view of how the strength of the prosecution's case and the presence or absence of a prior record influence the defendant's decision whether or not to testify.

TABLE 43

Frequency with which Defendant Testifies, by Lay of Evidence and Prior Record

	Defendant has			
	Criminal Record		No Record	
Case is —	Per Cent	Cases	Per Cent	Cases
Clear for acquittal	53	19	90	41
Close	80	187	94	303
Clear for conviction	73	331	88	262
Average all cases	74	537	91	606

The bottom row shows that the record is an important determinant of the defendant's decision to testify. If he has no record, he will elect not to testify in only (100 − 91 =) 9 per cent of the cases; if he has a record this percentage rises to (100 − 74 =) 26 per cent. Further, when the evidence is most favorable to the defendant — where the case is clear for acquittal or close — the defendant without a record testifies over 90 per cent of the time. This percentage drops, even for defendants without a record, when the case is clear for conviction. Again, when the defendant has a record and the case is clear for acquittal he elects to testify only 53 per cent of the time, suggesting that here counsel sees no reason to disturb a favorable situation by the disclosure of the record.

Another refinement can be added to the picture. The strategy game is complicated by the fact that it is not always true that the defendant's prior record will be disclosed if he takes the stand, nor is it always true that the record will remain unknown if he does not take the stand. Table 44 gives the pertinent information.[13]

[13] As noted in Chapter 9, differential knowledge of a prior record as between judge and jury may become a cause of disagreement.

TABLE 44

Jury's Knowledge of Defendant's Record

Jury	Defendant has a Record and —		Total Per Cent
	Takes the Stand Per Cent	Does Not Take Stand Per Cent	
Learns of record	72	13	59
Does *not* learn of record	28	87	41
Total	100%	100%	100%
*Number of Cases**	*1199*	*335*	*1534*

* Samples I and II defendants with prior record.

In 28 per cent of the cases where the defendant takes the stand the jury nevertheless fails to learn of his record, and, conversely, in 13 per cent of the cases in which the defendant does not take the stand, the jury learns of his record anyway. A variety of reasons, about which the judge seldom gives information, may cause either this disclosure or nondisclosure.[14]

We can give the data one more turn by asking whether the impact of a record on taking the stand varies according to whether the record is for a similar or a different crime. Table 45 sets forth the data and shows that, to some small degree, the defendant is more inhibited by the risk of disclosing a similar record. Except for the cases that are clear for acquittal, the percentage of defendants who testify on their own behalf is smaller — albeit by a very modest margin — if the prior record is for a similar crime than when it is for a different crime.

---

[14] One of the factors affecting a defendant's decision to testify will be the law concerning impeachment by means of the defendant's criminal record. Some jurisdictions bar impeachment where the conviction was remote in time, others may limit it to crimes that imply a lack of veracity, and still others bar impeachment unless the defendant has initiated evidence tending to show his good character. In addition, the record may have been revealed prior to the defendant's testimony as part of the evidence, or its sheer notoriety may obviate any attempt at concealment. See notes 8 and 9 above and Chapter 9, note 9. It would be interesting to learn whether defendants in states that tend to limit the scope of impeachment are more likely to testify.

The number of clear-for-acquittal cases in Table 45 is too small to warrant any inferences from the differences in percentages.

TABLE 45

Frequency with which Defendant Testifies, by Lay of Evidence and Type of Record

Case is —	Similar Record Per Cent	Cases	Different Record Per Cent	Cases	Total Record Per Cent	Cases
Clear for acquittal	60	5	50	14	53	19
Close	78	65	81	122	80	187
Clear for conviction	72	181	73	150	73	331
Average all cases	73	251	76	286	74	537

This then is the profile of evidence in the contemporary criminal trial. To inventory the various items of evidence has proved to be a relatively tractable task. However, to locate what it is in the evidence that produces judge-jury disagreement will be a far more formidable and subtle matter. The easy descriptions here may serve then as a kind of preface to the harder analysis of the jury as the trier of issues of fact.

CHAPTER 11

The Jury Follows the Evidence and Understands the Case

We begin our inquiry into what the jury makes of the evidence by establishing two basic propositions. The first is simply that, contrary to an often voiced suspicion, the jury does by and large understand the facts and get the case straight. The second proposition is that the jury's decision by and large moves with the weight and direction of the evidence. Taken together, these propositions provide a background against which to evaluate situations in which the jury disagrees with the judge on the handling of evidence.

The hypothesis that the jury does *not* understand the case has loomed large in the debate over the jury.[1] It has not infrequently been charged that the modern jury is asked to perform heroic feats of attention and recall well beyond the capacities of ordinary men. A trial, it has been argued, presents to the jury a mass of material which it cannot possibly absorb, and presents it in an artificial sequence which aggravates the jury's intellectual problem. The upshot is said to be that the jury often does not get the case straight and, therefore, is deciding a case different from the one actually before it.

Perhaps the most vivid spokesman in recent years for this challenge to the jury system was the late Judge Jerome Frank. In the course of a long criticism of the jury system, centered primarily on the jury's freedom to disregard the law totally

[1] Chapter 1.

and to do what it pleases, Judge Frank offers serious criticism of the jury's capacity to follow the facts. We quote here at some length his statement of the jury's difficulties.

Suppose, however, that the jurors always did understand the R's [rules]. Nevertheless, often they would face amazing obstacles to ascertaining the F's [facts]. For the evidence is not presented all at once or in an orderly fashion. The very mode of its presentation is confusing. The jurors are supposed to keep their minds in suspense until all of the evidence is in.

Can a jury perform such a task? Has it the means and capacity? Are the conditions of a jury trial such as to make for the required calm deliberations by the jurors? Wigmore, who defends the jury system, himself tells us that the courtroom is "a place of surging emotions, distracting episodes, and sensational surprises. The parties are keyed up to the contest; and the topics are often calculated to stir up the sympathy, or prejudice, or ridicule of the tribunal."

We may, therefore, seriously question the statement of Professors Michael and Adler that, unlike the witnesses, the jury "observes the things and events exhibited to its senses under conditions designed to make the observation reliable and accurate. In the case of what (the jury) observes directly the factor of memory is negligible." As shown by Wigmore, Green, and Burrill, the first of those comments surely does not square with observable courtroom realities. As to the second — that the factor of the jurors' memory is negligible — consider the following: theoretically, as we saw, the jury, in its process of fact-finding, applies to the evidence the legal rules it learns from the judge. If the jury actually did conduct itself according to this theory, it would be unable to comprehend the evidence intelligently until it received those instructions about the rules. But those instructions are given, not before the jury hears the evidence, but only after all the witnesses have left the stand. Then, for the first time, are the jurors asked to consider the testimony in the light of the rules. In other words, if jurors are to do their duty, they must now recollect and assemble the separate fragments of the evidence (including the demeanor of the several witnesses) and fit them into the rules. If the trial has lasted for many days or weeks, the required feat of memory is prodigious. . . .

The surroundings of inquiry during a jury trial differ extraordinarily from those in which the juryman conducts his ordinary affairs. At a trial, the jurors hear the evidence in a public place, under conditions of a kind to which they are unaccustomed: No juror is able to withdraw to his own room, or office, for private individual reflection. And, at the close of the trial, the jurors are pressed for time in reaching their joint decision. Even twelve experienced judges, deliberating together, would probably not function well under the conditions we impose on the twelve inexperienced laymen.[2]

In the counterpoint of the debate over the jury, its defenders have suggested several offsetting considerations. First, although the trial is not a perfectly logical enterprise, it nevertheless is based upon a highly structured argument. Again, it is not necessary that every member of the jury recall every fact of the trial record. In many instances it will suffice if only some members are able to do so and then make these facts available to the other jurors. The collective recall of the jury, it is argued, is certain to be superior to the average recall of the individual juror.[3]

When the challenge of not understanding is put most strongly, it becomes apparent that it goes to the heart of the jury system. If the jury with any great degree of frequency does not understand the facts, it is difficult to defend it. Further, even when the challenge is put somewhat less strongly, it becomes, at the least, a plea for blue ribbon juries, that is, for recruiting the jury, not from a representative sample of the people at large, but from an educated elite, who would be intelligent enough to handle the difficult, intellectual job.

Our concern is not to debate these points a priori, but rather to look to the data to see what we can learn about whether the jury does in fact understand.

It may come as something of a surprise that a survey of judge-jury disagreements can throw light on this particular issue.[4] One might have thought that the jury's understanding

---

[2] Courts on Trial, pp. 118-120 (1949).

[3] This point was brilliantly realized in the Reginald Rose film, Twelve Angry Men (1957).

[4] It is one of the chief advantages of a broadly gauged study that there is always more "take" from the design than one may at first in-

could be ascertained only by directly interviewing the jurors and conceivably by giving them some sort of test to measure their recall. Actually, however, the data yield powerful inferences concerning the jury's understanding. There are several converging lines of analysis.

The first runs as follows. If the jury misunderstands the facts of a case, it will then, of necessity, be deciding a different case from the judge, who presumably does understand the facts. And, if the jury is deciding a different case, whether or not it agrees with the judge will be a matter of chance. To the extent that, in actual fact, jury and judge agree considerably more often than chance would dictate, the hypothesis of substantial jury misunderstanding would seem defeated. The basic table of disagreements[5] provides critical evidence on this issue in two respects. The amount of agreement, 75 per cent of all cases, is so substantial as to make it highly improbable that much of it was caused by chance. Equally important, the disagreement, as we have seen, is highly directional, thus compelling the conclusion that misunderstanding cannot in and of itself be a major factor in causing judge-jury disagreement and, hence, cannot be a major determinant of the jury's behavior.

A second line of analysis is based on the reason-assessment materials previously summarized.[6] Two important points emerged. First, in 90 per cent of the disagreements it is possible to find a reason or reasons for the disagreement without recourse to misunderstanding of the case; hence, in the great majority of disagreements there is a plausible explanation which, by its nature, precludes the notion that the jury did not understand the case. More significant, the judge almost never advances the inability of the jury to understand as a

---

tend. For example, the comprehensibility index, Q. 11 of the Sample II questionnaire, was aimed at classifying the cases in terms of evidentiary difficulty. Its use in Tables 46 through 50 is one of these happy by-products.

[5] Table 23.

[6] Chapter 8.

reason for disagreement. Actually there is only one clear instance out of all of the disagreements where the judge states outright that the reason the jury disagreed with him was because of its inability to understand. In this case the charge was embezzlement by a city bookkeeper who had worked out an involved system to cover withdrawals. The trial lasted some ten days, and at the end the jury, after three hours of deliberation, acquits. While the judge notes that the jurors "all were poorly educated and an expert witness had to carry them through many steps of bookkeeping," he explicitly tells us:

> The jury simply was not able to understand the case which was perfectly presented. [I-0825]

The uniqueness of this case among the thousand instances of disagreement argues impellingly against any general hypothesis that the jury does not understand the case.[7]

The matter need not rest on inferences, good as these are. The Sample II questionaire furnishes data permitting a more direct approach to the problem. The judge was asked the following questions:[8]

Compared to the average criminal case, was the evidence as a whole —

    easy to comprehend?

---

[7] Even in this case, the misunderstanding appears not to have been the sole explanation; there were other reasons for the jury's disagreement, such as several sentiments about the defendant who was "an attractive woman" with a "loyal husband who was well liked," the "mother of a fine 12-year old boy," and "provided for her mother." Further, the judge notes that the defendant's expert witness offered testimony which "bordered on perjury," and that he was at the time of the trial up for disciplinary action [I-0825].

In six other cases there is at most a suggestion that the jury did not understand the case in some aspect, e.g., "It's doubtful the jury caught this" [I-0764]; "Many documents were offered and there was a likelihood of confusion" [I-19751 & 2]; in a narcotics case "Jury was too naive and lacked the worldly experience" [I-0791]. Perhaps most significant, in five of these seven cases the jury hangs. See also the cases in Chapter 30, note 8.

[8] See Appendix E, Sample II questionaire, Q. 11.

somewhat difficult?

very difficult to comprehend?

Table 46 provides an important map of how difficult the criminal case that goes to the jury actually is.

TABLE 46

Difficulty of Case as Graded by the Judge

	Per Cent
Easy to comprehend	86
Somewhat difficult	12
Very difficult	2
Total	100%
*Number of cases**	*1191*

* Sample II only.

Despite its simplicity the table makes an important contribution to the solution of the problem: it shows that the great bulk of cases are routine as to comprehension and hence unlikely to be misunderstood.[9]

We now make a critical analytic use of this distinction between difficult and easy cases. The analysis involves two steps: First, it will appear that the jury in several ways sufficiently acknowledges the difference between easy and difficult cases, so that we can be sure that the jury perceives the difficult cases as difficult. Second, if the jury has a propensity not to understand, it must be assumed that the propensity is greater for difficult cases than for easy cases. We thus reach a prediction that, *if the jury does not understand the case,* it will disagree with the judge more often in difficult cases than it does in easy cases.

There are at least two ways to test the jury's sensitivity to the difficulty of the case. There are the data on how often the

---

[9] There is other evidence that the bulk of cases are easy to comprehend. It will be recalled from Table 32 that only 43 per cent of the cases are classed by the judge as close on the evidence. Again, the average number of witnesses, as shown in Table 33, is seven. Lastly, a great many of the trials are short; 42 per cent of the trials take one day or less.

jury comes back to the court during its deliberations with an inquiry or a question. In the majority of cases the jury does not come back at all, once the deliberation starts.[10] But there are enough cases in which it does, to provide a helpful reading on whether the jury perceives the difference between easy and difficult cases. Table 47 shows that in difficult cases the jury comes back with questions about twice as often as in easy cases.

TABLE 47

Frequency of Jury's Coming Back with Questions
by Difficulty of Case

	Easy Cases	Difficult Cases*
Jury comes back	14%	27%
Number of cases	*1024*	*167*

* Somewhat Difficult and Very Difficult combined.

A second line of proof is a bit more complicated; it comes from data on jury deliberation time. One test of the jury's perception of the difference between difficult and easy cases is whether the jury deliberates longer in the difficult cases.

Table 48 shows in graphic form the general relationship between trial length and length of deliberation.[11] The points on this graph represent cases, grouped according to their average trial length, as indicated by the scale at the base; their height, indicated by the scale on the margin, gives the corresponding average length of deliberation for each group.[12] The line, as expected, has a rising slope; the deliberation time increases with the trial length. Specifically, the jury deliberates a little more than one hour for every trial day, except for the very brief trials, for which the deliberation lasts relatively longer, and for very long trials, which require a relatively shorter deliberation than one hour per trial day.

[10] Data on the jury coming back are provided in Appendix B.
[11] Additional data on deliberation time and trial length are found in Chapter 36.
[12] Theoretically, each individual trial could have been represented by a separate point, but for the purpose at hand this short cut suffices.

TABLE 48

Trial Length and Deliberation Time
(All Cases)

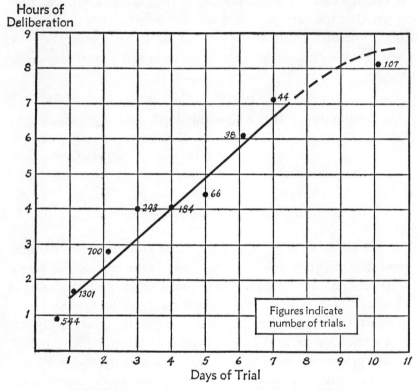

Hours of Deliberation / Days of Trial

Figures indicate number of trials.

* In bringing days and hours to a common denominator, we assumed the trial days to have 4 hours.

Table 49 then brings this segment of the analysis into sharper focus by showing the average length of deliberation time for cases of different degrees of difficulty when the trial length is held constant. For the purposes of this table we distinguish three degrees of difficulty: clear and easy, close and easy, and difficult, irrespective of whether clear or close on the evidence.

For any given length of trial, the jury deliberates longer in the difficult case than it does in the easy case. The conclusion is therefore justified that the jury does indeed perceive sensitively the different degrees of difficulty in the cases presented to it.

TABLE 49

Average Length of Deliberation by Difficulty of Case

Length of Trial	Clear and Easy Hours	Close and Easy Hours	Difficult Hours
Under 2 complete days	1.5	1.9	2.2
2 - 4 days	2.5	4.6	3.9
One week or more	4.0	5.5	9.0
Average deliberation	2.1	3.3	4.5
Number of cases	*618*	*406*	*167*

We are now ready to take the final step and present the judge-jury disagreement figures for the easy and difficult cases. The hypothesis is that *if the jury has any propensity to misunderstand the case,* it will be more likely to disagree with the judge in those cases it perceives as difficult. Table 50 provides the relevant data.

TABLE 50

Judge-Jury Disagreement as Affected by Difficulty of Case

	Clear Cases		Close Cases	
	Easy	Difficult	Easy	Difficult
Judge and jury disagree	9%	8%	41%	39%
Number of cases	*618*	*57*	*406*	*110*

The result is a stunning refutation of the hypothesis that the jury does not understand. While, as we can see,[13] jury disagreement is greater in close cases than in clear ones, there is virtually no difference between the frequency of disagreement when the case is easy and when the case is difficult; this holds true for the cases that are clear as well as for the close ones.

Finally, we pause to note that Table 50 offers the first opportunity to confront the results of reason assessment with the results of cross-tabulation and to take the compatibility of the one with the other as an important corroboration of both.[14]

[13] Chapter 12.

[14] See the discussion of confrontation in Chapter 7, The Logic of Explanation, at p. 99.

Reason assessment yielded almost no cases in which failure to understand was a reason for disagreement. The cross-tabulation presented in Table 50 yields the same result by revealing virtually identical frequencies of disagreement in easy and difficult cases. Thus, in our first try at confrontation we see that two methods of analysis — reason assessment and cross-tabulation — working independently of each other, yield congruent results.[15] We conclude, therefore, that for the law's practical purposes the jury does understand the case.

The discussion turns now from consideration of the jury's understanding of the facts to a first look at what the jury does with them. What can be said of the degree to which the jury follows the weight and direction of the evidence? To what degree is the evidence a determinant of the jury's decision? If some way could be found to organize or map the evidence in terms of the evidentiary strength or weakness of the cases, one could test the jury's response by running its decisions across such an evidence map.

There is, of course, no ideal way of determining the strength of the evidence in each case, but we can make two approximations: one, very simple, the other, fairly intricate. The simple approximation utilizes the judge's classification of cases as either clear or close. Using this distinction and adding as another dimension the way the judge himself decides the case, one can draw an evidential map in four gross categories:

1	2	3	4
Clear cases where the judge acquits	Close cases where the judge acquits	Close cases where the judge convicts	Clear cases where the judge convicts

This evidence map goes from the cases most favorable to the defendant to the cases least favorable to him. If the jury's

---

[15] In this instance a negative finding is supported by the confrontation of reason assessment and cross-tabulation. Elsewhere, affirmative findings will be tested.

judgment is in large part determined by the strength and direction of the evidence, one would predict that it would acquit most often in category 1 and least often in category 4, and that there would be a marked difference in its acquittal rate as we go from one category to the next. Table 51, which shows the jury's acquittal rate, indicates that this is indeed the case.

TABLE 51

Jury Acquittal in Clear and Close Cases

	1 Clear cases — judge acquits	2 Close cases — judge acquits	3 Close cases — judge convicts	4 Clear cases — judge convicts
Jury acquits	95%	74%	46%	10%
Number of Cases	60	142	374	615

In the strongest evidence category for the defendant, the jury acquits in 95 per cent of the cases; in the weakest category for the defendant it acquits in only 10 per cent of the cases; and in the middle categories, in terms of the strength of the case for the defendant, the jury, appropriately, acquits in 74 and 46 per cent of the cases, respectively. Thus, in these very broad terms, it is apparent that the jury's judgment does follow the direction of the evidence.[16]

A more complex map of the weight and direction of the evidence can be plotted by using various objective items of evidence information. Table 52 employs three variables in grading the evidence: (1) the strength of the prosecution's evidence (very strong, strong, normal); (2) the balance of contradictions (pro-defendant, neutral, pro-prosecution); and (3) the presence or absence of a criminal record.[17]

[16] One other aspect of Table 51 will be of considerable interest in later chapters. Even in the clear-convict cases the jury disagrees one tenth of the time, indicating that values or sentiments also mold its judgment.

[17] A word in explanation of these variables is necessary. The *record index* is comprised of three factors: Did the defendant have a criminal record? Did he take the stand? Did the jury learn of the record? We group in one class those defendants who take the stand and either have no record or are able to hide it from the jury; to these we add the

TABLE 52

Jury Acquittal Rate and Strength of Evidence

(Per cent jury acquittals of all verdicts in each cell)*

	Balance of Contradictions						
	Pro-defendant		Neutral		Pro-prosecution		
Strength of Prosecution's Case	No Record/ Stand	Record/ No Stand	No Record/ Stand	Record/ No Stand	No Record/ Stand	Record/ No Stand	Average
Normal	65	38	49	30	26	28	40
Strong	45	44	40	21	18	9	30
Very strong (confession)	31	13	30	17	21	12	21
Average	44		35		20		33

Total No Record/Stand   Total Record/No Stand

42   25

* Sample II only.

Looking initially just at the design of Table 52, we see that the strongest defense case is found in the upper lefthand cell

---

special group of defendants who do not take the stand, but of whom the jury learns, as it sometimes happens, that they have no record. All other defendants are classed in the other group on the rationale that either the record of which the jury learns or the suspicion of a record because of the refusal to take the stand may evoke a negative reaction.

The *contradictions balance* is derived from the following model, where (D) indicates an imbalance in favor of the defense and (P) an imbalance in favor of the prosecution:

Defendant Contradictions

		Major	Minor	None
Prosecution Contradictions	Major	—	D	D
	Minor	P	—	D
	None	P	P	—

The strength of the prosecution evidence is gauged "very strong" if there is a confession, "strong" when — although no confession is present — there is an eyewitness or expert or objective evidence, and "normal" when the prosecution offers simply the complainant and/or police.

where the defendant has no record, prosecution strength is normal, and there are contradictions in the prosecution's case; conversely, the weakest defense case is found in the extreme lower righthand cell, where the defendant has a record, the prosecution's evidence is very strong, and there are contradictions in the defendant's case. In a rough way the evidence can be said to move between these points of maximum strength for the defense and maximum strength for the prosecution.

Further, as one follows a row downwards, the strength of the prosecution's case increases, and, again, as one moves from left to right the strength of the prosecution increases as contradictions in favor of the defendant shift to contradictions that favor the prosecution's case. And, finally, moving from "no record" to "record" one expects the strength of the prosecution's case to increase. If then we accept Table 52 as a reasonable pattern of the weight and direction of the evidence, we can test once more the jury's response to the evidence by tracing the jury acquittal rates across the cells of the table.

The results corroborate strikingly the hypothesis that the jury follows the direction of the evidence. The highest acquittal rate (65 per cent) is in the upper extreme lefthand cell, where the defense case is the strongest, and one of the two lowest acquittal rates is in the extreme righthand cell, where the prosecution evidence is the strongest. Further, if one reads across the bottom row, the jury's average acquittal rate moves from 44 per cent to 35 per cent to 20 per cent, going, in terms of contradictions, from strong defense to strong prosecution; and, if one reads down the outer column, the jury's average acquittal rate declines from 40 to 30 to 21 per cent, as the strength of the prosecution's case increases. Finally, if we take the average of the cases where the defendant has no record as against the cases where he has a record, the acquittal rate declines from 42 to 25 per cent.[18]

Both the simple and the more complex evidence maps then tell the same story about the jury's performance, namely, that

[18] For criminal record as evidence, consult Tables 56 and 57.

its verdicts move basically with the weight and direction of the evidence.[19]

Having described in some detail the evidence involved in the criminal jury trial, having shown that the jury by and large does understand the case and get it straight, and, finally, having shown that the evidence itself is a major determinant of the decision of both judge and jury, we now return to the basic inquiry of this study: location of the sources of disagreement.

[19] The *judge's* acquittal rate also moves with the direction of the evidence, a circumstance which happily lends reality to Table 52 as an evidence map.

Judge Acquittal Rate and Strength of the Evidence
(Per cent Judge Acquittals of all Verdicts in each Cell)

Balance of Contradictions

Strength of Prosecution Case	Pro-defendant No Record	Record	Neutral No Record	Record	Pro-prosecution No Record	Record	Average
Normal	29	37	31	22	6	6	24
Strong	19	28	20	11	4	5	15
Very strong	13	0	10	3	3	0	5
Average	25		19		4		17

Total
No Record 21
Record 14

CHAPTER 12

A Preface to Evidence as an
Explanatory Category

The official view is that the jury's function is to try the facts. On that view all disagreement would arise over differences in the response of jury and judge to the evidence; evidence would be the sole explanatory category. As we have said, it is not clear that anyone has ever taken so literally the official view of the function of the jury. In any case, it is easy to draw on data to show that this view puts the function too narrowly.

Table 53, a refinement of information previously reported, summarizes the reasons for disagreements in term of facts and values.[1] Despite its simplicity, it will provide all the insights we need to put the jury's handling of the evidence in perspective.

TABLE 53

Facts and Values as Causes of Normal Disagreement

	Per Cent	
Disagree on —		
Facts alone	34 ⎫	Total facts 76%
Values and Facts	42 ⎰⎱	Total values 66%
Values alone	24 ⎭	
Total	100%	
Number of Disagreements	828	

[1] The Facts and Values data for all disagreements appear in Table 30. The current table is limited to the normal disagreements. Table 95 gives the corresponding data for cross-overs.

The table makes quickly two complementary points.[2] There are disagreements in which issues of evidence play no role at all. Some 24 per cent of all normal disagreements arise from disputes over values alone. The official view of the jury is not wholly true. But for many disagreements the explanation rests entirely on evidentiary disputes. Some 34 per cent of the normal disagreements are attributable to facts alone. The official view of the jury is not wholly untrue.

The decisive insight in Table 53, however, is to be found in the middle line, which shows that 42 per cent of all disagreements result from a response to both facts and values. The majority of the time the jury deals with values it deals also with facts (42 per cent in 66 per cent); the majority of the time the jury deals with facts, it deals also with values (42 per cent in 76 per cent). In the world of jury behavior, fact-finding and value judgments are subtly intertwined.

Behind this middle figure in Table 53 lies a central proposition about jury decision-making, what we shall call the liberation hypothesis. This category of cases presents two good reasons for disagreement: there is an evidentiary difficulty to which the jury may be responding and there is also a sentiment or value to which it may be responding. Would the jury have responded to one stimulus without the impact of the other?

---

[2] To some extent it is possible to make these same points by classifying the cases in terms of clear and close. The point to stress is that disagreements occur in clear cases as well.

Normal Disagreements in Clear and Close Cases

	Disagreements in each group %	Share of all disagreements %
Clear-Convict	14	24
Clear-Acquit	5	1
Close-Acquit	59	60
Close-Convict	32	15
		100%

Theoretically the per cent of *values alone* and of the two *clear* categories should match. However, one is 24 per cent and the other is (24 + 1 =) 25 per cent. The difference is due to the fact that the *clear-close* table is limited to Sample II.

The hypothesis is that in these cases both factors are needed to cause the disagreement.[3] The sentiment gives direction to the resolution of the evidentiary doubt; the evidentiary doubt provides a favorable condition for a response to the sentiment. The closeness of the evidence makes it possible for the jury to respond to sentiment *by liberating* it from the discipline of the evidence. For this explanation, the specific sources from which the evidential doubt arises are irrelevant. What matters is simply that, for some reason, there was doubt.

The point here is fundamental to the understanding of jury psychology and jury process. We know, from other parts of our jury study, that the jury does not often consciously and explicitly yield to sentiment in the teeth of the law. Rather it yields to sentiment in the apparent process of resolving doubts as to evidence. The jury, therefore, is able to conduct its revolt from the law within the etiquette of resolving issues of fact.

At times the judge himself comes close to making this point.[4] In a case where the judge notes that the jury sentiments were opposed to the law in question and where he had talked with the jury after the verdict, he stresses:

> There was deliberate effort on part of some jurors to hunt for doubt. [II-0035]

In a second case, a drunken driving case, in which the defendant had been badly injured in the accident and there was conflicting evidence of intoxication, the judge explains:

> There was no proof that he operated his car in an unlawful manner. . . . I think the jury felt that the defendant had

[3] We follow our convention and credit equally the evidentiary and the non-evidentiary factor in causing the disagreement; see pages 100 and 114. We are perhaps somewhat more confident here than elsewhere that both factors are really needed and that we do not have over-determination.

[4] Lord Devlin for example has put it in a flavorsome way: "I do not mean that they [the jury] often deliberately disregard the law. But if they think it is too stringent, they sometimes take a very merciful view of the facts." The Enforcement of Morals, p. 21 (1959).

suffered enough; that they looked for an excuse and felt that the blood test may have been inadequate. [I-0095]

However intriguing the notion that a major role of the evidence is simply to liberate the jury to follow a sentiment, it cannot explain everything. We are left, as shown in Table 53, with the one third of all disagreements — those falling in the facts alone category — for which by definition some other explanation is needed.

Two lines of explanation are suggested by the familiar legal concepts of the weight and credibility of the evidence. Obviously, if jury and judge come to different conclusions about pure issues of fact, it must in part be due to their making different responses to the credibility of the proof offered them. For some reason the jury may tend to believe certain evidence more than does the judge, or conversely to disbelieve it. This idea of differential credibility judgments reflects a commonplace expectation as to the role of evidence as a source of disagreement.

The law, however, adds a second and more subtle line of explanation. Some disagreements may result not because judge and jury evaluate credibility differently, but because they interpret differently the legal norm of "proof beyond a reasonable doubt." The jury may find the evidence as credible as does the judge and may weigh it the same as the judge, and yet may disagree and find the evidence wanting because in its view it falls below the required threshold.

It may be useful to summarize more formally now the three ideas we have advanced: In general, these then are the only routes by which the evidence can cause jury and judge to disagree.[5]

> (i) The liberation hypothesis. Disagreement arises because doubts about the evidence free the jury to follow sentiment.

> (ii) The credibility hypothesis. Disagreement arises be-

[5] There is perhaps a fourth hypothesis — *random* disagreement in close cases; see discussion in Chapter 14, note 4.

cause one decider accepts and the other rejects a given item of proof.

(iii) The reasonable doubt hypothesis. Disagreement arises because the jury will tolerate less doubt in convicting than will the judge.

Although the liberation hypothesis makes a most distinctive point about jury behavior, it does not admit of discursive treatment here, since it makes no difference what the evidence difficulty is which brings it into play. We can, however, trace further what we have called the credibility and the reasonable doubt hypotheses. The next two chapters are devoted to this task.

CHAPTER 13

The Credibility Hypothesis

We will look more closely now at what was called the commonplace hypothesis that judge and jury disagree in their handling of questions of fact because they make different judgments as to the credibility of given kinds of evidence. In its popular form the hypothesis touches a corner of the debate over the jury system itself. One major concern within the controversy over the system has been whether the judge or the jury is the more competent trier of facts. We already know that this issue, to a considerable degree, must be an inflated one, since the jury both understands the case and is disciplined by the evidence.[1] Nevertheless, it remains plausible that what disagreement there is between judge and jury over the evidence may arise because of what might be called the differential gullibility of the jury.

Yet one of the most striking impressions left by the judge's comments is that he almost never attributes disagreement to the jury's gullibility. In a rare case in which he makes this point, a police officer with a good record solicits a bribe to quash a bad check charge, and the judge, who would have convicted, explains:

> There was a remote possibility that complainant was falsifying the charge in order to avoid prosecution on the bad check charge. Could impress a jury, but not a judge. [I-1961]

Here, as we read him, the judge is offering the generalization that juries will be gullibly impressed by this kind of impeach-

---

[1] Chapter 11.

ment. An analogous remark is found in a disagreement in a narcotics case; the judge states:

> The defendant in this case, who incidentally had previously been tried and acquitted for the same offense, proved a defense which, although thought to be phony by the court, the jury apparently gave credence to. [II-0155]

Thus the popular view that there is evidence that "would impress a jury but not a judge" or that would be "thought to be phony by the court" but not by the jury is, we repeat, underwritten by the judge in only a few instances.

We cannot do much with the question whether judge or jury is a better trier of fact. But any contention that one or the other is better implies that they handle questions of fact differently. Whether they do presents the type of question we are equipped to pursue. Therefore, the remainder of this chapter seeks to locate any systematic differences in response to particular items of evidence.

The problem, although rich in human interest, is immediately beset with difficulties. There is today almost no real knowledge about how credibility judgments are formed, and a moment's introspection is sufficient to remind us how mysterious must be this process whereby we believe one person, suspect a second, and disbelieve a third.

This sense of difficulty only increases when we turn to the judge's comments. An occasional case offers a promising jury rule of thumb, as when the judge tells us, in a manslaughter case where the defendant stabbed the victim and pleaded self-defense:

> He immediately surrendered at the nearest precinct. The jury believed the defense of self-defense. [II-0203]

Here the homely criterion for credibility used by the jury, namely, that a man who voluntarily turns himself in is telling the truth, is exactly the kind of jury lore we would have liked to collect. The difficulty is that there are almost no comparable examples to report.

In other instances which at first appear promising, the judge

seems to suggest a recurring pattern where in conflicting testimony the jury in contrast to the judge opts for a particular
type of witness. Thus, in a series of child sex cases, the suggestion is that the jury has a distinctive tendency to believe
the accused adult as against the accusing young child.

> Child was only eight and a poor witness — could be led to say
> anything. . . . Jury was intelligent and mechanically applied
> reasonable doubt instruction to acquit. I was nonetheless
> certain, down in my heart I was sure that defendant did it.
> [I-0915]

> Defendant was charged with exposing private parts to eight
> year old girl. Defendant had 11 good character witnesses as
> to truthfulness and morality. [I-1585]

Such suggestions are arresting, but it is doubtful that they reveal a distinctive jury response. One would expect that in
these conflicts the choice between child and adult would be
extremely close, sometimes falling one way, sometimes the
other. And indeed this is the case. In a third example, where
the *judge* would have acquitted and it is the jury which convicts, the judge offers the familiar explanation, but the point
is reversed.

> I would hesitate to take the word of an eight-year-old boy in
> a case of this kind. A reasonable doubt was engendered in
> my mind. [II-1020]

Or once again in a sex case where it is the judge who acquits:

> Minor victim's story impressed the judge as fanciful and in-
> cluded criminal and underworld terms popular on radio and
> TV. [II-0206]

Ironically, it is when the judge's comments are at their best
in sensitivity and detail that the problem appears most perplexing. At times a judge will refer to no single specific item
of evidence, but to competing lines of proof, offering a series
of interacting clues that remind one of a detective story. In
such cases the credibility of any given item of evidence appears
to depend primarily on the context.

In one case the judge captures this interacting complexity

almost perfectly. The defendant is charged with breaking and entering, and the judge would have convicted. He offers the following vivid picture of the ambiguity in the evidence.

> Defendant opened an unlocked door to a private home and went in. The State's position was that the entering was with intent to commit grand larceny, the defense was that he was a yardman looking for work, and upon knocking at the door he heard someone from the inside call, "Come in." The sole question before the jury was one of intent. . . . There was testimony that on the desk in the living room was $70 in cash which defendant did not take and I believe this fact was the determining factor for the jury.
>
> I disagreed with the verdict of the jury because it was not shown that defendant ever had an opportunity to get the money, which was in the living room. When discovered, he was in the bathroom instead of the front part of the house where he would naturally have been had he entered upon invitation as he claimed. There was further testimony, unrebutted, that the grounds of the home entered were in the best condition of any yard in the neighborhood and as a matter of fact the yard had been mowed and the shrubbery trimmed only three days before. There was also uncontradicted testimony that the only equipment which defendant had with him for use as a yardman was a rake and a pair of clippers. He did not have a mower, an edger, or any of the other tools frequently used in that type of work in this section of the country. [I-0545]

The conflict of clues in the judge's description makes it evident how extraordinarily difficult it would be to generalize about credibility judgments from it.

We reach then something of an impasse. We cannot rely as firmly as elsewhere on reason assessment to test the hypothesis that the jury has, in matters of credibility, a distinctive cast of judgment. As the last example indicates, such judgments in large part depend upon the whole *gestalt* of the evidence and may well be ineffable. And again, credibility judgments must depend on nuances of demeanor often too tenuous for the judge's net.

The upshot is that we must turn from reason assessment to cross-tabulation for whatever help it can afford. The best we can hope for, taking some viable clues from reason assessment, is to trace the response of judge and jury to certain broad categories of evidence of the type outlined earlier.[2]

While this effort for the most part will prove unsuccessful, we do in the end locate one major category of evidence to which judge and jury respond differently, and obtain thereby one of the central findings of the study.

The first item of evidence we will consider is the challenged confession. In the past few decades the proper handling of confessions in criminal cases has been a topic of continual concern and controversy, often at the constitutional level, in American law. The Supreme Court, with ever-increasing stringency, has limited the occasions on which confessions can be said to be appropriately obtained,[3] and on this point the law is likely to continue to evolve. But once again the concern here is not with the policy issue but simply with whether jury and judge react differently to such evidence.

In a few instances the judge implies that a challenged confession is a source of disagreement. Thus in a prosecution for passing a bad check, where the defendant claims that he

[2] Chapter 10.

[3] In the past ten years or so constitutional doctrine as to confession has undergone a remarkable evolutionary growth, paralleling the development of cases on the defendant's right to counsel during the pre-arraignment period. See Meltzer, Involuntary Confessions: The Allocation of Responsibility Between Judge and Jury, U. Chi. L. Rev., v. 21, p. 317 (1954); Inbau and Reid, Criminal Interrogation and Confessions (1962); Way, The Supreme Court and State Coerced Confessions, J. Pub. L., v. 12, p. 53 (1963), and Note, An Historical Argument for the Right to Counsel During Police Interrogation, Yale L. J., v. 73, p. 1000 (1964).

In a recent controversial decision in this line of cases, the Court reversed a conviction based on a confession obtained during pre-arraignment interrogation when the defendant, after request, had not been allowed to see his attorney (though he was present in an adjoining room) and had not been warned of his right to silence. Escobedo v. Illinois, 378 U.S. 478 (1964).

confessed because of brutality by police officers, the judge notes:

> Unfavorable publication by one newspaper as to previous mistreatment of prisoners by officers, and circumstances under which confession was taken. Physical facts did show some question as to whether confession was voluntarily given. [I-1037]

Or in an auto theft case the judge reports:

> Only evidence against defendant was his confession. He denied it in court; only question was his credibility. Jury believed him when he said he lied when he signed the statement. [I-1037]

And again, in an indecent liberties case:

> A court could not have ignored the confession; the jury did. [II-0158]

In a somewhat similar vein, there is an arson case in which the judge tells us:

> Defendant's aunt was the owner of a house boat on which the defendant was living and which was completely destroyed by fire. Nine months later defendant made two written signed statements that he had set the fire. Later he pleaded not guilty and on trial repudiated both confessions. [I-1171]

After gleaning so limited a harvest from reason assessment, we turn to cross-tabulation. Table 54 attempts to measure just how much disagreement, if any, repudiated confessions cause. The rationale for such computation has been previously developed,[4] and the basic format will be repeated at various points throughout the study. The variables employed are required to keep things as homogeneous as possible;[5] the limitation to serious crimes is occasioned because disputed confessions, which occur in some twenty per cent of all cases, are hardly ever, as we saw, at issue in minor law violations.[6]

[4] See Chapter 7, pages 88 and 89.

[5] Why these particular variables have been selected will become clear in the course of the next several chapters.

[6] Compare Table 34, on the incidence of confession, with Table 40, which shows its relative frequency in selected crimes.

TABLE 54

The Effect of a Repudiated Confession on Normal
Disagreement for Close Cases of Serious Crimes
(Per cent disagreements of all cases in each cell)

	No Record/Stand		Record/No Stand	
	Sympathy	*Other*	*Sympathy*	*Other*
Confession	44%	73%	75%	29%
Number of Cases	9	22	4	24
No Confession	78%	56%	44%	34%
Number of Cases	40	94	18	71
Difference	− 34%	+ 17%	+ 31%	− 5%

Table 54 is inconclusive as to whether confessions have any
impact on judge-jury disagreement. In two of the four comparisons the results are negative. In these instances the cases
without confession produce more disagreement than the cases
with them. And the positive results are not impressive; when
weighed against the negative results they yield an over-all impact of only .6 cases out of 146, or less than one half per cent of
all disagreements where the judge would have convicted.[7]
Since the thesis that the jury is differentially skeptical of confessions receives such faint support from both reason assessment and cross-tabulation, we hesitate to draw a conclusion.

There is considerable popular lore about the unreliability
of the accomplice who turns state's evidence,[8] and the law itself has explicitly recognized the problem. In most jurisdic-

[7] This result is achieved by applying the "Difference" each time to the
respective number of confession cases, that is, $(- .34 \times 9 =) -3.06$, adding to this $(.17 \times 22 =) 3.74$, and so forth. The figure 146 represents
the total number of disagreements; it is obtained by multiplying the
percentage in each cell by its base. The rationale of this computation is
set forth in Chapter 7, The Logic of Explanation, and a more detailed
example of the computation is presented in Chapter 15. The corresponding computation for clear cases has been excluded because the
discussion here is restricted to cases with evidence problems.

[8] "He is bargaining and delivering the life and liberty of others for
a consideration. He has no morals and no honor, the truth means
nothing to him. He knows he is an outcast. . . ." Stewart on Trial
Strategy, p. 354 (1940). The author was a noted defense attorney.

tions the defendant is entitled to a cautionary instruction on the vulnerability of accomplice testimony,[9] and some jurisdictions go so far as to require such testimony to be corroborated.[10]

The judge notes with some frequency the unreliability of the accomplice as a key difficulty in the case, and occasionally spells out the suspected inducements for turning state's evidence.

> One of the State's witnesses was an alleged accomplice and it was urged in argument that the accomplice had been led to believe, if not promised, that he would receive leniency if he testified properly for the State. Other witnesses for the State were friends of alleged accomplice and I feel that this situation had its effect upon the jury. [I-0546]

And at times the judge complains about the law's own skepticism toward accomplice testimony.

> Indictment alleged police officer had set up another policeman on leave to permit his telephone to be used for bookmaking for $50 per month. Witnesses against him were co-conspirators. This was the re-trial of a former case in which he was convicted . . . but reversed by the Supreme Court because trial judge failed to charge broadly enough on effect of testimony of an accomplice or co-conspirator. New rule amounts in my humble opinion to almost the direction of a verdict of acquittal. . . . [I-1094]

More often the judge simply notes that the credibility of the accomplice was a chief issue.

---

[9] The following is a standard instruction. "It is the law that the testimony of an accomplice ought to be received with distrust. This does not mean that you may arbitrarily disregard such testimony, but you should give to it the weight to which you find it to be entitled after examining it with care and caution and in the light of all the evidence in the case." §829, California Jury Instructions — Criminal (1958).

[10] In these jurisdictions, in addition to the charge on the weight of such testimony and on the possible self-interest of the accomplice, the judge instructs the jury on the necessity for corroboration. E.g., State v. Moncayo, 94 Ariz. 390, 385 P.2d 521 (1963). The corroboration, however, may be circumstantial. Self v. State, 108 Ga. App. 201, 132 S.E.2d 548 (1963).

The jury apparently did not believe the testimony of the state's main witness who was an accomplice in the crime and a former friend of the defendant. [II-0229]

Government charged that defendant and accomplice (who pleaded guilty) stole pants from Railway Express office. Defendant had alibi. Trial lasted off and on for two weeks as repeated recesses had to be declared because government star witness, the accomplice, kept breaking down on the witness stand. Obviously sick accomplice may have been thought by the jury to be unreliable. [I-2047]

The chief witness for the prosecution was the accomplice who had turned state's evidence. The jury believed the defendant, a middle aged man of good reputation and no prior record. Good reputation of defendant as contrasted to a confessed thief as prosecution's principal witness. [II-0029]

Accused of burglary, no eyewitness could identify defendant. Evidence largely that of an accomplice. This was just a case where the jury felt that evidence of accomplice wasn't sufficient to overcome the presumption of innocence. . . . [I-0778]

Directed this time by a promising clue, we turn to cross-tabulation once again. Table 55, following the format of Table 54, is limited to serious crimes and makes our eight-cell comparison.

TABLE 55

The Effect of Accomplice Testimony for the
Prosecution on Normal Disagreement for
Close Cases of Serious Crimes

(Per cent disagreements of all cases in each cell)

	No Record/Stand		Record/No Stand	
	Sympathy	*Other*	*Sympathy*	*Other*
Accomplice	100%	44%	67%	33%
Number of Cases	1	9	3	6
No Accomplice	71%	60%	47%	33%
Number of Cases	48	106	19	89
Difference	+29%	−16%	+20%	0%

The results are surprisingly negative. In only two of the comparisons is there greater disagreement in the cases with accomplice testimony; the over-all net difference is actually negative.[11]

We are disposed to conclude that the accomplice hypothesis, too, fails of proof.[12] This is not to say that the jury may not be more skeptical of accomplice testimony than of other testimony; it is to say only that there is no difference in skepticism when compared to the judge.

The final item of evidence we wish to explore in terms of credibility is the defendant himself as a witness.[13] In various ways the comments of the judge, as would be expected, suggest that certain disagreements turn crucially on the credibility of the defendant. At times the judge's statement is simple and unadorned: "The jury believed the defendant's story and I did not." [I-4021] Or again, the outcome of an attempted rape case depends largely "on whether you believed the man or the woman." [I-0984]

Statements as broad as these are of small help, since they contain no clue as to why the jury believed the defendant while the judge did not; indeed, they do not advance matters much beyond the simple statement that there was a disagreement.

Sometimes, however, the judge's comments are more helpful, pointing up some feature of the defendant's personality, demeanor, or reputation.

---

[11] Once again the corresponding computation for clear cases has been excluded. For the computation see note 7 above.

[12] For certain other items it was possible to establish that there is no difference in judge-jury response. Thus, in the case of the expert witness, the judge never offers as a reason for disagreement the differential response to the expert's persuasiveness. When we proceed to test this by cross-tabulation, we find that the acquittal differential between judge and jury remains roughly constant, as we move from cases in which there were expert witnesses to those in which this factor was absent.

[13] As will become apparent in Chapter 15, there is risk of overlap between defendants with a good reputation and those who for other reasons evoke sympathy. The problem is discussed at p. 194.

Jury did not want to convict a man of good reputation by reason of some questions in the evidence. [II-0089]

Defendant very fine young man, well liked by citizens, high type. [I-0700]

Defendant made very good witness for himself. [I-0701]

Defendant was a young man of neat appearance with an excellent reputation in his neighborhood. [I-0788]

Gave the impression of an honest farm boy. [II-0049]

Sincere attitude throughout trial. [II-0334]

Good reputation of defendant as compared to a confessed thief as prosecution's principal witness. [II-0029]

While in none of these cases the defendant has a record, the judge notes explicitly at times the absence of a record as a key factor.

The defendant, a 19-year old boy — clean looking, good record. [I-0936]

Previous good record of the defendant. [II-0183]

Defendant had not been in trouble before. [II-0645]

Known to most of the jurors and had a clean record. [I-0587]

I believe there was sympathy for the defendant because of his prior good record. [II-0072]

Statements such as these suggest the possibility of objectively locating a type of defendant witness to whom judge and jury may have different responses. We venture, therefore, the hypothesis that the jury makes a differential credibility judgment on one large class of defendants: those who do not have records and who take the witness stand.[14] The hunch is that the presence or absence of a record would serve as an in-

---

[14] A word of caution may be in order. In this chapter and elsewhere the discussion of an isolated source of disagreement may or may not be the sole reason for disagreement in the particular case. Indeed in the majority of cases it will not be. See Table 27. For purposes of discursive treatment, we focus on the relevant reason alone and treat it as though it explained the disagreement by itself.

dex, rudimentary as it may be, of the complex *gestalt* and will separate defendants into two testable categories.[15] Table 56 sets out the relevant cross-tabulation.

TABLE 56

Effect on Normal Disagreement of the Defendant Who Has No Record and Testifies in Close Cases

(Per cent disagreements of all cases in each cell)

| Defendant | Defense counsel superior | | Other | |
	Sympathy	Other	Sympathy	Other
No Record/Stand	100%	74%	70%	56%
Number of Cases	12	23	61	136
Record/No Stand	57%	38%	59%	36%
Number of Cases	7	13	22	100
Difference	+43%	+36%	+11%	+20%

This time the cross-tabulation gives a positive result. All of the four comparisons yield an affirmative finding; 23.0 per cent of all disagreements where the judge would have convicted can be ascribed to the No Record/Stand factor.[16]

These results are further clarified in Table 57, which refines Table 56 by adding the distinction between serious and minor crimes.

Table 57 adds to our insight by showing that the bulk of the effect attributable to this defendant factor stems from serious crimes.

The jury's broad rule of thumb here, presumably, is that as a matter of human experience it is especially unlikely that a person with no prior record will commit a serious crime, and that this is relevant to evaluating his testimony when he denies his guilt on the stand. As to him, the presumption of innocence has special force. In contrast, defendants with records and defendants charged only with minor crimes evoke a different jury calculus of probabilities, which allows the jury and the judge, to see the credibility issue the same way.

[15] The composition of the Record/Stand index is given in Chapter 11, note 17.
[16] Again the computation follows the pattern of note 7 above.

TABLE 57

Effect on Normal Disagreement of the Defendant Who Has No Record and Testifies in Close Cases by Seriousness of Crime

(Per cent disagreements of all cases in each cell)

Defendant	Minor Crimes			
	Defense Counsel Superior		Other	
	Sympathy	Other	Sympathy	Other
No Record/Stand	100%	78%	90%	53%
Number of Cases	3	9	20	34
Record/No Stand	67%	—	100%	56%
Number of Cases	3	2	4	16
Difference	+33%	+78%	−10%	− 3%

Defendant	Serious Crimes			
	Defense Counsel Superior		Other	
	Sympathy	Other	Sympathy	Other
No Record/Stand	100%	72%	61%	57%
Number of Cases	9	14	41	102
Record/No Stand	50%	45%	50%	32%
Number of Cases	4	11	18	84
Difference	+50%	+27%	+11%	+25%

Our exploration of the credibility hypothesis results in some major conclusions. Apart from the point made by Table 56 and 57, judge and jury do not display different habits of mind or different criteria of judgment in evaluating credibility. Neither the one nor the other can be said to be distinctively guillible or skeptical. Nevertheless, Tables 56 and 57 make a major point for one great category of evidence: the defendant himself as a witness in serious cases, if he has an unblemished record. With regard to him, judge and jury show a systematically different evaluation, a difference which furnishes a substantial explanation for judge-jury disagreement.

From one point of view this finding is somewhat surprising.

It is not completely compatible with the original anticipations of what a distinctive credibility response would be like. Indeed, the category is so broad and so bland as to invite a competing explanation, namely, that the jury in criminal cases, more so than the judge, gives the defendant the benefit of the doubt. This is the idiom of the reasonable doubt hypothesis. And in concluding our discussion of the evidence, we turn now directly to it.

CHAPTER 14

A Different Threshold of Reasonable Doubt

The final notion of why judge and jury might disagree over issues of fact is that they have different standards of reasonable doubt, different thresholds for the proof required for conviction in the criminal case. As with credibility, the idea is another commonplace reflection of a popular view of the jury. And as with credibility, it turns out on closer analysis to involve an elusive and perplexing concept.

To be sure, in disagreement cases the judge often comments on reasonable doubt.

> In most acquittals by juries the defense stresses "reasonable doubt" and the court must instruct the jury that if there is such doubt the jury must acquit the defendant. [II-0030]

> Jury probably over cautious on reasonable doubt. [II-0212]

> Reasonable doubt of guilt. [II-0218]

> Insufficient evidence. [II-0251]

> Didn't feel state met burden of proof. [II-0079]

> Burden of proof not carried. I felt proof was beyond reasonable doubt. Jury did not and their conclusion was justified. [II-0420]

> Honest difference of opinion. [II-0441]

> It was a borderline case reasonable men could have decided either way. [I-0858]

At times the comment ties in with other issues as well.

Reasonable doubt and the fact that it was a circumstantial evidence case. [II-0547]

It was one which could go either way altho' I would have found defendant guilty. Jury may have felt defendant punished sufficiently in having killed uncle who was very close. [II-0584]

Child was only eight and a poor witness — could be led to say anything — Jury was intelligent and mechanically applied reasonable doubt instruction to acquit. I was nonetheless certain, down in my heart I was sure that defendant did it. [I-0915] [1]

Defendants were found with a deer about 30 minutes after legal hunting began. State attempted to show by circumstantial evidence that the deer had been killed by them the night before. Reasonable men could easily differ in their interpretation of the evidence. [I-0853]

Although the judges' comments are forceful, many of them are ambiguous. Often he is saying simply that the case was so close it could have gone either way, suggesting that the disagreement was random. At times, as in the case involving the credibility of the young child, he seems to be saying that the jury had a doubt which he didn't share; and at times, as in the deer-hunting case and the case where the defendant killed his uncle, the judge is attributing to reasonable doubt a jury dissent more correctly attributed to the pull of a sentiment. But he never quite says that the disagreement arose because judge and jury apply a different standard to reasonable doubt.

As we probe the ambiguities in the judge's comments, we are led to refine the basic idea of reasonable doubt as an explanation for disagreement. The difficulty is to locate an independent role for it. If all evidence disagreements could be explained by the influence of a sentiment, or by differential responses to particular items of credibility, or by randomness

[1] This is one of the several instances where we shall use the same case and even the same comment more than once because it is relevant to more than one line of analysis.

in the resolution of very close cases, there would be no need
for a reasonable doubt hypothesis. Indeed, in that event it
would be difficult to assign to it any meaning. We move,
therefore, to a narrower concept. If judge and jury, when un-
affected by a sentiment, make the same credibility responses
and yet disagree as to final outcome, and if they do this repeatedly and in the same direction, this disagreement pattern can
only be explained by their having different norms as to how
little doubt should be tolerated before convicting. On this
view reasonable doubt is a residual but indispensable category
for the complete explanation of evidence disagreements.

Perhaps these reflections can be brought into focus by a
homely analogy. Suppose two men were discussing marriage
plans for their daughters. They might both agree, other circumstances being equal, that they would prefer for a son-in-
law a doctor, and that a corporation executive would be next
most attractive, next a lawyer, next a university professor, and
then a civil servant. They would agree on the relative eligibility of men in these occupations, but one father might feel
that for him the threshold of eligibility would be at the level
of a corporation executive, while the other father might be
willing to settle for a university professor. Thus one father
would give his consent to the professor, whereas the other
would not. Yet the disagreement between the two fathers
would not arise over the relative merit and attractiveness of
university professors, it would arise simply because each has
a different threshold of attractiveness which a suitor for his
daughter's hand must meet.

This example suggests a simple model for the threshold
hypothesis as it affects judge and jury. Assume that the jury,
and the judge can independently rank all of the cases coming
before them according to the strength of the evidence, so that
they can be arranged in a continuous order from the weakest
prosecution case to the strongest. The cases can then be en-
visioned as a series of bars of varying height. If then, pursuant to the hypothesis, we assume that the jury requires proof

at a certain height before it will convict, but that the height required by the judge is measurably lower, we can plot the point at which the jury's threshold for conviction cuts the cases and can do the same for the judge's threshold. There will be some cases in which the prosecution's proof is so good that it will satisfy the jury's threshold and thus necessarily also satisfy the judge's threshold. Hence, in these cases, despite the difference in their thresholds, judge and jury will agree to convict. Similarly at the other end of the graph there will be cases in which the prosecution's proof is so weak that not even the judge's threshold will be satisfied, and once again, despite the difference in threshold, judge and jury will agree — this time to acquit. But between these two groups of cases, there will be an area in which the proof is strong enough to satisfy the judge's lower threshold but not strong enough to reach that of the jury. In these cases there will be disagreement; the judge will convict and the jury will acquit.

The model we have been describing is shown in graphic form in Table 58.

This then is a precise statement of the reasonable doubt hypothesis. Is there any empirical way to verify its operation in evidence disagreements?

We know from prior discussion that there is only loose support for it at best from reason assessment and the judge's comments, and it is also well beyond the reach of cross-tabulation. Nevertheless we can make a stab at verification. The essential logic is simple. We have said reasonable doubt is an indispensable, residual explanation. If it is operative there should be some cases of disagreement which cannot be explained in any other terms. To locate these cases, then, we must first abstract from the evidence disagreements those explainable on previously established grounds.

In this process of "purification" we first eliminate all disagreements attributable to the interplay of evidence problems with sentiment; here what has been called the liberation hypothesis will be considered a sufficient explanation. This expla-

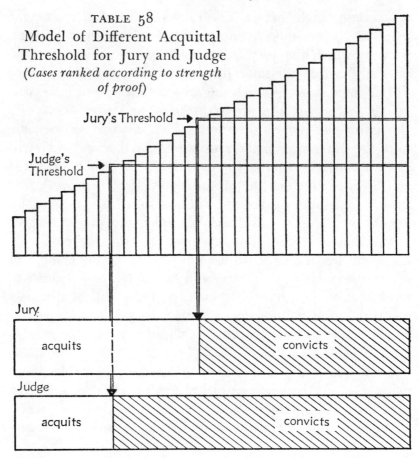

TABLE 58

Model of Different Acquittal
Threshold for Jury and Judge
(*Cases ranked according to strength
of proof*)

nation covers 46 per cent of the normal disagreements on evidence.[2]

From the remaining group we must remove the cases resolved by the differential credibility accorded by jury and judge to defendants without criminal records. This group comprises another 21 per cent[3] of the evidence disagreements.

The remainder requires one further purifying step in order

[2] The figure of 46 per cent is derived by applying the 42 per cent disagreements on Values and Facts from Table 53 to the basis of 753 cases which on the one hand excludes all Values Alone cases from Table 53 but adds the cross-over disagreements that have evidence issues.

[3] See Table 57.

to locate the true home of the hypothesis. One must expect that some disagreement between jury and judge in close cases is simply a random phenomenon. The cases are so close that reasonable men will decide them one way this time and another way the next time. .

If we assume that the 6 per cent cross-overs which remain at this point are such random deviations, then their equivalent on the normal-disagreement side would be 6 per cent of the cases.[4]

After this third step we are left with a residual 11 per cent of the disagreements spectacularly unamenable to specific explanation. We would argue that this very difficulty provides in itself a kind of proof that the reasonable doubt hypothesis is operative. The hypothesis predicts that there will be disagreements for which there is no explanation other than that the jury takes more generously than the judge the law's admonition not to convict unless guilt is proved beyond a reasonable doubt.

The various steps we have been tracing are summarized in Table 59.

As a methodological convenience we have assigned an extremely narrow and residual role to the reasonable doubt hypothesis in order to discover whether it is at all operative

---

[4] It should be understood that *random deviations* is merely a convenient term for events that cannot readily be traced to a particular cause, because they stem from a variety of causes so minute that they cannot be located individually. If, for instance, a coin is flipped, a great many small causes will determine whether one particular flip will end in heads or tails, and the individual outcome will be unpredictable. But the very fact that the result is determined by a multitude of minute causes makes it possible to predict, not the individual event, but the outcome of an aggregate of several throws; it will move around the 50-50 line. Similarly, judge and jury will in some cases produce random disagreements with each other. As to the frequency of these close-close cases, we are assuming that the residual of unexplained close cases in the cell with the smallest number of cases, the cross-over disagreement cell, determines this magnitude. As we saw it is 6 per cent of all disagreements. This assumption will reduce the so far unexplained balance of normal disagreements to its utmost minimum.

TABLE 59

Explanation for Disagreements on the Evidence

	Normal Disagreements (Per Cent)	Crossovers (Per Cent)
Liberation hypothesis (evidence *plus* sentiments)		10%
	46%	
Differential credibility of defendants without record who take stand		—
	21%	
Random disagreements in close cases		6%
	6%	
Jury's greater tolerance for reasonable doubt		—
	11%	
Total disagreements in which evidence was a factor		16%
	84%	

100%

Number of Cases   *753*

as an explanatory category.   Now that this has been established, there is no need to continue to view its sphere so narrowly.   It may well operate as well in other evidence areas, that
allocated to liberation and that allocated to credibility.   We
have no means of detecting how these factors may combine in
producing disagreement, and for the purpose of this study it
does not matter what the precise relationship might be.   It
is sufficient to have shown that the jury's more stringent view
of proof beyond a reasonable doubt is one explanation for disagreements between the two deciders in criminal cases.

It is well to remember a major point about the legal requirement that for conviction there be proof beyond a reasonable doubt: it is the normative or value judgment expressed
in this requirement.   It is a way of saying that we live in a
society that prefers to let ten guilty men go free rather than
risk convicting one innocent man.   This is, to be sure, an almost heroic commitment to decency.   In the end the point is
that the jury, as an expression of the community's conscience,
interprets this norm more generously and more intensely than
does the judge.[5]   If a society wishes to be serious about convicting only when the state has been put to proof beyond a

[5] We might for a moment add a speculation as to why the jury might
have a different threshold of reasonable doubt over and beyond the
likelihood that it reflects a distinctive value held by laymen.   It may
simply turn on the fact that the jury decides as a group and by unanimous verdict.   Given the ambiguity of the reasonable doubt formula,
it is likely that it is not understood in exactly the same fashion by all
jurors; hence, one could, theoretically, rank a population of jurors in
terms of their thresholds of reasonable doubt.   One could even assume
that the variation among individual jurors is no different from that
among judges and that the average for both groups would be at the
same point.   If then the group of 12 jurors decides close cases with a
higher cut-off point than does a single judge, the explanation may
reside simply in the unanimity requirement.   The jury, to avoid disagreement, would tend in the direction of its most stringent member.
One might, of course, object that the judge is not always an "average"
judge nor do any 12 jurors always represent the full range of thresholds.   It can, however, be mathematically proved that whenever the
distribution of thresholds among jurors is by and large the same as
among judges — the unanimity requirement will in the long run produce this threshold phenomenon, that is, given a sufficient number of
juries and judges drawn at random to confront each other.

reasonable doubt, it would be well advised to have a jury system. Undoubtedly it was something of this sort that Lord Devlin had in mind when he said: [6]

Trial by jury is not an instrument of getting at the truth; it is a process designed to make it as sure as possible that no innocent man is convicted.

[6] In a speech, "The Criminal Trial and Appeal in England," delivered at the University of Chicago for the Third Dedicatory Conference (Jan., 1960). Somewhat belatedly, we discovered an interesting confirmation of our theory, albeit from another century and another country. In his "Recherches sur la probabilité des jugements" (Paris 1837), the distinguished mathematician Poisson compared the conviction rate in the Belgian criminal courts for the years 1826 through 1829 with the corresponding rate for the years 1832 through 1834. During the first period cases were decided by a tribunal of three learned judges and the conviction rate averaged 83 per cent. During the second period when juries were substituted for the judges, the conviction rate dropped to 60 per cent. Since both judges and jury could convict with simple majority, Poisson concluded: "This can only be attributed to . . . the jurors having required, for conviction, a probability of the defendant's guilt above what the judge would find sufficient." (Page 371.)

*C*HAPTER 15 ISOLATES THE defendant as the third general source of the normal disagreements. He is the central figure in the criminal jury trial, and, as has always been thought, it makes a good deal of difference in the world of the jury who the defendant is. Out of the vast variety of human types that come before it, the jury is moved to respond only to some. The chapter then is a profile in depth of the sympathetic defendant.*

* For convenience we establish a special usage, "sympathetic," somewhat unusual in English, to describe the object or recipient of sympathy. This is in anticipation of English someday acquiring a word comparable to the French *sympathique,* the Italian *simpatico,* the Spanish *simpático,* or the German *sympathisch.*

CHAPTER 15

Jury Sentiments About the
Individual Defendant

It is popular lore that the jury is responsive to the variations among individual defendants, and it is generally assumed further that these variations make less, or even no difference to the judge. One would expect, therefore, that the variation among individual defendants is itself a major source of judge-jury disagreement, and in a general way we know[1] that this expectation is correct.

The question can perhaps be reformulated with greater operational precision by imagining for a moment a grand experiment under which each of our cases would be re-tried, with the defendant alone varying each time across the entire population of defendants.[2] If such an experiment were made, would the response of the jury vary as the defendants change? So massive an experiment is, of course, only a methodological fantasy, yet it serves to make more precise the hypothesis that the characteristics of the individual defendant are a factor in the jury's decision. As we shall see, the two more modest approaches available to us, cross-tabulation and reason assessment, approximate pretty well this experiment in varying defendants.[3]

We attempt here an almost heroic distinction: that between

[1] Table 29.

[2] It bears repeating that we are discussing the defendant who goes to jury trial, not the much broader spectrum of those who become criminals.

[3] See Chapter 7, pages 88 et seq., for the full discussion of this point.

individual characteristics that affect credibility[4] and characteristics that affect our sympathy. We rather rapidly get into
trouble. There is inevitably some overlap between response to
the person of the defendant and response to his capacity for
truth. A response to a cripple or a widow is more readily discernible as sympathetic than is a response to a good reputation.
Response to good reputation is only a shade, if that, away from
a credibility judgment, and as we have seen in Tables 56 and
57, the defendant's good record influences the jury as a matter
of evidence. Perhaps somewhat arbitrarily, therefore, we
treat reputation as belonging to evidence, and not as a personal
characteristic of the defendant, the topic of this chapter.[5]

Assuming then that, apart from credibility, there are areas
in which the characteristics of the individual defendant move
the jury to leniency, an intriguing issue arises as to what sort
of policy or judgment the jury is thereby expressing. To some
extent it will emerge as an expression of what might be rational
sentiments about punishment. But in many instances the jury
reaction goes well beyond this and rests on empathy of one
human being to another. After reviewing the details of the
jury's response, we return briefly to this puzzle at the end of the
chapter.

Complex lines of data have bearing on this topic of the individual defendant, and it will be convenient to divide the discussion into four sections: (1) a demographic profile of the defendant in criminal jury trials in terms of his age, sex, and race;
(2) a profile of those defendants who move the jury to leniency,
in terms of the judge's qualitative comments on them; herein
of reason assessment; (3) a summary profile of the defendants in

[4] At Tables 56 and 57.

[5] Also to be distinguished from response to the defendant as a person
is the specific sentiment on the law that the defendant has been punished enough, covered in Chapter 20. If the defendant has suffered
certain misfortunes between crime and trial, the jury may take
the view that life or providence has sufficiently punished him and that
further legal punishment would serve no useful social purpose. The
point under discussion in this chapter — although the distinction is
not without its difficulties — is that, not the defendant's fate, but his
intrinsic personal characteristics move the jury.

terms of a final *gestalt* classification of whether the defendant is *sympathetic, average,* or *unattractive;* (4) a statistical measuring, first by reason assessment and then by cross-tabulation, of how differences in the individual defendant affect disagreement between judge and jury.

We begin then with the simple description of the variety of personnel who stand as defendants before the jury. Of the various items of background information available, three prove to be worth reporting in detail: sex, race, and age.[6] Table 60 gives the breakdown.

TABLE 60

Criminal Defendants Before Juries, by Sex, Race, and Age

Sex	Per Cent	Race	Per Cent	Age	Per Cent
Male	93	White	73	18-20	9
Female	7	Negro	27	21-55	84
				Over 55	7
Total	100%		100%		100%
Number of cases	3576		3576		3576

Table 61 gives the comparable distributions from the 1960 census for the entire population.

TABLE 61

Adult U.S. Population by Sex, Race, and Age
(*1960 Census*)

Sex	Per Cent	Race	Per Cent	Age	Per Cent
Male	49	White	90	18-20	6
Female	51	Negro	10	21-55	69
				Over 55	25
	100%		100%		100%

[6] Both the Sample I and Sample II questionnaires provide this information. To the items of race, sex, and age, Sample II added data on

Some interesting contrasts emerge.   Although the general population is split almost evenly between men and women, crime is overwhelmingly a man's world; and whereas Negroes constitute roughly one tenth of the total population, they constitute a fourth of the criminal defendants in jury trials.   Finally, and not unexpectedly, defendants above the age of fifty-five are under-represented among the criminal jury defendants in a ratio of about three to one.   Crime, too, is not for the elderly.

In this gross profile the criminal jury defendant is likely to be male, white, and in the middle years of life.   And in fact some 54 per cent of our defendants fall into this category.[7]

It is possible to enrich the description by introducing the dimension of the specific crime categories.   Does the defend-

---

such items as reputation, marital and economic status.   It was decided not to pursue them here.   Reputation in the community is largely covered by whether defendant has a criminal record.   Marital status is to a great extent absorbed by age and rarely becomes a jury focal point. Economic status failed to discriminate simply because the vast majority of serious criminals happen to be not well off.   Some use of this data is made in Tables 83 through 86.

[7] There is some interest in observing how the three variables in Table 60 are interrelated.

Interrelationship of Sex, Race, and Age among Criminal Jury Defendants

	Race	
Sex	White	Negro
	%	%
Male	94	90
Female	6	10
	100%	100%

	Race		Sex	
Age	White	Negro	Male	Female
Under 21	9	8	9	5
21-55	83	88	84	92
Over 55	8	4	7	3
	100%	100%	100%	100%

The predominance of the male is almost as great among Negroes as among whites. Age patterns remain basically the same, except that the infrequent defendant over 55 is even more rare among the women.

ant profile in terms of sex, age, and race vary from one crime to another? Table 62 sets forth the pertinent data.[8]

TABLE 62

Sex, Race, and Age of Defendants by Crime

	Per Cent Female	Per Cent Negro	Per Cent Under 21	Per Cent Over 55	Number of Cases
Murder	11	43	10	4	210
Manslaughter	26	46	6	9	80
Negligent homicide	6	13	16	10	94
Assault	8	38	8	8	370
Rape	—	37	22	1	176
Mann Act	—	67	—	8	12
Prostitution, procuring, etc.	38	63	3	—	30
Incest	—	19	—	4	48
Indecent exposure	—	10	3	3	31
Sodomy	2	22	2	7	46
Molestation of a minor	—	18	5	31	38
Other sex crimes	23	10	6	12	31
Weapon laws	4	35	22	13	23
Arson	3	10	23	3	31
Robbery	1	33	19	8	229
Burglary	3	28	15	3	298
Larceny	10	32	10	3	182
Receiving stolen goods	4	24	12	4	51
Forgery	9	15	4	4	12
Fraud, embezzlement	10	7	1	11	131
Auto theft	2	26	19	—	111
Tax evasion	5	5	—	36	22
Bribery, official misconduct	—	8	—	23	39
Narcotics	6	60	7	1	192
Gambling	14	39	—	23	49
Liquor violations	16	28	5	11	133
Drunken driving	4	7	2	11	455
Traffic offenses	7	6	6	11	105
Mischief, public disorder	10	6	6	12	67
Family laws	10	19	9	6	77
Misc. regulatory crimes	4	7	2	11	46
Misc. other crimes	9	21	7	7	57
Average, all crimes	7	27	9	7	3576

[8] For convenience we reduced the roster of 42 crimes to 32.

Table 62 invites comment on the wide variations among defendants charged with particular crimes. Thus, the percentage of females indicted for manslaughter is unusually high; there is a disproportionately high number of Negroes involved in Mann Act cases, prostitution, and narcotics violations; and, conversely, a disproportionately low number of Negroes involved in the white collar crimes and notably in drunken driving. Finally, there is an almost Dickensian irony in the fact that three of the four crimes that are disproportionately high for the elderly are tax fraud, bribery, and molestation of children.

There is, of course, the interesting question of whether this differential spread reflects recruitment to involvement in the crimes or only the more specific recruitment to stand trial before a jury. In the two tables that follow we pause for a statistical digression to answer this question for the race and sex of the defendant. Given a certain incidence of arrests for a particular crime, say, 20 per cent Negroes or 10 per cent women, is the corresponding percentage of Negro or women defendants in jury trials about the same? If so, we would conclude that the race or the sex of the defendant does not affect the selective process by which it is determined whether or not a person accused of a crime will eventually come before a jury.

Table 63 gives the pertinent data for Negro defendants by comparing the percentages from Table 62 with the corresponding percentages of arrests as reported in the annual reports of the Federal Bureau of Investigation.[9]

The two rank orders compare well;[10] only five out of 21 crimes are grossly out of line.[11] Thus we would conclude

[9] For 1951. This was the last year in which these statistics were given in this detail.

[10] The rank order correlation is $\rho = 0.8$.

[11] A similar comparison was made for the female defendants. Again the rank order of crimes compares well ($\rho = 0.6$). The sequence is marred by two major discrepancies. Sex offenses and narcotics violations rank close to the top of the list of arrests, but both appear at the bottom of the list of jury defendants.

TABLE 63

Proportion of Negro Defendants and Arrests for Various Crimes*

	Defendants in Jury Trials		Arrests According to FBI Report	
	Per Cent	Rank	Per Cent	Rank
Disorderly conduct	6	1.5	20	6
Traffic offenses	6	1.5	25	7.5
Drunken driving	7	3.5	11	1
Embezzlement, fraud	7	3.5	14	2
Arson	10	5	26	9
Forgery	15	6	15	3
Sex offenses (not rape or commercial vice)	17	7	17	4
Family offenses	19	8	25	7.5
Receiving stolen property	24	9	31	12
Auto theft	26	10	19	5
Burglary	28	11.5	28	10
Liquor laws	28	11.5	46	16.5
Larceny	32	13	33	13
Robbery	33	14	37	14
Weapons	35	15	50	19
Rape	37	16	29	11
Assault	38	17	47	18
Gambling	39	18	51	20.5
Homicide	43	19	46	16.5
Narcotics	60	20	51	20.5
Commercial vice	64	21	39	15
Total average	27%		26%	

* These are the catégories carried in the FBI Report, and we adjusted our classifications accordingly. Compare note 8 above.

that whatever influence the type of crime has on the decision to select jury trial, the effect is by and large the same on white defendants as it is on Negroes. The fact that the over-all percentage of Negro arrests (27 per cent) is almost identical with the percentage of Negro defendants in our sample (26 per cent) is probably of little significance, since our sample comes from the southern states where Negro jury trials are relatively more frequent.[12]

The judge's assessment of characteristics of the individual defendant as reasons for disagreement between jury and judge normally takes the form of a specific descriptive comment about the defendant. Thus the process of reason assessment yields a colorful qualitative profile of the defendant which ranges over a much wider area than the flat demographic variables of sex, race, and age.

We begin with somewhat routine comments on age and sex. On occasion the judge notes either the relative old age or youth of the defendant as a distinctive circumstance. In the case of the young we are presumably facing the reluctance of the jury to mar an unblemished future; in the case of the old it is the reluctance to mar an unblemished past. We select a few illustrations from the judge's comments about the older defendant. It is apparent how readily other factors combine with old age to generate sympathy for the defendant.

> Tenant farmer — elderly. No criminal record, honest, hard worker. [II-1113 — drunken driving]

> Defendant was an old man. He made a rather pathetic appearance. [I-0202 — aggravated assault]

> Accused was elderly and, although a non-resident, good reputation established. [I-1027 — reckless driving]

In a substantially larger number of cases the judge finds it relevant to comment on the youth of the defendant.[13] Again,

[12] See Chapter 2 above. A proper regional sample of jury trials might conceivably reveal that Negro defendants are, on the whole, less likely to go before a jury, simply because jury trial is the more time-consuming and therefore more costly mode of disposition, either to the defendant or his assigned counsel. See Allen, Poverty and the Administration of Federal Criminal Justice, Report of the Attorney General's Committee (1963).

[13] Youth here may mean any age from 18 to the early twenties. Through an oversight the questionnaire was not gauged to pick up the precise age of the defendant within this range. This and the fact

a brief anthology of the comments will be sufficient to give the atmosphere.

> Youth and ignorance. [II-0408 — murder]

> Youth — not a bad looking youngster — sympathy for youth from a less-chance home. Father dead two years. [II-0006 — grand larceny]

> Young man; apparently remorseful; good family; good appearance. [II-0084 — negligent auto homicide]

> Young boy in difficulty; 18-year old boy; wife pregnant, and defendant unemployed. [II-0397 — receiving stolen goods]

> I think jury was sympathetic with the defendant, a young man aged 21, who looked clean-cut and whose mother was present with him during the entire trial. [II-0374 — petty theft]

The judge reserves some arresting prose for the infrequent cases involving female defendants. It turns out to be neither easy nor profitable to isolate the circumstance that the defendant is a woman from the circumstances that she can also be a widow, a mother, attractive, or may cry on the stand. The combination of characteristics that may appear together is vividly illustrated in an embezzlement case where the judge observes of the defendant that she

> . . . was (1) an attractive woman (2) claimed she had TB and wore a white mask throughout the trial (3) she had a loyal husband who was well liked (4) mother of a fine 12-year old boy (5) she provided for her mother (*numbers in the original*). [I-0825]

The jury in this case acquits, whereas the judge, resisting his sensitivity to the variety of the defendant's appeal, finds her guilty.

In some other cases the female defendant's profile is not so rich.

---

that the survey has no data at all on the juvenile offender in the technical sense, for whom, because of the separate court system, jury trial is not available, limits the significance of any analysis of the youth factor.

Mostly sympathy for defendant who was mother of several children and whereas complaining witness, a finance company. [I-0448 — fraud]

A refined lady who claimed a long course of harassment by [a man]. [II-0356 — assault and battery]

Lady; alien; Christmas time. [I-2006 — embezzlement]

An attractive young lady tried to an all-male jury. [I-2004 — illegal sale of liquor]

Blonde, young bride. [I-0508 — murder]

I believe that in this case, the jury was sympathetic with a woman who had no previous record and whose testimony showed she was not a heavy drinker. [I-0555 — drunken driving]

In still another group of cases it is not possible to separate strictly the response to the fact that the defendant was a woman from the response to that special form of self-defense in which an attractive wife defends herself against a bullying husband.[14]

There was evidence that husband had beaten wife and was a heavy drinker. Both had been married before. She was exceptionally good looking. [I-1748 — murder]

[14] Generally speaking, as Table 62 indicates, the crimes committed by women are so different that a simple comparison of acquittal rates for male and female defendants would reveal little.

For one crime however, homicide of a spouse, because of its symmetrical relationship, the comparison is meaningful. In this situation the female fares considerably better.

Homicide of Spouse
(*Judge Convicts*)

	Female Defendants %	Male Defendants %
Jury convicts	59	82
Hung jury	—	11
Jury acquits	41	7
Total case	100%	100%
Number of cases	*17*	*27*

The jury's view of self-defense in this and other domestic situations is dealt with in detail in Chapter 16.

Woman being badly beaten by a man she lived with. [II-0401 — assault and battery]

Sympathy for defendant because of decedent's treatment of her and her sorrow during trial. [I-0697 — murder][15]

Not unexpectedly the judge's most striking comments about the defendant go to characteristics other than race, sex, or age. One cluster relates to the very appearance of the defendant. The most obvious instance is the attractive defendant, a point already noted in the cases of the young and the female defendant. But even when the defendant is male and well over 21, the judge on occasion finds it relevant to comment on his attractiveness.

Well dressed and spoken; presented an overall good appearance. [II-1107 — theft]

Jury was composed of nine women who felt sorry for the young good looking defendant. [II-1058 — burglary]

Defendant was very handsome, personable man of 36 years of age. [I-1875 — incest]

At the other extreme, a defendant's handicaps may make a strong bid for sympathy, for instance when he is visibly in ill health or is crippled. While the judge sometimes tersely notes simply "crippled," he is often moved to describe the defendant in more sympathetic detail.

Defendant came into court with crutches. He was a crippled polio victim. He cried on the stand and obtained the jury's sympathy. [II-0383 — indecent exposure] [16]

[15] One last case deserves a note. The judge makes three points together in capsule form: "nice looking, has two small children, cried." [II-0734]

[16] Occasionally the point about the cripple gets into the law reports of a civil case. Consider this observation by a trial judge in reducing a personal injury verdict to $100,000: "I think that the members of the jury were unduly affected by sympathy. McKinney had a particularly winning and attractive personality and as he crept on his knees past the jury box to the witness stand and climbed upon the witness stand, he was quite an appealing sight." McKinney v. Pittsburgh, etc. Co., 57 F. Supp. 813 (1944). The problem of sympathy for the seriously injured looms of course much larger in personal injury cases than in criminal cases.

> Defendant had lost leg in Korea and presented a sorry spectacle. [II-0192 — statutory rape]

> Defendant had badly crippled and deformed back and this was played up for sympathy. [I-1868 — incest] [17]

> He was a very small man and had only one leg. [II-0154 — murder]

> Defendant was minus his right arm and had a very youthful appearance. [II-1009 — assault and battery]

> Defendant had received an injury during the war which might have affected his speech and ability to perform tests for intoxication. [I-3005 — drunken driving]

At other times the defendant may appeal to the jury by a display of emotion in the court room. He may break down and cry or appear repentant. It is a very special proof that the modern criminal trial is conducted in a sober key, that we find only a handful of cases in which the judge comments explicitly on the defendant's crying in court.[18]

At times the defendant might be well advised to let his wife cry for him. In what is certainly our most vivid instance of this, the judge notes:

> Jury of 11 women, one man; very sympathetic to defendant's wife. Lovely woman, impressed jury.

He then adds:

> Tears came to wife's eyes on witness stand and four of the jurors cried with her. [I-1573]

At least since the days of Aristotle[19] there has been discussion of the relevance of remorse to guilt and punishment. It

---

[17] We are left with the impression that fairly often in sex cases the crippled defendant earns some special sentiment from the jury, suggesting that perhaps the jury has sympathy for the sexual difficulties of the ugly.

[18] To be sure, there is an intrinsic bias here in favor of the female defendant. It must be easier for a woman to cry becomingly. We have just two cases in which a male defendant is reported crying.

[19] Nicomachean Ethics, Book III.1.

is thus a matter of considerable interest whether the jury responds to remorse or repentance. There are only a few cases in which the defendant's remorse is sufficiently marked to come to the judge's attention and his comments are not extensive.

A young Negro who apparently was sorry for his act. [II-0003 — murder, second degree]

Defendant very frank, said she was trying her best to break addiction habit. Husband killed in Korea. [I-1157 — narcotics]

Young man apparently remorseful. [II-0084 — negligent auto homicide]

Other characteristics of the defendant which the judge finds worth describing relate either to his family and family responsibilities or to his occupation and employment record.

The family may appear in court and be personally appealing or provide demonstrative evidence of the defendant's responsibilities. Or it may otherwise become known to the jury that the defendant has heavy family responsibilities. The judge's descriptions naturally tend to be fuller when the family is actually in court, and through his comments passes a gallery of patient and long-suffering mothers, tearful wives, pregnant wives, wives with babies in their arms, and, finally, a large array of small children.[20] It may be recalled from inventory of the evidence in the criminal trial,[21] that the defendant, in about one half of all cases, had family or friends as witnesses. The precise point here is not that the members of the family are appearing as witnesses, but that they appear as silent and suffering bystanders. In one case, answering the question,[22] "Were there extenuating circumstances in this

[20] The point recalls an observation by a distinguished reporter of the equities operating in a jury trial, André Gide: "The day before we had already seen a child appear . . . accompanied by her mother. Their appearance had certainly influenced the Court in favour of the prisoner and I believe that it contributed not a little to his acquittal." Recollections of the Assize Court, p. 24 (Wilkins trans. 1941).

[21] Table 35.

[22] Sample II questionnaire, Q. 14(a). See Appendix E.

case?" the judge checks, "No such circumstances," but then adds wryly: "Unless an obviously pregnant wife extenuates." [II-1124]

In other cases, the following comments appear relevant:

> The fact that the wife of one of the defendants was present and made a good appearance and seemed extremely agitated and concerned. The fact that she lost control of emotions in a quiet and inoffensive manner contributed to the result. [I-1026 — theft]

> Boy's mother present. She was old and looked poor. [II-0081 — disturbing the peace]

> Had three minor children and mother much in evidence. [II-0154 — murder]

> Wife and family in court throughout trial. [II-0279 — bribery]

> Mother was present with him during the entire trial. [II-0374 — petit theft]

There are just ten cases in which, as the judge saw it, the weight of the defendant's family responsibilities, although the family was not present in court, appeared to influence the jury. Since a great many defendants have family responsibilities,[23]

[23] The Sample II questionnaire had a question on whether or not the defendant had a family, the tabulation of which looks as follows:

Marital status	Per Cent
Single	41
Married (with minor children)	36
Married (no minors)	14
Divorced, widowed	9
	100%
Number of cases	1096

We could find no particular relationship between the marital status data and judge-jury disagreement. There may thus appear to be some inconsistencies between the judge's comments on the presence of the family and these results. If so, it is probably due in part to a defect in the question, since it fails to show whether the family were in court and, indeed, whether or not the jury knew of the defendant's family responsibilities.

it is something of a puzzle why in these few cases they become a decisive factor. When the burden is so great, the jury fears that by punishing the defendant they will punish his innocent family.

Defendant had six children. [I-1835 — assault and battery]

Youth of defendant — family — wife and child depending on him. [II-0426 — narcotics]

Middle-aged. Jury probably impressed by the fact that he was a belated college student with wife and children; were unable to overcome their sympathy in belief that defendant should be given another chance. [I-0422 — robbery]

This defendant was sole support of his wife and seven children. [II-0007 — drunken driving]

In the course of testifying, defendant without objection stressed the fact that wife was ill with broken back and unable to attend trial. [I-1027 — reckless driving]

These are examples of vicarious sympathy, of cases where the jury allows the defendant to be the beneficiary of his family situation and of the suffering his conviction would cause them.

The final category of descriptive comments covers what can be loosely called the work record or occupation of the defendant. Perhaps the most obvious source of appeal to the jury is the defendant who is a veteran, a point that some of the prior references have already touched upon. If the defendant happens to be still in uniform, he appears with impressive monotony to have an extra advantage.

Well dressed; attractive personality; ribbons on chest and sincere attitude throughout trial. [II-0334 — receiving stolen property]

Defendant was enlisted man in Navy. Subsequent conversation revealed that the jury did not wish to see defendant's record spoiled. [I-0416 — negligent auto killing]

They felt sorry for one of the defendants who had just been out of the Service for 30 days. [I-0670 — robbery]

Jury inexperienced and sympathetic toward defendant for being a member of armed forces who had just returned from Korea. [I-1347 — auto theft]

Jury was reluctant to return guilty verdict because defendant had just been discharged from the Armed Service. [I-3086 — liquor violation]

The fact that these officers had 12 and 15 years service and wore uniforms and ribbons in court. [II-0481-1 and 2 — assault and battery]

Defendant was an Air Force man in uniform, 20 years old. [II-0683 — drunken driving]

Other instances of the judge's noting a roughly comparable background characteristic include a few cases of students,[24] public office holders,[25] policemen,[26] and, finally, a case in which the defendant was visibly a clergyman.[27]

There are also a few cases in which the judge comments on the long and good employment record of the defendant, or, finally — to carry this roster to its bitter end — in a case where one convict kills another, on the fact that the defendant was a "model prisoner who had never had any difficulty." [I-3033]

The notably variegated characteristics of the criminal jury defendant may now perhaps be usefully summarized in tabular form. It should be emphasized that sub-categories in this area are highly arbitrary and hence of limited value. The basic fact is simply that, as the judge saw it, the defendant

[24] "College student with wife and children, [jury] unable to overcome their sympathy." [I-0422 — robbery] "College student, married, age 23." [II-1132 — murder]

[25] "Jury, being composed of normal people, it was difficult for them to believe that a normal appearing man, sheriff of the county where they lived, could commit such a repugnant and unnatural crime." [I-1381 — homosexual assault]

[26] "Sympathy for a rookie policeman." [II-1029 — manslaughter] "The jury knew he was an ex-police officer [who resigned because of this case]." [I-1391 — drunken driving]

[27] "Defendant was deacon of a Baptist church and had pastor and several church members present in court room." [I-1428 — reckless driving]

had something special about him which set him apart from others, and that characteristic was a cause of the jury's reaction. Table 64 summarizes the descriptive material we have reported.[28]

TABLE 64

Summary of Reasons for Jury Sympathy in Normal Disagreement Cases

	Number of Cases
Personal Characteristics	
Cripple, illness	24
Youth	47
Old age	12
Woman, Mother, Widow, Lady	22
Occupation	
Serviceman, veteran	20
Student	6
Police, official	12
Clergyman	1
Good employment record	5
Other occupational reasons	6
Family	
Family testified or present	23
Pregnant wife, young children	8
Large or difficult responsibilities	10
Other family reasons	4
Court Appearance	
Generally good, attractive	23
Repentant, crying	10
Sympathy unspecified	12

The discussion thus far has underscored the variety among criminal jury defendants. Our purpose now is to see what measurement we can bring to that variety. It has been seen that quite different policies may move the jury when it re-

[28] There are as a rule more instances for each characteristic than we have quoted for illustrative purposes. For instance, Table 64 shows 22 cases in which disagreement turned at least in part on the fact that defendant was a woman.

sponds to the young defendant and his future, to the aged defendant and his past, to the repentant defendant, the defendant's wife faced with losing a provider, or to the defendant who is a be-ribboned veteran to whom society might be thought to owe some gratitude. Nevertheless, it seems that all these diverse reactions have a common denominator. The defendant has a personal characteristic which in some general way marks him, in the eyes of the jury, as *sympathetic.*

In designing the Sample II questionnaire we asked the following question:[29]

> As a person, did he [the defendant] create —
>
> _____ Sympathy?
>
> _____ Unattractive impression?
>
> _____ An average impression?

As a result we can classify all defendants in terms of whether the over-all *gestalt* they created was sympathetic, average, or unattractive. We will show that this threefold classification captures all of the relevant variation among criminal defendants. It serves as an adequate summary of the demographic profile and of the more detailed qualitative profile. We are, therefore, in the happy position of having a summary term through which we can trace and test the impact of the variety of defendants on the jury.[30]

In pursuit of this line of analysis we shall first show, in Table 65, the incidence of the sympathy *gestalt* for the three demographic variables.

Table 65 reveals significant differences in the incidence of sympathy aroused by the various categories of defendants. Defendants under twenty-one have the highest sympathy index (+17), women defendants rank next (+11), then older defendants (+8), down to the Negro defendants who show a negative sympathy index (−7), indicating that these defendants appear on balance unattractive to the jury. Table 66 now

[29] Sample II questionnaire, Q. 20(a). See Appendix E.

[30] The term has much the function here that "tolerance" had for Stouffer's study of attitudes toward communism. See Chapter 4, note 9.

TABLE 65

Sympathy Index* of Defendants by Sex, Race, and Age

| | Sex | | Race | | Age | | | Total |
| | Male | Female | White | Negro | Below 21 | 21-55 | Over 55 | |
	%	%	%	%	%	%	%	%
Sympathetic	18	30	22	13	29	17	32	19
Average	65	51	62	67	59	66	44	64
Unattractive	17	19	16	20	12	17	24	17
Total	100%	100%	100%	100%	100%	100%	100%	100%
Number of cases	1112	79	840	351	123	993	75	1191
Sympathy index *	+1	+11	+6	−7	+17	0	+8	+2

* The index, designed to provide a simple measure of sympathy evoked by any given group, is the percentage of sympathetic defendants minus the percentage of unattractive defendants. Thus, for male defendants the index is (18 − 17 =) + 1.

TABLE 66

Jury Disagreement Where Judge Convicts: by Sex, Race, Age, and Sympathy

(Per Cent Disagreements of All Cases in Each Cell)

| | Sex | | Race | | Age | | | Total |
	Male	Female	White	Negro	Below 21	21-55	Over 55	Average
Sympathy	57	43	57	53	58	56	50	56
Number of cases	165	21	148	38	31	135	20	186
Average	27	27	27	25	17	28	27	27
Number of cases	589	30	426	193	63	534	22	619
Unattractive	14	7	13	14	21	12	12	13
Number of cases	170	14	118	66	14	153	17	184

traces how age, sex, and race are related to judge-jury disagreement, when sympathy is held constant.

The table enables us to see the combined relationship between sympathy and sex and race and age, the demographic characteristics that were found to be related to sympathy. As we read the table across, we find relatively little variation in the level of disagreements. To be sure, there is some: particularly between the two sexes, and some concerning the defendants under 21. That group, for instance, shows high normal disagreement even for unattractive youngsters, suggesting that youth may be a motive for disagreement beyond the sympathy normally created by young defendants.[31] By and large these differences are minor if compared with those engendered by the different levels of sympathy. We generalize therefore, for the analytical purpose of studying the individual defendant, that the sympathy-average-unattractive formula captures the bulk of the significance of the variety of criminal defendants as classified by the demographic variables.

The same point holds for the qualitative profile. If one considers the cases in which the judge gives as a reason for disagreement with the jury some characteristic of the defendant, such as his being crippled, young, having a pregnant wife, or being a war veteran, we find that in the overwhelming majority of these cases the judge checks the defendant as sympathetic. In fact, in over 90 per cent of the cases in which the judge is moved to comment on an attractive distinguishing characteristic of the defendant, he has rated the defendant as sympathetic.

As the first wing of the argument, we, therefore, conclude that the relevant variety of criminal defendants is sufficiently captured for the purpose of this study by the three gestalt terms: sympathetic, average, and unattractive. In consequence we are now in a position in Table 67 to reduce to a simple quantitative summary the variety among criminal jury defendants.

[31] The female defendants prove, of course, a special problem, insofar as their crimes are so different from those of the males.

TABLE 67

Distribution of Jury Sympathy Among Defendants

	Per Cent
Sympathetic	19
Average	64
Unattractive	17
Total	100%
Number of cases	*1191*

The simplicity of Table 67 could scarcely be improved upon; yet it makes some powerful points. It shows that almost two thirds of all defendants are in effect fungible; whatever their individual differences from each other, they are not sufficient to make the defendants significantly different individuals in the eyes of the jury. This means that, in roughly two thirds of all trials, the jury could not have been moved to disagreement by any special response to the idiosyncratic variety of defendants. Further, there is an interesting symmetry; the defendant is seen as sympathetic with roughly the same frequency as he is seen to be unattractive.

The most striking thing about Table 67 however is that it brings us to the position where we can test by cross-tabulation the impact of differences among individual defendants in judge-jury disagreement. Before making this computation, we pause to recall what we learned on this point from reason assessment. We reported earlier[32] that 11 per cent of all disagreements were credited to the defendant factor. Indeed, the qualitative profile of the defendant, given earlier in this chapter, was nothing more than an inventory of the individual reason assessments. If our underlying methodological theory is correct, the cross-tabulation should yield essentially the same result — and as we shall see, it does.

Table 68 makes the relevant comparison. It compares the jury disagreement rate for sympathetic defendants with all

[32] See Chapter 8, note 16, and Table 29. Occasionally we refer to tables of total disagreement where the figure for normal disagreements is the same.

other defendants for eight subgroups. The eight groups are required because they reflect other variables that are known to affect significantly the disagreement rate, namely, whether the evidence was clear or close; whether defense counsel was superior or not; and whether a defendant who had no record took the stand.[33]

TABLE 68

Effect of the Sympathetic Defendant on Disagreement
*(Where Judge Convicts)**

| | No Record-Stand | | | |
| | Close | | Clear | |
Per cent jury disagreements	*Superior Defense Counsel*	*Other Counsel*	*Superior Defense Counsel*	*Other Counsel*
sympathetic defendants *Number of cases*	100% 12	70% 61	13% 8	35% 48
other defendants *Number of cases*	74% 23	56% 136	30% 10	10% 231
Difference	+26%	+14%	−17%	+25%

| | Record or No Stand | | | |
| | Close | | Clear | |
Per cent jury disagreements	*Superior Defense Counsel*	*Other Counsel*	*Superior Defense Counsel*	*Other Counsel*
sympathetic defendants *Number of cases*	57% 7	59% 22	75% 4	48% 25
other defendants *Number of cases*	38% 13	36% 100	13% 15	9% 274
Difference	+19%	+23%	+62%	+39%

* Total number of disagreements = 293.
Total number of cases = 989.

The bottom line of Table 68 discloses that in 7 out of the 8 comparisons the sympathetic defendant engenders a higher dis-

[33] The effect of the Record-Stand variable in Table 68 has been measured in Tables 56 and 57. The importance of the Clear-Close distinction emerges from Chapters 10 through 14. The significance of counsel as a necessary variable will be established in Chapter 28.

agreement rate. Thus the cross-tabulation confirms the findings from the reason assessment that the individual defendant makes a difference.

But Table 68 enables us to make a further step of considerable importance. We can estimate from it just *how much* disagreement the defendant factor causes. The rationale of this computation has been developed earlier;[34] it will suffice to illustrate the procedure by making the computation here for one of the eight subgroups, conveniently for the first column of Table 68.

The theory of cross-tabulation holds that only the excess of disagreement in the sympathetic defendant column can be credited to this factor, since, even without it, disagreement reaches 74 per cent. Thus, the total amount of disagreement engendered by the sympathetic defendants in this group equals $(100 - 74 =)$ 26 per cent of the disagreements in the twelve sympathetic defendant cases, or (26 per cent of 12 =) 3.1 cases.

If this computation is repeated for the other seven groups, we obtain the following numbers, reading from left to right:

$$
\begin{array}{rcrr}
26\% & \text{of} & 12 = & 3.1 \\
14\% & \text{of} & 61 = & 8.5 \\
-17\% & \text{of} & 8 = & -1.4 \\
25\% & \text{of} & 48 = & 12.0 \\
19\% & \text{of} & 7 = & 1.3 \\
23\% & \text{of} & 22 = & 5.1 \\
62\% & \text{of} & 4 = & 2.5 \\
39\% & \text{of} & 25 = & 9.8 \\
\hline
& \text{Total} & & 40.9
\end{array}
$$

The cross-tabulation thus credits 40.9 disagreements to the defendant factor. Since the universe of disagreements comprised 293 cases, the defendant factor accounts for (40.9 divided by 293 =) 14 per cent. The reason assessment showed the defendant factor responsible for 11 per cent of all disagreements.[35] Cross-tabulation now provides us with the companion figure of 14 per cent, a quite satisfactory corroboration.

[34] Chapter 7, The Logic of Explanation, page 88.
[35] Table 29.

Since we know the frequency with which the sympathetic defendant occurs in our trials, and how often he causes disagreement, we can take the analysis one step further and compute the power of the factor. The power is defined as the ratio of the impact to the frequency with which the factor occurs. The total impact is 40.9 disagreements credited to the sympathetic defendant; the frequency is 187, the total number of sympathetic defendants in the table. Relating the two measures we see that the power is $(41 \div 187 =)$ 22 per cent, that is, the factor causes the jury to disagree once every five times it is present.

The 22 per cent figure conceals a metaphor. We can say that the power of the sympathetic defendant is *equivalent* to causing judge-jury disagreement 22 out of 100 times it occurs. Actually, because the defendant factor is so often only a partial reason, it has an effect roughly twice as often.[36]

There is one last statistic to add. Since the sympathetic defendant causes disagreement 1 out of every 5 times he is present, and since he is present roughly 1 out of 5 times, the sympathetic defendant causes disagreement in $(1/5 \times 1/5 =)$ 1/25, or 4 per cent, of all cases.

Given the thesis about the individual defendant presented in this chapter, we would predict that an *unattractive* defendant would have a converse effect on the jury. Where the judge acquits the presence of this factor will at times induce the jury to disagree with the judge and convict. This turns out to be the case.[37]

In the end we can only report out the jury's unmistakable response to the variety of human beings that appear before it. We cannot with any confidence carry further the analysis of what sentiment or policy it is thereby expressing. In all likeli-

[36] We learn this from reason assessment; compare Tables 26 and 29.
[37] The influence of personal characteristics of the defendant in producing cross-over disagreements is discussed at Table 97.

hood it must often be subliminal for the jury. And in any event it would seem that the capturing of this human variety by the summary terms must blunt the delicacy of the sentiments that may be evoked as the jury's empathy moves from the widow to the beautiful girl to the cripple to the veteran. We obviously confront here a deep human response to other humans.[38] At this point we have exhausted not only our data but our insight.

[38] We know, of course, that the Sympathetic Defendant is but a collective term for many very different sentiments that deserve more subtle analysis than can be provided here. Some sense of the formal literature on empathy may be found in Jekels, Zur Psychologie des Mitleids, Imago, v. 16, p. 5 (1930); Kohut, Introspection, Empathy and Psychoanalysis, J. Amer. Psychoanalytic Assn., v. 7, p. 459, and especially pp. 463, 464 (1959); Schafer, Generative Empathy in the Treatment Situation, Psychoanalytic Quarterly, v. 28, p. 342 (1959).

*I*N MANY WAYS THE jury is the law's most interesting critic. In an impressive number of cases we find that the explanation for disagreement is that the jury's sense of justice leads it to policies which differ from official legal policies. The disagreements thus engendered have been classed under jury sentiments on the law. Detailed exposition of these sentiments yields in effect a casebook of jury law.

The next twelve chapters review these matters. We take up now in Chapters 16 through 19 what might be thought of as the major sentiments on the law; they constitute two thirds of the cases in this entire category. Chapter 16 deals with the jury's expanded version of the law of self-defense; Chapter 17 sketches the extent of a jury policy that would excuse the actor because of participation of the victim and would extend legal ideas of contributory fault. Chapter 18 gives expression to the jury's perception that for a wide variety of reasons, and whatever the nature of the crime, some kinds of offending conduct are too minimal to be dealt with by law. These first three policies cut sharply across crime categories.

Chapter 19 explores whether the jury ever rejects certain categories of crime. Despite the historical importance of this jury role, it is a commentary on the convergence of modern law and community sentiment that this list of unpopular laws is relatively short and the crimes on it are minor.

CHAPTER 16

The Boundaries of Self-Defense

It is fundamental to our criminal law that under special circumstances the intentional infliction of violence is justified. The special circumstances are that the complainant has engaged in an act of aggression against the defendant so immediate and so dangerous as to make self-help the only practical recourse. The law grants the attacked party the privilege of returning violence with violence, that is, the privilege of self-defense. Indeed, self-defense is regarded so seriously that at times it is permissible in law even to kill.

Self-defense is, by and large, the principal defense that can be offered in those crimes of violence in which it is clear that the defendant did perform the act in question; it looms large in cases of murder, manslaughter, and assault and is by nature confined to those three crime categories.[1]

The law has hedged the privilege with a complex series of restrictions under a general formula that retaliatory violence is condoned only in the face of immediate violent attack,[2] and

---

[1] The over-all frequency of the self-defense factor depends therefore on the frequency of crimes of violence, which constitute about one in five cases, and in turn on the frequency of disagreement in these crimes, which is about one in four cases. The discussion is thus limited to about 5 per cent of the cases. Nevertheless, self-defense is fourth most powerful of the sentiments on the law. From one perspective, the incidence of this factor is considerable. In about 30 per cent of the disagreements in crimes of violence, the defense turns on this issue.

[2] In this summary we omit certain details of the law of self-defense, such as the obligation to retreat, mistake, and the defense of another, because they are not relevant to the jury cases discussed. For con-

only to the extent that such retaliation is necessary to repel or forestall the attack. Thus defensive violence is not permitted against mere provocation, however aggravated or however likely to cause a man to lose his head.[3] Nor is violence allowed for reprisal after the attack has clearly ended, however strong or understandable the temptation for such reprisal may have been. And even when the defendant is making a prompt and necessary response to aggression, he is not permitted to use excessive force.[4] In brief, the law is jealous of self-help and makes only grudging concessions to it.

One would expect that the jury's response to provocation and aggression would not match precisely the elaborate calculus by which the law has defined the privilege of self-help, and that cases with aggressive victims would offer a lively source of judge-jury disagreement.

As a prefatory matter we note that in a considerable number of disagreements involving crimes of violence, the issue of self-defense appears to be operative simply as a source of evidentiary dispute. In innumerable tavern brawls and domestic squabbles where violence finally erupts, there is genuine dif-

---

sideration of these and other factors, see American Law Institute, Model Penal Code §3.04, Tent. Draft No. 8 (1958) and Perkins, Criminal Law, pp. 899, 910-911 (1957).

[3] Provocation may be a mitigating circumstance but cannot justify self-defense. Ordinarily, the physical aggression must go beyond mere words or gestures so as to cause apprehension of an immediate and serious harm. See Perkins, pp. 43-56.

[4] If there was more force than necessary to repel the initial attack, the defense of self-defense fails. In recognition of possible inequities from such a rule, the Austrian Criminal Code provides, at §2, for the misdemeanor of excessive self-defense to fit the case where the defendant, though not the original wrongdoer, has exceeded the reasonable boundaries of responsive violence without excuse, such as from shock or terror. The availability of such a solution in the calculus of self-defense might have obviated some of the judge-jury disagreements that follow. The Illinois Criminal Code of 1961 has a provision that will in some cases provide relief for the otherwise strict dichotomy of justified or not justified self-defense. In §9-2-b there is provision that an otherwise intentional killing will be classified as manslaughter if the defendant, though mistakenly, believed that the circumstances permitted what was in fact excessive force. 38 Ill. Stats. Ann.

ficulty in reconstructing what actually happened and therefore in deciding whether the victim or the defendant was the aggressor. If there is nothing more in the picture, these cases are viewed simply as instances of evidence disputes of a type already explored.[5] Our special interest here is with the cases of violence in which something more than this issue of fact is present and in which it can confidently be said that the jury's disagreement is a response, in part at least, to its own normative judgment about exactly what aggressive behavior justifies violent self-help.

We begin with the cases that are closest to legal self-defense. The victim has been a violent aggressor, has threatened serious harm, and the defendant's violence is in response to violence initiated by the victim. What causes the judge and jury to disagree is that in each of these cases, at the time the defendant acts, the threat of violence to him is no longer immediate enough to satisfy the legal rule. These then might be called cases of *reprisal*[6] rather than of self-defense. The first case provides an almost perfect illustration. The defendant is charged with assault for shooting at the victim. The full story is complex. Victim and defendant get into an argument on a country road because the victim has driven his automobile so as to force the defendant's car into a ditch. An hour or so later, the victim comes to the defendant's house, calls him out, and shoots at him with a pistol. At this point, the defendant goes back into his house, comes out with a rifle, and shoots into the victim's retreating automobile. He is charged with

[5] See Chapters 10 through 14.

[6] The doctrine of reprisal in international law permitted a state the use of force short of war to exact from a citizen or citizens of another state compensation for a wrong done one of its own citizens, when the wrongdoer and the state of the wrongdoer had refused to render justice. Reprisal is like self-defense in the requirement that the countermeasures taken be proportionate to the wrong done, but unlike it in that the response is separated in time and taken only after recourse has been made to legal process. See Colbert, Retaliation in International Law (1948).

pointing a deadly weapon. The judge would have convicted; the jury acquits. It is quite clear that at the time he shoots the defendant is in no immediate danger from his assailant and that he deliberately shoots in order to harm his assailant. The judge readily explains the disagreement:

> I believe the jury was outraged by the fact that P drove to defendant's home, called the defendant out to the highway, kicked open the door, and fired the pistol at defendant almost without warning. I believe the jury felt that the entire incident had been provoked by P and that defendant, who was at home, should not be punished because of his actions after he had been shot.

Two other circumstances here are worth a word. The victim is not injured, but merely shot at; had he been wounded or killed the jury's response might have been different. The jury rule of law implicit in this case need be no broader than that amount of force the defendant used is justified, even though there is no immediate threat to the defendant, when the conduct of the victim has been outrageously provoking. Further, the jury directs that the defendant pay court costs, and the judge observes:

> Apparently they felt that defendant was not entirely in the right as he fired at P as P drove away. [II-0834] [7]

In a second case, the defendant and his son-in-law get into a fight during a drinking bout, and the defendant is severely beaten by the son-in-law. The defendant then goes home and later shoots and kills the son-in-law as he enters the house. The judge finds murder in the first degree; the jury, murder in the second. Presumably the jury is reacting in part to the

---

[7] As noted, the jury, though it acquits the defendant, assesses costs against him, under a special Pennsylvania rule. The judge would have fined the defendant one hundred dollars. Since our survey was made, that provision of the Pennsylvania law has been declared unconstitutional, on the ground that if a defendant has been found not guilty he need pay nothing. Giaccio v. Pennsylvania, 34 Law Week 4099 (Jan. 19, 1966). We would predict that this appellant, although he helped himself, will have hurt others: juries that cannot anymore acquit and assess costs will now sometimes convict.

prior provocation of the deceased. The judge, however, cannot accept this as self-defense, and states:

> The defense of the accused was self-defense. However, the defendant was armed and the deceased was not. And the defendant could have held him off by turning on the lights and holding him at gunpoint rather than hiding in the dark and shooting him. [I-0669] [8]

In another example of reprisal "a rough young gang" threatens the defendant and his friend; the defendant goes home, obtains a gun, returns to the scene, and shoots wildly three times, one bullet killing a bystander across the street. On these facts the judge finds second degree murder, the jury, manslaughter. The judge explains that "defense counsel was able to persuade court and jury on danger of mobs and gangs and that the defendant was compelled to protect himself." [I-1563]

Lastly, where a defendant is forcibly ejected from a tavern by the victim and gets up and fatally wounds the victim in the stomach with a knife, the judge finds manslaughter and the jury acquits. It appears that the defendant, small in size, found himself among a group of Negroes, many of them large men. The judge explains that on his view the use of the knife was not necessary for the defense of the accused. He suggests the following explanation for the jury's acquittal.

> A sole Puerto Rican among several colored people and he may have acted in fear of large size victim and others around him. [II-1052] [9]

---

[8] This is in sharp contrast to the previous case, where the defendant shoots and misses. [II-0834] The difference in the degree of leniency suggests that the jury is more interested than the law in how things turn out. The jury's disagreement goes only to charge where the harm is serious, but it acquits where it is slight. See Chapter 18, *De Minimis*.

[9] One or two other such cases may be noted. Where the defendant, after a brawl, is ejected from a saloon and returns some time later to fire a shot into the saloon, killing the man who ejected him, the judge finds murder, the jury manslaughter. [I-0639] These cases illustrate not only the jury's response to reprisal but also its views of the legal limits of excessive self-defense. There is one further case in which excessive force is squarely the issue that produces disagreement, the

It is a basic characteristic of the jury to expand a legal concept by analogizing to other situations.[10]   Thus far in these analogies to reprisal the jury has not gone much beyond the formal legal doctrines of self-defense.   Other cases will push the ambit of the analogy further.

We move next to the situation in which *property* rather than life is being defended.   Here, again, the jury extends a more generous privilege of defense than does the law.   The victim in one such case is caught stealing gas from the defendant's automobile and truck at a lumber camp.   He had been warned off twice before that very night, but this third time he is caught in the act.   The defendant's story is that, after a warning, he shoots at the victim with a rifle from a distance of about 30 feet, killing him.   The judge, commenting on the jury's acquittal against his finding of murder, says simply:

> The jury evidently took into consideration the fact that there is much gas stealing in our logging operations.   [II-0187] [11]

There are similar cases.   Illustrative is one where the defendant, a tavern owner, is charged with intentionally aiming a firearm; the judge finds him guilty but the jury acquits.   It appears that the defendant, seeking to stop a riot in his tavern,

---

judge saying second degree murder and the jury acquitting.   The defendant uses a knife against an unarmed man.   The judge notes: "I expected the jury to acquit, on the ground of self-defense.   My personal opinion, however, was that the defendant was guilty of manslaughter, because, although the deceased was the aggressor, I thought the defendant used more force than was necessary for his own protection." [I-1880]

[10] Reasoning by analogy has been said to be the basic method used by judges in developing the common law; the definitive analysis is Levi, An Introduction to Legal Reasoning (1949).

[11] In a very similar case, where an Australian farmer shot a chicken thief, the jury convicted of manslaughter but public pressure from among the farmers mounted to such heights that the Attorney General released the man after only two months in prison on his own recognizance.   See Morris, The Slain Chicken Thief, Sydney L. Rev., v. 2, p. 415 (1958).   Jury sentiments that result from a bad local situation may, of course, operate *against* the defendant.   See Chapter 30, note 8 (II-1192), where a defendant charged with arson comes before jurors who know that recently there had been several unexplained fires in the area.

fired a shot to the ceiling and gun in hand ordered all colored patrons to leave. There is a dispute about whether he had intentionally pointed the gun at the complainant. The judge indicates that there was possibly some race prejudice in the jury's verdict, but it can be read simply as an instance in which the jury is willing to permit the tavern owner this degree of force as a way of quelling a disturbance in his place of business. [I-1342]

In a variation on the property defense theme where the judge finds assault with a deadly weapon and the jury acquits, we learn only that the assault of a neighbor on the defendant's property was the "outgrowth of a difference with defendant's 12-year old boy over a dog." [I-0449] The case shows the jury permitting the use of force, even with a knife, to evict an unwelcome intruder from one's property.

Next there are cases in which the victim's aggression does not literally threaten violence but is simply at the level of *harassment or insulting provocation.* It is a distinctive characteristic of the law that it does not privilege a man to respond to an insult with violence. The famous "When you call me that, smile!" standard may have been the rule of the frontier and may be close to the popular mores, but it is not the law.[12] It is of special interest, therefore, to trace the jury's reaction when the defendant has responded in anger — as might the majority of men.

At times the judge makes the point fully explicit: a defend-

[12] "The English language has a number of words and expressions which by general consent are 'fighting words' when said without a disarming smile." Chaplinsky v. New Hampshire, 315 U.S. 568, 573 (1942). However, the insulted party has a civil remedy in some states. See Wade, Tort Liability for Abusive and Insulting Language, Vand. L. Rev. v. 4, p. 63 (1950). Nowhere in American criminal law does it seem that language, however provocative, justifies physical reprisal, though uttering "fighting words" may be a criminal act. Provocation is, as noted, relevant in sentencing and, if serious enough, may reduce a murder charge to manslaughter. The question in the end will be whether the actor's loss of self-control arouses sympathy enough to call for mitigation. See Mod. Pen. Code, Tent. Draft No. 9, App. A (1959).

ant is charged with striking a victim on the nose, and the judge finds assault and battery; the jury acquits. There is apparently only one blow, and the case might well be regarded as *de minimis*. The judge adds:

> The evidence showed that the complaining witness had for days been doing all he could to irritate the defendant and I feel sure that the jury felt that the defendant acted in the same manner they would have acted under the circumstances. [I-3111]

Here is the judge's explanation of disagreement in another case where the defendant is charged with threatening violence.

> The fact, I believe, that complaining witness was a quarrelsome individual; they believed defendant had right to threaten complaining witness because of remarks complaining witness made about defendant. [I-1640]

Again, there is a dispute between two "ladies" at a bar where, after an argument, the defendant pushes the complainant off a bar stool, thereby breaking her hip. The judge finds assault and battery; the jury acquits. The judge explains:

> I think the jury felt that both were guilty, and overlooked the part of my charge where I said the names called defendant by prosecutrix would not excuse attack on prosecutrix by defendant. [I-1552]

Or when the defendant, an elderly lady, strikes the victim, and the jury acquits, the judge tells us:

> Defendant was a refined lady who claimed a long course of harassment by complaining witness. [II-0356]

Finally, in a curious case the victim is a dog which the defendant shoots in his own backyard, and the defendant is charged with firing a gun within five hundred feet of a dwelling. The judge finds him guilty, but the jury acquits. The judge comments:

> This dog was one of those dogs that make night and day miserable with their barking and fighting. [II-1121]

This cluster of insult and provocation cases offers an insight into the moderation of the jury's revolt against the law. Under some circumstances the jury, in a marked departure from the formal rule of law, will recognize an insult as sufficient aggression to privilege violence. What is impressive here, however, is the amount of defensive force which the jury allows. The jury's rule, restated, is that it will permit minimal force — something like the one-punch battery — in reply to an insult.[13]

Occasionally however, even where this defensive reaction to provocation results in serious harm, the jury may still take a lenient view. The most picaresque illustration involves a quarrel between two convicts working on a road gang. One is charged with killing the other by hitting him with a hoe. The judge finds second degree murder; the jury acquits. The judge's explanation merits full quotation.

> I believe the jury found the defendant not guilty because the defendant was shown to be a model prisoner who had never had any difficulty with either the guards or other prisoners while the victim was noted for his "lipping." In this particular case, the testimony was uncontradicted that the deceased kept picking at the defendant and walked some several feet toward him during which time he threatened to "kick his ass" and during his approach to the defendant had a hoe in his hand. The testimony was extremely weak as to any effort made by the deceased to harm the defendant, but I am certain that the jury felt that the defendant was a pretty good old Negro and that the deceased was a person who was a born troublemaker and went out of his way to bring on this difficulty. I do not believe the jury was concerned as to whether or not the deceased made an effort to strike the defendant.

And as a final comment the judge discloses how he too felt about the case.

> It was certainly a case where the defendant had the sympathy of everyone in the courtroom. [I-3033]

[13] This one-punch rule is relevant also for analysis of the jury's *de minimis* sentiment, and one or two of the cases will be restated with different emphasis in Chapter 18 at pages 265-266.

It is not altogether easy to fit this case into the pattern of prior cases; here, after all, the victim was killed. However, there are additional circumstances: it was a quarrel between Negroes in the deep South;[14] the defendant had been a model prisoner and was sympathetic as a person whereas the deceased apparently had been obnoxious and unsympathetic as a person. And beyond these factors there was the special environment: both were convicts on a road gang and there was, therefore, no way for the defendant to walk away from the harassment.

Another case again shows the jury tolerating real harm in response to insult and provocation. Here the situation appears unpromising; the defendant, a young man, is charged with assaulting a man of about sixty-five. The judge finds aggravated assault, yet the jury finds only simple assault. The judge provides the clues to the jury's motivation.

> The prosecuting witness was noticeably belligerent and aggressive. He had abused the father of the defendant the morning of the afternoon assault and the defendant was following it up. [I-0022] [15]

This sequence of cases on provocation appropriately closes on a case in which the defendant shoots and kills one of his partners in the offices of a multimillion-dollar concern. There are no eyewitnesses and the defendant pleads self-defense. The trial discloses, however, that the defendant was ousted recently by his partners, and in his view, they were refusing to pay him what his share was worth. The judge

---

[14] The view that crimes between Negroes may be taken less seriously by the jury is treated in Chapter 26.

[15] We might add a curious case in which the operator of a tavern kills a patron. The judge finds second degree murder, which the jury by a compromise verdict reduces to aggravated assault, even though the victim died. The judge comments: "This was the case of a colored juke joint operator getting mad at some remarks of a patron; leaving the place and coming back and shooting deceased. Claim of the defense was without merit and the case made by state was a perfect one. Jury, as is so often the case, by its verdict, acted as a pardon board." [I-0479]

attributes the jury disagreement to sympathy. He catalogues the woes of the defendant:

> Defendant was sick and had been ousted from a large firm which he founded, without reasonable compensation. He had a heart attack and a nervous breakdown shortly before the shooting. He was a very small man with only one leg. [II-0154] [16]

The judge finds first degree murder; the jury, looking at all the circumstances, makes it murder second degree.

We can see that the jury's responses to provocation and harassment are based on a delicate calculus indeed. At one point, an insult may be enough to justify a single-punch attack, while at another point a long course of financial harassment will cause the jury to shade the penalty for killing, or, as under the terrible circumstances of the chain gang case, even acquit.

A substantial number of violence cases in which judge and jury disagree arise between husband and wife, or at least within a domestic context. In a loose way, all are suggestive of the self-defense, provocation theme. They fall into two general classes: cases in which there has been a long background of domestic strife which then suddenly erupts in a decisive act of violence or cases in which the violence is occasioned by unfaithfulness, and where the so-called "unwritten law" seems to be invoked. Both these types of domestic quarrel are likely to have in common that the parties are the only witnesses to the event and that the prior background has built up a degree of tension that can trigger off violence on the slightest provocation. This is a point which the jury can be taken to understand introspectively.

We will begin with the cases in which there has been a prior

[16] This case carries the suggestion of a sentiment covered in Chapter 20, Defendant Has Been Punished Enough. Here, however, a good deal of the "punishment" comes from the activities of the victim, making the case more one in which the defendant, at least in the eyes of the jury, can claim some justification for his violence.

background of brutality on the part of the victim. In a first case, where the judge finds second degree murder and the jury, manslaughter, the judge makes explicit this slow building up of domestic tension. The defendant shoots and kills her husband when he intercepts her taking a ride with another man. There is "testimony that deceased assaulted wife over a period of seven years." The judge's final comment is:

> A typical homicide resulting from tension and emotion between husband and wife, a divorce pending and a long record of abuse by husband. [II-0546]

A somewhat similar case ends in a disagreement on charge, with the judge finding second degree murder, and the jury second degree manslaughter. The defendant fatally stabs her boy friend when he is threatening her. The judge reports that the deceased had "a reputation of violence with women." [II-1147] In yet another case, a wife is accused of stabbing her husband, thereby severing an artery and causing death. The judge finds manslaughter; the jury acquits. There had been a prior quarrel and the wife claims she was in fear at the time; the judge adds:

> Nice looking; has two small children; cried. [II-0734]

To take a further illustration, a wife shoots her husband during a quarrel while he is sitting in a chair reading a newspaper. The judge rates the case as clear and the disagreement as "without any merit" [17] and he gives the following clue to the jury's response in acquitting. The victim was "accused of

---

[17] The defense of self-defense may seem absurd, where the "aggressor" is shot while allegedly reading a newspaper, but the view of the jury is not so literal-minded; the whole history of physical abuse is evoked by the threat of any given moment and becomes part of the immediate peril. The law too will at times stretch the limits of what is to be considered immediate peril. For example, murder may be mitigated to manslaughter even in the absence of immediate provocation when the accused has been subjected to prior ill treatment and at the time of the slaying entertains a reasonable belief that such misconduct will continue. In one case, where a wife shot her husband to death after he fell asleep on the couch while watching television, the Supreme Court of New Jersey in reversing a conviction for murder, because of

bootlegging liquor and abusive treatment of family." [II-0151]

In an almost classic version, a wife shoots her husband with a rifle after an all-night drinking session. The judge notes that there was evidence that the husband, a heavy drinker, had beaten his wife. The jury acquits. The judge finds first degree murder and adds: "She was exceptionally good looking." In this combination of circumstances, it may not be too surprising to learn that it took the jury but nine minutes to reach its verdict. [I-1748] [18]

In these cases the jury doubtless is responding to several factors, but high among them are prior brutality and domestic tension.[19] At times, however, it seems sufficient for the jury that it is a young wife who kills her husband, even if there was no background of tension and brutality. The cases are in an unnerving way suggestive of the plot of the recent lighthearted Italian film "Divorce, Italian Style." [20]

---

prior abuse, stated: "In taking this view, we merely acknowledge the undoubted capacity of events to accumulate a detonating force, no different from that of a single blow or injury." State v. Guido, 40 N.J. 191, 211, 191 A.2d 45, 56 (1963).

[18] See Chapter 36 for a brief analysis of the length of jury deliberation. For additional light on the cases concerning female defendants, see the statistics in Chapter 15, note 14, showing how the jury tends to favor the woman in these domestic situations.

[19] Another case illustrates how many factors may converge in a domestic situation to produce a judge-jury disagreement. The wife shoots and kills her husband during a drunken brawl. She intends to wound but not to kill, and the case is tried under the felony murder rule. Both the victim and the defendant seem unattractive; the defendant is described by the judge as a "helpless, pointless soul who drank heavily herself. At one point during the trial she made a dramatic declaration of love, spoiled it by being unable to resist telling of fervid relations a few hours prior to the shooting, followed by decedent's acknowledgment of her prowess as a sexual partner." The judge goes on to say, "Community thought itself well rid of decedent: Refused to take seriously the quarrel of twisted, drunken personalities. . . ." In addition there is the circumstance that "the decedent had for four to five years frequently beaten accused when intoxicated. The beatings were severe and relatively frequent." [I-3083] We comment on aspects of this case on page 283.

[20] Although there it is the husband who believes himself privileged to eliminate his wife.

There is an overlap in such cases with Sympathy. In one case where the judge would have found second degree murder while the jury acquits the wife, the judge simply says:

Sympathy for defendant who was 20 years of age. [I-0612]

And in another, where the judge finds murder second degree, and the jury acquits, the judge states:

Blonde, young bride shot middle-aged husband after some drinking by both. Self-defense pleaded. [I-0508]

The cases provide formidable evidence that the jury is sympathetic to the wife who alleges self-defense, and that sympathy progresses geometrically with the youth and attractiveness of the wife.[21]

There is an occasional domestic quarrel in which it is not the wife who is the defendant. Thus, where a son shoots and kills his stepfather during a quarrel between the father and the mother in which the father was abusing the mother, the judge finds manslaughter; the jury acquits. The judge notes:

History of father abusing mother physically in presence of defendant. [II-0408]

And in a final somewhat analogous case, it is the husband who shoots the wife and is the beneficiary of a jury acquittal. Here the gun discharges in the course of a struggle. There is at least a suggestion of the domestic tension excuse in this disagreement on whether the defendant should have prevented the accident:

The defendant was a police officer, whereas the wife, the victim, was a stranger here. No doubt that a difficulty arose between them and it's likely that the wife was the aggressor; I would have convicted him of involuntary manslaughter for I thought that there was no necessity for the killing or his failure to prevent the shooting; he was much stronger and could have subdued her without difficulty. [II-0963]

In the domestic cases considered thus far, the mitigating circumstance has been the background of tension; we will now examine the other group of domestic quarrels, the *unwritten*

[21] See the cases in Chapter 15 at pages 201-203.

law cases, in which the unfaithfulness of the victim is the trigger. These cases touch the outer limits of the self-defense
analogies; yet they can be viewed as presenting a classic form
of provocation and the defense of a vital interest.

Where a Negro woman throws lye in the face of her common law husband, seriously burning him, the judge finds aggravated assault; the jury acquits. The comment reveals the
telltale circumstance.

> Sympathy for woman who had been wronged by a man who
> had failed to get a divorce, had three children by her, and was
> about to leave her. [II-0401] [22]

The judge then adds a reference to "another woman." And
in a second case a young girl shoots and kills her boy friend
after his refusal to marry her. The jury disagrees on charge,
finding manslaughter. The judge finds second degree murder. The judge notes:

> Defendant had borne a child by victim several weeks prior to
> the killing. [I-0697]

It has been said that hell hath no fury like a woman scorned,
and these two cases strongly suggest that the jury at times takes
this insight into account.

In another group of cases the third party in a love triangle
becomes the victim. [23] In the first instances the attack is made

---

[22] In still another case, a woman throws lye in the face of her common
law husband and is again the beneficiary of jury leniency. Here, however, the jury settles for assault and battery while the judge finds aggravated assault. In both of these lye-throwing cases the parties are
Negro, and in the second case the judge thinks this to be the decisive
circumstance: "The defendant and common-law husband were colored
people. If they had been white, I think the verdict would have been
guilty on the first charge. Our juries are loathe to hold colored to as
high standards as white people." [I-0195] For a general discussion of
this view, see Chapter 26.

[23] The most intriguing of the third party cases is one where the defendant, separated from a wife who had a reputation for unfaithfulness, shoots and kills a man in the kitchen of the wife's home. The victim is 72 years old and the defendant shoots him 13 times. The judge
finds first degree murder; the jury manslaughter. [I-0681]

by the wife on the other woman. In one, the judge's description of the facts runs as follows:

> Prosecuting witness, a woman, was badly cut by knife by defendant, a wife who contended prosecuting witness was taking defendant's husband away with illicit relationship. Evidence showed this to be true, which evidence was allowed in case under defendant's plea of insanity. Jury believed defendant and under "unwritten law" found defendant guilty of lesser offense of assault with a weapon and fixed a fine of 1-cent and costs.

The judge adds a comment on the jury's failure to go all the way to an acquittal.

> The jury thought the prosecuting witness deserved "a whipping" but that defendant went too far. [I-0008]

In another instance the defendant goes to the home of the other woman, breaks in, and, in a struggle, fells her with an iron pipe, fracturing her skull. While there are ambiguities as to who was the aggressor in the quarrel, the judge's final comment indicates that he attributed the acquittal to non-evidentiary considerations on the part of the jury.

> This is a case in which the jury was not interested in the finer distinctions of criminal law. [I-0421] [24]

To round out the report of the jury's response to self-defense, it is necessary to look briefly at a final group of cases which have in common that the victim is a *police officer* engaged in making a forcible arrest, and the defendant, for one reason or another, resists with violence. It comes as something of a surprise to find that, in this situation, the jury at times shows a special indulgence for the defendant. It is tempting to see in this sequence a trace of the jury's once clas-

---

[24] This catalog of triangle cases could be illustrated further but without adding to the point. In a final case where the judge would have given capital punishment, and the jury finds second degree murder, the judge sums up: "Perhaps the so-called unwritten law." [II-0418]

sic role of protecting the citizen against official tyranny.[25]

The first case[26] involves atrocious assault and battery on the person of the chief of police in a small community. The background description leaves little doubt as to the source of the jury's reaction.

> While the Court sitting without a jury would have found him guilty, there was no difficulty for the Court to understand why a jury of laymen would find the defendant not guilty. The police chief and his witnesses were six-foot, one-inch men, weighing over 200 pounds, and the defendant was about 5 ft. 7, weighing about 118 pounds . . . . The police made the arrest without a warrant and beat the defendant up before they got him into the car, and after getting him into the car the alleged assault on the complainant took place, after which the defendant was overpowered and his two hands were hand-cuffed to one leg. It is Court's opinion that the inhuman treatment of the defendant throughout the arrest and after the arrest made the jury feel, I presume, that he had received un-usual punishment and the verdict was prompted to discipline the officers which, in the Court's opinion, the jury was entitled to do. While the Court could have dismissed the treatment angle and based its decision on the assault, it is very under-standable how the jury reached its verdict. As a matter of fact, the rough treatment of prisoners by arresting authorities is so well known that it is difficult to get convictions where police or prosecuting detectives are involved [I-1085] [27]

In a second case the defendant, a twenty-two-year-old boy of Greek extraction, is standing in a dark doorway with his girl friend when he is approached by a police officer. A scuf-fle ensues, as a result of which the defendant is charged with assault. The officer is off duty and out of uniform, and it ap-pears that there is no evidence that the defendant was engaged

[25] There is however evidence within the sample against this. In two cases the jury is more lenient than the judge to the arresting policeman. In both the victim's resistance results in death. For discussion of jury ambivalence, see Chapter 31.

[26] In each of these disagreements distance between judge and jury is total: the jury goes all the way to acquittal.

[27] This aspect of the case is treated again in Chapter 23, Improper Police and Prosecution Methods.

in any violation of the law. What makes the jury's support of the citizen against the police official understandable in this case are two additional background factors which the judge reports.

> The police victim in this case was the brother of the mayor and the defendant's brother was also a member of the police force and had been pressuring the defendant to plead guilty out of fear of repercussions for his job as a policeman. [I-1406]

As a result of these pressures the defendant had originally pleaded guilty; he was later permitted, however, to withdraw the plea and to take his chances on a jury trial.

In another case the defendant is charged with resisting arrest in a tavern, and the judge notes:

> Jury thought officer too severe in making arrest.

In further commenting on the reasons for disagreement the judge adds an interesting insight into the strategy of the defendant.

> Sympathy for respondent. Officer was unsympathetic; natural taking of respondent's part against officer. Respondent tried his own case, claimed he didn't have money to hire a lawyer. Jury thought law was picking on him. [II-0068] [28]

In a neat blend of police aggression and domestic quarrel the defendant is charged with assault with a dangerous weapon on a police officer who attempts to enter the defendant's home to arrest him, without a warrant, for a misdemeanor. The defendant, in turn, claims the police officer is trespassing and had no excuse for entering the house. The jury sides with the defendant and acquits. With some additional facts, however, the true flavor of the case emerges. It appears that the defendant was beating his wife and that things got sufficiently serious so that the wife's brother called the police. But before the police arrived defendant and his wife had patched up their quarrel and the brother had departed,

---

[28] The defendant without counsel may win sympathy on that ground alone. See Chapter 28 at page 368.

apparently to avoid the embarrassment of confronting the police. Understandably, the defendant himself was none too happy to see the police; understandably too, the police theory that he was still engaged in beating up his wife, thus justifying an arrest, was not persuasive to the defendant, who proceeded to resist with force. Nor, as it turned out, was the police theory persuasive to the jury; they deliberated for exactly five minutes. [I-1456]

A final case provides perhaps the strongest illustration of the depth of the jury's sentiment against use of excessive force by the police. The defendant actually kills a policeman; yet the jury acquits. The police attempt to arrest the defendant for reckless driving with a house trailer. There is an imbroglio over the arrest, and the police finally move in with tear gas grenades. The defendant, in resisting, uses a gun, and a policeman is fatally wounded in the affray. The judge appends a note disclosing that it was later discovered that the defendant had been involved in a similar controversy with the police in another county. But since the jury did not learn of this, it must have seen the case as one of a man "defending his home" against an almost military assault by the police, with the result that he is granted high privileges of defense. [I-0489]

TABLE 69

Summary of Reasons for Jury Disagreement on
Self-Defense

	Number
Reprisal	8
Defense of property	4
Provocation, harassment, insult	11
Domestic quarrel — background tension	10
Domestic quarrel — "unwritten law"	12
Police aggression	10
Total	55

Tracing it in different contexts, we have now completed the profile of jury sentiment with respect to self-defense. It may be useful in conclusion to provide a quantitative summary of the shades of self-defense we have been exploring.[29]

It is a noticeable characteristic of the jury's response that except in the police cases its stance often carries it only to disagreement on charge. Its view is not so much that the defendant was blameless, but that in light of the provocation by the victim, the defendant's punishment should be moderated. Unable to control the punishment directly and unwilling to let the defendant off, the jury can only exercise its option in these cases to disagree on charge. Table 70 shows the relative frequency of such disagreements in this sequence of cases.[30]

TABLE 70

Self-Defense Compared to Other Issues: Normal
Disagreements on Guilt and Charge

	Disagreements over Self-Defense %	Disagreements for Other Reasons %
On guilt	67	84
On charge	33	16
Total	100%	100%
Number of cases	55	773

Occasionally a judge makes this point patent, as in a domestic quarrel case where the judge finds murder in the second degree, the jury finds manslaughter, and the judge explains:

> I feel that the jury found the defendant guilty of the lesser offense in the hope that it would influence the court in fixing punishment. [I-3112]

In the end the jury protest reflected in this long sequence

[29] To avoid repetition, not all the cases totaled in Table 69 are discussed in the text.

[30] The opportunity for disagreement on charge is much more frequent in crimes of violence, which permit self-defense. Thus we cannot be certain whether the table reflects this opportunity or a distinctive jury attitude which is moderating its disagreement. Compare an analogous jury reaction to the crime of rape in Chapter 17.

of cases speaks for itself: an impatience with the nicety of the law's boundaries hedging the privilege of self-defense.[31] We are reminded of a familiar epigram of Justice Holmes in a self-defense case, which captures in large part the sense of the jury's realism: "Detached reflection cannot be demanded in the presence of an uplifted knife." [32]

[31] Compare however the jury's sentiment *against* the greater leeway of Texas self-defense: "In Texas, the law of self-defense permits a man to stand his ground and defend himself if he believes that he is in danger of death or serious bodily harm. He need not retreat. Nevertheless, in self-defense homicides we regularly, indeed invariably, find jurors who candidly admit that they could not find a person innocent by reason of self-defense unless he had retreated and done everything possible to avoid the killing. These people frequently persist in this sincere view even when told specifically by the judge what instructions he must give under the law. Such people are, of course, entitled to their beliefs, but a defendant is entitled not to have them on a jury." (From the Statement of William F. Walsh, Esq. Hearings before the Subcommittee on Improvements in Judicial Machinery of the Committee on the Judiciary, U.S. Senate, 90th Congress, 1st Session, U.S. Government Printing Office, 1967.)

[32] Brown v. United States, 256 U.S. 335, 343 (1921).

Contributory Fault of the Victim

It took several centuries of Anglo-American legal evolution for the rather sophisticated idea to emerge that the state is the other party in interest in a criminal case.[1] For some purposes, however, it is characteristic of the jury to continue to see the criminal case as essentially a private affair.

In both tort and crime the role of the victim may, of course, become relevant. The victim may consent to the conduct or he may generate a privilege of self-defense. In tort, however, there are additional rules which tend to disqualify the plaintiff because of some participation on his side, such as contributory negligence or assumption of risk.[2] But in theory there

---

[1] The distinction between criminal and civil proceedings was probably unknown to ancient law, or if it existed it was indeed a blurred one. The two bodies of law were, as Winfield noted, "a viscous intermixture." In general all claims were civil and were pursued on the initiative of the injured party, but, on the other hand, every cause of civil action was a punishable offense.

It is only late in history that the distinction between tort and crime emerges. The state's arrogation to itself of the primary prosecution for certain injuries is a relatively recent development. See Pollock and Maitland, History of English Law, v. 2, pp. 519, 572 (Camb. 2d ed. 1952); Maine, Ancient Law, Ch. 10, The Early History of Delict and Crime (1861); Allen, Legal Duties, p. 222 (1931). A concise summary appears in Winfield, The Province of the Law of Tort, pp. 190-191 (1931).

[2] "Contributory negligence is conduct on the part of the plaintiff, contributing as a legal cause to his damage, which falls below the standard to which he is required to conform for his own protection," Prosser on Torts, §51 (1955). "[Assumption of risk] bears some resemblance to the notion of consent in intentional tort. . . . Whatever [it] means, it is clear that it requires both knowledge of the risk on the

is no comparable concern with the victim in criminal law.

The topic then is the tendency of the jury, in crimes with victims[3] to weigh the conduct of the victim in judging the guilt of the defendant. The cases show a bootlegging of the tort concepts of contributory negligence and assumption of risk into the criminal law.

We begin with three homicide cases in which the victim's participation is almost insanely reckless. In one case the defendant and the victims apparently had been playing "chicken," [4] that is testing each other's nerves by competitively reckless driving. The jury acquits, and the judge offers in explanation:

> Because the jury did not follow the charge of the court, they saw some evidence of contributory negligence on part of person assaulted. Contributory negligence is no defense in the laws of this state to criminal actions. [I-1763]

In a parallel case it appears that the victim has suggested a game of Russian roulette, and the defendant obligingly puts

---

·part of the plaintiff and a free choice to assume it." Gregory and Kalven, Cases and Materials on Torts, p. 204 (1959).

[3] The term "victim crimes" may perhaps require explanation. For most crimes, the distinction offers no problem. Thus, crimes such as murder and assault by definition involve a victim, whereas gambling and other regulatory crimes clearly do not. Crimes which might or might not involve a victim, such as arson or reckless driving, were classified by inspection according to the individual circumstances of the case.

[4] The term is a pejorative characterization of the loser's courage. Ordinarily cars are set on a collision course; a variation, two cars headed for a precipice, the winner the last to abandon his car, achieved classic status in the James Dean film, Rebel Without a Cause (1955). The view that such conduct is "insanely reckless" is one that even the delinquent gangs who occasion it appear to share. "The notion that one should 'live fast, die young, and leave a beautiful corpse' might be romantically attractive to a few gang boys, but . . . [those] who persist in extreme aggression or other dangerous exploits are regarded generally as 'crazy' by the other boys." Short and Strodtbeck, Group Process and Gang Delinquency, p. 224 (1965); see especially Ch. 11, Aleatory Risks Versus Short Run Hedonism.

the gun to the victim's head.   The defense to the resulting homicide charge is that the victim actually was attempting to commit suicide: some evidence of threats of suicide was introduced at the trial.   The jury convicts only of manslaughter.   The judge, disagreeing, states that it was the victim's suggesting Russian roulette which caused the jury's verdict. [II-0108]

Finally, in a negligent homicide case, a woman is charged with killing a close friend.   The parties had been drinking and playing with a .22 caliber revolver, each taking turns firing it at random and playfully snapping it at each other.   On one of these rounds when defendant happened to be holding the gun, it went off, killing the victim.   The jury disagrees with the judge and acquits.   [II-0025]

The contributory fault theme is found in a more familiar form in a series of negligent automobile homicide cases in which the party killed appears to the jury to also have been negligent,[5] and accordingly the jury acquits the defendant.

> Reluctance of jurors to be severe concerning driving conduct of others, especially with possibility that deceased driver may also have been negligent.   [I-0788]

> Victim, who drank to excess, walked or staggered across the road.   [II-0700]

> Defendant travelled too fast, but woman (deceased) may have darted into path.   [I-0091]

In other cases it is the negligence of a third party, related to the complainant, that moves the jury.   In a negligent automobile homicide case where the passenger in the car collided with is killed, the judge states:

> Case fairly clear on facts.   Negligence of driver of car in which deceased was riding, although no defense in criminal charge, had effect on jury.   [I-1216]

[5] See Chapter 24 for the discussion of inadvertent crimes.

Here the jury is in effect importing into criminal law the special doctrine of imputed negligence from tort law.[6]

In a radically different context the jury response is similar. Where the defendant is charged with molestation of an eleven-year-old girl and the jury hangs, the judge offers the following explanation of the jury's inability to reach a verdict:

> I believe the jury considered matters other than issues involved, to wit: why had the mother permitted the defendant to come to the house and why had not the mother complained earlier? [I-1375] [7]

Where the defendant drives onto the scene of a previous accident which was inadequately marked off with warnings and negligently kills an ambulance driver, the jury finds the defendant guilty only of drunken driving. As the judge notes, the negligent third party on this occasion is an agent of the state.

> Jury refused to send defendant to penitentiary, apparently deciding that greater warning should have been given by officers in charge at the scene or they should have kept the lane of traffic open for use by others who desired to pass the scene. [II-0711]

[6] "During the latter part of the nineteenth century a good many courts imputed the negligence of the third person to the plaintiff in a number of situations, because of theories of a fictitious agency relation, which are now generally recognized as fiction and nothing more, and are no longer regarded as valid." A.L.I. Restatement of the Law of Torts Second, Tent. Draft No. 9, Ch. 17, §485, p. 53 (1963).

[7] Similarly in an indecent exposure case a wife, who went to some trouble in alerting her husband to come to the window and look at the exposed defendant, may have been considered responsible for "contributing" to the completion of the crime. [II-0433]
In statutory rape cases involving older girls there is often a strong suggestion that the parents are as much to blame as the defendant. "Testimony of the girl's father that he bought hard liquor which the defendant and her father had consumed." [I-0738] "The parents had at one time urged marriage between her and the defendant, but a license could not be obtained because of the girl's age." [I-1052] "Suspect jury blamed her parents rather than the young man." [I-0781]

Thus far the jury has been dealing with what in tort would be readily recognizable as contributory negligence. The idea is still evident in a series of fraud cases where the jury seems to be endorsing W. C. Field's bon mot: "You can't cheat an honest man." In one case the defendant, through a series of misrepresentations, sells poor quality goods. The judge notes:

> The victims actually received a poor grade of roof paint for their money; they were looking for a bargain and got beat at it. [I-3051]

In a second case the defendant is charged with misrepresenting to the victim the threat of prosecution for a liquor violation and thereby obtaining money from him for "fixing" the non-existent violation. The jury acquits. [I-1506] Similarly, the jury hangs in a case where the defense is that the prosecutrix, an elderly woman intent on separating from her husband, drew their life's savings from a joint bank account and gave the money to the defendant to hold until after the divorce proceedings were terminated. The defendant claims he returned the money; the prosecutrix denies this. The jury does not ignore the fact that the victim appears to have been trying to take advantage of her husband in the divorce proceedings. [II-0603]

There is also a somewhat obscure case in which the defendant, a contractor, is charged with having remodeled a kitchen in the complainant's home without having the license required by law. The victim is described by the judge as a "very forward woman of Russian extraction, over eager and evasive." The crime in this case appears to be trivial, and, one surmises, there has been a falling out between the contractor and the complainant which is the real cause of the criminal prosecution. But, one also suspects that the complainant had originally selected this contractor because in operating without a license he was cheaper than a more respectable contractor would have been. The acquittal, therefore, may be taken as one more instance of the jury's weighing the guilt of the defendant in the light of the overreaching of the complainant. [II-0631] [8]

A slight variation is supplied by a group of property crime cases in which the dominant theme is that the victim's carelessness has somehow tempted the defendant to commit the crime. The jury regards this too as a kind of contributory negligence. In one case the defendant, while purchasing some cattle, loads one more than he bought and is charged with grand larceny. The jury acquits, and the judge explains:

> Sales ring known to be careless in not supervising the loading and unloading of purchases. [I-1644]

In a similar case in which the jury again acquits:

> Defendant charged with stealing a calf at a livestock auction; defense was that he bought four calves and the subject calf was delivered to him by error of auction employees. [II-0743]

There are also traces of the same point in a fraud case where the jury acquits and the judge notes that "loose practices had prevailed for many years" in the defendant's store. [II-0953]

In the next group of cases the victim is, at most, stained by some general immorality which has left him vulnerable to the crime. As will be seen, the jury extends its analogy to cover this group of victims.

Perhaps the most vivid instance of this type of jury moralizing is a case where the defendant is charged with rolling a drunk. The judge finds grand larceny; the jury, petty larceny, and the judge explains:

> The prosecuting witness intoxicated at the time of the theft had been around to the taverns and solicited sexual inter-

---

[8] The jury's reaction to the grasping victim may also be perceived in cases where moral guilt is clearly divided between victim and defendant but the state prosecutes only one side. Thus in an extortion case the jury acquits a public official who was allegedly bribed by operators of a gravel pit seeking special operating advantages. [II-0311] And similarly, in a second case where contractors give a kickback to an official of the town highway department in order to obtain a contract, the jury acquits. [II-0279]

course and the jury did not see fit to impose a heavier crime on the defendant. This is what I think motivated the jury. [I-0762]

Other examples are less clearly pointed. Where the jury acquits in a case of petty theft, the victim has charged the defendants with the theft of articles from his person while he was asleep after a drinking party. The defendants, admitted prostitutes, claim that the articles were given to them in payment for services. The jury may, of course, simply have believed the defendants rather than the complainant, although the judge did not. It seems likely, however, that the jury was not too fussy about resolving the precise issue of fact and was rather taking the view that a victim who consorts with prostitutes should not be heard to complain about a petty theft. [I-0941-1 & 2]

Similarly, in a homicide case where the judge finds second degree murder, the jury, manslaughter, the decisive circumstance is that the quarrel took place in a brothel. The judge states:

> The jury would only convict of manslaughter because witnesses for both the state and the defense were all prostitutes, dope peddlers, pimps, or a combination thereof. The deceased went to a house of prostitution operated by defendants and got into a fight over the price charged. [I-1358-1 & 2]

In the cases described thus far the jury appears to be reacting to an assumption of risk involved in frequenting sordid environments. Its curious concern with collateral immorality does not stop here however.[9] In a domestic violence case where the judge finds aggravated assault and the jury acquits, it appears that "defendant and the injured party had been living in adultery." The judge comments:

> Injured party was not seriously hurt and jury evidently felt that past life of both parties was a contributing factor to the difficulty. [I-1758]

---

[9] This sentiment may also be reflected in situations where victim and defendant join together in preliminary drinking bouts. See the cases in this chapter at pages 254-257 below.

And where the defendant is charged with armed robbery, the jury acquittal is influenced by the following circumstance:

He (defendant) admitted extra-marital relations with complaining witness. [II-0030]

This rationale is also suggested for a disagreement on charge in an assault case where the victim is a married woman who "had had illicit relations with the defendant for many years." [I-0921] [10]

A number of disagreements arise in cases of forcible rape. Because of the distinctive legal problem here, the jury's response might have been treated as a sentiment in its own right. But these cases show so strong and interesting a resemblance to the assumption of risk theme that it seems congenial to discuss them here.

The law recognizes only one issue in rape cases other than the fact of intercourse: whether there was consent at the moment of intercourse. The jury, as we come to see it, does not limit itself to this one issue;[11] it goes on to weigh the woman's conduct in the prior history of the affair. It closely, and often harshly, scrutinizes the female complainant and is moved to be lenient with the defendant whenever there are suggestions of contributory behavior on her part.

The rape cases are numerous enough to permit the analysis to proceed by cross-tabulation as well as by reason assessment. We begin with reason assessment.

In cases of this nature the judge will often make explicit the assumption of risk sentiment in his comments. Where a young defendant is charged with raping a seventeen-year-old girl and the jury acquits, the judge explains bluntly:

[10] There is some suggestion in the last few cases of vindictiveness or spite on the part of the complaining witness. At one point we thought this sentiment would emerge as an independent category, but in the end there were no further cases.

[11] There are, of course, cases where the issue of consent is restricted to a resolution of the facts alone and no problem on the law sentiment arises. These cases involve evidentiary matters such as are treated in Chapters 10 through 14.

A group of young people on a beer drinking party. The jury probably figured the girl asked for what she got. [I-1922]

At times the point is unmistakable simply in his narrative of the facts.

Complaining witness and defendant were formerly married and had two children. During the past year they had been going together with a view toward reconciliation and remarriage. The defendant had apparently spent much time and many evenings at the complaining witness' home. She denied any prior intercourse during the period since the divorce, but he claimed it continued after the divorce. The jury was of the opinion that if it was in a course of conduct which she had accepted, she was in no position to complain of her leading him on. [I-1457]

There is a series of other cases in which the point is not quite so explicit but in which the judge notes circumstances suggesting something akin to assumption of risk on the part of the victim.

The complaining witness alleged after several beers she entered car with defendant and three other men and was driven to cemetery where act took place. [II-0232]

Woman involved went to public dance and was picked up by defendant. Then went to night club and permitted defendant to take her home over unfrequented road . . . woman involved twice married and divorced, age 33. [I-1634]

Prosecutrix and defendant strangers to each other; met each other at dance hall. He undertook to take her home . . . rape occurred in lonely wooded area, she drinking but not drunk. He much more under influence. [I-0488]

In these rape cases the jury acquits. But often it expresses disagreement by finding the defendant guilty of a lesser charge, suggesting a refinement of its policy. The jury's stance is not so much that involuntary intercourse under these circumstances is no crime at all, but rather that it does not have the gravity of rape. If given the option of finding a lesser offense, the jury will avail itself of it. However, if this option is not available, the jury appears to prefer to acquit the defendant rather than to find him guilty of rape.[12]

This rewriting of the law of rape to accommodate the defendant when the female victim has taken the risk is on occasion carried to a cruel extreme. There are cases in which the situation is clearly aggravated by extrinsic violence, but the jury is still lenient to the defendant.

In one such case the judge tells us:

> This was a savage case of rape. Jaw of complaining witness fractured in two places.

Nevertheless the jury acquits when it learns that there may have been intercourse with the complainant on prior occasions. The judge adds:

> The parties knew each other and went out together on several occasions and on evening in question had been drinking.
>
> . . . Defendant claimed he had been having intercourse with complainant prior to occurrence. [I-0653]

In another case the jury's reaction is equally disturbing. Again the rape appears to have been brutal. Three men kidnap a girl from the street at 1:30 in the morning, take her to an apartment, and attack her. The judge states:

> It developed that the young unmarried girl had two illegitimate children; also defendant claimed she was a prostitute. No evidence of prostitution was introduced except by defendant's testimony. [I-0642]

He calls the verdict "a travesty of justice."

We turn now to the possibilities of cross-tabulation. There are in all 106 cases of forcible rape of an adult woman. Table 71 sets forth the verdict pattern.[13] Of a total of 75 cases where the judge convicts, there are 20 normal disagreements and 3 hung juries.

[12] See Chapter 16, The Boundaries of Self-Defense, at Table 70, for the tendency of the jury in crimes of violence to disagree on charge when afforded the opportunity.

[13] Table 71 differs from the verdict pattern for rape given previously in Table 19, because here the hung juries are left undistributed. The disagreements on charge will be considered in the subsequent analysis.

TABLE 71

Verdict Pattern for Forcible Rape Cases*

| | | Jury | | |
		Acquits	Convicts	Hangs
Judge	Acquits	24	6	1
	Convicts	20	52	3

$N = 106$

* The figures in this table and the ones that follow it do not represent percentages but the actual Number of Cases.

Table 72 then divides these cases into two categories suggested by the reason assessment: *aggravated rape,* a generic term of art, includes all cases in which there is evidence of extrinsic violence or in which there are several assailants involved, or in which the defendant and the victim are complete strangers at the time of the event; *simple rape,* another term of art, includes all other cases, that is, the cases in which none of the aggravating circumstances is present. This classification, at best a somewhat crude restatement of the hypothesis furnished by the reason assessment,[14] serves to discriminate the jury's responses very sharply.[15]

[14] Constructs such as "aggravated" and "simple" rape provide a good illustration of the difficulties of cross-tabulation for a study such as this. We lacked the foresight to ask a series of questions about the cooperativeness of the victim and hence must proceed by such indirect clues as whether there was more than one attacker or whether victim and defendant were strangers. Cf. Sample II questionnaire in Appendix E, Q. 32, which establishes the degree of relationship between victim and defendants. Thus, this distinction can match only imperfectly the insight furnished by reason assessment. While it is true that there will be little chance that contributory fault is present in the cases grouped as aggravated rape, it is hardly true that every simple rape case involved such a fault.

[15] The differences are so sharp and the total number of cases so small that it seemed unnecessary rigor to introduce here our customary variables; see e.g. Table 68. Because of the form of the table it is convenient to use raw normal disagreement percentages as the crucial measure

TABLE 72

Verdict Pattern for Aggravated and Simple Rape

| | Aggravated Jury | | | Simple Jury | | |
	Acquits	Convicts	Hangs	Acquits	Convicts	Hangs
Judge Acquits	11	4	—	13	2	1
Judge Convicts	5	42	2	15	10	1
			N = 64			N = 42

Per cent jury
acquittal when
judge convicts: **12%** (5 + 1* out of 49)   **60%** (15 + ½* out of 26)

* Hung juries are here counted as ½ acquittal.

While in the aggravated rape cases the percentage of jury disagreement is 12 per cent, in the simple rape cases it shoots up to 60 per cent.

The analysis can be taken an important step further if we consider the disagreements on charge and examine more closely the 10 cases of simple rape in Table 72 where judge and jury agree to convict. It happens that in all these cases the jury was given the option of finding a lesser charge, and in all but one case the jury exercised this option. In 4 of these cases the judge agrees with the jury on the lesser charge. In 5 the jury convicts of the lesser charge, but the judge convicts of rape, leaving only one agreement on guilt where the jury convicts on the major charge. The statistical consequences of this are summarized in Table 73, which shows the verdicts in simple rape cases in terms of the response to the major charge of rape.

The result is startling. The jury convicts of rape in just 3 of 42 cases of simple rape: further, the percentage of disagreement with the judge on the major charge is virtually 100

TABLE 73

Verdict Pattern for Simple Rape Cases:
Rape Charge Only

		Jury		
		Acquits*	Convicts	Hangs
Judge	Acquits*	(13 + 4) 17	2	1
	Convicts	(15 + 5) 20	(10 − 9) 1	1

$N = 42$

* Acquittal here means acquittal from the major charge of rape, even if convicted of a lesser charge.

per cent ($20\frac{1}{2}$ out of 22). The figures could not be more emphatic. Read in conjunction with the reason assessment, Table 73 permits the conclusion that the jury chooses to redefine the crime of rape in terms of its notions of assumption of risk. Where it perceives an assumption of risk the jury, if given the option of finding the defendant guilty of a lesser crime, will frequently do so. It is thus saying not that the defendant has done nothing, but rather that what he has done does not deserve the distinctive opprobrium of rape.[16] If forced to choose in these cases between total acquittal and finding the defendant guilty of rape, the jury will usually choose acquittal as the lesser evil.

In the final cluster of cases illustrative of the contributory fault sentiment, it is easier to isolate the unifying circumstance than to understand why it moves the jury to leniency. With an insistent regularity the judge reports that the defendant and the victim have been "drinking together." The sugges-

[16] Compare the proposal for the new Austrian penal code which provides for a lighter penalty: ". . . if the offense [forcible rape] on account of the woman's relation to the man, or for some other reason, may be considered less serious. . . ." Draft of the Penal Law Commission, Vienna, p. 462 (1953).

tion is that in some way this activity marks a crucial assumption of risk. The cases tend to have a familiar plot. Victim and defendant drink together, a quarrel starts, at the climax of which violence erupts, and the victim is either injured or killed. Since both parties have been drinking, there are always evidence problems as to precisely what happened, problems of self-defense, problems of determining the state of mind of the defendant. But over and beyond this is the constant theme that the parties, both the victim as well as the defendant, have been simply drinking together.

All drinking. [II-1066-1, 2, & 3]

Drinking, began swearing at each other. [I-1795]

Defendant and victim . . . prior to the commission of the crime had been . . . drinking. [II-1033]

Parties had been drinking together. [II-0146]

A friendly drinking party at defendant's house. [I-1854]

All parties and witnesses had been drinking. [I-1446]

Crime occurred after some drinking by both. [I-0508]

A bunch of men in a bootlegger's home on a Sunday afternoon. [I-1725]

The complaining witness obviously had spent considerable time in the bar prior to the altercation. [I-0202]

Both parties had been drinking and I feel the jury felt that part of the trouble had been induced by drinking. [I-1552]

Then in series of domestic violence cases, there is much the same story. There are, of course, other sentiments at work in these cases, but it is still impressive how carefully the judge notes the drinking that preceded the violence.

After all night drinking. [I-748]

During a drunken brawl. [I-3083]

After much drinking. [I-1735]

There was much drinking all around. [I-0077]

This jury preoccupation with the drinking of the victim is extended to a series of robbery cases in which the victim is drunk and the incident occurs in the immediate vicinity of a tavern. The judge describes one such case where the jury acquits, as follows:

> Defendant came in saloon where M was drinking. M knew defendant and bought him a drink. M then put $39 in his shirt pocket and both left together to go to another place. In the dark outside, defendant attacked M and took his money. [I-0501]

Again, in an auto theft case where the jury acquits, the judge notes:

> The offense occurred during a Saturday night drinking party between three men, one of whom owned car and defendant was one of them. [I-0693]

One final illustration suggests again that the drinking theme is a mitigating factor in more than just tavern brawls and domestic quarrels. The defendant is charged with negligent homicide when, as a result of drunken driving, he kills a passenger in his car who was also drunk. The jury acquits and the judge comments:

> There was no marked reckless conduct proved . . . . Coupled with this was the fact that deceased was also drunk, so there was nothing to arouse the jury as in a case where an *innocent* third person is killed. [I-0764] (Emphasis added.)

As we said at the outset it is not easy to know what to make of this jury sentiment, but the sheer incidence of the judge's comments on the victim's drinking compels recognition of it as a source of disagreement. It tends to slip into other categories, and one cannot draw too nice a line. Doubtless, as in the tavern brawls, the drinking may simply proliferate evidence problems for the jury. In the domestic violence cases it may be merely a last twist added to already existing tension.[17]

[17] For a further discussion of domestic violence cases, see Chapter 16, The Boundaries of Self-Defense, at pages 231-236.

Or the jury may see the drinking of both parties as demeaning the case, and we may have impatience expressed in what we call the "plague on both your houses" theme.[18]   Finally, at least some of these drinking cases are simply further illustrations of the moral stain idea discussed earlier.[19]

It bears repeating that it took centuries for the law to come to the position that the state is the other party in a criminal case, a view which, as we have seen, the jury does not entirely embrace.   The jury's point which connects the negligent homicide to the fraud to the rape to the drunken brawl is that insofar as the victim is disqualified from complaining, there is no cause for intervention by the state and its criminal law.

[18] See the discussion of these cases in Chapter 18, *De Minimis.*
[19] Page 247.   There seems to be no suggestion — despite the judge's preoccupation in these cases with drinking — that the jury is exonerating the defendant because of his intoxication.   For a discussion of jury leniency where intoxication appears to have induced a "change of character" in the defendant, see Chapter 25, pages 335-336.

CHAPTER 18

De Minimis

We now turn to a third major jury sentiment on law, the sense of which is adumbrated by the legal maxim *de minimis non curat lex,* although, as we shall see, the jury sentiment reflects a somewhat richer idea.[1] The issue posed by the jury's response in these cases is whether there ought not be some cut-off point for a legal system below which controversies and complaints will be considered too trivial to be dealt with formally.[2] American criminal law has no official *de minimis*

---

[1] The maxim had its original application in Roman law under the formulation *De Minimis non curat praetor,* ordinarily translated "the law does not concern itself with trifles." The rationale is variously applied in law and in equity, and is an explicit canon which threads all law. In damage actions the *de minimis* concept may be invoked to deny jurisdiction, or on appeal, to construe a minor monetary discrepancy as nonreversible error. In equity cases, jurisdiction is refused on *de minimis* grounds — the maxim is equity does not stoop to pick up pins. For a review of cases where *de minimis* has been applied, see the annotation in Am. L. Rev., v. 44, p. 168 (1926).

[2] The rationale is captured in a case that achieved some fame among the Austrian bar. Hugo Sperber, a criminal lawyer known for his wit, is remembered, among other things, for having made a brilliantly brief closing argument for the defense in a larceny prosecution for the theft of poultry. "May it please the Court," he said with a shrug of deprecation, "one chicken!"

André Gide notes the *de minimis* response in the journal of his experience as a juror. "The accused was acquitted, not because there was any doubt of his guilt, but because the Jury considered that there was no call for a sentence in this trifling matter . . . several of them were indignant that the time of the Court should be taken up with such bagatelles, which, they said, happened daily everywhere." Recollections of the Assize Court, p. 8 (Wilkins trans. 1941).

principle making it a valid defense that the wrong done was a trivial one.[3]

To be sure legislatures have left many kinds of minor wrongs outside the domain of the criminal law, on the ground that they are too unimportant to merit state intervention. It is also true that there are types of criminal offenses that fall into desuetude because the community, by and large, has come to think of them as too petty for complaint. And it must be a chief aspect of the prosecutor's discretion that trivial complaints are screened out of the system. What this response in the disagreement cases suggests, therefore, is that the jury has a somewhat narrower view than the prosecutor or the legislator of what constitutes an offense serious enough to rise to the dignity of the criminal law.[4]

[3] There is, however, provision in the Model Penal Code for judicial discretion to dismiss certain prosecutions because of trivial aspects in the case. See Proposed Official Draft §2.12, p. 43 (1962). By way of comparison, §153 of the German Code of Criminal Procedure provides: "Minor misdemeanors (Ubertretungen) shall not be prosecuted if the accused's guilt was small and the consequences of his act insignificant, unless there is a public interest in a judicial decision of the case"; §153 adds with regard to felonies: "In a case where the court on a finding of guilty could dispense with a penalty, the prosecutor may with consent of the court decide not to prosecute, or to quash such a prosecution any time before the beginning of the trial." It is also of interest to see in which situations the German courts may dispense with a penalty even though the accused was found guilty of a felony: this may be done in the case of high treason if the accused has voluntarily desisted from his conduct and thereby averted its success (§82), or if the preparatory actions have not reached the state of attempt (§138); similar provisions obtain for the crimes of sabotage (§129) and conspiracy (§138). Other situations are: perjury committed only to avert criminal prosecution of the accused or his family (§157), or if the perjured testimony was rectified in time (§158); incest between in-laws (§173); sodomy if the accused is under 21 (§175). The reasons for the court's discretion in these situations differ from crime to crime, but they will strike a familiar chord at various points of this discussion of the jury's sentiments on the law.

[4] The problem may have a different resonance, however, in civil law. The remarks of Justice Cardozo in defense of a petty civil claim illuminate the point. Where a hotel resident sued for damages in an action growing out of a dispute over a hotel kitchen fee of one dollar for the

In an important sense the law meets the jury halfway by graduating penalties radically. Thus, it anticipates the jury's point that the theft of one thousand dollars may be intrinsically different from the theft of ten; it not only calls the latter petty theft, but attaches a proportionately less severe penalty to it.[5] Again, the magnitude of the offense is presumably a major consideration for the discretion of the judge in sentencing.

It is something of a surprise that the jury's principle cuts across crimes and in an interesting and subtle way. Table 74 shows the distribution of *de minimis* disagreements in the various crimes. Roughly three quarters of the *de. minimis* cases are found among the serious crimes, murder not excluded.

The theory then, it should be stressed, is not that the jury is progressively more lenient the less serious the crime, although there is some evidence that it does make such a response.[6] Every crime, however precisely its boundaries are

---

preparation of plaintiff's own spareribs, Cardozo stated: "To enforce one's rights when they are violated is never a legal wrong, and may often be a moral duty. . . . A great jurist, Rudolf von Ihering, in his 'Struggle for Law,' ascribes the development of law itself to the persistence in human nature of the impulse to resist aggression, and maintains the thesis that the individual owes the duty to himself and to society never to permit a legal right to be wantonly infringed. . . . The plaintiff chose to resist a wrong which, if it may seem trivial to some, must have seemed substantial to him. . . ." Morningstar v. Lafayette Hotel Co., 211 N.Y. 465, 468, 105 N.E. 656, 657 (1914). Thus, while the individual may win approval in jealously protecting his civil rights, however small, the question is whether the state in the criminal case may do the same.

[5] Some criminal codes go even further in their distinction of various grades of theft. The German code, for instance, defines *Mundraub* as the lowest grade of petty theft: "Who commits larceny with respect to food or other objects of domestic use in small amounts or negligible value for the purpose of immediate use." §370, No. 5. And in §248a the code provides another intermediate category, larceny of objects of "little value" under "economic duress."

[6] There is evidence of this in comparable crimes, e.g., for serious assault jury disagreement is 20 per cent, but it rises to 24 per cent when the assault is simple; in burglary it is 15 per cent, but for breaking and entering it is 22 per cent.

drawn, may cover violations of very different gravity; this is true for first degree murder as it is for drunken driving. Some cases will be at the lower cut-off point, but the jury occasionally takes it upon itself to move this cut-off point up.

TABLE 74

De Minimis Disagreements by the 42 Crime Categories

	Number of de Minimis Disagreements		Number of de Minimis Disagreements
Murder	15	Robbery	3
Manslaughter	5	Burglary	2
Negligent homicide	1	Auto theft	2
Aggravated assault	18	Mail theft	—
Simple assault	9	Other grand larceny	7
Kidnaping	—	Petit larceny	5
Prohibited and concealed weapon	2	Receiving stolen goods	3
		Embezzlement	3
Forcible rape	4	Fraud	5
Statutory rape	16	Forgery	3
Incest	—	Extortion	—
Sodomy	—	Arson	—
Molestation of a minor	2	Gambling	3
Indecent exposure	7	Game laws	1
Commercial vice	—	Liquor (tax)	—
Other sex crimes	2	Other liquor offenses	6
Drunken driving	7	Other regulatory offenses	—
Other traffic offenses	4	Narcotics	1
Miscellaneous public disorder	2	Perjury	—
		Tax evasion	2
Malicious mischief	2	Escape	—
Non-support and other family offenses	3	Bribery, official misconduct	1

We turn to the individual case and to reason assessment. The first group is perhaps the most obvious one, *property crimes where the harm done is quantitatively very small.* The cases provide a roster of minutiae:[7] theft of two pieces of lumber [II-0380]; theft of a few frankfurters [II-0710]; robbery of $2 [I-0670]; sale of lottery slips in the amount of $1.10 [II-1081]; "property taken in truck amounted barely to some pennies" [I-0972]; "so little property" [I-0223]; receiving stolen property "amounting to $10" [II-0402]; theft of "articles of little value" from a chain store [I-1441]; receipt of stolen pillows valued at $10 [II-0412].[8]

Two familiar caveats need be noted again lest the simplicity of the jury's response be overstated. The sentiment is often embedded in the resolution of evidence issues.[9] The sentiment is often found in conjunction with other jury values.[10] Not infrequently the additional factor is the jury's fear that the punishment would be disproportionate to the small offense; it has this feeling rather than the feeling that *any* punishment would be excessive.[11] Or the additional factor might be that extrinsic circumstances have punished the defendant enough in view of the small harm involved, and these circumstances coupled with the slight harm make the defendant a sympathetic case.[12] Finally, the complicating factor might be that the general crime category itself is somewhat unpopular

[7] Occasionally the judge seems oddly baffled, as in a prosecution for the embezzlement of $10: "Damned if I know. Maybe it's too close to Christmas. The evidence in this case is the clearest I've ever seen. The defendant was married with five children. Also small amount involved." [I-0695]

[8] There is, of course, always a possibility that these minor thefts have been selected by the prosecution from a larger pattern of crime by the particular defendant because of the ease of proof. But the judge's comments support the impression that the given charge is all there is.

[9] See Table 53 and the discussion of the liberation hypothesis in Chapter 13.

[10] See the discussion of overdetermination in Chapter 7 at page 100 and Table 28. The special point in the text, however, is not the combination of one major reason category with another, but that within the law sentiment category the sub-category *de minimis* often combines with other sub-categories.

[11] See Chapter 21, Punishment Threatened Is Too Severe.

[12] See Chapter 20.

with the jury, and a minimal instance of such a crime is likely to be viewed with special skepticism.[13] Despite these conspicuous overlappings with other categories, it remains a key to the explanation of the disagreements that these cases involve *de minimis* harms.

A few illustrations will be helpful to give the rounded impression. Where the defendant is charged with a minor theft, the point is that he is a second offender and a conviction, therefore, would be a conviction for a felony. While the judge would have found him guilty, the jury hangs ten to two in favor of acquittal. The judge states:

> The jury or at least 10 jurors did not want to send a man to prison on a felony charge for taking one or two wieners. [II-0710] [14]

The same point is evident in a case in which two men rob a hitchhiker of two dollars. The judge finds the defendants guilty of robbery; the jury, although it is clear that violence was used, finds them guilty only of petty larceny. This is a striking example of a compromise verdict, where the jury reaches an apparently irrational result on the evidence in order to retain some hold over the appropriate penalty. The law distinguishes sharply between grand and petty larceny but treats all theft involving force as robbery. The jury's verdict appears to be an effort to introduce into law the category of "petty robbery." Again, the judge makes the point perfectly clear.

> The jury felt that the penalty for robbery was too severe since the amount robbed was only $2. [I-0670-1 & 2]

Where the defendant breaks into a filling station and steals some pennies, cigarettes, and a few candy bars, the judge convicts of burglary but the jury finds only petty larceny. This

[13] See Chapter 19, Unpopular Laws.

[14] In a similar case a bad check amounted to $6.31, and it was a third offense. [I-1737]

time the jury creates the category of petty burglary. [I-0972] [15]

Much the same note appears if extrinsic factors have punished the defendant. Where the defendant was charged with stealing two pieces of lumber, the additional stimulus to leniency is that he had been in jail awaiting trial. The judge says:

> The jury felt sorry for the defendant because he had been in jail for over two months and the lumber allegedly stolen was worth $2.50. I think the jury had a Jean Valjean complex. [II-0380] [16]

Interaction of *de minimis* with an unpopular crime category is illustrated by two cases involving the sale of lottery tickets, a crime the prosecution of which, as we shall see, is unpopular.[17] The defendant is charged with selling six numbers slips in the amount of $5.64 to customers in a smoke shop. This time the defense argues the *de minimis* point directly:

> The defense minimized entire proceedings . . . made little of it.

And the judge makes this closing comment about the case:

> This is typical of small misdemeanors. The jury rarely convicts unless the evidence is overwhelmingly beyond reasonable doubt. [I-1558] [18]

There are other cases where *the harm though small cannot be so readily measured in dollars.* In the most outlandish of

---

[15] In a case of receiving stolen property where the jury hangs eight to four for acquittal, the judge explains: "Case involved so little property that some of the jury didn't feel it wanted to convict a man of a felony under these conditions." [I-0223]

[16] For further jury reactions to the defendant's having been in jail while awaiting trial, see Chapter 20, The Defendant Has Been Punished Enough.

[17] Gambling violations are treated with in Chapter 19, Unpopular Laws.

[18] In another gambling case the defendant is a waitress; again, the amount is trivial: "The alleged violation was not aggravated and only two lottery slips were found on the premises where the defendant was employed. Furthermore, the two alleged lottery slips totalled the small sum of $1.10." [II-1081]

these the defendant comes upon a parked police car with its motor running and the key left in the ignition. He enters the car, shuts off the motor, pockets the key, and casually watches the police return and frantically look for it. After some ten minutes he presents the key to the policemen who promptly arrest him. Since there is absolutely no evidence problem, the judge is forced to convict of malicious mischief; but the jury hangs, albeit with ten jurors voting for conviction. The judge adds:

> Because of the notoriety and some of the humorous aspects of the case, we had difficulty in getting a jury. Finally, the two jurors holding out for acquittal thought the charge was too serious (although no mention had been made of a penalty) and refused to be swayed by the other 10. [I-1398] [19]

Then there are several instances of minor battery, of what might be called the one-punch fight, in which the judge convicts of assault and the jury acquits. Thus, where the defendant is charged with striking a city administrator a single blow while in the administrator's office, the court explains its disagreement with the jury as follows:

> They felt the incident was too unimportant to punish the defendant further. [II-0225]

In such simple cases, however, there are often complicating overtones of self-defense. Where the defendant is charged with punching the victim in the nose, the judge states:

> The evidence showed that the complaining witness had for days been doing all he could to irritate the defendant and I feel sure that the jury felt that the defendant acted in the same manner they would have acted under the circumstances. [I-1311] [20]

---

[19] One might have expected that more than two jurors would have been in favor of acquittal in this case. The explanation would appear to reside in the trouble the judge reports in selecting a jury after newspaper publicity. Presumably the many who thought the matter was a prank had been disqualified.

[20] The cases are discussed more elaborately in conjunction with the self-defense theme in Chapter 16.

Thus, one may not simply conclude that the jury has a tendency to treat minor batteries as below its threshold for the criminal case. In the calculus of the jury, provocation may become sufficient aggression to justify the one-punch rebuttal.

As one moves down the scale from trivial harm, one would expect the jury's *de minimis* reaction to be strongest in cases where there was *literally no harm at all,* and we do find the judge at times offering the absence of harm as the reason for the jury's disagreement with him.

The first examples come from cases of drunken driving,[21] since it requires only the act of driving while drunk, and no damage need be caused. In several cases where the driving has caused no accident the judge convicts while the jury acquits, and the judge specifically notes the absence of harm as a reason for the jury's disagreement.

> Defendant had not damaged personal property and was arrested when pulling away from parking place. [I-1460]

> This defendant was guilty but accident was not involved and juries do not seem to want to convict drunken drivers. [II-0772]

In one case where there was an accident but only property damage resulted, the judge comments:

> In this state juries do not seem to want to convict in drunken driving cases, even where an accident occurs if it is only property damage. [II-0773]

Again, in a reckless driving case the judge states:

> Jury seems reluctant to convict in Traffic Court appeals unless it is shown there has been an accident — seem to put themselves in defendant's position. [II-0790]

A final case carries the idea of drunken driving without harm a step further. As a technical matter the crime of

---

[21] Other aspects of the jury's reaction to drunken driving are discussed in Chapter 19, Unpopular Laws. See also the analysis at Tables 130-131.

drunken driving is committed if a man drives while drunk, it is no defense that he drove well.[22] This nuance does not often come to the surface, but in at least one instance the defendant is charged with drunken driving, his third offense, and the police testify that he was definitely drunk. The jury acquits and the judge says in explanation:

> The fact that officers testified that they saw nothing wrong in the way he drove. [II-0622]

In theory the no harm rationale could also be extended to attempts. The matter does not lack perplexity since we are equating the gravity of attempted murder where no harm is done to a completed theft of say two dollars.[23] In only an occasional case, however, can we detect this type of jury reaction.[24] Where the defendant threatens to shoot a married woman with whom he has been living illicitly for many years, the judge convicts of first degree assault, the jury of second degree. The judge notes:

> Jury felt that woman was not in real danger. No harm done. [I-0921]

[22] The Ohio statute is typical: "Operation of vehicle while intoxicated. — No person who is under the influence of intoxicating liquor, narcotic drugs, or opiates shall operate any vehicle, streetcar, or trackless trolley within this state." 4511.19 Rev. Code (1963).

[23] There is a famous puzzle in American law as to why there should be any punishment at all for attempt. Arnold, Criminal Attempts — The Rise and Fall of an Abstraction, Yale L.J., v. 40, p. 53 (1930). But see Wechsler, Jones and Korn, Inchoate Crimes in the Model Penal Code of the American Law Institute; Treatment of: Attempt, Solicitation and Conspiracy, Columbia L. Rev., v. 61, p. 571 (1958). In any event American law has used the concept of attempted crime very sparingly. The Model Penal Code however proposes that liability be imposed "in a broader class of cases where dangerousness of character is plainly manifested." Model Penal Code, Tent. Draft No. 10, Art. 5:01, p. 68 (1958).

[24] Two further disagreements over attempts should be mentioned. In a narcotics violation case the defendant attempts and fails to obtain a morphine derivative by using a forged prescription. [II-0972] There is also a molestation case where the defendant asks two young girls to have intercourse with him but makes no effort to touch them. [II-0383]

A disagreement in a federal bribery case provides an unusual example with which to bring this segment of the discussion to a close. The defendant is charged with having bribed a government official in order to get his job classification advanced. There is an evidence difficulty in the case, but the distinctive circumstance seems to be that the defendant's work was excellent; he had saved the government over a million dollars, and all his superiors recommended promotion. Thus, the defendant bribed an official for a promotion to which he was clearly entitled. The jury acquits. [I-1949]

In a few cases the harm caused by the defendant is kept minimal because *the crime is detected so quickly that the victim suffers no loss.* Where the defendants are charged with the theft of some sailors' wallets but are immediately caught, the jury acquits. The judge explains:

> Where there was no loss, because wallets were immediately recovered after snatching, the jury was reluctant to convict of a felony. Probably they would have convicted if charge was purse snatching. [I-0331]

In an auto theft case the defendant is apprehended a few hours after he has taken the car; there is no damage. There is a strong evidence dispute as to whether the defendant had the owner's consent to drive the car for purposes of inspection, and in this context the jury gives the defendant the benefit of the doubt because "there had been no harm to the car." [I-1347] [25]

In the embezzlement case the defendant, an employee, is de-

[25] "Juries, in their wisdom, have over the generations recognized the transgression for what it really is — the theft of a ride rather than a car; and prosecutors have found it extremely difficult to obtain convictions in such cases. Therefore, wise judges and district attorneys, anticipating jury reactions, usually reduce such charges to the offense of disorderly conduct or the misdemeanor of petit larceny." Botein and Gordon, The Trial of the Future, p. 116 (1963). For a legislative recognition of this point see Chapter 25, note 16.

tected with the money before she has a chance to leave the premises. Defense counsel played up the fact that she had not yet converted the money to her own use. The judge would have convicted of embezzlement; the jury finds petty larceny. [I-2006]

These last few cases of crimes technically complete but quickly frustrated provide an easy bridge to the next facet of the jury's theory of small harm — cases where *restitution* has been made after the crime. The jury's formula might be said to be: a cured harm is no harm. Its response raises two points of general significance. The jury is taking a circumstance which the law recognizes as a legitimate factor in sentencing and is treating it as relevant in determining guilt.[26] And, the jury appears to be saying that if the complainant has been satisfied, there is no need for state intervention, thus reflecting the private origins of the criminal law. Here again the modern jury does not find it easy to distinguish between the purposes of tort law and of criminal law.[27]

Two such restitution cases involve income tax violations where the tax has been paid prior to the trial. In each case the judge comments specifically on restitution.

> The fact that defendant amended his tax debt and made full payment of his income tax return before the trial. [I-0779]

And again:

> Also defendant paid most of the taxes found to be due and prior to the time he had been contacted by income tax agent had hired a CPA to take care of his tax return. [I-2030]

[26] Some European codes go beyond this and offer immunity if restitution is made prior to prosecution, as in §187 of the Austrian Criminal Code. And it has been noted that embezzlement is the least prosecuted crime in the United States because of restitution: "The practice of foregoing prosecution where restitution is made or arranged for is so frequent and widespread that it tends to reduce embezzlement to a merely private transaction, the defalcation being viewed as damage that can be fully repaired by the payment of a certain sum of money — like a breach of contract." Hall, Theft, Law and Society, p. 311 (2d ed. 1952).

[27] See the discussion in Chapter 17, note 1.

Similarly, where the defendant is charged with passing a forged check for $22.50 and the jury acquits, the judge notes that restitution had been made. [II-0193] [28]

Finally, a hit-and-run case involves an unusual form of "restitution." The charge is leaving the scene of an accident without reporting it, but the defendant repents and reports the accident later, which persuades the jury to acquit him. [I-1029]

It is tempting to argue that restitution moves the jury not so much for *de minimis* reasons but because it is a conspicuous gesture of repentance on the part of the defendant. [29] Sometimes, however, when restitution comes from a third party, not from the defendant, the jury is nevertheless moved to leniency. For example, in a case of auto theft by a bailee, the car is recovered fairly promptly, and storage and damage charges are paid by the defendant's parents. [I-1730]

The distinguishing circumstance in still another group of cases is the *reluctance of the complaining witness to prosecute,*[30] a reluctance which somehow becomes known during the trial. Presumably in these cases the jury's logic again is that if the victim does not want to prosecute, there cannot have been much harm done, and there is, therefore, no reason why the state and the criminal law should intervene.

In a securities fraud case, the judge tells us:

[28] There is a disagreement case where the defendant is charged with receiving stolen property and restitution appears to function primarily as evidence of his state of mind. The defendant purchased two stolen rifles worth $200 from a young boy for $30; he argues that he bought them only to return them and, in fact, did so when the owner repaid the $30. [II-1191]

[29] How repentance moves the jury is discussed in Chapter 15, pages 204-205.

[30] Both restitution and reluctance to prosecute may occur together. In one such case the defendant is charged with burglary of his place of employment and the property is valued at $40. He was drunk at the time of the offense and made restitution within a week; on trial he evokes sympathy, as the judge puts it, "because of poverty and difficulty in making restitution." Understandably the complainant is reluctant to prosecute and the jury acquits. [II-0263]

Woman who was the victim had purchased stock in a mine that was only a hole in the ground, was a personal friend of the defendant, and her attitude as a victim was such that the jury could infer that she was not anxious to prosecute. [I-0087]

In a larceny case where only small amounts of grain had been taken, the judge notes, "prosecuting witness was not strong; did not want to prosecute." [I-0970] [31]

A more poignant example is a negligent automobile homicide case in which a young bride-to-be was killed and her family is reluctant to prosecute the bereaved defendant, her fiancé. [I-0913]

The remaining examples of this reluctance sentiment are dramatic in that each involves violence in an affair or marriage.[32] Perhaps the clearest is the case in which the judge would have convicted of assault with attempt to commit murder while the jury acquits. The action takes place on a yacht, and there appears to be no doubt that the defendant shot the victim after a fight. The court relates that defendant and victim were "sex perverts" and continues:

> The complaining witness was very reluctant to testify against the defendant and stated that they were still friends and indicated that he did not want the defendant prosecuted. There was never any question but that the defendant did the shooting and that the testimony before the jury was that immediately following the shooting the complaining witness asked the defendant why he did it. I think the jury must have felt that if the person injured did not desire conviction, the state should not be concerned. [I-3121]

[31] There is some suggestion of reluctance in cases where there is an embarrassment at being involved. In a securities fraud case the victims "were unwilling witnesses . . . had never filed a complaint against the defendants and seemed to be hopeful that they would eventually find 'the pot of gold at the end of the rainbow.'" [I-1951] The jury response to the complainant who comes with unclean hands is discussed in Chapter 17, Contributory Fault of the Victim, particularly at page 246.

[32] These may be taken as a variant of the domestic violence cases discussed in Chapter 16, The Boundaries of Self-Defense, at pages 231-236.

In the second case a husband fires at his wife but the gun does not discharge. The judge finds assault with intent to murder; but the jury finds the defendant not guilty by reason of insanity. The judge reports:

> Also wife, whom he was accused of attempting to murder, changed her position and testified for her husband and against her own complaint. [II-0678]

In another case involving a husband and wife the judge again finds the husband guilty of assault with intent to murder; the jury finds him guilty of assault only. The parties are Negroes and the judge, after making a point about a lower standard of responsibility,[33] adds:

> The jury was also probably influenced by the fact that the parties had resumed marital relationship and were living together at the time of the trial. [I-0041]

The jury here is almost literally importing the idea of condonation from family law into criminal law.[34]

It is obvious by now that the simple idea of minimal harm is expanded by analogy as the jury deals with it. There remain three important analogic phases to the concept. First, there are cases in which the application of the criminal category makes the law, as interpreted by the jury, lose its point; in these cases what has become minimal is the social harm which was the original predicate for the crime category. Second, there are cases in which, because of an accident of time, value, or age, the defendant's conduct just misses being legal and is therefore minimal as marginal. And, third, there are cases where the jury as much as says "a plague on both your

[33] The point is critically evaluated in Chapter 26, A Note on Crime in a Subculture.

[34] Condonation results when a married partner, though legally entitled to a divorce because of certain acts of the opposite partner (brutality, adultery, desertion, etc.) continues or resumes the marriage in such a way as to constitute forgiveness. Thereafter, the forgiving partner is barred from the right to a divorce, unless, of course, it happens again. See Madden, Domestic Relations §§90, 91 (1931).

houses." Each is a somewhat complex story and we will bring this chapter to a close by considering each in turn.

There are three good examples of the jury response to *minimal social harm:* the sale of liquor to minors who are members of the armed forces; indecent exposure before an adult woman; and statutory rape of an unchaste girl.

Perhaps the readiest illustrations of minimal social harm come from the few cases involving the sale of liquor to minors who are servicemen. In one such case the judge states:

> A 19-year-old sailor was sold a bottle of beer. . . . The jury seemed to feel that if a boy can be taken and forced to fight, he can buy and consume a bottle of beer. [I-0140]

And in another case the judge echoes:

> Sailors drinking in other lands should drink here too, if they are in uniform. [I-0190]

The other two categories of minimal social harm are more difficult to document; we can proceed at least as much by cross-tabulation as by way of the judge's reason assessment. Indeed, the point about indecent exposure comes to light entirely through cross-tabulation. We were encouraged to pursue the hunch that the jury might distinguish between exposure to an adult woman and exposure to a child by coming upon the distinction in the writings of the psychiatrist Benjamin Karpman.[35] Armed with this hypothesis we proceeded to cross-tabulation.

---

[35] "The important and practical factor is the question of the type of individual before whom the offender exposed himself. In the case of indecent exposure before children, we have an actual social menace, because of the potentially dangerous effect of the offense on the immature mind. In the case of indecent exposure before an adult, however, we have a public nuisance. There is no potential danger involved. Mrs. Grundy knows what a man's sex organs look like; and she should know, if she has any sense at all, that any man who chooses to exhibit them on a street, in a park, or before an open window is a victim of mental aberration and belongs in a mental hospital rather than a jail. It is true that she may not like to be confronted with the sight of a man's sexual organs in a public place; that such an exhibition may offend her sensibilties; but she suffers no harm, nor is she in any danger of harm.

TABLE 75

Verdict Pattern for Indecent Exposure

		Jury	
	Acquits	Convicts	Hangs
Judge Acquits	4	1	—
Convicts	12	11	3

$N = 31$

Per cent jury
acquittal when
judge convicts: 52% $(12 + 1\frac{1}{2}$* out of 26).

* Hung juries are counted as $\frac{1}{2}$ acquittal.

Table 75 contains 26 cases where the judge would have convicted; only in 11 cases does the jury agree with him. Table 76 divides these cases according to whether the exposure was, in Karpman's terms, a public nuisance or an actual social menace.

Cross-tabulation suggests[36] that the jury considers exposure to an adult victim to be different from exposure to a child victim and that the implicit rationale is the one stated.[37] The puzzle perhaps is that the judge does not perceive this reason

She is a grown woman who knows 'the facts of life,' and she is not going to be mentally injured by such an exhibition, as a child might be to whom it represents something which the child does not understand. There should be complete separation of cases of Indecent Exposure into those which utilize children as their object and those which are confined to exhibition before adults. It is not what the man does which is important, but the potential effect of what he does on the individual before whom he does it." The Sexual Offender and His Offenses, pp. 460-461 (1954).

[36] It is worth noting that the jury does not stay all the way with the hypothesis; there are two cases in the adult exposure group where the jury agrees to convict. It happens, however, that in both cases the defendant has a prior record for exhibitionism, indicating that while the jury views indecent exposure to adults as a nuisance rather than a threat, the nuisance, if repeated, may warrant conviction.

[37] Once again the jury rationale has some support in the law elsewhere: "[Indecent exposure] is only punishable . . . if it is committed

TABLE 76

Indecent Exposure to Adults and Children

To Adults Only

	Jury		
	Acquits	Convicts	Hangs
Judge Acquits	—	—	—
Judge Convicts	6	2	2

N = 10

Per cent jury
acquittal where
judge convicts: **70%** (6 + 1* out of 10).

To Children

	Jury		
	Acquits	Convicts	Hangs
Judge Acquits	4	1	—
Judge Convicts	6	9	1

N = 21

Per cent jury
acquittal where
judge convicts: **41%** (6 + $\frac{1}{2}$* out of 16).

* Hung juries are counted as $\frac{1}{2}$ acquittal.

for disagreement with anything like the clarity he shows in
most cases.[38]   At best he notes "no one got hurt." [II-1073]   Or,
"Did not take the matter too seriously."   [II-0405]

---

in connection with a child under fifteen years of age or is of a nature
to cause grave offence to another person's feelings."   See Rudholm,
Swedish Legislation and Practice Concerning Sexual Offenses, in Sexual Offences, A Report of the Cambridge Department of Criminal
Science, p. 454 (1957).   The Belgian code provides more severe punishment if the act of exposure is committed in the presence of a child
under sixteen.   Id., p. 497.

[38] For the discussion of possible limitations of the reason assessment
method, see Chapter 7, page 96.

We now turn to the third sub-category of minimal social harm, statutory rape of an unchaste girl. In such cases of statutory rape, the jury apparently fails to see any harm in corrupting the already corrupted. The criminal codes in several jurisdictions reflect the point.[39]

Proceeding to cross-tabulation, the over-all fourfold table for statutory rape is as follows.

TABLE 77

Verdict Pattern for Statutory Rape

	Jury Acquits	Jury Convicts	Jury Hangs
Judge Acquits	7	—	1
Judge Convicts	16	40	6

$N = 70$

Per cent jury
acquittal where
judge convicts: **31%** (16 + 3* out of 62).

* Hung juries are counted as $\frac{1}{2}$ acquittal.

As a first step in refining the pattern, we will remove the thirteen cases in which the child victim was not yet in her teens; in these cases the consensual aspects of statutory rape cannot be truly present. The verdict pattern for statutory rape when the girl is at least thirteen years old is shown in Table 78.

We next divide the cases on the basis of whether or not the victim had a bad reputation.[40] Table 79 gives the relevant figures.

[39] For example, Fla. Stat. Ann. §794.05(1) (1965): "Any person who has unlawful carnal intercourse with any unmarried person, *of previous chaste character,* who at the time of such intercourse is under the age of eighteen (18) years, shall be punished," etc. (Emphasis added.) The statute adds that the defense of previous unchastity fails if the defendant was its cause.

[40] This reputation of the victim question appears in the Sample II questionnaire, and as a result the number of cases drops to 16.

TABLE 78

Statutory Rape of Females 13 Years and Older

		Jury Acquits	Jury Convicts	Jury Hangs
Judge	Acquits	7	—	1
	Convicts	16	28	5

$N = 57$

Per cent jury
acquittal where
judge convicts: **38%** $(16 + 2\frac{1}{2}$* out of 49).

* Hung juries are counted as $\frac{1}{2}$ acquittal.

TABLE 79

Statutory Rape by Reputation of Victim

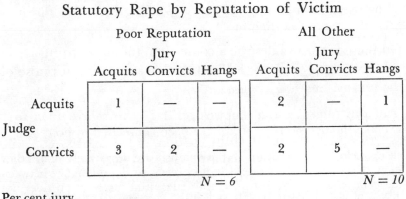

		Poor Reputation Jury Acquits	Jury Convicts	Jury Hangs		All Other Jury Acquits	Jury Convicts	Jury Hangs
Judge	Acquits	1	—	—		2	—	1
	Convicts	3	2	—		2	5	—

$N = 6$ $N = 10$

Per cent jury
acquittal where
judge convicts: **60%** (3* out of 5).   **29%** (2* out of 7).

* Hung juries are counted as $\frac{1}{2}$ acquittal.

Although the number of cases is small, the distribution moves
in the direction of the hypothesis.[41]

[41] In this simplistic form the table can be only a weak proof. But
the hypothesis is striking and the results plausible. There remains,
however, an ambiguity in the message from Table 79. The jury's reaction to the poor reputation of the girl may be simply to her credibility
as a witness and not a response, as we have suggested, to a sentiment.
The ambiguity is reduced by classifying the cases from Table 79 into

This time we find the point vividly covered in the judge's comments. It is given perfect expression in one of our most dramatic cases. The defendant is the rector of a church and the victim, his niece, was deserted by her parents and taken in by the rector and his wife and supported for over three years. The sixteen-year-old girl is described by the judge as mature. She "had been very promiscuous and was pregnant by another at the time of the offense." Her description of the act at the trial, we are told, was "without shame." The human drama immanent in the judge's report suggests that the girl is the seducer, producing a situation which bears a striking resemblance to Maugham's story "Rain." As the judge tells it:

> His niece through marriage was good-looking but extremely hard to handle. In spite of her aunt and uncle watching her closely, she had much sexual experience. The uncle had chastised her a month before by spanking her. She threatened to get even with him.

On these facts, and despite a confession, the jury acquits.

The judge is moved to a memorable statement in praise of the jury system.

> In this case of carnal knowledge, if I were called upon to make the decision I would have been compelled to hold him

---

clear or close cases. Although the numbers are desperately small, they show that even in clear cases the jury reacts to the difference between the good girl and the bad girl, thus suggesting its reaction does not derive from the credibility issue.

Poor Reputation of Victim of Statutory Rape in Clear Cases

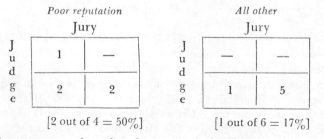

	Poor reputation Jury			All other Jury	
J u d g e	1	—	J u d g e	—	—
	2	2		1	5
[2 out of 4 = 50%]			[1 out of 6 = 17%]		

No analogous comparison for close cases is feasible because there are even fewer of those.

guilty according to the strict interpretation of the law. Yet if he had been guilty, he would have lost his place in society, his wife would have divorced him . . . maybe the jury could look past the confession; the court could not. The jury, not knowing the cold technicalities of the law, could conscientiously bring in this verdict. [I-0929]

In another statutory rape of a girl fifteen years old, the judge explains the disagreement as follows:

This was a typical case of the jury not paying much attention to the law and acquitting because they thought the girl was already a bad girl and had initiated the chain of events. I suspect the jury blamed her parents rather than the young man. The parents had taken her to a dance and had given her whiskey. She disappeared during intermission. [I-0781]

In still another disagreement, in which it is disclosed to the jury that there had been other acts of intercourse, the judge adds:

The girl involved was a few months short of statutory age. She obviously enjoyed the experience and the jury just would not convict. [I-1210] [42]

One last statutory rape case deserves brief mention. The victim is a "bold and brazen" fifteen-year-old girl "with a bad reputation proved pretty conclusively by the defense." The jury finds the defendant guilty of corrupting the morals of a minor, only because at the time of the trial it appears that the girl was pregnant. As the judge puts it:

---

[42] Several other cases contain comments much along the same line: "A belief that the girl was too free with favors." [I-0738] "The complainant, a colored girl of 15, denied that she was going to accept his advances and that she, however, went outside the car three times to let off water and then went back for more punishment." [I-1092] "Natural reluctance of jury on the scantily corroborated testimony of a 14-year old complainant who could have been found by the jury as inviting the attention the respondent gave her." [I-0835] "Prosecutrix and mother immoral." [I-0571] "All parties were drinking and complainant invited the act." [II-0284] "Reputation of the defendant as opposed to complainant. The court could not have ignored the confession; the jury did." [II-0409] And, finally, in one case it was relevant that the girl had been posing for "nude photos." [I-1597]

> If she had not been pregnant, the jury probably would have
> let defendant go. [II-0272]

The jury is thus tugged in opposing directions by its sentiments, and its verdict is a compromise between them.[43]

At this point we come to a cluster of disagreement cases
which are *de minimis* in still another sense; here the violation
is minimal or *marginal in terms of where the law draws the
line*. The defendant's conduct has just missed being legal.
The legal boundary may be drawn in terms of time, of value,
or of age. We offer a few illustrative cases for each of these
boundaries.

Game laws prescribe the times of day when hunting is permissible. In one case the applicable statute prohibits in-
season hunting between 5 P.M. and 5 A.M. and proscribes the
carrying of an uncased gun during that interval. The defendant, returning from a rabbit hunt, is charged with having a rifle in the back seat of his car at 5:30 P.M. The judge
convicts; the jury hangs. The judge makes it clear that in
this jurisdiction game laws are unpopular per se. Further,
the defendant proffers two excuses: that he had been unavoid-
ably detained by a blowout and that he had his gun covered
with a blanket, thereby complying with the statute. There
is, however, the additional fact that the defendant's ille-
gality consisted of being just thirty minutes late. [II-1117]

The same sentiment is evoked in a reckless driving case
where the defendant is charged with going sixty-five miles
per hour in a fifty-five-mile zone. It appears further that the
speed limit was sixty-five miles per hour before sundown and
fifty-five miles per hour after sundown. The defense was that

---

[43] The judge pointed out that the verdict is a compromise, noting
that if her reputation was so bad, the defendant could not be legally
guilty of contributing to her delinquency, although he could be guilty
of statutory rape. This example of a compromise verdict could scarcely
be improved upon. The jury in effect applies its rule that you cannot
corrupt the corrupted to defeat the statutory rape charge, and then by
a special alchemy it finds the defendant guilty of corrupting the morals
of a minor because of the girl's pregnancy.

it was still "daytime" when he was arrested. The judge would have convicted; the jury hangs. [II-0508] [44]

The problem of value boundaries arises in connection with the distinction between petty and grand larceny. In a case of illegal "self-service" [45] the defendant is charged with the theft of several cases of beer in a state where the limit for grand larceny is placed at property worth $25. The prosecution charged the defendant with the theft of nine cases, a total value of $29.61; the defendant admits taking seven cases worth $23.03. The judge finds grand larceny; the jury, petty larceny. The judge regards the jury as having simply given the defendant the benefit of the doubt on an issue of evidence. But we suspect that the jury was moved by the consideration that even if the defendant had taken the larger quantity as the prosecution charged, he would have been less than five dollars over the statutory line. [I-1881]

It might be thought that statutory rape would furnish good examples of marginal transgressions of the age boundary, as the age of the girl approached the statutory limit. There is variation in the statutory limits; conduct may be statutory rape in one state but not in another.[46] Occasionally the judge mentions this point in explanation, as in the case previously noted where he tells us the girl "was just a few months short of statutory age." [I-1210]

---

[44] The judge in this instance, although he calls the case close, rates the resultant hung jury as "without any merit." See Chapter 34 for a general discussion of the judge's critical reaction to the jury verdicts with which he disagrees.

[45] This occurred in a small town, and the defendant knew the proprietor of the store. On his theory, he "borrowed" refreshments for an after-hours party, with the alleged intention of paying when the store opened.

[46] The age limit for statutory rape varies widely among the states, ranging from seven years (Delaware) to eighteen (Kansas). A minority of the states retain the common law age of consent of ten years. The majority of jurisdictions distribute between the ages of twelve and sixteen, some states providing for a penalty differentiation within those years. For a complete summary, see Model Penal Code, Tent. Drafts Nos. 1, 2, 3, and 4, Appendix A, Comment §207.4(10) (1956).

However, if we test this hypothesis by a cross-tabulation of the statutory rape cases, we get only the faintest corroboration. The problem is that most girls in the sample close to the statutory age are girls with poor reputations. It is therefore difficult to test the age factor independently. Also, prosecutor discretion has presumably kept the best of these cases from coming to the jury.

The last major group of cases illustrative of the jury's *de minimis* response is somewhat awkward to characterize. Here one senses jury impatience with the fact that it has been asked to deal solemnly with matters of the sort presented, and a distaste for the issues. The impatience and the distaste may arise simply because *the matter is trivial or because the parties are in some way unattractive or even worthless*. The judge's pen is unusually sharp when he explains this source of disagreement, suggesting that the explanation is congenial to him as well as to the jury. A curious aspect is that the jury is lenient not out of a sense of sympathy for the defendant so much as out of a sort of contempt for both the parties and their controversy.

In a larceny case in which the sum of $360 is "filched" from a gambling game, the jury acquits, showing thereby a nice sense of what is contraband. The judge comments:

> Gambling involved. Jurors as individuals believed funds used in gambling could not be subject to larceny, and I feel this entered into their considerations. [I-1026] [47]

The jury, however, may make the same point even in cases where very serious harm results. Thus, in a case where a wife kills her husband, the judge finds murder in the second degree, whereas the jury acquits. The judge pauses for a long description of the unattractiveness of both parties.

---

[47] Compare the decision of the former German *Reichsgericht*, which reversed a judgment of guilty on a charge of theft, holding that a fellow thief who appropriates to himself the loot from a common cache does not commit theft. RG 11/438.

The killing had been during a drunken brawl. Accused personified helpless, pointless soul, who drank heavily herself; at one point made a dramatic declaration of love, spoiled it by being unable to resist telling of fervid relations a few hours prior to the shooting, followed by decedent's acknowledgment of her prowess as a sexual partner.

The judge concludes:

Community thought itself well rid of decedent. Refused to take seriously the quarrel of twisted drunken personalities, although both had been a source of police irritation for years. [I-3083] [48]

In a third example the defendant, a woman claiming self-defense, knifes the man she has been living with. The jury acquits, the judge finds aggravated assault and battery. His comment follows:

Jury all female, defendant a woman. Victim and defendant very low grade. Jury probably recognized guilt but attitude was "why bother," I suspect. [II-0473]

There is a homicide case which the judge rates as first degree; the jury as second degree murder. The judge notes:

Parties had been drinking together; impatience of the jury with injuries growing out of drunken brawl. [II-0106]

At times the *de minimis* perspective of the jury strikes a sour note to the contemporary ear. Thus, in a manslaughter case where the jury acquits, the judge states:

The parties were both Indians and jurors can't get excited about the fact that one Indian kills another Indian. [I-2029]

In the cases just described substantial harm, it seems, has been viewed by the jury as somehow trivial.

In a companion set of cases, not only are the parties un-

---

[48] This case and several that follow contain a theme which overlaps with other law sentiment categories. Compare the self-defense disagreements, where domestic tension is taken as provocation, at pages 231-234, the contributory fault disagreements, where prior to the harm the victim and defendant were drinking together, at pages 254-257, and Chapter 26, A Note on Crime in a Subculture.

attractive but the harm itself is petty. These are the typical barroom brawls.

In a tavern case where the defendant is charged with cutting the victim with a broken beer bottle, the judge explains "assault in a tavern and not regarded as serious as if in another type of business." [II-0419] Again, in a case where three men are charged with using an ax, a hoe handle, and a crowbar, to beat up two others in a barroom the judge not unexpectedly finds aggravated assault. The jury finds simple assault and the judge explains:

> The five fellows involved in the fight were five of a kind, all had been drinking, all had previous criminal record, all were poor citizens. [II-1066-1, 2, & 3]

The underlying impatience of the jury with this type of case is made explicit in a final example where the defendant is charged with assault and battery arising from a fist fight outside a tavern and the jury acquits:

> The jury evidently decided it was not going to stay all night on a petty case. [I-0458]

It may now be helpful to draw together in summary form the striations in the jury's view of *de minimis*. Table 80 sets out the relative frequency of the sub-categories we have been tracing.

TABLE 80

A Summary of the *De Minimis* Sentiments

Trivial harm	51
No harm, attempt	18
Restitution, cured harm	11
Reluctance to prosecute	14
Small social harm	19
Marginal illegality	17
Plague on both houses	31
	161

As we bring this lengthy summary of three major sentiments on the law to a close, certain caveats bear repetition. Very often the jury's response is made possible only by the presence of evidence doubts in the case.[49]   Very often too there are other reasons for disagreement.   Further, spelling out the jury's concepts of self-defense, contributory fault or *de minimis* into the various subcategories necessarily has a touch of artificiality; the jury's analogizing is more a reaction to a single *gestalt*.

Yet we should not qualify too much.   The prediction from this discussion is that cases having a *de minimis* cast or a note of contributory fault or of provocation will present distinctively frequent occasions for disagreement between the two deciders.   The jury will exercise its de facto powers to write these equities into the criminal law.[50]

[49] See discussion of the liberation hypothesis, Chapter 13, pages 165-166.

[50] Our assertion that the American law has no official de minimis rule (p. 258 above) requires amendment.   In People v. Thomas, 54 Cal. Rptr. 409, 414 (1966), the court reversed a conviction for the possession of marijuana in minute quantities, quoting People v. Leal (50 Cal. Rptr. 777, 413 P.2d 665 (1966)) and People v. McCarthy (50 Cal. Rptr. 783, 413 P.2d 671 (1966)): "the principle 'de minimis non curat lex' is applicable even to this serious accusation."

C H A P T E R   1 9

Unpopular Laws

It will be recalled that when earlier[1] we looked at the four-fold tables for the forty-odd crime categories, we could not readily find any law against which the jury could be said to be in revolt, as it was a generation ago against Prohibition and a century and a half ago against seditious libel. Today the jury's war with the law is modest, and its sentiments cut across crimes to respond to distinctions the law does not make.

Nevertheless, there are a few crimes in which the disagreement arises largely out of the jury's antipathy to the crime itself, although the rate of disagreement is not far out of line. These crimes have two factors in common. First, they are by and large sumptuary, and we thus appear to be picking up some of the traditional hostility to sumptuary legislation.[2]

[1] Chapter 6.

[2] Sumptuary laws attempt to regulate personal expenditures or activities on social or moral grounds; They are the supreme expression of paternalism in government. The so-called blue laws are examples. See Encyc. Soc. Sci., v. 14, p. 466 (1934).

Blackstone treats them as offenses against the public health and economy: "[Here] may also be properly ranked all sumptuary laws against *luxury,* and extravagant expenses in dress, diet, and the like; concerning the general utility of which to a state, there is much controversy among the political writers. . . . Next to that of luxury, naturally follows the offense of [gambling], an offense of the most alarming nature; tending by necessary consequences to promote public idleness, theft and debauchery . . ." As to game laws, "[T]he only rational footing upon which we can consider [game law-violations] as a crime is, that in low and indigent persons it promotes idleness and takes them away from their proper employments and callings." Commentaries, v. IV, pp. 170-174 (1791).

More explicitly, the jury's response is keyed to its perception that in these crimes widespread violation is tolerated. And since almost everybody is doing it, it seems a violation of the principle of evenhanded justice to single out this particular defendant for prosecution.

The Sample II questionnaire elicited reactions to the following question:[3]

What is the community's sense of justice with respect to this type of crime?
☐ In *complete accord* with the letter of the law
☐ Regards the law as *too severe*
☐ Regards the law as *not severe enough*
☐ Don't know

Table 81 shows the results when crimes are ranked by the relative frequency with which "too severe" is marked.[4]

TABLE 81

Crimes Ranking Highest on "Law Is Too Severe"

	Per Cent "Too Severe"	Number of Cases * (= 100%)
Game laws	57	7
Liquor laws	55	38
Gambling	29	14
Drunken driving	20	112

* Sample II.

For our purposes Table 81 provides a handy outline of the unpopular crimes.

We begin with game law violations. There is a long history of enmity toward prosecutions for such violations, reach-

[3] Q. 15. The question is somewhat ambiguous in that it fails to make clear whether the law is too severe generally or only under the special circumstances of the case.

[4] There are other crimes whose severity index reaches 20 per cent, e.g., tax and miscellaneous regulatory crimes, but the cases are too few and the comments on them unilluminating. The average proportion of "too severe" for all crimes is only 8 per cent.

ing back to the controversies in eighteenth century England between poachers and gentry.[5] In America the crime appears largely in the form of hunting protected animals or hunting out of season or after hours. And, as might be expected, in regions in which hunting is a popular pastime, prosecutions are not likely to sit well with the jury. Where two defendants are charged with the special crime of killing a doe and the jury hangs, the judge notes simply:

People generally do not like the game law. [I-0964]

In a case where the charge takes the form of hunting deer at night with a flashlight, the jury acquits again, and the judge's comment sounds the same note.

There is a strong resentment in this area against convictions in game law violation cases. [I-13091 & 2]

In another case the judge observes:

To the best of my recollection, there has never been a game law violation verdict of guilty in this county. [II-1117]

In a final game law illustration — the jury again acquits — the general unpopularity of the crime is, as the judge describes it,[6] buttressed by a private reason suggesting why this defendant was singled out.

---

[5] Poaching was not restricted to an occasional trespass by a hungry or spirited peasant. Some illegal hunting was part of an organized effort to keep the urban black market and the rising middle class supplied with gentry fare. This led the large landowners to set up spring guns to protect their game, and to distinguished debate in the House of Commons: "Their object is to preserve game; they have no objection to preserve the lives of their fellow creatures also, if both can exist at the same time; if not, the least worthy of God's creatures must fall — the rustic without a soul — not the Christian partridge — not the immortal pheasant — not the rational woodcock, or the accountable hare." The Selected Writings of Sidney Smith, p. 231 (Auden ed. 1956).

[6] The case [II-0501] has the same judge as the prior case [II-1117].

One of the jurors afterwards said the jury was influenced by the statement of one of its members that defendant and game warden had trouble over a woman. [II-0501]

The second category involves *gambling*. Although distinctions are suggested by some variety in the fact situations, the jury's response is general. Thus, where the charge is operating a numbers racket and the jury acquits, the judge states:

Many of our jurors play the numbers. Not illegal. It is only a violation to sell numbers — and in small doubtful cases such are our verdicts. [I-1569] [7]

In another case the judge observes:

Playing numbers is not an offense. Many jurors play them and will not convict in 50 per cent of the cases. [I-1579]

In still another gambling case where the jury acquits, the defendant had been able to operate his numbers game with great circumspection, and hence with a minimum of records. The judge provides the reason.

I think there was ample testimony before the jury upon which it should have returned a verdict of guilty. However, juries in this area have a great reluctance to return a verdict where they find no tangible evidence of a lottery ticket. [I-3118]

The remaining gambling cases illustrate much the same point. Thus, where the defendant is charged with being a bookmaker and the jury acquits, the judge states:

It seems somewhat difficult to get verdicts in bookmaking cases, because it is legal to bet at a race track but if a bet is placed just a few miles away, it is illegal. There seems to be a very strong sentiment that this distinction is unreasonable. [I-1084]

There is one last significant illustration. The defendant, president of the local chapter of the fraternal order of the

---

[7] In another numbers case the judge states that from an informal poll after the trial he discovered that, "Several of the jurors played the numbers themselves." [I-1558]

police, helps arrange a stag party, one of whose lesser divertissements is a dice game; he is indicted for having established
a gambling setup.   Once again the judge convicts and the jury
acquits, although it apparently has a surprisingly hard time
with the case.   After eleven hours of deliberation it reported
back to the court that it was divided 6 to 6.   The case has obvious political overtones.   The judge tells us that the "D.A.'s
intervention brought about this case."   He also notes that the
community thinks the law is too severe and gives as one reason
for the disagreement the fact that:

> Other similar violations had gone unnoticed.   [II-0139]

There are a few other cases that are convenient to discuss
here, although the crime charged is technically misconduct in
office.   In two of these cases a police officer or prosecutor is
accused of dereliction of duty in failing to suppress gambling
operations [I-1097 and I-10005]; in a third case a police officer
is charged with having permitted the use of his own phone in
a bookmaking operation. [I-1094]   In all these cases the judge
would have convicted, while the jury acquits.

Since the jury does not rank gambling very high among the
sins, it is only to be expected that it would not be too critical
of the police for not taking gambling seriously either.   In the
case where the prosecutor was indicted, the judge's description
of the facts has a familiar ring to those who live in big cities.

> The assistant prosecutor led a raiding party on a small pri
> vate garage where a dice game had been set up but had not
> yet gotten under way.   The crap tables were in place, the win
> dows blacked out, and the door bolted from the inside.   Com
> plaints could have been made against the operator, the dealer,
> and the owner of the premises for conspiracy; instead the
> assistant prosecutor shipped the few assembled prospective
> players back to their homes in another county and took no
> further action.   [I-1097]

The jury in these gambling cases is moved by two considerations.   It considers artificial the legal distinction between sell-

ing lottery tickets or numbers slips and buying them.   By legal-
izing all gambling in one state, by allowing track betting in half
the states, and by even having the state run lotteries in some
states,[8] the law has narrowed the possible area of criminal activity here so much, that the jury has difficulty in treating any
segment of gambling as a crime.   We have seen the jury's
sense of equity triggered by the law's failure to draw a distinction which the jury thinks the law should draw.   With
respect to gambling, the situation is exactly reversed.   The
jury is moved to leniency because in its eyes the law draws
one distinction too many,[9] thus creating an artificial boundary
between what is permissible and what is criminal.

As the judge comments indicate, gambling is so widespread
an activity in our society that many of the very jurors who sit
on these cases engage in it themselves or have acquaintances
who do.   There is, then, a special embarrassment in trying to
persuade jurors to convict a defendant for doing something
that they themselves or their friends do in their daily lives.
The moral seems to be that, unless the state wants to be more
serious and stringent in the regulation of gambling, the jury
will not cooperate in efforts to regulate part of it through the
criminal law.

As noted earlier, the Prohibition era provided the most intense example of jury revolt in recent history.   Our *liquor*

[8] "While most of our states have statutes that forbid virtually all
gambling, there is one state which in fact lives on it; it not only encourages and solicits the business but even permits your being politely
turned out if you come only to watch.   As recently as 1906, betting on
horses was permitted only in three states: Kentucky, Maryland, and
New York. Today about half of our states allow betting on horses or
dogs, provided the bet is placed at the track and the pari-mutuel system is employed.   But in all but one state it is a crime to place the
very same bet with a bookmaker."   Zeisel, The Law, Gambling, and
Empirical Research (Review of Tec, Gambling in Sweden), Stan. L.
Rev., v. 17, p. 990 (1965).

[9] This phenomenon is repeated in the cross-over cases.   There the
jury's impatience with legal distinctions favoring the defendant causes
it to disregard them and convict. See Chapter 31.

violation cases pick up some notes, albeit faint, of these Prohibition era sentiments.[10]

In a Kentucky case where moonshining in violation of federal law is involved and the jury acquits, the judge comments:

> Routine whiskey case where violations of federal tax law pertaining to moonshining are prevalent. [I-2034]

Again, where the defendant is charged with selling beer in a dry county and the jury acquits, the judge notes simply:

> Difficult generally to convict bootleggers. [I-0808]

And again, where the defendant is charged with selling liquor in a dry territory and the jury acquits, the judge notes:

> This particular county adjoins the Mississippi River and alcoholic drink is sold just across the bridge. A very great number of persons maintain the belief that the law against selling such alcoholic drinks should not be enforced, and it is extremely difficult to get a conviction no matter how strong the evidence may be. [I-0732]

This brief look at liquor and the jury is rounded out with a case against a barmaid for selling liquor to a minor aged

---

[10] These sentiments are more generalized than sentiments prevailing in the days of Prohibition, when the jury acquittal ratios in trials for violation of the National Prohibition Act varied widely by regions. Thus for 1929-1930 the acquittal rate for liquor violations for 8078 trials in the federal system was 26 per cent. For the 15th District (Kansas, Nebraska, Oklahoma) it was 13 per cent; for the 1st District (New England), 48 per cent; for the 2d District (New York) it was 60 per cent. Ann. Rep. Commissioner of Prohibition (1930).

Turning to our sample, it is of some interest to see the judge-jury disagreement rates by type of liquor violation:

Liquor production in violation of	Disagreement Rate	Number of Cases
Federal tax laws	33%	25
State tax laws	8%	26
Illegal sale		
in dry territories	27%	32
in wet territories	8%	15
to minors	31%	35

nineteen. The jury acquits, and the judge rates the verdict as without merit. But he offers several helpful comments.

> Prevalent practice of minors being able to buy beer — reportedly some of the jurors are extremely liberal as far as intoxicants are concerned and jurors reported that there was deliberate effort on part of some jurors to hunt for doubt. [II-0035] [11]

Although the gambling, game law, and liquor law violations do not bulk large in number, the judge's comments on them suggest a persistent theme of jury hostility to particular types of criminal regulation. Further, in many of them the sentiment is fed by what the jury regards as an inconsistent line between legal and illegal conduct, be it between betting at the race track and betting in town, or between selling liquor on one side of the Mississippi or the other. The theme that violation of the law has become widespread and open recurs and brings with it the embarrassment that it is difficult to find a jury whose members are not close to the conduct they will be asked to judge. On the other hand, it is perhaps a sign of the strength of the society and of the democratic congruence between the people's sense of justice and the law that this best evidence of jury sentiment against special crime categories is so modest.

One final unpopular law which illustrates the general theme is driving under the influence of intoxicating beverages, or more simply, *drunken driving*.[12] The jury's response to drunken driving turns out to be interesting and complex, and in part determined by factors having little to do with senti-

[11] The judge's final comment reminds us of a theme from the gambling cases: "Also after verdict was returned it was learned that the wives of several of the male jurors were employed as barmaids."

[12] This law is not altogether unpopular. The jury's attitude toward drunken driving is ambivalent, reflecting the wide differences in national attitudes toward liquor. Thus, the cases in the sample show a relatively high proportion of cross-overs. See note 10 above and Chapter 31, page 406. For geographic variations in the jury sentiment towards drunken driving, see Chapter 37, Tables 130-131.

ments on drinking. In many cases the issue seems to be entirely evidentiary, with the jury showing hostility to the use
of drunkometers and alcometers, so frequently relied upon in
these cases. Then too, the penalty for drunken driving is
often the mandatory loss of the driver's license for a year, a
penalty which the jury regards as overly severe.[13] In an occasional case it is the stringency of the law's definition of the
crime that offends the jury; the crime is driving under the influence of liquor and does not require that the defendant in
fact drive badly, or even that he be drunk in the popular sense,
if there is the necessary proof of alcohol in his blood.[14]

For the purposes of this chapter, however, we are concerned
with cases in which the judge notes an underlying community
sentiment against the crime. In a substantial number of
drunken driving cases the judge detects such a community feeling and offers it as an explanation for disagreements.[15]

A classically blunt statement of the sentiment comes in a
case from a small mining community in the West. The charge
is drunken driving, second offense, and the evidence appears
to have been overpowering. The defendant was weaving as
he drove, and the car finally left the road and turned over.
Several bottles of beer and a small, empty bottle of vodka
were found in the car, and a blood test showed the high alcohol content of 0.344 per cent.[16] The defendant's explanation, as the judge repeats it, strikes the ear as over-plausible.

> His defense was that he was not drunk at the time of the acci-
> dent, but, after the accident, because of the pain he felt he
> drank the vodka. The car went off the road when he tried to
> pick up a cigarette he had dropped on the floor of the car.

Since the defendant took the stand, the jury learns of his prior
record of drunken driving. Nevertheless, it acquits. The

[13] See Chapter 21, Punishment Threatened is Too Severe.

[14] For the presumptions of law following upon the various levels of
alcohol content in the blood, see Chapter 9, note 13.

[15] An analogous sentiment has been reported in the English experience. See Appendix C.

[16] Or over twice the amount of alcohol required in most states to
establish the presumption that the defendant is "under the influence."

judge rates the verdict as "without any merit," but he leaves us in no doubt as to why the jury acquitted.

This is a mining community and the men in the community will not convict in gambling and drunken driving cases. Women in the community refuse jury duty. Of 50 women asked to serve on the present jury panel, 49 refused. The one woman on the panel did not happen to be called, so the jury consisted of all men. [II-0317] [17]

The jury revolt is less intense in the remaining cases, but hostility to the law is still discernible.

These cases show fewer guilty verdicts than any other kind. It depends on how many people on the jury imbibe alcohol as to how many verdicts come out guilty. [I-1592]

Most jurors are drinking men themselves, and, therefore, biased. [I-1745]

No eyewitness saw him actually driving; and lenient attitude toward drinking in the community. [II-0127]

I think these jurors were inclined to be lenient about drinking anyway and I think they would be lenient toward the defendant. [II-0052]

I understand that jurors in this county hesitate to convict persons for drunk driving. In my opinion the verdict was shocking. [II-0127]

Juries do not seem to want to convict in drunken driving cases, even where an accident occurs if it is only property damage. [II-0773]

Few convictions in this type of case. [II-0500]

Hesitance to convict on part of jurors who drive and drink. [I-0486]

Some members of jury were favorable to drinking. [I-1365]

At times the jury sentiment appears as a refusal to approve the distinction between being drunk in the loose sense and being under the influence of liquor in the legal sense.

[17] There is a cluster of cases with like comments, e.g., "Some beer drinkers on jury," [I-0703] or "All male jury." [I-1739] See Chapter 37.

Many people are very tolerant of this offense and demand show that the defendant is drunk or intoxicated. [I-0384]

Or again:

Notwithstanding the court's instruction, the juries fail to distinguish between being under the influence of intoxicating liquor and drunk. [II-0340]

Many of the cases, of course, illustrate the difficulty already noted in the gambling, game law, and other liquor violation cases, namely, selecting a jury not tainted with the crime it is asked to condemn. One comment gives homiletic expression to the moral dilemma the jury is faced with in cases of this kind.

Perhaps some members of jury thought "There but for the Grace of God go I." [I-1537]

The difficulties in jury selection are often commented on. The vulnerable composition of the jury is at times credited directly to the skill of defense counsel.

The defense was careful to get jury of people who drink; a strategy that is used in cases of this kind. It is my opinion that jurors who drink are inclined to be sympathetic to defendant when he makes a good appearance and expect more proof of alcoholic influence than the law requires for conviction. [I-3134]

The historic role of the jury as a bulwark against grave official tyranny is at best only dimly evident in its contemporary role as a moderate corrective against undue prosecutions for gambling, game, and liquor violations and, to some extent, drunken driving. As we review these instances of disagreement, it is apparent that jury reaction against unpopular laws is complex: to some extent the jurors see themselves as on trial but for the grace of God, to some extent the jury resents the sumptuary interventions, and to some extent the jury objects to the penalty. Beyond these points there is the recurring theme that the prosecution of the particular defendant seems to be selective and to violate the ideal of evenhanded administration of justice.[18]

[18] For other aspects of the jury's principle of evenhanded justice, see Chapter 22, A Note on Preferential Treatment.

W E CONTINUE WITH OUR review of the jury sentiments on the law, presenting in the next eight chapters what might be best thought of as the lesser sentiments. Although these sentiments represent only about one third of the total sentiment category, they embody ideas of high interest and are essential for a complete grasp of jury equity.

CHAPTER 20

Defendant Has Been Punished Enough

The jury's attitude toward punishment emerges as one of the pervasive themes of this study.[1] In a few situations, however, this reaction is so distinctive as to merit brief, separate discussion.

One such situation arises when for one reason or another the jury feels that the defendant at the time of trial, has *already* been sufficiently punished, so that the addition of further punishment would be excessive. The readiest occasion is where the defendant himself is hurt as a consequence of the crime. In one case the defendant fires a shot into the family

[1] At several points in the previous discussion we have noted that the jury considers factors legally relevant to punishment as relevant to guilt. In one sense the disagreement on charge is a reflection of this. In Chapters 21 and 22 we continue to explore other jury reactions to punishment. Finally, in Chapter 35 we review the jury's response to the death penalty.

In general under American law the jury does not deal with penalty. But there are important exceptions. In the overwhelming majority of capital punishment jurisdictions in cases of first degree murder the jury determines whether the death penalty, mandatory life imprisonment, or some lesser penalty shall be imposed. In a fifth of the states, chiefly in the South, the penalties for all cases are determined by the jury, within the framework established by the legislature, and in three states the jury sets the penalty only for certain specific offenses. The judge may, in some jurisdictions, reduce the jury-imposed sentence. Statutes are collected in table form in American Law Institute, Model Penal Code (Tent. Draft No. 9), App. D., pp. 121-126 (1959). For an analysis of the judge-jury penalty scheme, see Note, Statutory Structures for Sentencing Felons to Prison, Colum. L. Rev., v. 60, pp. 1134, 1154 and Notes 136, 137, and 143 (1960); also George, Sentencing Methods and Techniques in the United States, Fed. Prob., v. 26, p. 33 (1962).

home of his estranged wife. The judge finds him guilty of shooting with intent to kill; the jury convicts only of the lesser charge of pointing and discharging a firearm. The decisive circumstance appears to be that the defendant's shot did not injure anyone, but when the brother-in-law shot back in self-defense, he seriously injured the defendant. The "punished-enough" theme comes through in the comment of the judge.

> Defendant had long experience of marital strife with his wife. Jury felt since the only person hurt was defendant himself they could not punish him further. [I-1356]

In a drunken driving case where the jury acquits, the moving circumstance is again that the defendant himself is badly injured in the accident. The judge states:

> I think the jury felt that the defendant had suffered enough; that they looked for an excuse and felt the blood test may have been inadequate. [I-0095]

Sometimes, in the jury's eyes, the defendant has been sufficiently punished by the death of a loved one. In a prosecution for negligent auto homicide the victim is the intended bride of the defendant, a twenty-one-year-old member of the Air Force. It is clear from the judge's description of the case that not only the jury but the parents of the girl as well feel that the defendant has been punished enough by the event.

> Her mother and father were character witnesses for the defendant and he makes his home with them when not on duty. Defendant had never been in trouble and it was obvious that the family of the girl did not want him convicted. [I-0913]

In another case, a tavern fight, the defendant accidentally kills a relative who had attempted to intercede. The judge captures the point of the jury's disagreement.

> Jury may have felt defendant punished sufficiently, having killed uncle who was very close. [II-0584]

The punishment need not always involve physical harm to the defendant or someone close to him. There is a drunken driving case where the defendant, a police officer, had been requested to resign and in fact had already resigned prior to the trial; this circumstance is brought out indirectly. Arguably, the jury feels here that losing his position is enough punishment for this particular offense. [I-1391]

Indeed the jury may respond to the punished-enough sentiment even when the victim in the case is a stranger to the defendant. Thus the jury acquits a high school senior, who has killed a ten-year-old while negligently using a rifle. The judge, after describing the defendant as a boy of "high moral character, religious, clean-cut appearing," offers the following explanation of the disagreement:

> The jury felt that having the charge and killing on his conscience was sufficient punishment. [II-0284]

We get just a glimpse here of the profound but disturbing idea that at times the crime may be its own punishment.

The pattern of these cases indicates that the jury is again employing a delicate calculus.[2] It is not simplistically treating every injury to every defendant in the course of a crime as a punishment. It appears to weigh this factor only when the crime has been a crime of negligence[3] or where the crime has been limited to an attempt.

The punished-enough theme is found in a second group of cases in which there has been long imprisonment while the defendant awaited trial. It is customary for the judge in sentencing to give the defendant credit for the time he has already spent in jail; the jury, however, would at times not only give him credit but would set him free. The point is most obvious if the offense itself is considered trivial, as in the case where the defendant was charged with stealing two pieces of lumber. He had already spent two months in jail.

---

[2] Compare the calculus employed in the "privilege" to commit a one-punch battery in response to provocation. See Chapter 16, The Boundaries of Self-Defense.

[3] Inadvertence as a crime is treated in Chapter 24.

The jury felt sorry for the defendant because he had been in jail for over two months and the lumber allegedly stolen was worth $2.50. [II-0380] [4]

The sentiment may be present, however, even when quite serious harm is involved. In a domestic quarrel, the defendant shoots and wounds his common law wife so seriously that she is in the hospital for almost a year. The trial is not held until her discharge, with the result that the defendant spends the interval in jail awaiting trial. This circumstance seems to be a major factor in moving the jury to acquittal. [I-1206]

In one set of circumstances the jury carries the punished-enough theme a wild dimension further. The defendant is charged with the rape of his ten-year-old daughter and at the first trial of his case is found guilty and sentenced to life imprisonment. On appeal, a new trial is granted with a change of venue. At the second trial the jury hangs. The case is tried a third time, and it is for this third trial that we have the judge-jury report. At this trial it is disclosed that the defendant has at that point been in jail for thirteen months. The extraordinary reaction of this third and last jury, which acquits, is set forth by the judge as follows:

> They were out just 30 minutes. The jury took up a collection of $68 and gave it to the defendant after the case was over. [I-3067] [5]

A final variation on the punished-enough theme arises where the defendant has been plagued by such misfortune, dating from the time of the crime, that the jury feels life or providence has already punished him sufficiently. This equity is illustrated in a case of income tax evasion which brings to mind

---

[4] In one case of auto theft the jury is influenced by the fact that the defendant had languished in jail for six months. The judge adds, "Unknown to the jury it was for a misdemeanor conviction in the adjoining county for driving while intoxicated." [I-1730] To complete the irony, the defendant at the time of the drunken driving arrest was driving the stolen car.

[5] It should be added that the jury knew that the defendant had nine children.

the story of Job. During the period for which the defendant, originally well-to-do, is charged with failing to file tax returns, he was subject to misfortunes which the judge inventories as follows:

> Defendant did not testify but the evidence shows that, during the years in question, his home burned, he was seriously injured and his son was killed. Later he lost his leg, his wife became seriously ill and several major operations were necessary. About three years before the trial, his wife gave birth to a premature child which was both blind and spastic. These, however, are only a portion of the calamities the defendant suffered during the years he failed to file his income tax return. [I-2030]

The jury cannot bring itself to add to the misfortune of the defendant. The judge gives full recognition to the point, adding:

> This is a typical case of the jury exercising the power of pardon. [I-2030] [6]

It is not simply that the jury has sympathy, as it does, for the crippled, blind, and unlovely, but that the sequence of misfortunes visited upon the defendant seems to stem from the commission of the crime and to be so extreme as to make the defendant appear to be the victim of divine retribution.

[6] This is as good a place as any to note that at least one legal order, the Canon law, has built such general equity considerations into the system itself. There, *Legis in casu speciali relaxatio* is to be granted for a "just and reasonable cause," more specifically defined as *necessity, charity,* or *utility* which is to be assessed in proportion to the gravity of the law dispensed. Canons 80 and 84. See Cicognani, Canon Law, pp. 833, 852 (2d ed. 1934).

CHAPTER 21

Punishment Threatened Is Too Severe

In this chapter we seek to mark off another distinctive response to penalty. The cases are unified by the jury's perception of a gross discrepancy between the offense and the anticipated punishment.

In the first few illustrations the jury weighs the extra-legal consequences of a conviction along with the legal penalty itself. The impending penalty to which it is responding is not a fine or a jail sentence but rather the loss of a job. In its calculus the loss of a job may add to the legal penalty, whatever it may be, and make the total penalty for the defendant's conduct too severe. Where, for example, two Air Force officers are charged with aggravated assault, the jury finds them guilty only of simple assault. The judge explains the ensuing disagreement as follows:

> Both defendants appeared in uniform and ribbons with 12 and 15 years respectively in Service. Jury was sympathetic and feared that conviction on a higher degree of crime would cause them to be discharged from Service. [II-0481-1 & 2]

In a second case the defendant, a railroad engineer with an excellent work record, is charged with drunken driving and the jury acquits. The judge commented:

> A conviction probably would have caused defendant to lose his job. Jury believed that such penalty would be disproportionate to offense committed. [II-0128]

The jury's reaction in these cases may engender some perplexity. It is surely one of the more durable dilemmas of

criminal law that we cannot control all the extra-legal consequences of a criminal conviction — even if we were to try
harder than we do.   If the jury is so responsive to the extra-
legal consequences of criminal convictions, how can it be per-
suaded to convict as often as it does?   The cases suggest some
limiting factors: the nature of the job is particularly visible, as
with an Air Force officer or a railroad engineer or a minister,[1]
and the possibility of formal disciplinary action is particularly
likely.   Occasionally the point is extended to other employment situations where for some reason the loss of the job becomes salient.   Thus, where a youngster is involved in a juvenile brawl, and the boy's mother, who "was old and looked
poor," is in court, the judge explains:

> The boy had a job at Sears and if convicted probably would
> have lost his job. [II-0081] [2]

Moving from extra-legal punishment to legal punishment,
we are confronted with the fact that in the great majority of
states and in the federal system the jury does not officially
know what the penalty will be.[3]   And if the jury inquires
about the penalty, as it occasionally does,[4] it is generally told
by the judge that it is not their concern.   Nevertheless, the
threatened penalty may come to dominate the deliberation, because the jury guesses at the magnitude of the legal penalty, or
because it has special reason to know what the penalty actually is.

[1] A vivid instance where the jury takes into account that the defendant is a cleric is detailed in Chapter 18, page 278.   As is clear
there, many other factors besides defendant's status were operating.

[2] In at least one instance the secondary consequence is a variant of
the loss of a job.   In an auto homicide case, where the jury acquits, the
defendant is an attractive young man in his first year of college.   The
judge notes that the "risk of dropping out of college if convicted was
one of the factors which influenced the jury to acquit." [II-0831]

[3] Unless, of course, the jury is to set the penalty.   See Chapter 20,
note 1.

[4] Information on the frequency and nature of jury requests will be
found in Appendix B.   The jury comes back with questions in 17 per
cent of all cases.   In the cases with requests, it asks about penalty 9
per cent of the time.

A series of negligent automobile homicide cases presents a situation in which the jury is disposed to guess at the penalty. In these cases the jury is uncertain what the penalty will be but fears that, since death is involved, it will be serious. The judge's view is that the momentum to acquit is generated primarily by an impression of the penalty, and that if the jury had known what the actual penalty would be, it would be less disturbed. As one judge puts it:

> Substantial justice may have been done, although I thought the boy should have been subjected to some punishment, since his carelessness contributed to loss of life. Perhaps it would be best if we were permitted to inform jury of minimum and maximum penalty. This offense was a misdemeanor but jury didn't know whether he would go to the penitentiary or county jail, or whether his punishment would be a fine only. [I-0778]

The judge in another case states the problem in almost identical fashion.

> The jury was influenced by fear that the defendant would receive harsh penalty when he shouldn't. Didn't realize that Court would consider all facts. [I-0764]

And in yet a third case, where once again there is acquittal, the judge, although unsympathetic to this response, elaborates the basis for it.

> In this case there appears to be no justification for the verdict which the jury returned. I could only say that defendant was a young man who held a fairly responsible job and the jury may have felt that incarceration for up-to-20 years might serve no purpose except to ruin the defendant's life without being helpful to the deceased or his family. I find that, although the jury understands that the matter of punishment is for the Court, they are many times reluctant to return a verdict of guilty where the penalty can be severe. [I-0538]

The most substantial and striking evidence of this special sentiment is furnished in drunken driving cases. The jury's response has several sources. Prosecution for this crime, with its overtones of an anti-liquor policy, is, as we have noted, somewhat unpopular,[5] moreover, the cases often involve special evidence problems connected with blood and breath tests. The fact relevant here, however, is that the mandatory loss of the driver's license for a year is a widely prevalent penalty, and the jurors, as members of the driving public, have good reason to be fully aware of it. The judge is often precise in pinning the jury's disagreement to the feeling that this loss of license is a disproportionate penalty for the routine case of drunken driving.

> The jury was instructed that in the event of conviction, the State Highway Patrol would revoke his license for one year. The jury thought this too severe. [I-0989]

> Everybody knows that operating privileges are revoked for one year. [I-1592]

> One of the penalties of guilty in such cases is revocation of drivers license for one year. [I-1314]

> Juries generally feel punishment (loss of license for one year) is too severe and are reluctant to convict except in aggravated cases. [II-0467]

The judge may add that the defendant is a working man and that the suspension of his license would be particularly harsh.

> I have come to the conclusion that one of the basic reasons for the jury's refusal [to convict] is the belief on the part of the jury that to suspend the license of a working man for one year is too severe a punishment. [II-0830]

Again:

> I think the jury decided that they were not going to cause the man to lose his operator's license because it would seriously affect his making a living. [II-0827]

And again:

> Where as in this case defendant's occupation requires use of his car, juries seem reluctant to return a guilty verdict. [I-0536]

[5] See Chapter 19, Unpopular Laws, at pages 293-296, and Chapter 37 at Tables 130-131.

Perhaps the clearest instance of the impact of the drunken driving penalty comes in a case in which the judge explains:

> This was the second offense for driving while intoxicated for this man, and if convicted it carries a six-year suspension of driver's license together with a fine of not less than $50 and a sentence to confinement. This was not mentioned during the trial, except the prior conviction record of driving while intoxicated, but the jurors know of the six-year suspension and the prison term and it is awfully hard to get a conviction even with a blood test. [I-1789]

In one last illustration the defendant is an elderly tenant farmer with no criminal record and "an honest, hard worker." The jury acquits, and the judge gives the following reason.

> Big thing is that in Indiana conviction of drunken driving at that time carried mandatory suspension of driver's license for one year. Juries normally will not find guilty because of this. [II-1113]

The judge then adds a comment indicating that the state legislature too has noticed the frequent jury acquittals in drunken driving cases.

> Law now changed to give only 60-day suspension of license for first offense.[6]

A memorable chapter in the history of the English jury concerns its response to excessive punishment in the early nineteenth century when England had an incredible list of some 230 capital offenses. The jury then felt the death penalty so

---

[6] This is a prime example of a legislative change in direct reaction to a jury response. Defendants appear to note such jury reactions too. Thus, when the penalty for drunken driving was made stricter recently in California, the number of requests for jury trials rose sharply. See Chapter 2, note 27.

Sometimes the legislature, rather than yield, has attempted to circumvent community response to an unpopular penalty by eliminating or refusing to grant trial by jury for that class of violations. While the state constitutions insure the right to jury trial, the right depends on its availability at the time of ratification. See Chapter 2, note 5.

disproportionate for most crimes that it conspicuously refused to convict. Finally, in 1819, the bankers themselves petitioned Parliament to remove the death penalty from the crime of forgery, since it had become almost impossible to obtain a conviction for that crime.[7] By grading punishment to "fit the crime" and reserving capital punishment for only the most severe crimes, the criminal law of our day has met the jury more than halfway.[8]

What is left, therefore, of this once great source of jury nul-

[7] This was true of many other crimes as well. While declining elsewhere, the number of capital crimes in England had increased from about 50 in 1700 to 230 or so in the early nineteenth century, accompanying the social and economic upheaval during the beginnings of the Industrial Revolution. Due to the long and arduous efforts of early champions of penal reform, such as Sir Samuel Romilly and the members of the Society for the Diffusion of Knowledge upon the Punishment of the Death, a revulsion of feeling set in; juries started systematically to nullify capital crimes by refusing to convict or by convicting of a lesser offense. A complete account will be found in Radzinowicz, A History of English Criminal Law and Its Administration from 1750, v. 1, Parts IV and V (1948). See also Report from the Select Committee on Capital Punishment, p. viii (1931). For the history of capital punishment in the light of the modern British movement to abolish the death penalty, see Report of the Royal Commission on Capital Punishment (1953), and Christoph, Capital Punishment and British Politics (1962).

A recent example of jury nullification comes from Norway: "Judges have expressed the view that the high minimum penalties [for sex offenses] have had an adverse effect on juries, who are not inclined to give a verdict of guilt when the offender is liable to a penalty which they think disproportionate. Another effect was that the public prosecutor sometimes waived the prosecution in cases which perhaps ought to have been brought before the court, feeling that the punishment which the court would be bound to inflict, would be too severe." Andenaes, Norwegian Legislation and Practice Concerning Sexual Offenses, in Sexual Offenses, Report of the Cambridge Dept. of Crim. Sci., p. 466 (Radzinowicz ed. 1957).

[8] It might be thought that the jury would exhibit a different disagreement pattern in states where it has the task of setting the penalty. The hypothesis would be that if the jury had such control of the penalty this would lessen disagreement by providing the jury with a means of accommodating equities in the particular case. Under elaborate testing, however, the hypothesis failed.

lification are these somewhat scattered instances.[9] Even with the more modest sentences of today, the jury at times finds the penalty so disproportionate to its view of the offense that it is moved to acquit the defendant rather than subject him to that penalty.[10]

[9] To which we add a narcotics case in which the jury's usual propensity to go along with the law in such cases is tempered by a consideration of the threatened penalty. Here the jury hangs, and the judge leaves no doubt as to why. "His youth, previous good record, and the mandatory 5 years penalty account for the hung jury. The statute provides a mandatory minimum sentence of 5 years with no probation or suspended sentence." [II-0426]

[10] We cannot resist the wry observation that this study of judge-jury disagreement would have been a great deal easier to make if a lengthy list of capital crimes still obtained. Again (see note 6 on page 190) we find support from Poisson's "Recherches sur la probabilité des jugements" (Paris 1837). At one point he draws attention to the increase in the ratio of guilty verdicts of French juries after 1831:

1831	53.9%
1832	58.9%
1833	59.0%

In all these years at least 8 guilty votes were required for conviction; but beginning with 1832, the jury was permitted to add to the verdict a finding of "extenuating circumstances," with the result that the jury now brought back 5 more convictions in every hundred trials. (Page 391.)

CHAPTER 22

A Note on Preferential Treatment

This chapter presents still another variant of the jury's re-action to the "fit" of punishment. The cases have in common that the crime involves multiple parties and that the jury has become aware that a partner in the crime is receiving treat-ment different from that accorded the defendant. The situ-ation thus opens on the large theme of evenhandedness in pun-ishment,[1] and one might well anticipate a rich and varied jury reaction. But the story requires little more than a note.

In the first group of illustrations the discrepancy in treat-ment is aggravated for the jury because the dominant partner in the crime is receiving the more lenient treatment. These then are cases where in the jury's eyes the differentiation in treatment, if any is warranted, is moving in the wrong direc-tion.[2]

The most vivid instance of this is a burglary of a liquor store committed by a white man and two Indians. As the judge himself views the matter, it is a case of "a white man getting

[1] There are, inevitably, analogies between this and other chapters. The preferential theme is relevant to Chapter 19, Unpopular Laws, where the defendant may appear to the jury to have been singled out for prosecution. The theme is also suggestive of Chapter 21, Punish-ment Threatened Is Too Severe; here too the penalty imminent upon conviction is not according to scale when the jury considers all the participants in the crime.

[2] It may help to formalize the relationships thus: equal roles are punished unequally, or unequal roles are punished equally; or unequal roles are punished unequally so that the defendant with a lesser role is threatened with the greater penalty.

uneducated Indians in trouble." To make matters more un-
balanced, the principal has entered a plea of guilty and received a suspended sentence. In this posture of affairs the
jury acquits both Indians,[3] and the judge is clear as to why.[4]

> I believe the fact that this defendant and his accomplice,
> both Indians, the latter having a very low mentality, were
> being tried, while the white man . . . was the admitted
> leader, caused the result. The white man testified and it
> was manifest that he was the leader.

The judge adds a final comment.

> I am not so sure the verdict was not proper justice under the
> circumstances. [I-09382]

This extreme imbalance is found in another burglary case
where the dominant party, thirty-one years old, has pleaded
guilty and received leniency, while the teen-aged defendant is
left to stand trial alone. The jury acquits and the judge once
more is firm in explanation.

> Jury didn't feel that instant defendant should receive same
> punishment or more. [I-0969]

These two cases, since both involve guilty pleas, suggest an
interesting qualification. They are the only cases, out of
many in the sample, in which the jury reacts against leniency

---

[3] One of the two Indians would have been acquitted by the judge:
"Evidence was clear that he was drunk and asleep at the time;" and the
judge adds that the joint trial was a mistake. The Indian whom the
judge would have convicted thus becomes the beneficiary both of the
obvious innocence of his co-defendant and of the jury's antagonism to
the special treatment shown to the principal.

We have already met a case in which one defendant withdrew a
guilty plea to take his chances with a co-defendant and their joint trial
resulted in acquittal for both. See Chapter 9, page 125. For the reverse effect in the cross-over situation, see Chapter 30, note 8.

[4] The judge implies that the verdict in this case might have been
different if the crime had been committed in the next county. "The
Indians live on a reservation in an adjoining county. They are no
problem here and the jury's prejudices would be in their favor and
not against, as is more likely the case in the county of their residence
where drunken Indians are a problem." See Chapter 37.

"earned" by a guilty plea.[5] It is somewhat surprising that
the jury is not more offended by preferential treatment of defendants who cooperate with the prosecution. It indicates perhaps that the jury has a realistic tolerance of the guilty plea
bargaining mechanism and, like the prosecution, is willing to
pay some price for cooperation. But as the cases suggest, the
price has its limit. The jury will not pay when the divergence
between the cooperating partner and the defendant becomes
too great.

The partner in crime in a second cluster of cases appears not
to have been prosecuted at all, and the defendant is perceived
by the jury as left holding the bag. In the first, the defendant,
"an attractive young lady," is tried before an all male jury on a
charge of attempting to transport liquor into a dry state. The
judge explained:

> [S]uggestion was made "she was taking rap" for someone else.
> In the civil case for forfeiture of the liquor . . . tried con-
> temporaneously . . . the jury held in favor of the govern-
> ment. [I-2004]

In another violation of liquor laws in a dry territory the defendant is charged with operating a night club to the outrage
of some local citizenry. The jury hangs; the judge remarks:

> The jury was reluctant to return a guilty verdict because the
> defendant had just been discharged from the U.S. Marine
> Corps and was fronting for local hoodlums who actually oper-
> ated the place in his name. [I-3086] [6]

A few cases suggest an analogous problem where two defendants are tried together and at some point in the trial the
judge directs an acquittal for one of the defendants. Such a

[5] The credibility of the accomplice who turns state's evidence is
analyzed at pages 174-177.

[6] In another liquor violation case it again appears that the dominant
partner has not been prosecuted. Here the defendant is charged with
aiding and abetting in the maintenance of a still by allowing it to be
operated on his property, and the principal is not on trial. The jury
acquits. [II-0609]

move, in the eyes of the jury, tends to weaken the prosecution's case in general; it may, however, also arouse some sense of unequal enforcement of the law with respect to the defendant left to stand trial.

One involves a complicated corporate fraud. The trial starts with two defendants, the president of the corporation and the chief accountant. The judge directs an acquittal [7] for the president,[8] and the jury then acquits the accountant. The judge explains:

> Counsel for the remaining defendant, the CPA who prepared the statement, rested heavily upon the theory that this client was an innocent dupe and assuming the statement was false, the client knew of no falsity when he prepared it. I believe if the case was given to the jury with both defendants the jury would have found them both guilty, but with the principal free, the jury was unwilling to convict the agent. [I-1963]

Finally, in a few cases the discrepancy in roles is so great that the jury cannot see the defendant's conduct as criminal at all. In a fraud case where the jury acquits, the judge explains:

> Defendant was jointly charged with another defendant; the co-defendant had been previously tried before the Court (the jury did not know this) in another department. The money was paid to him. My thought is that the jury figured that the co-defendant was the real criminal. [I-0018]

[7] The judge, if he finds the evidence insufficient as a matter of law to sustain a guilty verdict, may command the jury to acquit the defendant. This case is one of four disagreements in which one of the defendants obtains such a directed acquittal. The other cases are: theft of an outboard motor [II-0352]; husband and wife fraudulently obtaining a loan [II-3109]; and receiving stolen property [II-1107-2]. In none of these cases, however, is the directed acquittal of the co-defendant offered as the reason for disagreement; the judge simply notes it as one fact in the case.

[8] The judge directs for the president because of the "paucity of the evidence." There is more than a suggestion that the judge is aware of the beneficial effect this move may have for the remaining defendant. But he prefers to see the accountant go free rather than risk a jury verdict on the president. For other glimpses of such judicial strategy, see Chapter 25, note 7.

Similarly, in a bribery case where again the jury acquits, the judge states:

> The acquittal was due to belief of the jury that the employee received no part of the money for himself but merely acted for his superior. [I-1853]

In the end, there is little disagreement generated by the problems of multiple party crimes and the equity of the minor role. Here the law in its distinctions between principals and accessories has met sufficiently the jury's sense of justice.

There is a somber postscript, however. The jury, as it will turn out, is highly sensitive to equality of treatment and inequality of role when the death penalty is at issue.[9]

[9] See Chapter 35.

CHAPTER 23

Improper Police and
Prosecution Practices

One of the great controversies in American constitutional law has arisen over the appropriate sanction for enforcing the law against illegal searches and seizures by police officials. About fifty years ago the United States Supreme Court adopted the rule that in federal cases the sanction against the illegal garnering of evidence by the police was the exclusion of that evidence from the trial — even if it meant, as it usually did, acquitting a guilty defendant.[1] So dramatic a legal rule, of course, came under frequent criticism, especially for the anomaly of punishing the police by letting the defendant go free.[2] To many, the preservation by this rule of citizen privacy against police intrusion seemed a quixotic democratic luxury. Nevertheless, in 1961 in *Mapp v. Ohio*[3] the Supreme Court, in one of its most celebrated reversals of constitutional doctrine, extended this federal rule to the state courts.[4]

This reference to constitutional law provides a useful pref-

[1] Weeks v. United States, 232 U.S. 383 (1914).

[2] "On the one hand, it is demonstrable that two effects of the exclusionary rule are to produce a troublesome grist for the courts and to return rascals to the practice of their nefarious trades. This much is certain. On the other hand, there is no convincing evidence that the exclusionary rule significantly improves police practices (though one would think it would)." Wigmore, v. 8, §2184a, p. 52 (McNaughton rev. 1961).

[3] 367 U.S. 643.

[4] See Allen, Federalism and the Fourth Amendment: A Requiem for Wolf, [1961] Supreme Court Review, p. 1.

ace to the tracing in this chapter of a special jury sentiment. What unifies these cases of disagreement has much the same rationale. The jury acquits the defendant in protest against a police or prosecution practice that it considers improper.

We cannot be sure whether the jury acquittals reflect simply indignation over the practice — an indignation which then works to the benefit of the defendant — or whether the jury is deliberately following the strategy of imposing a sanction on the police and prosecution. In at least one case there is a glimmer of conscious strategy: the defendant, tried for breaking and entering, is not represented by counsel and is acquitted. The judge regards the acquittal as a "violent miscarriage of justice." He is moved to interview the jurors afterwards and receives a variety of explanations for their verdict. But by one juror he is told that:

> [U]ntil the state provided a public defender, he would let everyone go free. [I-3113] [5]

In a drunken driving case where the jury acquits, the judge explains:

> Defendant claimed police refused to let him call his wife or an attorney for a night and a day. [I-0709]

In a case where the defendant is charged with selling liquor to a minor, the jury's resentment stems from a different aspect of the trial.

> In the selection of a jury, one or two prospective jurors indicated they would be prejudiced where a defendant was not in the courtroom to tell his side of the case and I feel that this influenced the jury which was finally sworn in. [I-3049] [6]

[5] As noted in Chapter 28, p. 352, it was not until 1963 that, through the Gideon case, counsel became mandatory. It is tempting to say that this particular juror was simply running a little ahead of the United States Supreme Court.

[6] The defendant was not in the courtroom, because counsel had come hoping for a continuance. "Counsel for the defendant requested a continuance before the jury was seated in the box, which continuance was refused by the court inasmuch as the case had been set for trial for over a month and there was no showing made as to why the defendant was not present."

Occasionally, references to improprieties are connected with confessions.[7] The following is a good indication that the jury may not so much consider the credibility of the confession as the impropriety of the method by which it was obtained. In a burglary trial in which the jury acquits, the judge explains:

> Principal witnesses were [State] Bureau of Investigation men. They may not have been as careful as they should have been in advising defendant of his rights, and letting him see an attorney speedily. I admitted a statement obtained from him, over objection, but enough was presented to jury to give impression that there might have been an attempt to railroad him, so to speak. Attempt was not bad, but there was a little odor. [I-0786]

Confessions apart, there is one extraordinary case which we have already met in which the jury's acquittal is regarded by the judge as a direct protest against police brutality. The case is tangential to the theme under discussion because the defendant is charged with assaulting the chief of police of a small community. However, the judge's comment is worth quoting a second time.[8]

> It is the Court's opinion that the inhuman treatment of the defendant throughout the arrest and after the arrest made the jury feel, I presume, that he had received unusual punishment and the verdict was prompted to discipline the officers which, in the Court's opinion, the jury was entitled to do. While the Court could have dismissed the treatment angle and based its decision on the assault, it is very understandable how the jury reached its verdict. As a matter of fact, the rough treatment of prisoners by arresting authorities is so well known that it is difficult to get convictions where police or prosecuting detectives are involved. [I-1085]

The case is a good illustration of a phenomenon we have noticed many times in comparing judge and jury. The judge is

---

[7] The effect of a repudiated confession on judge-jury disagreement is analyzed at Table 54. See also Chapter 13, note 3.

[8] There are overtones of self-defense in the case: the defendant was only half the size of the victim. The case is discussed in Chapter 16, page 237.

sensitive enough to the jury view to describe it with almost affectionate detail, but he cannot bring himself to yield to the very equities he describes with such empathy.

The next group of cases reflects the jury's protest when the police "trap" a defendant into committing a crime for which they later arrest him.[9] In a drunken driving case where the jury acquits, it appears that the police stood by and watched the defendant, suggestively unstable, get into his car and begin to drive away. The judge explains:

> The sheriff could have prevented the defendant from committing the crime. The sheriff watched the defendant get into his car and drive away. The sheriff then gets into his car and promptly arrests him. [I-1639]

In a prostitution case where the jury hangs, the pivotal fact appears to be that the defendant, the operator of a massage parlor, had agreed to furnish a prostitute to an undercover police officer. [II-0633] In a second prostitution case where the jury acquits, the judge notes an aura of entrapment and suggests it as a basis for the jury's doubting the credibility of police witnesses. As the judge puts it:

> The case presented the issue of credibility as between the defendant and the police officer who entrapped him. Jury chose to disbelieve the officer. [I-1859]

A similar sentiment emerges in an embezzlement case where a bus driver is charged with collecting cash fares and converting them to his own use. The jury acquits, and the judge assigns the cause:

> Not only was the defendant of good reputation and small amount was involved, but also case worked on by professional spotters. [I-1423]

Another case presents the basic theme but with a perfect crime twist. As we fit the pieces together from what the judge tells us, a restaurant owner works out a scheme to get revenge

[9] The jury is here expanding the legal doctrine of entrapment. See Bancroft, Administration of the Affirmative Trap and the Doctrine of Entrapment: Device and Defense, U. Chi. L. Rev., v. 31, p. 137 (1963).

on the defendant, who has been seeing his estranged wife. He
tips off the police that the defendant is planning a burglary of
the living quarters in the rear of the restaurant. He then,
through an intermediary, somehow induces the defendant to
enter the premises. A policeman is waiting in the back of the
restaurant, having, as the judge puts it, "staked out a trap
there." The husband's strategy is to set up a situation in which
the policeman would be privileged to shoot the defendant.
But the strategy misfires when the defendant kills the policeman. The judge makes explicit that enough of this plot
came through at the trial to move the jury to refuse to convict
for murder and find the defendant guilty of voluntary manslaughter.

> The jury felt because defendant was seeing owner's estranged
> wife and later married her, that the owner was out "to get"
> the defendant and had his agent entrap defendant into break-
> ing into owner's restaurant. [II-0948]

The jury's reaction is quite remarkable: It responds, even
though it is not the government but a private third party who
is doing the entrapping.[10]

The final group of cases expands this idea of a differential
view of improper police practice. In these cases it appears to
the jury that the defendant is arrested only because in some respect, other than the crime, he irritates the police. The point
is nicely captured in a comment on a drunken driving case.

> Testimony showed, and this was admitted, that the defendant
> did drive across the center line and forced the troopers on to
> the shoulder of the road which admittedly caused them to
> become angry, at least momentarily. [I-0536]

And in a reckless driving case, the judge explains the disagreement:

> Unfavorable impression of prosecution witness (policeman)
> who admitted stopping defendant and questioning him sub-

---

[10] In part the jury's reaction comes also from the realization that the
principal defendant is not before them. See Chapter 22, A Note on
Preferential Treatment.

sequent to date of alleged offense. Gave the impression that defendant was being heckled by police department. [I-0412]

A drunken driving prosecution develops a variant of the Good Samaritan parable and furnishes a last word for this chapter. The oddity of the defendant's behavior seems to have made a considerable impression on the judge.

The police had been dispatched to the scene of an accident. While crossing the roadway one officer fell on the ice and broke his leg. He was removed to the side of the road to await an ambulance. The other officer, together with a civilian, attempted to direct traffic at the scene. The defendant, who was driving on the road, saw the police officer who had been injured and asked the other officer if he could be of assistance. He was told that it would not be necessary and was asked to move on. After passing the scene he made a U turn and again passed where the officer was lying and asked to help. Again he was told to move. He repeated the same procedure two more times and after the ambulance arrived at the scene and the officer was placed in it the defendant followed the ambulance a distance of about three miles over icy roads to the hospital. He left his car, came into the emergency room, inquired of the injured officer if this wasn't some kind of civil defense test and was informed it was not. The injured officer said that then the defendant gave his stretcher a push and started to walk away. (This was vigorously denied by the defendant.) The other officer then arrested him for operating a motor vehicle while under the influence of alcohol. The arresting officer testified that on the first three occasions when the defendant passed the scene he did not smell any alcohol on the defendant. On the fourth occasion he did, but said he did not arrest the defendant as he was only interested at the time in directing traffic and further that he did not see anything wrong with the defendant's driving. [I-1396]

CHAPTER 24

A Note on Inadvertent
Conduct as Criminal

There is a well-known observation of Justice Holmes' that even a dog knows the difference between being stumbled over and being kicked.[1] Anglo-American criminal law has taken this epigram to heart, for it includes very few instances where non-intentional conduct is made criminal. Indeed, the only major instance is the crime of negligent homicide; in most jurisdictions no crime is committed if the victim of a negligent act is only hurt, no matter how severely. Furthermore, most statutes require that the act, to qualify as a crime, be more than simple negligence, that is as "gross" or "willful" or "wanton." [2]

Some legal scholars[3] have argued that even so modest a set of

[1] The Common Law, p. 5 (Howe ed. 1964).

[2] The American Law Institute, Model Penal Code now includes a few crimes of negligence or recklessness. See §§210.4 (negligent homicide), 211.2 (recklessly endangering another person), and 220.2 (causing or risking catastrophe), Proposed Official Draft (1962). Paragraph 335 of the Austrian Code makes negligent wounding a crime, and §431 even the negligent endangering of the safety of another.

[3] E.g., Jerome Hall: "The relevant ethical principle expressed in terms of *mens rea*, that penal liability should be limited to the voluntary (intentional or reckless) commission of harms forbidden by penal law, represents not only the perennial view of moral culpability, but also the plain man's morality." General Principles of Criminal Law, pp. 133-134 (2nd ed. 1960). This view of course is not intended to cover the quasi-criminal infractions regularly tried in traffic and municipal courts, where the law imposes strict liability for various forms of inadvertent behavior.

The concept of strict liability for more serious crimes has come under increasing criticism. See A.L.I., Model Penal Code, Tent. Draft No. 4.,

rules goes too far, and that for ethical, scientific, and historical reasons negligence should be excluded entirely from penal liability.

Inadvertent crime promises, therefore, an interesting point of policy on which to poll the jury's sense of justice. But we come up at best with only a handful of helpful cases.

To begin with there are, as just noted, few negligent crimes on the books and hence few opportunities for the jury to react to this matter.[4] Moreover, the jury's reaction to the fact that the conduct is negligent tends to combine with other sentiments such as that defendant has been punished enough by injury to himself or to a loved one in the course of the crime,[5] or, more often, that the defendant is exonerated by the contributory fault of the victim.[6]

In a sense, therefore, much of the story of the jury and inadvertent crime has already been told. The fact that the conduct is not intentional may, in our idiom, liberate the jury to respond to these other sentiments.

Not unexpectedly, several of the disagreements turn on disputes as to where the line defining negligence should be drawn, and this is especially true where the law requires willful or wanton conduct. Thus, in an automobile homicide arising out of a head-on collision, where the defendant, who had been drinking, was on the wrong side of the road, the judge explains the jury's acquittal:

Perhaps some difficulty in understanding and applying the difference between wanton negligence and simple negligence. [II-0576]

---

comments 2.05. For a concise discussion on the issue of the use of criminal sanctions in the absence of mens rea, see also Packer, Mens Rea and the Supreme Court, 1962 Sup. Ct. Rev. 107, arguing that the idea of criminal responsibility based upon the actor's failure to act as carefully as he should affords an important and largely unutilized means for avoiding the tyranny of strict liability in the criminal law.

[4] In our sample negligent homicide accounts for less than 3 per cent of all cases.

[5] See Chapter 20.

[6] See Chapter 17.

The difficulty over the standard is made even more explicit in the judge's comment on a second case of involuntary manslaughter:

> Court viewed act of defendant in driving his car at speed in excess of 60 m.p.h. in a 30 mile zone, and passing another car in the area on defendant's left side where victim was at time of impact, as gross negligence; jury thought otherwise. [II-0700] [7]

And in another automobile homicide case, where the jury finds only violation of the hit-and-run statute, the judge complains:

> Law on involuntary manslaughter involves too much proof on part of Commonwealth; should be amended. [II-0488]

And where the defendant had been subject to great fatigue at the time of the fatal accident, the judge states:

> The jury felt great sympathy for the defendant. I am sure the crucial issue as to whether defendant had been criminally negligent was considered by only two members of the jury. [II-0084]

Occasionally, however, the jury comes close to saying that negligence alone cannot be a crime. Thus, where defendant pulled out in front of two approaching cars, colliding with one and killing a passenger, the judge's explanation is general.

> Juries in this state will not convict persons for negligent homicide. I knew the verdict would be not guilty. [I-3070]

At times the judge underscores a point previously noted in the discussion of unpopular crimes — the jury is sensitive about judging conduct as criminal which they might engage in themselves. The next case illustrates the point. The defendant is alleged to have run a red light, causing a collision and thereby the death of a passenger in the other car. The jury acquits, and the judge is more discursive as to the underlying source of the jury's leniency.

---

[7] The jury however does find the defendant guilty of the lesser offense of reckless driving.

Experience has indicated it is extremely difficult to obtain a guilty verdict in a misdemeanor manslaughter case. Ordinarily there is no evidence of willfulness on the part of the defendant. Juries sometime feel same thing could happen to them. In this case, defendant apparently inadvertently ran red light, causing collision. Cases involving extreme speed, etc., result in more convictions. [I-0414]

This theme also appears in a case where the defendant collides with a boy on a bicycle and where once again the jury acquits.

Hesitate to convict where the negligence is only slight or where it appears that it could happen to anyone, including members of the jury, if they were momentarily inattentive to their responsibility. [II-0677] [8]

Virtually all of our examples of inadvertent crime come from automobile homicide cases. We will look now at the few other cases of negligence.

In one odd case a prison guard is charged with negligently permitting the escape of a prisoner. It appears that after delivering food to the prisoners the guard leaves several doors unlocked and fails to observe that one prisoner is not in his cell. Overpowered and then locked in the cell himself, he is forced to surrender his car keys to two escaping prisoners. On this record the judge finds criminal negligence; the jury does not. The judge rates the jury verdict as "without any merit" and charges the jury with having completely ignored the evidence. The sources of the jury's leniency are perhaps disclosed in other comments of the judge. He describes the defendant as "rather dull and stupid," and the defendant offers as a defense that "I had not been properly trained as a guard." [II-0300] There seems to be reluctance on the part of the jury to hold

---

[8] Occasionally a traffic violation in which no accident has occurred comes before the jury. In one such case the judge explains: "Jury seems reluctant to convict in Traffic Court appeals unless it is shown there has been an accident — seem to put themselves in defendant's position." [II-0790]. Cf. page 266.

the defendant to the standard of a professional prison guard.[9]

Other cases involve the negligent use of firearms. In one such case the accident occurs while the parties are hunting. The judge finds the defendant guilty of negligent wounding; the jury hangs. The judge reports:

> The statute makes it a criminal offense to carelessly shoot or wound a human being while hunting. The negligence involved is simple as compared to criminal negligence. Juries are slow to convict. [I-0837]

A final illustration, another hunting accident, shows how stubborn a jury's resistance to the whole idea of inadvertent crime can be. The victim is a thirteen-year-old boy in a leather coat with a fur collar. The defendant claims he thought he was shooting a bobcat. The judge's reasons for calling the verdict a "miscarriage of justice" follow.

> The average case of an accidental shooting while hunting would scarcely merit a prosecution; and this is the first such case in the 30 years I have been about the courts of this county. This time, though, the District Attorney was well justified in bringing the case to trial. By a series of diagrams and photographs, some posed, the D.A. established to the satisfaction of any experienced person that the shooting was completely wanton, entirely lacked any justification. It is hard to believe that the defendant could have believed he was shooting at anything but a human being. Hard to see how the jury could not have been shocked into action. [I-0278]

[9] Not surprisingly, tort law has worked out refinements on the standards of required care, which criminal law has had little occasion to develop. The readiest example is that of the rural doctor who cannot be expected to perform at the level of a metropolitan specialist; the degree of his skill and learning has been held to be limited to that ordinarily possessed by physicians practicing in similar localities. Cf. Ferrell v. Ellis, 129 Iowa 614, 105 N.W. 993 (1906).

CHAPTER 25

On Insanity and Intoxication

In tracing jury sentiments we have found for the most part that where there is a policy controversy in the criminal law, the jury is likely to be moved by the competing considerations and make its own resolution of the conflict, usually a generous one for the defendant. But curiously, on the great debate over full personal competence and responsibility, much exercised in the literature these days,[1] the jury seems disengaged. The point is especially true with respect to the controversies over insanity as a defense and the debates over the M'Naghten

[1] Under the traditional M'Naghten doctrine the defense of insanity is established if the accused either did not know what he was doing or did not know that what he was doing was wrong. The adoption of the Durham rule by the criminal courts in the District of Columbia has given new focus to the debate. Under that rule the defense is established if the unlawful act is shown to have been the product of a mental disease or mental defect. This formula has been rejected by various federal courts. See, e.g., the detailed review in Sauer v. United States, 241 F.2d 640 (9th Cir. 1957). From the growing literature on this issue consult: Symposium, Insanity and the Criminal Law — A Critique of Durham v. United States, U. Chi. L. Rev., v. 22, p. 317 (1955); Krash, The Durham Rule and Judicial Administration of the Insanity Defense in the District of Columbia, Yale L.J., v. 70, p. 905 (1961); and Simon, The American Jury — The Defense of Insanity (1966).

In the Simon study, another segment of the Jury Project, some one hundred juries heard and deliberated in an actual courthouse on a mock experimental case presented by soundtrack to keep trial events and testimony constant. The experiment tested jury reactions, under three different sets of instructions: (a) following the M'Naghten rule, (b) following the Durham rule, and (c) under instructions which left the rules essentially to the jury itself. An additional variation concerned the psychiatric testimony.

rule. There is however some evidence that the jury does dissent from the law's position that total drunkenness is only a limited defense.

Appraisal of insanity pleas is not a pressing business for the jury today. The defense of insanity is raised in only 2 per cent of all the cases and three quarters of these are homicide cases; further, it may be recalled that the psychiatric expert appears in less than 2 per cent of all cases.[2]   And even where the defense is raised, it is almost never a source of disagreement.

A few of our cases give possible clues as to a distinctive jury reaction, although, on closer inspection the disagreement between jury and judge seems to evaporate.   In just two cases does the jury find the defendant not guilty by reason of insanity while the judge would have found him guilty.   One involves a son who shoots and kills his step-father, who, after a long history of mistreatment of the boy's mother, was physically abusing her in his presence.   After the verdict the defendant is committed to the state hospital. [II-0408]   The case, however, tells us little about the jury and insanity and seems easier to understand as a jury extension of self-defense when there is extreme provocation.[3]   Since the judge finds the defendant sane, this appears to be a sharp and relevant disagreement until we notice that the judge would have simply placed him on probation for a few years.   The difference between probation and commitment for temporary insanity is surely not great.

The second case also involves temporary insanity.   The charge is assault with attempt to murder in a case of domestic violence.   The jury's acquittal of the husband "by reason of temporary insanity" seems largely predicated on the circumstance that the wife dramatically reverses her stand and testifies on behalf of her husband at the trial.[4]   Although again the

[2] See Table 38.

[3] This case is also discussed in Chapter 16, The Boundaries of Self-Defense, at page 234.

[4] The case is discussed in Chapter 18, *De Minimis,* under the theme of the reluctant complainant, at page 272.

judge finds the defendant sane and guilty of the attempt to murder, he would have placed him on probation for just two years. [II-0678]

There is one of the rare references to the M'Naghten rule in another case, but once again the disagreement is too narrow to illumine a distinctive jury attitude. As the judge describes it, the defendant, a young man, "killed a young farm wife of his employer, together with an unborn child and a three-year-old child without apparent motive." The principal defense is insanity; the jury finds first degree manslaughter and the judge, first degree murder. The judge observes on the insanity issue:

> The question of insanity was determined under the M'Naghten rule. Under that rule, I believe he was sane, so did the jury. [II-0643]

The judge explains that the jury's greater leniency in this case stemmed from the fear that conviction of murder would carry the death penalty. On the judge's view the jury is sufficiently responsive to insanity to save the defendant from the death penalty, but no more;[5] it is willing to find him guilty and expose him to the penalties of first degree manslaughter.[6]

There is only one other case containing an explicit reference to the M'Naghten rules, and it is not appreciably more helpful. The defendant is charged with having poisoned his wife. The judge notes:

> The defendant had a long record of mental trouble both in the Army and since his discharge. He was admittedly suffering from mental abnormality, not, however, amounting to insanity under the M'Naghten rules in force in this state. [I-0869]

[5] See Chapter 35.

[6] There are two ironies in the case. First, as the judge indicates, the jury was wrong about the possibility of the death penalty as a matter of law. Even on a verdict of murder, it could have been imposed only if the jury so recommended. Second, even on the jury's lesser verdict, the judge sentenced the defendant to life imprisonment, the maximum penalty he could have received for murder, unless the jury had recommended the death penalty.

The jury apparently agrees and finds the defendant guilty of manslaughter; the judge's verdict would have been murder. But the judge adds a revealing comment about his own strategy

> The Court allowed the jury to consider whether leaving potassium cyanide in the house constituted criminal negligence which would support a verdict of manslaughter. The jury took this opportunity to bring in a verdict of less than murder. [I-0869] [7]

Thus these last cases suggest, albeit faintly, that the jury inclines toward a concept of reduced or diminished responsibility, under which insanity would mitigate but not exonerate.[8]

The question of diminished responsibility is put in another form in the case of a nineteen-year-old unmarried girl whom

---

[7] There are other instances of the judge's leading the jury to equity. Where defendant was charged with selling heroin to an undercover agent of the Narcotics Bureau, the jury finds him guilty of possession without intent to sell, a misdemeanor. The judge explains: "They obviously did not want to convict the defendant of selling. . . . With guidance from the court, juries often find the defendant in narcotics cases guilty of the lesser crime of possession, where the sale is solely to support defendant's own habit. This would have been a plea, but district attorney does not accept pleas from sellers." [II-0198] Compare the selective use of the judge's control powers discussed in Chapter 33.

[8] This is a concept which American law has not embraced apart from the recognition that gross intoxication may be incompatible with specific intent such as the deliberate premeditation required for a first degree murder charge. But see Taylor, Partial Insanity as Affecting the Degree of Crime — A Commentary on Fisher v. United States, Calif. L. Rev., v. 34, p. 625 (1946), and Weihofen and Overholser, Mental Disorder Affecting the Degree of a Crime, Yale L.J., v. 56, p. 959 (1947). The 1957 English Homicide Act recognized diminished responsibility, 5 & 6 Eliz. 2, CH. 11, §2. Borderline insanity is its essence. Regina v. Walden [Eng. 1959], Weekly L.R., 1008, 1012. The Model Penal Code includes a concept of diminished responsibility in capital cases, proof of which will avoid the death penalty: "[E]vidence that the capacity of the defendant to appreciate the criminality [wrongfulness] of his conduct or to conform his conduct to the requirements of law was impaired as a result of mental disease or defect is admissible in favor of sentence of imprisonment." A.L.I., Model Penal Code §4.02 (2), Proposed Official Draft (1962).

the state charges with the murder of her minutes-old baby. The judge convicts of murder, the jury, only of voluntary manslaughter.   The judge explains:

> Infanticide in this state is unknown; we try homicide of infants under the homicide statutes. [II-0021] [9]

A final case presents on its facts a classic insanity situation but somehow still misses being a useful illustration of the jury's response to insane behavior.   The case tells a strange and terrible story of a young, married college student, handsome and well-to-do with no prior record, who after a long period of drinking visits a fifty-year-old woman living alone in a trailer court occupied mostly by GI college families.   He is charged with a pointless and fantastic murder which the judge describes thus:

> Dismemberment of female breast, invagination by knife, throat cut; even pet dog killed.

And in describing the defendant, the judge said:

> Handsome, fine looking parents and brothers. As hard to believe involvement of his type in this crime as of your own son. On the other hand, he was cold, flat, and controlled in all responses.

[9] Many modern criminal codes accept the jury's reduction of this type of homicide to manslaughter, giving recognition to the vulnerable state of mind in which a mother finds herself after giving birth, usually unassisted, to an illegitimate child. See the English Infanticide Act, 1 & 2 Geo. 6, c. 361. (1) (1938). "Before the passing of the Infanticide Act, 1922, heartrending scenes occurred when young girls who had killed their illegitimate children were found guilty of murder and had to face the dread ordeal of being sentenced to death. Almost everyone in court might realise that the sentence would never be carried out; but the girl herself, and her distraught mother at the back of the court, would unfortunately be the exceptions. The Act of 1922 removed some but by no means all the occasions on which the law demanded the obscene mockery of a death sentence that was not seriously intended." Williams, The Proof of Guilt, p. 300, London (1955).

For a discussion of whether the law of homicide might make further special dispensations, see Kalven, A Special Corner of Civil Liberties — A Legal View 1 (Symposium, Morals and Medicine and the Law), N.Y.U.L. Rev., v. 31, p. 1223, esp. pp. 1234-1237 (1956).

The defense appears not to have put the insanity issue squarely but rather to have highlighted other facts such as intoxication and unconsciousness.[10]   The judge finds second degree murder; the jury hangs, with eight jurors voting for conviction.   The judge suggests a clue as to what might have influenced some of the jury.

> The very horror of the crime by a youth of better than average background may probably have made some jurors feel that defendant could not have known what he was doing. [II-1122]

The materials on intoxication are a good deal more interesting than those on insanity.[11]   In general the law has taken a firm stand against voluntary intoxication as a defense.   Even if the defendant was grossly drunk, the law will only allow the defense that he was unable to form a specific intent, such as that required for assault "with intent to kill."   But even though he is grossly drunk and in fact does not have an intent, the law still holds him liable for assault and in this sense imputes an intent to him.   This curious set of compromises in the criminal law on intoxication has often been criticized.[12]

---

[10] The defense of momentary unconsciousness is raised in two further cases.   In an automobile manslaughter case the jury apparently accepts the defense claim of a blackout and reduces the charge.   [II-0488]   In the second, a murder case, the jury again reduces the charge to manslaughter, where the defendant claims to suffer from "variation of consciousness" due to hypoglycemia.   The judge comments, "First defense of this kind in my rather long experience in criminal law."   [I-0172]

[11] There is a small group of cases which offer coercion as a defense, but it does not appear that the jury is any more responsive to it than the law has been.   In any event, there is no indication that the jury takes a distinctive view about coercion, and the few disagreements in the sample seem to result from credibility problems.

[12] Hall, General Principles of Criminal Law, p. 553 (2d ed. 1960). Hall suggests: "Certain astute critics . . . have argued that a solution of the problem requires penalization for the voluntary intoxication and complete exculpation for the harm committed under gross intoxication."   Section 523 of the Austrian Penal Code, for example, punishes as a misdemeanor the commission of a felony while in the state of complete drunkenness.   The American Law Institute, Model Penal

It cannot be said that there is any jury-revolt against the present law, yet there is evidence that the jury is aware of the problem and is moved to leniency if the defendant was drunk. The response is a narrow and subtle one. If due to intoxication the defendant has done something that is utterly out of character for him, the jury may be moved to charge the crime to "demon rum" and not to the defendant.[13]

Thus, where an employee in a chicken dressing plant is charged with knifing the foreman of his department, the defense is that he was drunk at the time and does not remember what happened. The jury finds him guilty only of a lesser charge. The judge emphasizes that the defendant had a good reputation and that his frankness in admitting that he was drunk was impressive. The judge adds:

> Unusual for defendant to admit he was drunk. Ordinarily, this defense does not appeal to a jury, but in this case it did since he was known to most of the jurors and had a clear record. [I-0587]

In a similar case drunkenness combines with restitution to make the defendant a sympathetic character in the eyes of the jury.[14] Here the defendant, an employee in a sandwich shop, commits burglary on the premises. The jury opts for a lesser charge, and the judge offers the following explanation:

> Defendant was under the influence of intoxicant at the time and made full restitution, a week after the crime, to the victim who was reluctant to prosecute. [II-0263]

Code rejects voluntary intoxication as a defense unless it negates an element of the offense or is pathological. Pathological intoxication is defined as grossly excessive in degree, given the amount of the intoxicant, to which the actor does not know he is susceptible. §2.08(1), (4), and (5)c, Proposed Official Draft (1962).

[13] In the view of the common law, this is to take one vice as the excuse for another. " 'A drunkard,' says Sir Edward Coke, 'who is *voluntarius daemon,* hath no privilege thereby; but what hurt or ill soever he doth, his drunkenness does aggravate it.' " Blackstone, Commentaries, v. IV, p. 26 (1791), citing Coke, Inst., v. 1, p. 247.

[14] See the discussion of restitution as a ground for jury leniency in Chapter 18, *De Minimis,* pages 269-270.

Where the defendant is charged with killing a man with a knife in a tavern quarrel while drunk, the jury again responds to the impact of liquor on a normally good character. It acquits, although the judge finds second degree murder. The defendant "was a good worker, friendly with everyone, never heard anybody say an unkind thing about him." [II-1203]

Where a defendant is charged with second degree murder for having killed his friend "while both were drinking at a Saturday night party," the jury finds only manslaughter. The judge sees clearly the sentiment of the jury.

> Defendant killed victim while intoxicated; otherwise wouldn't have done so. Apparently was sorry for his impulsive act. [II-0003]

The alteration of character theme is suggested more dramatically by the next case. The defendant, a young man in his early twenties, is accused of forcing three boys, with ages ranging from nine to twelve, to engage in homosexual practices. The jury acquits. The judge reports:

> Defendant testified that he was so intoxicated that he did not know what he was doing and even at the date of the trial did not remember what occurred on the night the offense was alleged to have been committed. All witnesses for the state including the boys alleged to have been assaulted, testified that he was "bad drunk."

The judge also tells us that the jury came back to request a re-reading of the instructions, "particularly as to drunkenness being a defense if defendant was intoxicated to the extent he could not have had requisite intent." Normally the jury shows hostility to homosexuality, especially with younger partners;[15] in this case, however, the defendant's extreme drunkenness serves to establish him in the eyes of the jury as not a true, or at least not a conscious, homosexual. The judge adds:

> I think that the fact that defendant had no previous record and was badly intoxicated on the night in question was the controlling factor in this case. [I-3044]

[15] Homosexuality has the lowest net leniency rate among the sex crimes, except for commercial vice. See Table 19.

Where intoxication cannot be said to take the defendant out of character, the jury may nevertheless react to it on the ground that it blunts a requisite criminal intent, expanding thereby the law's response to the problems of intent. In an odd case the defendant is charged with receipt of stolen property. A burglar gave the defendant a stolen watch as a gift, in itself an unusual instance of the crime of receiving stolen goods. The source of the jury's disagreement is explained in the following comment of the judge.

> Lack of intention to keep the watch and drinking to such an extent he did not know what he was doing. [II-0445]

In another case the defendant borrows a friend's car in order to see a girl friend. He gets drunk, drives to a neighboring town where he parks in front of a bar, and later comes out to find the car stolen. He is charged with theft and with the special statutory offense of joy-riding.[16] The judge finds him guilty of both charges; the jury acquits. The judge stresses that the defendant was an alcoholic, drunk at the time. Rating the jury's response as "without any merit," he adds.

> I feel that the jury must have thought that since the defendant was very intoxicated during the course of his joy riding that he could not have been guilty of taking this car with the intent of currently or temporarily depriving the owner of its possession. Of course, they were instructed that voluntary intoxication is no defense. [II-0708]

In a final case the intoxication operates to take the sting out of the defendant's conduct and to make him appear playful rather than criminal. Here the defendant, a college student, enters a restaurant while drunk, places a toy gun in the back of the waitress, demands the contents of the cash register, and then flees without the money. He is indicted for attempted

---

[16] To establish the crime of joy-riding, it is sufficient to prove that the defendant intended to use the car without permission, even if he intended to return it. E.g., Cal. Vehicle Code §10851. Some states refuse the joy-riding distinction and provide for the same punishment, usually one year and/or $1000, for auto theft "temporarily or otherwise." E.g., Ill. Rev. Stat. 95½, §4-102(a) (1963).

robbery. It appears that there was some prior record of the defendant's playing jokes like this, but two bartenders testify on his behalf, along with faculty members and fellow students. The judge places the jury's disagreement in part on the ground that "they believed that alcohol was really to blame as perhaps it was." [I-0422]

CHAPTER 26

A Note on Crime in a Subculture

It is commonplace that American society is to an unusual degree not a single homogeneous culture; in a favorite word of social science, the society is pluralistic. Conceivably, the law might recognize cultural differences and apply different norms to subcultures within the society, as indeed British colonialism appears to have done on occasion.[1] But only in rare instances has American law encountered this issue. The examples that come to mind are of religious sects such as the Mormons and the Quakers. In the case of the Mormons the law has forced them to accept the general standard of monogamy,[2] while in the case of the Quakers, when the law recog-

---

[1] Consider, for example, the following instructions to the jury in the trial of an aboriginal for murder: "The strict statement of the rule is that a reasonable man has to be deprived of his self-control. You may use these words . . . as meaning a reasonable native inhabitant of Australia. You may draw a distinction between the amount of provocation which is needed before the ordinary reasonable being, such as you are, could lose his self control, and the lesser [degree of provocation], if you think it applies, needed before an aboriginal of Australia loses his self-control." Again, in a murder case in Northern Australia where the significance of the time interval between provocation and the act was at issue, the judge instructed as follows: "If the accused in this case were a white person I should have to tell you as a matter of law that the defence of provocation would not be open because . . . a sufficient time had elapsed between the time he was wounded and the time he struck [the victim] for passions to have died down. But the accused is not a white man. . . ." Howard, What Colour is the "Reasonable Man"? Crim. Law Review, 1961, pp. 41-46.

[2] Reynolds v. United States, 98 U.S. 145 (1878). See the discussion in Kurland, Religion and the Law, p. 21 (1962).

nized their distinctive claim it did this in the form of a general exemption for conscientious objectors.[3]

In this study, in a handful of disagreements, the judges' explanations seem to open suggestively onto this large theme of subculture. But while these comments are insistent, there is a good deal of doubt that this time they succeed in isolating a special jury sentiment.

Not unexpectedly, the cases have a racial cast.[4] In crimes of violence committed by Negroes against Negroes, or Indians against Indians, the jury is, as the judge sees it, moved at times to leniency because it views the defendant as not fully acculturated and therefore incapable of white standards of self-control.

It scarcely needs mention that this explanation, uncongenial as it is to contemporary mood, tends to speak more in the language of contempt than in that of tolerance.

In the end, the theme remains evanescent. The materials are sketchy and crossed with other interpretations. Thus, we do little more here than report out these cases.

In a case from the South a Negro woman shoots and kills her husband; the judge would have given the death penalty on a finding of first degree murder, the jury reduces the charge to first degree manslaughter, and the judge comments:

> Negroes are not held to the same moral responsibility as white people. . . . Negroes kill each other without reason other than the immediate urge at the time. . . . Community

[3] It has been a notable feature of the various draft laws that Congress made an exemption from military service for citizens who by religious training and belief are conscientiously opposed to war. The treatment of the alien with such scruples in the naturalization cases has provided a famous chapter in Supreme Court adjudication. United States v. Schwimmer, 279 U.S. 644 (1929); United States v. Macintosh, 283 U.S. 605 (1931); Girouard v. United States, 328 U.S. 61 (1946). Compare In re Summers, 325 U.S. 561 (1945) (admission to the bar denied). See generally Sibley and Jacob, Conscription of Conscience — The American State and the Conscientious Objector, 1940-1947 (1952).

[4] One can easily think of other groups on the outskirts of society that might qualify for special sentiment, e.g., homosexuals, nudists, and derelicts.

regards the law as too severe for some Negro cases because of lack of moral sense. [II-0077]

In another case from the South where a Negro man and woman living in the same house get into a quarrel and the man kills her with a shotgun, the judge explains the disagreement in much the same way:

This verdict in my opinion is due somewhat to the fact that juries give much more latitude to colored folks than to white. They know how liable colored folks are to act on impulse by shooting and cutting. [I-0478]

In another instance of domestic violence, this time however from the North, a wife throws lye into the face of her husband. The jury finds only simple assault, and the judge explains the disagreement:

Defendant and common-law husband are colored. If they had been white, I think the verdict would have been given on the first charge. Our juries are loathe to hold colored people to as high standards as white people. [I-0915]

There are two further illustrations of the theme in cases of Negro-Negro violence.

Probably because of the fact that defendant and his wife were illiterate Negroes and the jury did not feel like holding the defendant to the same responsibility as it would a white man under the same circumstances. [I-0041]

If this had been a white man he would have been convicted. Negroes in cases of this type receive more than equal rights; juries seem to think it's okay for them to cut, if it's another colored person that is cut. [I-0894]

The point may not be confined to Negroes. There is more than a suggestion of it in a homicide case where the judge, after giving other reasons for the disagreement, states:

None, except the parties were both Indians and jurors can't get excited about the fact one Indian kills another Indian. [I-2029] [5]

[5] Compare Case I-3287: "A hillbilly venereal affair."

Despite the emphasis with which the judge's comments have been made[6] there are substantial difficulties with accepting this sub-culture explanation. To begin with, there are not enough cases to persuade. The explanation is couched in simple general terms[7] and requires no more than Negroes in a crime of violence; yet we have many disagreement cases in intra-racial crimes of violence which the judge explains on other grounds while keeping silent about the sub-culture theme.[8] More troublesome, the few cases we have here are largely instances of *domestic* violence between Negroes. We have already seen that the jury is sensitive to domestic tension and is ready to treat its eruption into violence on generous analogy to self-defense.[9] At best then the Negro sub-culture point would be reduced to the thesis that the jury is especially willing to acknowledge domestic tension as a mitigating factor where Negroes are involved. This may be true, but it must be a

[6] There is a kind of corroboration for the point in urban police practice. "An officer [in a Detroit Negro precinct] learned that a Negro woman had seriously stabbed her husband with a pair of scissors. The husband commented that there had been a little argument and requested transportation to the hospital. The officer, who had served in the precinct for some time, had reported to such calls in the past and had received similar responses. Although the conduct constituted a felonious assault, no official action was taken." LaFave, Arrest — The Decision to Take a Suspect into Custody, p. 110 (1965).

[7] For the importance of such stylistic clues in evaluating an explanation see Chapter 7, pages 95-96.

[8] The over-all verdict pattern for intra-racial crimes offers no confirmation. See note 15 below.

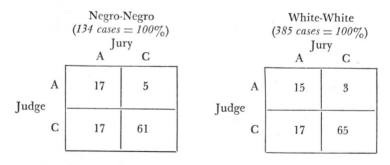

Negro-Negro
(*134 cases = 100%*)

		Jury A	Jury C
Judge	A	17	5
	C	17	61

White-White
(*385 cases = 100%*)

		Jury A	Jury C
Judge	A	15	3
	C	17	65

[9] These cases are discussed in Chapter 16, pages 231-236.

subtle matter indeed when we recall the readiness of the jury's response to the blonde young wife who shoots her husband. In our society, we suspect, domestic tension is not a distinctive attribute of the married Negro.

As a sort of postscript of dissatisfaction with this line of explanation, we would note that we may have one case too many: the defendant, a Negro, shoots the mother of his child. The jury finds murder in the first degree and the judge comments that the verdict "was fully supported by the proof." But he would have found only second degree murder, because the defendant was a Negro and the real reason was "just anger and resentment." He then goes on to say:

> The ancestors of this defendant came from the jungle of Africa only a few generations ago. Society expected too much from him. He killed the woman because he had insufficient intelligence to solve his problem any other way. [I-0482]

The power with which the judge puts this to explain his own verdict rounds out the doubt that we have located a distinctive jury sentiment.[10]

Originally we expected the study to yield considerable evidence on whether or not the jury is color blind. Actually it has been possible to collect only a few scattered findings. The Negro appears as defendant more frequently than the Negro share of the population would predict,[11] although he elects jury trial proportionately.[12] He is at some disadvantage in the quality of counsel, even when we control for economic position.[13]

The Negro defendant, furthermore, is less likely to be seen

---

[10] This example of a judge giving expression to an alleged jury sentiment is to be distinguished from the phenomenon of ambivalent sentiments where, on the same issue, different juries take opposite stands, e.g., "wet" and "dry" juries. See the discussion of ambivalence in Chapter 31, and data collected in Table 100.

[11] See Tables 60 and 61.

[12] See Table 63.

[13] See Table 86. This will be shown in Chapter 28, The Impact of the Lawyer.

as sympathetic, a factor established as a major influence on jury leniency.[14] Finally, there is the possible offset, examined in this chapter, that in *intra*-racial crimes the Negro may occasionally be the beneficiary of an unfriendly sentiment.

There is some awkwardness in announcing these conclusions at a time when the most controversial aspect of the American jury is the spectacle of southern juries in civil rights cases. To be sure there is a sense in which this southern reaction transcends hostility to the Negro, as in the Liuzzo case, where a white defendant was charged with killing a white woman. In any event, this study has no data on this problem. Two points need be made. First, the field work for this study ended before the present wave of civil rights activity began. Second, however, the sample, even if drawn seasonably, might easily miss the spectacular but relatively infrequent case.[15]

[14] Table 66.

[15] Civil rights cases apart, the limitations of the sample make it impossible to say anything about inter-racial crimes. What little we have, however, shows a precarious imbalance in favor of the white defendants, but the number of cases in the White vs. Negro group is very small.

Serious Crimes by Race of Defendant and Victim
(Per Cent Jury Disagreement Where Judge Convicts)

| | Clear | | Close | |
Defendant-Victim	No Record Stand	Other	No Record Stand	Other
N-N	9	—	64	41
Wh-Wh	15	17	63	39
Difference	−6%	−17%	+1%	+2%
N-Wh	7	—	58	8
Wh-N *	—	50	67	100
Difference	—	−50%	−9%	−92%
* Number of Wh-N cases	—	2	3	1

"Almost without any exception non-European [read: black] prisoners, who constituted the overwhelming bulk of persons accused, elected to be tried by a judge with or without assessors. Thus almost at the strike of a pen the jury system [without black jurors] began to disappear." (Leslie Blackwell, Of Judges and Justice, Cape Town, 1965, p. 112.)

An Anthology of
Non-recurring Sentiments

The detailed survey of jury sentiments on law ends with a residuum of cases in which the jury is clearly reacting to a law sentiment but where the particular sentiment, however vivid and important, appears in only a single case. This is but another way of saying that these sentiments were so specific as to defy classification into one of the broader categories of reasons. We have, therefore, a small number of disagreements on law sentiments which are, so to speak, left over.[1] Unlike the earlier chapters which showed how the jury expanded by analogy a core sentiment, this chapter is a collection of idiosyncracies, an anthology of non-recurring sentiments.

In the first case the defendant, the operator of a bowling alley, is charged with violating the child labor laws by employing minors. The defendant has an attractive personality, a good reputation, and is generally liked in the community. The judge's explanation of the jury's acquittal is totally convincing.

> Jury would not go along with state law. Figured poor kids could make some money and keep 'em off street. Place was well operated and not a bad place to work. [I-0700]

[1] There is perhaps some arbitrariness in deciding that these explanations defy classification. The cases, at any rate, clearly bespeak sentiments on the law and are so few in number that it makes no appreciable difference whether we treat them as idiosyncratic or analogize them to the previous sub-categories.

It is not easy to see what sensible generalization could be made from the sentiment the jury expresses here. Clearly it is not hostile to criminal enforcement of child labor laws, rather, the case is an example of the law's failure to do equity in the classic sense; here, because of its generality, the law is found to apply to a case where the policy behind the law is not in fact involved.

A different jury policy is reflected in a child stealing case in which the jury acquits while the judge convicts. The defendant met a fourteen-year-old girl on a cattle ranch. The two eloped and lived on another ranch until they were located by her parents. The defendant, charged with removing a minor from her home,[2] is acquitted. The jury may well have thought that this particular charge made little sense as a matter of policy once the couple were married, and happily so. The judge tells us:

> Fourteen year old, rather well developed, and stated she loved the defendant. She was glad to be married and away from the tribulations at home. [I-0056]

A third sentiment is suggested where the defendant is charged with passing a worthless check. His story is that the complainant asked him for a loan, whereupon, as a joke, he signed a check in blank and gave it to her, and she filled in the amount of $1000. There were no funds in defendant's bank account. The judge finds a technical violation; the jury acquits. At least three odd points converge to explain the jury's response here. First, as the judge indicates, it believes the defendant's story that the whole thing was a joke.[3] Moreover,

---

[2] Some states have, apart from their kidnaping law, a provision threatening with imprisonment "a person who maliciously, forcibly or fraudulently takes or entices away a child under the age of seventeen years with intent to detain and conceal the child from its parent. . . ." Ariz. Pen. Code §13-841 (1956).

[3] We have met with two other cases where the defense was that the apparent crime was committed in a spirit of fun. In each the jury acquits, suggesting that it may have a broader sense of humor than the law. See Chapter 18 at page 265 [theft of keys to a police car, I-1398] and Chapter 25 at page 337 [robbery with a toy gun, I-0422].

there is the suggestion of some spite on the girl's part in finally presenting the check for payment. And indeed it is not altogether easy to see what evil results from giving a worthless check as a loan. [I-1073]

There is a case where the government itself appears to the jury to be cast in the role of a private litigant, exploiting the criminal law, in order to collect a debt. The jury will have none of it. The defendant, a concessionaire under contract to the government to pay rent on the basis of income received, is charged with criminally defrauding the government by making false reports as to sales. The judge makes the theme clear.

> Jury probably became convinced that controversy was in reality an issue or dispute over rent due and was not truly a criminal matter. It is evident to me that the jury was firmly convinced that the issue was civil rather than criminal.

And he continues:

> While I would have convicted the defendant, I am not at all sure but that the jury was in accord with substantial justice, although contrary to the technical violation conclusively established by the evidence. [I-1975]

A further strand of jury sentiment is furnished by a federal income tax evasion case where the defendant is charged with not having reported his full income. He defends on the ground that he accurately reported his net income since he had incurred special business expenses in the form of black market bonuses paid for materials needed in his business. The jury, thus given a chance to test the public policy against black market bonuses as legitimate business items, votes to acquit the defendant. [I-2053]

This particular series of cases is brought to a close with a case where the defendant, charged with failure to support an illegitimate child, defends on the arresting ground that "to force him to provide for an illegitimate child would force a hardship on his wife and legitimate children." [I-0430] The jury nods and acquits.

*C*HAPTER 28 ON THE lawyer is in texture comparable to Chapter 15 on the defendant, and it brings to a close our lengthy survey of the reasons for the normal disagreement. We appropriately hold it until the last so that the materials on which the lawyer must operate and which he tries to exploit are already before the reader.

It is tempting for the lawyer to see himself as the central figure in the drama of the criminal trial; he is often a producer, in many ways a director, and certainly a chief actor in it. But there is a limiting factor: the lawyer's role is played within an adversary system.

This chapter traces the situations in which an imbalance in the lawyers' skill causes a disagreement between judge and jury.

CHAPTER 28

The Impact of the Lawyer

It is a point of fascination to the trial lawyer to find out how important he really is. And, it is one of the more popular assumptions about the jury that it tends to "try the lawyers," that, unlike the judge, it is susceptible to the skill and rhetoric of trial counsel and that he may well be a major determinant of the jury's decision. The very legends of the bar's heroes, of the Erskines, the Choates, the Darrows, imply that lawyers of their caliber would make a decisive difference in any case; a view that is given perfect poetic expression in Benêt's "The Devil and Daniel Webster," where it will be recalled Webster is so skillful an advocate that he wins a case against the Devil himself, in a trial in which both judge and jury are of the Devil's choosing.

In its more sober moments the bar must feel some perplexity in separating its role from the myriad other factors which bear upon the decision of a case. While our study does not remotely exhaust the rich significance of the lawyer's role, it provides a first systematic insight into it.

The role of the lawyer in the criminal case has been acquiring great constitutional prestige. The right of a criminal defendant to counsel has occupied the United States Supreme Court with increasing frequency in the last thirty years, and recently there has been something of a constitutional revolution in this area. For a long time the Court had read the Sixth Amendment as requiring only the Federal Government to provide counsel for federal criminal defendants unable to afford one. After handling the obligation of the states on a case by case basis, the Court in 1963, in *Gideon,* went the whole way and held that the states too have an obligation for counsel comparable to that of the Federal Government.[1] The impressive official view today is that the role of counsel in a criminal trial is so critical and important that where necessary it is an obligation on the Government to see that the role is filled.[2]

The study does not touch however, except incidentally, on the problem of the indigent defendant without counsel. Rather, it deals with the more subtle imbalance that results from the unequal performance of opposing counsel, an imbalance which the law cannot easily correct. While this issue may lack the dramatic impact of the indigent defendant without counsel, it is not without its broader implications. It would disturb if the outcome of criminal trials were recurringly determined not by the merits of the case but by the happenstance of which counsel was superior.

[1] Gideon v. Wainwright, 372 U.S. 335 (1963).

[2] Counsel was not always regarded as so important. Not until 1836, for instance, did English law recognize the right of a defendant to be represented by retained counsel in all felony cases. The development of American constitutional law on the point dates from the Scottsboro case, Powell v. Alabama, 287 U.S. 45 (1932). Not until 1938 in Johnson v. Zerbst, 304 U.S. 458, did the Court hold that the Sixth Amendment required the appointment of counsel in all federal criminal trials. The major precedent prior to Gideon was Betts v. Brady, 316 U.S. 455 (1942), which limited the states' obligation to provide counsel to cases where absence of counsel would be "highly prejudicial." In the years following, the Court, on a case-by-case basis, specified just what it considered highly prejudicial. This body of law has now largely been superseded by the Gideon case. But it is not yet clear just how far this decision goes, whether, for example, it covers all misdemeanors. It also remains uncertain to what extent incompetence of defense counsel will be treated as a constitutional shortcoming.

The legal developments have been widely commented upon. See for instance, Report, U.S. Atty. Gen. Committee on Poverty and the Admin. of Fed. Crim. Justice (F. A. Allen, ch., 1963); Israel, Gideon v. Wainwright: The "Art" of Overruling, 1963 Sup. Ct. Rev., p. 211. For a less technical account see Lewis, Gideon's Trumpet (1964) which first appeared as a series of three articles in the New Yorker magazine.

As to the continental European situation, in general the codes of criminal procedure provide that in a trial above the misdemeanor level the defendant must be represented by counsel.

The lawyer, of course, cannot work independently of the merits of the case as the jury sees them. His role is to accentuate those factors of the case likely to move the jury to his side — the very factors that have been traced in detail in the preceding chapters. It seemed appropriate, therefore, to have reserved the discussion of the lawyer's role, so as to have behind us a full sense of the materials on which he works.

Since the data on this point are of some complexity, it will be helpful to divide the discussion into three major subsections:

(i) Data on how often and in what particulars one counsel is superior to his adversary.

(ii) Detailed comments provided by the judge in the course of his reason assessment as to precisely what technique or characteristic of the lawyer establishes his margin of superiority.

(iii) An effort to measure the impact of the defense counsel on disagreements, first by reason assessment and then by cross-tabulation.

The chapter accordingly has a long plot line. It begins with some simple but fresh descriptive data about the incidence of disparity between counsel.

The Sample II version of the questionnaire asked the following question:

Was the case tried equally well on both sides?

☐ Yes
☐ No, prosecutor was better
☐ No, defense lawyer was better[3]

---

[3] The questionnaire for Sample I asked the question somewhat differently:

Was the defendant's attorney an experienced trial lawyer?
☐ Yes ☐ No

Was the prosecuting attorney an experienced trial lawyer?
☐ Yes ☐ No

If one question was answered "yes" and the other "no," imbalance of counsel was inferred. Where both questions were answered "yes" or "no," counsel were regarded as equal.

The response to this question, giving the trial judge's vote on the lawyer, provides unique information on the quality of legal counsel in criminal trials in the United States today.

Since the judge's ratings are general, they serve to disclose only major disparities in ability and skill; lawyers rated as equivalent may still differ substantially in important respects. It is therefore safe to infer that when the judge does report a disparity between lawyers, the difference will be a substantial one.

Table 82 gives the major descriptive statistic: the frequency with which defense counsel was superior to the prosecutor and, conversely, the prosecutor superior to defense counsel.

TABLE 82

Relative Strength of Prosecutor and Defense Counsel

	Per Cent
Superior defense	11
Balanced	76
Superior prosecution	13
Total	100%
Number of cases	3576

Table 82[4] makes two important points about the functioning of the criminal trial system. In a surprisingly large number of cases the judge rates counsel as equal and thus establishes that

[4] Table 82 gives the combined results for Samples I and II, which separately yield the following data:

	Sample I	Sample II
	%	%
Defense superior	11	11
Both equal	76	77
Prosecution superior	13	12
	100%	100%
Number of cases	2385	1191

for three fourths of the criminal trials no problem of a serious imbalance of counsel exists.   To the extent that there is an imbalance, it is roughly as often in favor of the defense as it is in favor of the prosecution.   Whatever the impact of superior counsel on the jury may be, Table 82 is in a general way highly reassuring as to the evenhandedness of our trial justice.[5]

This basic profile of the legal representation for criminal defendants can be refined along various dimensions, such as economic status, race, and the nature of the crime charged.   Table 83 sets forth the relevant data on the defendant's economic status, a factor one would expect to bear heavily on the imbalance of counsel.

The total frequency of imbalanced counsel is about the same in each group, but the direction is different.   The impoverished defendant's counsel is slightly more likely to be inferior and less likely to be superior than counsel for defendants above the poverty level.

---

[5] The data do not, it should be observed, tell anything about the level of skill at which this even-handedness is achieved.   Equality of counsel may result from inferior performance on both sides, and superiority may result simply from the advantage that mediocre counsel has over inferior counsel.   Some light is thrown on this by the information from the Sample I question, which was put in terms of "experience" of counsel (see note 3 above).

	Equal Counsel
	%
Both experienced	91
Both inexperienced	9
	100%
Number of cases	*1820*

The data give added assurance as to quality of counsel; whenever counsel are equally matched, they are so for the most part because they are both experienced.

We must assume that the judge's rating is not limited to the lawyer's performance in the courtroom, but covers as well the degree of his preparation, which especially in criminal cases may often reflect economic status.   See Table 83 below.

TABLE 83

Economic Status of Defendant and Imbalance of Counsel

	Average and Well-to-Do %	Poor %
Superior defense	12	9
Balanced	78	78
Superior prosecution	10	13
Total	100%	100%
Number of cases (Sample II)	682	509
Imbalance	(12 − 10 =) 2%	(9 − 13 =) − 4%
Difference	6%	

Turning to another factor, Table 84 gives the over-all picture of how well-represented Negro defendants are. Using our measure of disparity, it can be seen that the quality of counsel furnished to Negro defendants, as contrasted to white defendants, is inferior in 5 per cent of the cases, but once again the imbalance is small.

TABLE 84

Race of Defendant and Imbalance of Counsel

	White %	Negro %
Superior defense	12	7
Balanced	76	81
Superior prosecution	12	12
Total	100%	100%
Number of cases (Sample II)	839	352
Imbalance	+ 0%	− 5%
Difference	5%	

Since the impact of both race and economic status on the quality of legal representation raises points of considerable interest, it is worthwhile to pause and refine these comparisons. Table 85 shows, as expected, that there is a correlation between race and lower economic status. The proportion of poor defendants among Negroes is markedly greater (58 per cent) than among whites (36 per cent).

TABLE 85

Race and Economic Status

	White %	Negro %
Average and well-to-do	64	42
Poor	36	58
Total	100%	100%
Number of cases (Sample II)	*839*	*352*

To make the comparison as exact as possible, one would like to see how much of the counsel imbalance is due to economic status and how much to race. Table 86 gives the needed information.

TABLE 86

Economic Status, Race, and Imbalance of Counsel

	White		Negro	
	Average %	Poor %	Average %	Poor %
Superior defense	13	12	7	6
Balanced	75	76	84	80
Superior prosecution	12	12	9	14
Total	100%	100%	100%	100%
Number of cases (Sample II)	*534*	*305*	*148*	*204*
Imbalance	+ 1%	0%	− 2%	− 8%
Difference	1%		6%	

Table 86 makes it evident that the economic imbalance of counsel affects primarily the Negro defendant; being poor leads to less adequate representation only for the Negro defendant.[6] Nevertheless, we are again surprised that the dis-

[6] It turns out that for the white defendant the relative frequency of superior defense as compared to superior prosecution is the same, whether he comes from an average or poor background. For the Negro there is an obverse imbalance, even if he comes from an average background and more so if he is poor.

parity is not greater. Even the impoverished Negro defendant has in $(80 + 6 =)$ 86 per cent of all cases counsel equal to or superior to that of the prosecution.

We did not have the foresight to ask whether counsel was privately hired, appointed by the court, or provided by a public defender or other sources.[7] It may well be that the lack of disparity between prosecution and defense in the representation of the poor criminal defendant is due, in large part, to counsel from such auxiliary sources, which would be a highly significant point. In any event, all of the data converge on the benign conclusion that the representation of the poor criminal defendant, once the case goes to trial, is better than might have been expected.[8]

Determining the disparity of counsel by crime adds another insight into the process by which trial counsel is recruited. Does the imbalance of counsel vary from crime to crime? The balance between defense and prosecution, of course, depends not only on the quality of defense counsel but on the quality of his opponent. Here is another connection between trial tactics and game theory.[9] Where should the strategists for prosecution and defense allocate their skilled players?

Table 87 lists for all crimes the percentage of cases in which there is superior defense counsel and the percentage in which there is superior prosecution counsel, together with the resulting measure of imbalance.

The unthinking expectation might be, in keeping with television programs, that homicide would show the highest superiority of defense counsel. Actually, homicide has an al-

[7] The various sources of counsel are evaluated in Silverstein, Defense of the Poor in Criminal Cases in American State Courts (1965). See note 11 below.

[8] This does not solve the problem of representation prior to trial. The Gideon case and our data concern the presence of counsel only at the trial stage, leaving untouched the aid of counsel in the often crucial preliminary stages. Cf. Escobedo v. Illinois, 378 U.S. 478 (1964).

[9] We have had other occasions to relate the two: for the choice in the area of guilty pleas and jury waiver, see page 26; and for cases in which counsel must decide whether he should let a defendant with a record testify, see pages 144-145.

TABLE 87

Imbalance of Counsel by Type of Crime

	(1) Superior Defense %	(2) Superior Prosecution %	(1)—(2) Net im- balance* %	Number of Cases
Income tax evasion	32	5	+ 27	22
Perjury	32	5	+ 27	19
Gambling	22	6	+ 16	49
Kidnaping	23	8	+ 15	13
Game laws and other regulatory offenses	26	15	+ 11	46
Arson	10	—	+ 10	31
Negligent homicide	13	5	+ 8	94
Fraud, embezzlement, extortion	16	9	+ 7	142
Prostitution, Mann Act	21	14	+ 7	42
Drunken driving, traffic offenses	13	10	+ 3	560
Simple assault	17	15	+ 2	78
Narcotics	11	10	+ 1	192
Homicide	9	8	+ 1	289
Receiving stolen goods	−8	8	—	14
Escape	—	—	—	51
Serious assault	12	13	− 1	292
Burglary, breaking and entering	10	12	− 2	298
Non-support, other family laws	9	12	− 3	77
Rape	6	10	− 4	176
Larceny	14	19	− 5	170
Liquor laws	7	12	− 5	133
Other sex crimes	9	14	− 5	194
Robbery	9	15	− 6	229
Mail theft	8	17	− 9	12
Bribery, misconduct	—	13	− 13	39
Forgery, bad check	9	24	− 15	112
Public disorder	15	34	− 19	67
Auto theft	3	22	− 19	111
Concealed weapons	—	22	− 22	23
Total all crimes	11%	13%	− 2%	3576

* Percentages for "balanced counsel" are omitted; they can be computed by subtracting the sum of (1) and (2) from 100.

most perfect balance, a defense superiority of only one percentage point: a murder trial is important not only to the defense, the prosecution too tries to assign its better counsel to such cases.

The crime-by-crime data in Table 87 generally re-enforce the impressions of evenhandedness gained from Table 82. For the vast majority of crimes the imbalance for either defense or prosecution does not reach 20 per cent, and for the majority of serious crimes, whatever imbalance there is, is found on both sides, so that the net imbalance is small.

The categories that do show some major imbalance do not admit of easy generalization, except perhaps that several of the crimes with a favorable defense balance, such as income tax evasion, gambling, embezzlement, fraud, and prostitution, are such that one might risk the observation that the crimes that pay, also pay for skilled counsel.

The figures thus far have lumped together the cases in which the prosecutor was superior to defendant's counsel and the cases in which defendant was without counsel. We now look separately at this critical group of cases.[10] The striking point is that in only 2.7 per cent of jury trials is defendant without counsel.[11]

Table 88 lists the no-counsel cases by crime.

[10] It turns out occasionally that to be tried without counsel may work to the defendant's advantage. In a few cases the jury tends to side with the defendant simply because it considers such a trial basically unfair. See below, page 368. See also Case I-3113, on page 319.

[11] That this surprisingly low figure is not far out of line finds support in a national survey on the indigent defendant and the problem of representation. Silverstein, Defense of the Poor in Criminal Cases in American State Courts (1965). The data permit the estimate that on the average 21 per cent of all defendants were without counsel (derived by us from that study's Table 28). This comprises defendants who pleaded guilty, where most of the non-representation occurred, and those who went to trial. Further, the proportion of defendants without counsel in bench trials was relatively larger than in jury trials. Since the problem was aggravated in the South (see Table 89 below) and since our sample underrepresents the South, our over-all percentage of defendants without counsel is probably on the low side.

TABLE 88

Defendants Without Counsel by Type of Crime

	Per Cent of This Crime	Number of Cases
Disorderly conduct	28	67
Mail theft	8	12
Simple assault	5	78
Larceny	5	170
Liquor (violation)		
Non-support	4	77
Drunken driving and traffic violations	4	560
Burglary	3	298
Aggravated assault	3	292
Auto theft	1	111
Robbery	1	229
Rape	1	176
Other sex crimes	1	194
All other crimes	—	1179
Total all crimes	2.7%	3576

Finally, Table 89 gives the cases by region.

TABLE 89

Defendants Without Counsel by Region and Crime

	Serious Crimes	Minor Crimes
	(Per Cent of Trials in Each Area)	
Pacific and Mountain	1	5
Midwest	1	1
Middle Atlantic and New England	1	1
South Atlantic, East South Central	6	12
West South Central	—	7

Read together, Tables 88 and 89 permit some major observations on the problem of legal representation for the indigent defendant. While Table 88 shows that on occasion defendants have been tried for serious crimes without counsel, the clear majority of these cases are minor crimes. More important, Table 89 shows that when the cases are grouped by region, nonrepresentation in serious crimes emerges as a visible problem primarily in the South.

Since not all of these defendants without counsel were un-
represented because they were indigent (some refused counsel), the data compel the conclusion that even prior to the
Gideon case, the legal system, outside of a few southern states,
had been doing a good job of seeing that no defendant who
wanted counsel in a serious criminal trial came to trial without one. The *Gideon* decision thus closed only a small, albeit
important, gap, and the change in doctrine had a solid foundation in the widespread recognition of the principle.[12]

We turn now to reason assessment for insights. These cases
to be considered indicate the frequency with which the judge
thought the lawyer a factor in causing disagreement; they also
provide an interesting profile of lawyers' techniques and characteristics rated as important by that seasoned observer, the
trial judge.

To be sure, the judge frequently does no more than observe
that the superior defense counsel was "clever" [I-0092] or
"excellent" [I-1937] or "skilled" [I-0104] or "experienced"
[I-1634].[13] But often he provides a more specific image of the
defense counsel's superiority.

At times the judge sees it as residing in the quality of the
closing argument. Thus, in an incest case he tells us:

> Defense attorney delivered a brilliant argument and in my
> opinion this argument meant the entire difference between a
> verdict of guilty and one of not guilty. [I-0684]

To much the same point is the comment in a case of breaking
and entering where the jury acquits three defendants.

> Defense attorney made a very impassioned plea, lasting three
> hours and twenty minutes, in which he dealt with reasonable
> doubt and in which he attacked the credibility of state's wit-

---

[12] This is evident from the arresting circumstance that in the Gideon
case an *amicus* brief was filed for the state governments of twenty-two
states, three of them southern, urging adoption of the principle.

[13] There are thirty-four cases in which there is only such abridged
comment.

nesses largely on the ground that a reward had been paid for the apprehension of the accused. [I-0552-1, -2, & -3]

The time-honored technique of explaining "reasonable doubt" in a closing argument is again noted in another breaking and entering case.

I think this was another case where experienced defense counsel was able to convince the jury that beyond a reasonable doubt meant beyond all possible doubt. [I-0541]

These references to closing arguments are admittedly sketchy, and are infrequent enough to cast some doubt on the widespread assumption that the jury is especially vulnerable to demagogic oratory. Only in these few cases was the closing argument significant enough in the eyes of the judge to provoke a comment from him.

More frequently, counsel demonstrates his superiority in the handling of some other aspect of the trial, such as the introduction of evidence, or cross-examination. At times the compliment is backhanded.

Defendant's attorney was successful in getting a highly prejudicial, irrelevant matter before the jury by asking irrelevant questions, objections to which were sustained by the court. [I-0036]

Again, in a fraud case where the jury is moved to acquit, the judge enters a comparable observation about the —

Distinctive defense counsel, who obfuscated the jury by bringing in extraneous testimony attacking complaining witness's credibility. [I-1040]

On occasion, however, the judge can be quite affirmative about the skill of counsel in cross-examination. Thus, in an incest case where the jury acquits, he comments:

Defendant signed a confession verifying the girl's story. A skillful defense counsel demonstrated successfully that the two county detectives should have been out digging ditches. [I-1875]

And again, in a case where defendants are charged with breaking into a granary at night, the judge writes of the cross-examination:

> One witness was too positive of the identification of tire marks in the first instance. His claim of general knowledge of tire treads was badly shaken on cross-examination by exhibit to the jury . . . of a truck tire of the size in question which had actually a different tread from which he had testified all truck tires of that size and make had. [I-0786] [14]

And in a rape case:

> With cross-examination, defense counsel made it appear that prosecutrix was a prostitute without substantial evidence. [I-0045]

In the cases so far it is the professional skill and technique of defense counsel that mark his superiority. In another cluster of cases the impact of counsel depends more on his personality and social status. Thus, in a robbery case where the jury is hung, the defendant, as the judge sees it, has the benefit of what might be called innocence by association with counsel.

> Defendant had not been in trouble before. He was defended by a young, honest and sincere lawyer who had known defendant before and believed the fantastic tale told by defendant. The honesty and decency of defense attorney rubbed off on the jurors who were hearing their first case. [I-0645]

At times the attractiveness of counsel's personality is the decisive factor: "Defense attorney young, sincere and appealing" [I-0223], or again, "able, congenial, likable defense counsel helped." [I-1568] The most vivid of these comments comes from a trial for a game law violation, where the judge tells us:

[14] In this same case the judge offers details on other effective moves made by counsel, which are discussed in Chapter 23: "Principal witnesses were [state] Bureau of Investigation men. They may not have been as careful as they should have been in advising defendant of his rights and letting him see an attorney speedily. I admitted statement obtained from him, over objection, but enough was presented to jury to give impression that there might have been an attempt to railroad him, so to speak. Attempt was not bad, but there was a little odor. Defense attorney was very capable."

Defendant's attorney is one of the old timers and very colorful. He grunts and laughs and disparages witnesses' testimony
on the other side by holding his hands to his ears. The court
had to cut him down several times. But everybody likes Mr.
R, the defense attorney. [I-0964]

In a few cases from rural communities the judge makes the
somewhat unusual point that defense counsel was effective
with the jury because the jurors were obligated to him. In one
such case, a drunken driving prosecution where the jury hangs,
the judge puts it this way:

The defendant's lawyer had been practicing at the local bar
about 35 years and has had a tremendous number of clients,
many of whom felt obligated to him in one way or another.
Doubtless some of the jurors were under his influence.
[I-0034] [15]

In all of these cases the judge has noted some affirmative
strength of defense counsel. It may be convenient to summarize the various descriptive factors we have been reviewing.
Table 90 sets forth such a summary.

TABLE 90

Sources of Strength of Defense Counsel

Professional skills		
Summation	7	
Cross-examination and handling of evidence	9	
	—	16
Personality and status		
Attractive personality	8	
Jurors obligated to him	3	
	—	11
Undifferentiated		34
Total		61

In a sizable number of cases the judge rates defense coun-

[15] In an assault case, the same judge reports: "Defense attorney personally knew all jurors." [I-0008] In still a third case he repeats almost
verbatim the comment quoted in the text. All three cases come from
a small town, and quite possibly the judge is talking about the same
lawyer.

sel as superior simply because the prosecution performs poorly. Here again, in many instances the judge makes only a general comment about "poor prosecution" [I-1151] or "inexperienced deputy district attorney" [I-0110] or "inefficiency of prosecuting attorney." [I-0629]

But on occasion there is a more specific criticism which sharpens the profile of lawyer performance. In an income tax violation for which the jury acquits, the judge states "presentation of government case was sloppy and hypertechnical." [I-2053] At other times the prosecution appears to have made a bad tactical move in the course of the trial. In a drunken driving case: "Prosecution offered a bottle that could not be identified by its witnesses which created doubt from the beginning." [I-0052] And in a case of receiving stolen property the prosecutor makes a classic mistake.

> The prosecutor during the cross-examination of defendant requested him to try on one sport coat. It did not fit him. This obviously impressed jury that the defendant did not receive coat for his own use. [I-0318]

Often the prosecutor's error lies in his failure to stress a particular point or to pursue a line of inquiry. In a case of petty theft where the jury acquits, the judge tells us that "prosecutor failed to stress concealed articles taken to defendant's apartment as an indication of guilt." [I-0194] In another income tax disagreement it is "failure of state's attorney to present all the facts." [I-0838] And where the defendant is charged with violating a voting registration law, the judge feels that the defendants lied in one important respect, but "the point was not adequately argued by the prosecution and the jury did not appreciate its significance." [II-0291]

Similarly, in a drunken driving disagreement:

> Jury failed to evaluate testimony of police officer that defendant admitted to drinking seven or eight bottles of beer. Prosecution failed to question along this line. [I-0082]

Perhaps the most vivid example of a prosecution oversight

occurs in a grand larceny case in which a confession is challenged. The judge notes that the prosecutor lost a fine chance to impeach the defendant:

> Many of the facts which defendant stated were discussed at the time of her confession, were facts which, based on the entire record, were wholly unknown at the time of the confession. [I-3117] [16]

It may again be convenient to summarize the instances of prosecution deficiencies just reviewed. This is done in Table 91.

TABLE 91

Tactical Errors by Prosecution

Hypertechnical	1
Oversight	7
Poorly prepared	9
Too eager	1
Antagonistic	2
Total	20

There remains one interesting corner of the data, the situations in which defense counsel is able to turn weakness into strength. Here the very inexperience of the defense counsel creates sympathy for the defendant on the part of the jury; thus, the imbalance of skill between prosecution and defense produces a reversal of impact. In a murder trial the judge notes:

> Defendant's attorney was appointed by the court. He had just been admitted to the bar and this was his first jury trial. [I-0038]

And in a burglary case, the judge observes:

> Defense counsel young and inexperienced. May have been sympathetic. [II-1038]

[16] In one case the judge observes that the prosecution missed a point of law. On a charge of drunken driving he notes: "Also no instructions were given on what constitutes operating a motor vehicle while under the influence of intoxicating liquor." [I-0692]

And most explicit is another burglary case where the jury hangs. The judge reports:

> Although there may have been some sympathy for the defendant because of his youth, I believe that some of the jurors very definitely were sympathetic to young defense counsel who during his argument told the jury this was his first jury trial. [I-1846] [17]

Perhaps a fitting conclusion to this profile of the factors that make a lawyer effective can be made by reporting a few cases where the defendant appears without counsel and reaps advantage from this fact. Thus, in a case of reckless speeding, the judge sums up the problem:

> It is difficult to prosecute a case when the defendant is not represented by counsel. [I-0515] [18]

The most poignant of these cases, surely, is the one where a recent law school graduate — as his own first case — successfully defended himself against a charge of statutory rape. [I-0835]

We have now traced the incidence of superior defense counsel and have reviewed in detail the judge's sketches of what makes one lawyer better than another. We move now from qualitative to quantitative analysis. How much difference does the superior defense lawyer make?

In the aggregate this question has already been answered. We know from the reason assessment summary[19] that 4 per cent of all normal disagreements can be credited to the lawyer's

[17] Presumably, this is a technique defense counsel cannot use often. We are reminded, however, of an eminent Austrian attorney, Richard Pressburger, who continued defending cases into his old age and acquired some secondary renown by winning more than one of them before a jury on the plea that this was to be his last case before the bar.

[18] Similarly, in a drunken driving case, the defendant representing himself excelled in his cross-examination of the policeman and thus gained not only an acquittal but a newspaper feature story on his behalf which the judge sent to us. [II-0340] There are six such cases, where apparent superiority for the prosecution boomerangs.

[19] See Chapter 8, note 16, where the figure is rounded off to 4 per cent.

performance. We approach the question now through cross-tabulation. Table 92 compares the incidence of jury disagreement in cases having superior defense counsel with comparable cases in which defense counsel was not superior. To insure maximum homogeneity of the cases to be compared, the comparison is made for eight subgroups, each of which represents a factor known to affect disagreement.[20]

The bottom line of Table 92 gives the measurement. In all but two of the eight groups (the third and fifth), the cases with superior defense counsel produce a higher incidence of jury disagreements.[21] Following the computation procedure discussed earlier, and applying the per cent difference to the number of cases with superior defense counsel we arrive at a figure of 9.9 cases in which the disagreement can be credited to counsel.[22] Since the total number of disagreements in Table

---

[20] The rationale for this procedure is provided at pages 88 and 89. Compare the measurement of the Record-Stand factor, Table 57, and the Sympathy Factor, Table 68. The computation of the effect of Superior Defense Counsel uses the same basic data in the same format as Table 68, the only difference being the variable measured. For how the measurement is made on a cell-by-cell basis, see the discussion in Chapter 15, page 216.

[21] In one of the two reversals, the amount of judge-jury disagreement is virtually equal (57 per cent and 59 per cent). In general such reversals are the visible effect of the impossibility of ever keeping all cases comparable in a survey analysis. The assumption on which the computation rests is that these fluctuations will compensate each other, hence the average of all these differences can be relied on.

[22] The cell-by-cell computation reading across is as follows:

(1) Difference %	(2) Number of Cases	(1 × 2) Effect in Cases %
+ 30	12	+ 3.6
+ 18	23	+ 4.2
− 22	8	− 1.8
+ 20	10	+ 2.0
− 2	7	− 0.1
+ 2	13	+ 0.3
+ 27	4	+ 1.1
+ 4	15	+ 0.6
	Total	+ 9.9 cases

TABLE 92

Effect of Superior Defendant Counsel on Jury Disagreement Where Judge Convicts

| | No Record/Stand | | | | Record/No Stand | | | |
| | CLOSE | | CLEAR | | CLOSE | | CLEAR | |
	Sympathetic Defendant	Other	Sympathetic Defendant	Other	Sympathetic Defendant	Other	Sympathetic Defendant	Other
Superior defense counsel	100%	74%	13%	30%	57%	38%	75%	13%
Number of cases	12	23	8	10	7	13	4	15
Other counsel	70%	56%	35%	10%	59%	36%	48%	9%
Number of cases	61	136	48	231	22	100	25	274
Difference	+30%	+18%	−22%	+20%	−2%	+2%	+27%	+4%

92 is 293, superior counsel accounts for $(9.9 \div 293 =)$ 3.4 per cent of all disagreements.

The approach via reason assessment having yielded a weighted figure of 4 per cent, we thus have a highly satisfactory confrontation between the two methods.

One other important question can be answered with the data from Table 92, namely: What is the *power* of superior counsel to effect disagreement between jury and judge? How does the effectiveness of superior defense counsel in producing disagreement relate to the frequency with which there is such counsel? As to the frequency of the factor, the table shows that defense counsel is superior in 92 of the 989 trials, which is 9.3 per cent or roughly 1 out of every 11 trials.[23]

The power of the factor is measured by relating 9.9, the number of cases in which defense counsel causes judge-jury disagreement, to 92, the frequency with which the factor occurs. The power thus is $(9.9 \div 92 =)$ 10.8 per cent; superior defense counsel then has the power to cause a disagreement in approximately 1 out of every 9 cases in which it is present.

We know by now that this figure is an abstraction. In actual fact the superior defense lawyer has *some* effect not 10.8 per cent of the time, but 25 per cent of the time when the factor is present.[24] It is credited with only part of the effect, the balance of credit going to other factors operative in the cases.

There is but one final statistic on the over-all effect of superior defense counsel. Since the factor appears in 1 out of 11

[23] The incidence of superior defense counsel, as shown earlier in Table 82, is 11 per cent, but this is *for all trials*. The 9.3 per cent figure referred to here is limited to the incidence of superior defense counsel in *cases where the judge would convict* (i.e., the universe of the normal disagreement). The 92 cases are obtained by adding the top line in Table 92.

[24] We know from Chapter 8, Table 26, that the incidence of superior defense counsel as a factor in producing disagreement is about 9 per cent, without taking into account its combination with other factors in the case. When this is done, i.e., when the reason is weighted, the figure reduces to about 4 per cent, as shown in Chapter 8, note 16. The 25 per cent figure is derived by multiplying the *power*, which is about 11 per cent, by the ratio between counsel as an unweighted and a weighted factor $(11 \times 9/4 = 24.7$ or rounded, 25 per cent).

trials, and since it causes disagreement once every 9 times it is present, a disagreement is caused by superior defense counsel in ($\frac{1}{11} \times \frac{1}{9} =$) $\frac{1}{99}$, or in a little more than 1 per cent of all trials.

From this analysis of the effect of superior defense counsel we would predict that *inferior* defense counsel should, conversely, produce an increased number of jury agreements when the judge convicts and an increased number of cross-over disagreements when he acquits. Both predictions turn out to be correct.[25]

This chapter began by acknowledging the lawyer's great interest in and great expectations as to his own role. The final estimate of a 1 per cent impact on the system appears to deflate.[26] But the figure should not be misread. In 25 per cent of the cases in which defense counsel is superior he will have some share in moving the jury toward disagreement. But more important, the lawyer's role is not exhausted by consideration of the disagreement cases alone, since in the vast majority of trials, counsel on both sides are evenly matched. And indeed it might be well said that the great role of the defense lawyer, as an institution, is to keep the trial process in balance so that the adversary system can function.[27]

[25] The role of the superior prosecutor is analyzed in Chapter 30; as to the over-all view, see Table 135.

[26] The view of one of England's great trial lawyers is worth noting in this context: "The late Mr. Justice Rigby Swift, a most forceful judge, was once dining at a mess dinner on circuit, when he was greeted, triumphantly by the circuit leader: 'Well, Judge,' he said, 'I had a good win before you to-day.' Rigby Swift was never one to mince his words. 'How dare you say you had a win before me? ' I sit in Court to see that justice is done. In my Court justice *is* done. No counsel ever wins a case before me.' The learned judge was very nearly right. I have known so many advocates, good advocates and very good advocates, bad advocates and very bad advocates, and in the result I am satisfied that at least ninety per cent of all cases win or lose themselves, and that the ultimate result would have been the same whatever counsel the parties had chosen to represent them. But of the remaining ten per cent it is not so easy to speak with any certainty." Patrick Hastings, Cases in Court, p. 329 (1953).

[27] His significance in *agreement* cases is discussed in Chapter 38.

W E ARE JUST halfway through the task of this study. In our search for a rounded theory of jury decision-making we must now confront those disagreements which, in our idiom, cross over, the cases in which the judge is more lenient than the jury.

Chapters 29 through 32 cover the explanations for the cross-over phenomenon. As would be expected, these explanations are in the large parallel to those for normal disagreements. Chapter 31 covers the jury's pro-prosecution sentiments on the law, and Chapter 30 investigates the cross-over stimulus for the remaining categories of evidence, differential communication, the lawyer, and the defendant. The other chapters frame the discussion: Chapter 29 will serve as a preface, Chapter 32 is an epilogue. It looks into what the judge does when confronted with a verdict more severe than the judgment he would have rendered.

Preface to the Cross-over Phenomenon:
The Judge Is More Lenient
than the Jury

A theory of jury decision-making must explain judge-jury disagreements, whatever their direction. In the materials presented thus far we have become so habituated to the jury's being the more lenient decider that there is point in pausing for a moment to adjust our thinking to a reversal of the jury role.

The very existence of the cross-over phenomenon raises some major questions. In studying the disagreements in which the jury is more lenient than the judge, we have come to understand what we have called the jury's sense of equity, or its modest war with the law. It is understandable that the jury should at times acquit a defendant in defiance of the law. But it is not so apparent what the reverse of this means, the situation in which the jury finds guilty a man whom the judge and the letter of the law would acquit. After studying these cases we shall come to think of the jury not so much as an institution with a built-in protection for the defendant, but rather as an institution which is stubbornly non-rule minded. Bringing the cross-over cases into our ken effects a major reorientation in perspective about the jury.

A second problem, closely connected with the first, is whether on the whole these cross-over disagreements are so like normal disagreements that all we can say is that this time the particular jury happened to come out on the other side of the judge. If this turned out to be the case, much of our theorizing about the jury up to this point would lose its significance. We would be left with the not very exciting conclusion that juries vary, some leaning in one direction and some in the other.[1] The alternative possibility which, as we shall see, largely prevails, is that the cross-over case is intrinsically different and that the basic explanation for the jury's apparent reversal of role lies in the different stimulus which these cases present.

A first indication of this basic asymmetry comes from the lower frequency of the cross-overs. Over-all, as the basic four-fold table on guilt showed, there are about eight normal disagreement cases for every cross-over case.[2] More important, a first inquiry into the explanatory structure of the cross-overs reveals a dominant characteristic which distinguishes them from the normal disagreements. Table 93 shows the proportion of cases which are close on the evidence.

TABLE 93

Disagreement Cases with Evidence Reasons

	Cross-overs	Normal Disagreements
	%	%
Evidence	96	76
Other	4	24
Total	100%	100%
Number of cases	*134*	*828*

The suggestion is that the explanation for cross-overs resides largely in the handling of evidential difficulties.

As expected, other factors join with evidence to play a role in producing cross-overs. Two of the factors which served us well in the explanation of normal disagreements pose no puzzles as explanations here. If the case is tried with a prosecutor

---

[1] See discussion in Chapter 37, Methodology: No Two Juries and No Two Judges Are Alike.

[2] The precise figures are 19.1 and 2.7 per cent. But see the text at page 380.

who is markedly superior to defense counsel, it is totally ex-pectable, when the adversary advantage lies in this direction that, the prosecution may at times be able to swing the jury, though not the judge, to its side. Similarly, when a case has been differentially communicated and the jury knows some-thing detrimental to the defendant that the judge does not know, or where the judge knows something favorable to the de-fendant which the jury does not know, it is no surprise that cross-overs at times result.

The situation becomes more complicated with respect to sentiments that concern the defendant. It would appear at first that just as some defendants are attractive and arouse the jury's sympathy, so others are unattractive and alienate the jury. But the matter cannot be so simple. It is understand-able that the jury may, on occasion, be moved by sympathy to acquit an otherwise guilty defendant. But the reverse proc-ess would require that the jury out of antipathy would convict an innocent defendant.

Table 93 has already pointed to the direction in which the explanation must lie. Since virtually all cross-over cases are close on the evidence, it is likely that the unattractiveness of the defendant will bear primarily on the jury's decision by way of reducing in their eyes the defendant's credibility.

Thus, four of the five categories which serve to explain the normal disagreements have ready roles in explaining the cross-over phenomenon as well. What appears more problem-atic, however, is whether there can be sentiments on the law distinctively in favor of the prosecution.

To be sure, some of these sentiment disagreements will turn indeed on nothing more than the fact that not all juries are alike and not all sentiments are held uniformly by the en-tire population. Some people will tend to be lenient toward violators of liquor and drunken driving laws, because of their general liberalism toward liquor, while others led by extreme disapproval will react exactly in the opposite way. Juries re-cruited at random from a wide population will thus produce both normal disagreements and cross-overs.

In a majority of cases, however, the jury sentiment is responsive to something intrinsic and recurring in the legal situation. We find prosecution equities which are as specific, for example, as *de minimis* is a defense sentiment. As a rule, these prosecution oriented sentiments move the jury to override some point of law which renders the defendant's conduct non-criminal, but only in a technical sense.

It will thus be useful to establish a distinction for future use. When the sentiment is distributed in the population such that some feel very strongly one way and some equally strongly the other way, as in the liquor example, we will speak of an *ambivalent* sentiment which then may produce either a normal disagreement or a cross-over. When the sentiment is on the whole, unidirectional, either in favor of the defendant, or in favor of the prosecution, we will speak of a *pure* sentiment.

Table 94 provides an over-all view of the explanation of the cross-overs in terms of the categories; for purposes of comparison we list the parallel data for the normal disagreements.

TABLE 94

Summary Explanation of Cross-overs

	Unweighted *		Weighted †	
	Cross-Over	Normal Disagreement	Cross-Over	Normal Disagreement
	%	%	%	%
Sentiment on the law	48	51	24.4	29.7
Sentiment on the defendant	20	22	8.6	10.8
Evidence	96	76	64.0	53.0
Jury or judge only knew	3	6	1.4	2.4
Superiority of counsel	4	9	1.6	4.1
Total			100.0%	100.0%
Number of cases	*134*	*828*	*134*	*828*

* The numbers indicate the percentage of disagreements in which this factor played *any* role irrespective of the presence of other factors. Since, therefore, one case may be counted several times, depending on how many factors are operating, the sum total of these two columns is more than 100 per cent.

† Here each case is counted only once; if it involves several factors they share in each case in proportion to the total number of reasons in the case.

Each factor, except evidential disagreement, is less important in engendering cross-overs than it is in causing normal disagreements. The difference is, relatively speaking, most marked in the case of superior counsel.

Another significant aspect of the cross-overs is shown in Table 95, paralleling an important table for the normal disagreements.[3] It shows how judgments of facts and judgments of values are interrelated in cross-over cases.

TABLE 95

Facts and Values: Cross-over Disagreements

	Per Cent	
Facts alone	35	96% Facts
Values and Facts	61	
Values alone	4	65% Values
Total	100%	
Number of cases	*134*	

Table 95 makes explicit that what we have called the liberation hypothesis operates in almost two thirds of the cross-over cases.

Still another comparison throws light on the nature of the cross-over disagreements. Table 96 indicates that the crossover is, as a whole, not as sharp a disagreement as the case where the jury is more lenient than the judge.

TABLE 96

Cross-overs and Normals by Type of Disagreement

	Cross-Over %	Normal Disagreement %
Disagreement on —		
Guilt	54	66
Charge	18	17
Hung jury	28	17
Total	100%	100%
Number of cases	*143*	*920*

[3] The comparable data for normal disagreements will be found in Table 53. The Facts and Values distribution for all disagreements is provided in Table 30.

Twenty-eight per cent of all cross-overs are hung juries, compared to 17 per cent of the normal disagreements; and correspondingly, only a little more than half of all cross-overs are disagreements on guilt, as compared with the normal disagreements, where two thirds turn on the issue of guilt.

Finally, we should repeat a word about the sheer magnitude of the cross-over phenomenon. The proportion of these disagreements is, as we have seen, relatively small, but it is important that we do not misread their significance. We know that a chief reason for the relative infrequency is found in the rules and customs as to waiver. The defendant has the right to waive a jury trial and to opt for a bench trial, by and large, whenever he thinks that will be preferable. If we assume that the defendant's counsel has some insight into jury behavior, the right of a defendant to waive a jury works in practice as an option to remove a potential cross-over from the universe of jury trials.[4]

In the discussion that follows then we take up the second half of our task — tracing the importance of the cross-over to a full theory of jury behavior.

[4] See Table 3 for the incidence of waiver for selected states, and see also the discussion of waiver in civil as against criminal cases in Chapter 5, page 65. Following is a comparison of the incidence of cross-over cases in jurisdictions with high, moderate, low, and very low jury waiver rates. The hypothesis would be that cross-overs tend to be lower in high waiver jurisdictions, because there, counsel, influenced by custom, is more likely to forego jury trial if he senses the danger of a cross-over. The data in our sample offer some modest confirmation on this hypothesis.

Waiver Rate	Per Cent Cross-overs
High (65% and over)	4.1
Moderate (50-64%)	4.7
Low (25-49%)	5.1
Very low (under 25%)	5.4

The average cross-over frequency in the states for which we know the waiver rate is somewhat above the average for all states.

CHAPTER 30

Four Factors Explaining Cross-overs

We begin the more detailed review of the reason categories which explain cross-overs by considering more or less together the evidence factor and the defendant.

A distinctive feature about cross-overs is that they are almost all close cases. Hence when sentiments are operative, they occur in the context of evidentiary problems.[1] It follows that we cannot attempt a sharp distinction between those things which make a defendant unattractive and those which make him unbelievable; a distinction, in other words, between characteristics of the defendant that make the jury uneasy about him as a person and those which, in the jury's eyes, impeach his veracity.

As we see these cases, they range across a spectrum, moving from close cases where the defendant's unattractiveness as a person is emphatic in the judge's explanation, through cases where the unattractiveness slides into demeanor, and, finally, on to cases in which the issue is largely evidential and the person of the defendant is not salient.

We begin then with the cases in which the evidence is close and the judge is emphatic about the unattractiveness of the defendant. In one cluster the defendant seems to have prejudiced the jury because of some immoral or vulgar behavior

---

[1] Table 93 establishes that only 4 per cent of the cross-over disagreements are based exclusively on non-evidentiary reasons. The cases, discussed in Chapter 31, note 11, all stem from sentiments on the law. In the normal disagreement cases only 62 per cent show this combination of the defendant factor with evidence problems.

collateral to the crime. Thus, in a homicide case which the judge would have reduced to involuntary manslaughter, the judge states:

> The defendant was charged with beating his companion on a joint fishing trip to death with his fists. The testimony showed that during a drunken orgy the defendant and decedent engaged in perverted sexual intercourse. It is probable that this fact weighed heavily with the jury. [I-0040]

Again, in a commercial vice case where the jury finds guilty a man and woman whom the judge would have acquitted, the evidence is circumstantial and the judge explains:

> Certain elements of the prosecution were legally weak, but the jury was probably impressed by the loose morals of both defendants. Evidence of lewd and vicious language of the parties made an undeniable impression on the jury. [I-02931 & 2]

In another disagreement on guilt the use of vulgar speech again seems to impress adversely. The defendant, accused of disorderly conduct, resisting arrest, and assault, is convicted on all charges by the jury, while the judge would acquit. The judge believes that the defendant, a foreigner with language difficulties, misunderstood the cause of his arrest but grants that influential on the jury was the "vile, profane language attributed to the defendant which he did not deny." [II-0354]

It is not quite clear how one should best generalize about these cases. It would seem awkward to hold that juries tend to disbelieve people who use vulgar language. Perhaps the best we can say is that the jury does not give the benefit of the doubt in close cases to those defendants whose behavior it finds offensive.

In other cases, the unattractive aspect of the defendant's personality seems more closely tied to his demeanor in presenting evidence. In the first illustrations the defendant does not take the stand to testify, and there is thus the suggestion that the jury will make credibility judgments of demeanor so long as it can see the defendant, whether or not he testifies.

The charge in one case is violation of the Mann Act. The judge concludes that there was no evidence that the defendant had taken money from prostitutes, although his co-defendant had. By way of explanation the judge adds:

> This defendant did not take the stand but because of his association with the white victims and because of the loss of sight in one eye, he may have made a bad impression on the jury. [II-0897]

Juxtaposed against this Cyclopean image of vice is a case with the tintype of virtue. Again, the defendant refuses the stand, but the jury learns much from her demeanor.

> The defendant gave the picture of a pious old fraud. She took her seat in plain view of the jury with a big cross swinging from her neck and thereupon opened her bible in front of her. Then she brought out a bottle of smelling salts, preparing herself spiritually and mentally for any eventuality. [I-1802]

Normally, of course, the characteristic relates to the manner of testifying. In an attempted rape case, which the judge, in disagreement with the jury, reduces to assault because he does not completely believe the complaining witness, he remarks:

> Defendant did not make a good impression. He was insolent looking and smart. [I-1555]

Again, in a drunken driving case where the disagreement is on guilt, the judge reminds us of the usual difficulty in these cases: "The case turned entirely on credibility of the witnesses." He adds:

> Defendant, a blowhard and smart aleck, sought to impress the jury with the weight of his influence and importance of social connections. [I-1363]

In another cross-over on guilt, an assault case, part of the disagreement is ascribed to the defendant's bad record, including three previous assaults. The judge adds:

> Also his personality was such as to prejudice him before a jury. [I-1858]

These then are the cases of disagreement in which, while the evidence is close, the unattractiveness of the defendant has been specifically and emphatically called to our attention by the judge.

It may be helpful to pause for a moment to look at the matter from the standpoint of cross-tabulation. It will be recalled that in the second questionnaire we collected information on whether the defendant evoked sympathy, made an unattractive impression, or made an average impression, and further that all defendants distribute as follows:[2]

Sympathetic	19
Average	64
Unattractive	17
	100%

Using a rough counterpart of the analytic technique employed on the role of the individual defendant in normal disagreements, we can make some measurement of the impact of the unattractive defendant on the cross-over. Table 97 presents the computation.[3]

TABLE 97

Effect of the Unattractive Defendant on Cross-over Disagreements on Guilt

	Record / No Stand		No Record / Stand	
	Prosecution Superior	Other	Prosecution Superior	Other
Unattractive	100%	36%	50%	63%
Number of cases	2	11	2	8
Other defendants	60%	25%	—	18%
Number of cases	5	57	9	108
Difference	40%	11%	50%	45%
Attributable cases	0.8	1.2	1.0	3.6

[2] Reproduced from Table 67.

[3] The method of computation is the same as used in previous cross-tabulations, with the standard variables; evidence is collapsed since almost all cases are close. See Chapter 15, page 216, and Chapter 28, note 20.

We find that 6.6 cases or roughly 13.7 per cent of the cross-overs on guilt[4] are attributable to the defendant factor. This is fairly congruent to the previous estimate of 8.6 per cent derived from reason assessment.[5]

This brief survey of the unattractive defendant tends to corroborate the explanation of a theoretical difficulty discussed in Chapter 29.[6] Although it is now clear that the jury is often alienated by the unattractiveness of the defendant, we find no cases in which the jury convicts a man, so to speak, for the crime of being unattractive. In the cases examined it is apparent that there is always a considerable link, in the eyes of the jury, between the unattractiveness of the defendant and his credibility.

The focus of the discussion shifts now from cases where the unattractiveness of the defendant was a principal feature to cases where court and jury are wrestling directly with problems of credibility, and where the jury, in contrast to the judge, resolves these issues in some way against the defendant.

We begin with a disagreement which is very different from those we have been discussing. In a drunken driving case, although there appears to have been reasonable evidence of guilt, the judge is moved to acquit the defendant who, as he describes him, emerges as uniquely attractive:

The defendant was such an honest witness and of such good character that I was personally convinced that he was not un-

[4] The normal disagreements are expressed as a proportion of all cases in which the judge would have convicted; the cross-over disagreements are expressed as a proportion of all cases in which the judge would have acquitted. For reasons of convenience the cross-over confrontations are restricted to disagreements on guilt only, excluding the few cross-overs on charge. The cross-overs on charge have, however, been taken into account in the normal disagreement computations by subtracting them in each cell from the normal disagreements on charge.

[5] See Table 94, weighted.

[6] See page 375.

der the influence at the time of his arrest to the extent that he
had violated the statute, although there was ample evidence to
the contrary. [I-1264]

The arresting thing in this case is that the defendant, despite
his appeal, does not move the jury at all. They look to the
other evidence in the case and convict.

In a second, somewhat similar case, it is more apparent
why the jury does not respond to the attractiveness the judge
finds in the defendant. The case, a burglary prosecution,
merits fuller quotation because of the subtlety of the point the
judge sees and some of the jury misses:

> A child in the house of a Mrs. M awakened the household
> claiming that she had seen a man in her bedroom. The older
> children saw a man who resembled the defendant running
> from the place and getting into a car. The defendant was ar-
> rested in his car a short distance away and some school papers
> belonging to one of the older children were found in his car.
> He claimed that he had been friendly with one of the older
> girls and had driven her home from high school which ac-
> counted for the papers. Girl denied this but made a very
> poor witness. Defendant had a prior record for burglary.

The difficulty in the evidence is the presence of the school
papers in defendant's car. It is on one hand an illogical theft,
yet the defendant stoutly corroborates the complaining witness that his acquaintance with the older daughter is remote.
On this evidence the jury hangs. The judge explains why he
would acquit the defendant:

> It was fairly clear to me that he probably knew the girl very
> well but decided to risk conviction than ruin her reputation,
> and thus refused to admit he entered the house to keep a date
> with her. [II-0601]

The case is a good illustration of how complex credibility
issues are and how difficult it necessarily is to isolate in any
recurrent pattern factors which account for disagreement.
Here the judge is sensitive enough to the total picture to pick
up the defendant's gallant but hidden gesture. He is thus
led to acquit while some of the jury, looking only at the ap-

pearances of the matter, would draw a common sense conclusion of his guilt.

Two other cross-overs reveal again the discriminating insight of the judge. In both cases the defendant, in an apparent effort to make a good case better, tells a story which neither the judge nor the jury believes. The jury, having found him not credible in one part of his testimony, rejects the rest of it and convicts; the judge, sensing the foolish motivation of the defendant, is able to separate the false part of the defendant's story from the true. The jury in these cases is following the old credibility maxim, *falsus in uno, falsus in omnibus*, whereas the judge, if we are to match maxims, separates the wheat from the chaff.

In the first illustration, a drunken driving case, the defendant claims the arresting officer beat him gratuitously and severely and apparently gets somewhat carried away with the injustice of it all. The judge, who does not believe this account of police brutality, is willing nevertheless to give the defendant the benefit of the doubt that he was not under the influence. The jury convicts and the judge explains:

> Defendant's testimony convicted himself — too much for jury's credulity. [I-1701]

In a second such case, the defendant's disbelieved story again concerns police brutality. The charge is possession and operation of an illegal still, and the judge explains:

> I am of the opinion that the fact that the defendant testified that the sheriff beat him almost to death while he was in custody prejudiced the jury.

The judge then nails down the interpretation of the case by adding: "I myself doubt defendant was beaten." [I-0032]

In the last cases discussed it is clear why, on the surface, the defendant would appear to be unreliable and guilty, and it is also clear why on closer examination he might appear to be reliable and innocent.

We have one further illustration of the judge's capacity to

fence off the less credible component in a case. In a drunken driving trial the judge explains:

> The principal witness for defendant . . . made a terrible witness, contradicted her testimony in a former trial and generally messed up the whole proceeding. This woman was so bad in her testimony that the jury probably thought both she and the defendant were lying. [I-0752]

In another group of cross-overs, conflict in credibility judgments, although present, is a good deal less dramatic. The judge describes explicitly what there was about the defendant that might have led the jury not to believe him; he is, however, moved to decide in the defendant's favor because of a general weakness of the total prosecution evidence in the case. Thus, where he is deciding in favor of the defendant, the judge nevertheless tells us:

> Defendant made a very poor witness. [I-1164] Defendant fell down on cross-examination. [I-1129] Too eager, gave too many details. [II-0138] Did not give clear answers. [II-0383]

In discussing normal disagreements where credibility was the issue, we noted there was little data to suggest that the jury tended to be differentially gullible.[7] In the cross-over cases the question, of course, is the opposite; it is whether the jury as an appraiser of credibility is more biased than the judge.[8]

---

[7] See Chapter 13.

[8] Mention should be made of a few cases in which the disagreement in the handling of the evidence arises because of sloppiness on the part of the jury. For example, there is an arson case in which the judge's comment suggests that because of a local problem the community had simply grown impatient and eager to convict somebody: "There have been a number of incendiary fires in this county, police have been unable to apprehend guilty party." [II-1192] Again, in a narcotics case, the defendant, a Chinese crew member on a merchant ship, shared quarters where a supply of heroin was found. The co-defendant in pleading guilty exonerates the Chinese from any participation in the crime and persuades the judge of his innocence. The jury, however, convicts, and the judge observes: "Jury evidently convicted on the theory of guilt by association and strong suspicion." [I-2061]

It is somewhat reassuring that there are so few cases in which possible jury bias or irresponsibility in handling issues of fact appears to be responsible for cross-over disagreements.

We come then to the end of the reason assessment exploration of cross-over disagreements involving evidence factors. It will be remembered that in normal disagreements due to evidential disputes we located one specific matter on which the jury and judge recurringly made different credibility estimates, namely, cases in which the defendant has no record and takes the stand. It is tempting, therefore, to inquire whether this process is reversed in the case of the cross-over and whether the response of the jury to defendants who have records and do not take the stand is systematically more harsh than that of the judge. To test this we make the customary cross-tabulation, keeping the standard factors constant, and compare the defendants with a record or who do not take the stand with all others. Table 98, a rearrangement of Table 97, sets out the results.

TABLE 98

Effect of a Record or Failure to Testify on Cross-overs on Guilt

| | Unattractive Defendants | | Other Defendants | |
	Prosecutor Superior	Other Counsel	Prosecutor Superior	Other Counsel
Record or No Stand	100%	36%	60%	25%
Number of cases	*2*	*11*	*5*	*57*
No Record, Stand	50%	63%	—%	18%
Number of cases	*2*	*8*	*9*	*108*
Difference	50%	−27%	60%	7%
Attributable cases	*1.0*	*−3.0*	*3.0*	*4.0*

Table 98 shows that the hypothesis of a negative credibility judgment is corroborated; we can attribute 5.0 cases or 10.4 per cent of the cross-overs to the differing response of judge and jury to this type of defendant (one who has a record or fails to testify). Table 98 lends support to the legal tradition which so closely guards the disclosure of a prior record in a criminal case.[9]

At the end of the discussion on the role of the evidence in causing normal disagreements, we were able to build a model showing the various modes in which evidence comes into play, and even to make rough measurements.[10]

The obvious challenge here is whether a comparable table can be made to show the role of evidence in causing cross-over disagreements. The answer is basically no. It is however pos-

[9] Table 98 receives some corroboration from a number of references by the judge to this as a factor; a few examples will suffice: "Some women on the [hung] jury reasoned from three prior guilty pleas that he must have been guilty this time." [I-0750] "Jury knew of defendant's bad record." [I-1616] "Defendant had a record with several assaults." [I-1858] "Defendant has a bad reputation." [I-0586] "Defendant had a prior record for burglary." [II-0601] "This defendant did not take the stand." [II-0897]

The recent controversy over the fair trial and free press issue has highlighted the law's concern with the possible prejudicial aspects of a prior criminal record. Attorney General Katzenbach has already imposed some restrictions on such disclosure, and in a recent speech he indicated that these may be made still more severe. See his address to the American Society of Newspaper Editors, Free Press and Fair Trial, April 16, 1965. Federal Register Doc. 65-4112, v. 30, p. 5510.

[10] For convenience we reproduce here the data that appears in Chapter 14 as Table 59.

	Normal Disagreements %	Cross-Overs %
Liberation hypothesis (evidence *plus* sentiments)	46	10
Differential credibility of defendants without a record who take the stand	21	—
Random disagreements in close cases	6	6
Jury's greater tolerance for reasonable doubt	11	—
Total disagreements in which evidence was a factor	84%	16%
Total	100%	
Number of cases	*753*	

sible to make the first two steps and indicate the area of the liberation hypothesis and the role of specific judgment as to credibility. After this, we are left with at least 25 per cent of the evidence cross-overs which we cannot pinpoint; and this marks the end of analytic possibilities.[11]

It was a distinctive feature of the explanation of normal disagreements that on occasion the disagreement resulted simply from the differential communication of the case to the jury and the judge, so that they were not deciding quite the same case. As it turned out, this category plays only a very limited role in explaining normal disagreements, and it is not surprising, therefore, that there are only a handful of cases which suggest that differential communication is a source of the cross-over case.

A first illustration is offered by a trial in which the jury knows something which the judge does not know and where this extra knowledge influences its less lenient decision. In a homicide case, the judge finds the death accidental, whereas the jury convicts of involuntary manslaughter. The distinctive circumstance is that the jury somehow, from sources outside of the trial, knows of the defendant's repute and even that he has a criminal record, whereas the judge does not learn of these matters until after the verdict is in. As the judge puts it by way of explanation:

> The defendant was not well thought of locally and that fact was known to the jury but not by the judge until after the verdict. [I-1616]

Other illustrations concern factors, known only to the judge, which favor the defendant. In one case the judge knows that the chief prosecution witness in a charge of conspiracy to solicit

[11] There is no way of determining whether an *inverse reasonable doubt* hypothesis can be maintained, to the effect that some juries some of the time underestimate the level of doubt the law and the judge will tolerate in convicting. We have no way of determining whether this interesting possibility exists, because we cannot reverse the process used in Table 59.

bribes has pleaded guilty; armed with this additional insight the judge weighs the prosecution evidence differently from the jury and is led to acquit the defendant. [I-1520] In a final illustration, it is the judge's knowledge of the legal process and of the significance of certain moves by the prosecutor that is relevant. The defendant is charged with drunken driving and there is apparently a close question of credibility, but the judge is guided by his extra knowledge to a different conclusion about the weight of the prosecution's case. The precise circumstance is that the defendant's driving results in a death, and the judge explains his personal logic:

> It is my further thought that had the officers not been in doubt about the defendant's intoxication, he would have been charged with involuntary manslaughter. [I-0547]

The judge is thus reading the selection of the charge by the prosecutor as an admission of weakness which, when coupled with the difficulties of the evidence, is sufficient to persuade him not to convict. The jury presumably is not in a position to draw a comparable inference.

We dealt at length with the impact of the lawyer in producing normal disagreements. The story there was told chiefly in terms of the impact of superior defense counsel, although on occasion the imbalance is due primarily to inferior prosecution. Our inquiry now turns to the consequences of the opposite imbalance of counsel.

The judge's comments about counsel in the cross-over cases are not particularly detailed. More often than not, it is the maladroitness of the defense counsel rather than the superiority of the prosecutor which catches his attention. Thus, in a disorderly conduct case where the judge would have acquitted but the jury convicts, the judge points a finger at defense counsel:

> The conduct of counsel for the defense became so argumentative and obnoxious that the court threatened to hold him in

contempt. This conduct may have helped to influence the jury. [I-0151] [12]

At times through a tactical error defense counsel fails to make clear to the jury a point the judge is nevertheless able to pick up. In a prosecution for receiving stolen goods the judge apparently believes the defendant, although he is a poor witness, whereas the jury does not; the judge attributes the cross-over in part to a failure of defense counsel to bolster the defendant, the owner of a small store:

> Failure to call character witnesses. [II-0138]

In another case the judge attributes the disagreement to the failure of the defense counsel to follow up a lead which might have discredited the motivation of the complaining witnesses. The charge is attempted robbery of two women while they were sitting in a parked car in a gas station at 3 A.M. The judge[13] notes:

> There are indications that the two complainants were Lesbians who were interrupted by the defendant. The unskilled defense attorney was not alert enough to follow up the implications. [I-3006]

It remains to turn once more to cross-tabulation and thereby to measure the impact of this factor. To test this we again introduce our customary matrix, keeping the factors we have found to be significant constant, and compare the cases in which the prosecutor was superior to the remaining cases in which he was not. Table 99 then shows the role of counsel in causing the cross-over.[14] It is seen that 1.2 cases or about 2.5 per cent of cross-overs on guilt may be ascribed to the influence of counsel. This is very close to the estimate of 1.6 per cent which reason assessment yielded.

[12] Strangely, the best examples of the negative impact of counsel occur in a cross-over disagreement on the death penalty. See Chapter 35, page 441.

[13] The judge in this case is a woman.

[14] The estimate of the role of counsel will not be complete until we assess his effectiveness in the agreement cases. See Table 135 in Chapter 38.

TABLE 99

The Effect of the Superior Prosecutor on Cross-overs on Guilt

	Unattractive Defendants		Other Defendants	
	Record or No Stand	No Record, Stand	Record or No Stand	No Record, Stand
Prosecutor superior	100%	50%	60%	—%
Number of cases	2	2	5	9
Other counsel	36%	63%	25%	18%
Number of cases	11	8	57	108
Difference	64%	−13%	35%	−18%
Attributable cases	1.3	−0.3	1.8	−1.6

CHAPTER 31

Pro-prosecution Equities

In a preface sketching in broad outline the "cross-over tendencies" of the jury, we noted that a substantial number of cross-over decisions were due in part to sentiments on the law which made the jury side with the prosecution, and that sometimes the sentiment was a *pure* prosecution equity and sometimes it was simply an *ambivalent* response. The business of this chapter is to survey in detail the nature of these pure and ambivalent sentiments.

We begin with a narcotics prosecution which captures the complexity of the cross-over phenomenon by showing both types of sentiment. The defendant is charged with the sale of narcotics, but the sale is made "to an undercover agent who knew the defendant from high school acquaintanceship." The defense is not that the defendant did not commit the act, but that he was entrapped into doing it. The judge would have accepted the defense, but the jury convicts. And the judge blames the "public attitude" toward narcotics violations. [II-0937]

Although the judge is emphatic about the popular hostility toward narcotics violations, it is possible to detect an additional nuance in the jury's reaction. We learned earlier that the jury had some modest tendency to support the prophylactic rules against improper police procedure, particularly with respect to entrapment, and that on occasion this sentiment is a factor in producing disagreements where the jury is more lenient.[1]

---

[1] The normal disagreements involving entrapment as a defense involve evidence issues as well, and a distinctive jury sentiment barely emerges. See Chapter 23, pages 321-322.

This narcotics case suggests the possibility that the public is in fact ambivalent about civil liberties values such as the norms against entrapment, and that for some of the public it is nonsense to free a guilty man for the sake of such norms.

A series of sex crimes offers a good illustration of the nature and source of a pure prosecution response. In each of the cases the defendant has engaged in some sort of sexual behavior which, for one reason or another falls short of the legal definition of the crime. But in each of the cases the jury is so outraged by the defendant's conduct that it overrides distinctions of the law and finds him guilty as charged. These then are instances in which the law's precision emerges as more pro-defendant than does the jury's appetite for equity.

In a case where a father is charged with attempting a sexual assault on his thirteen-month-old-daughter, the jury finds him guilty of the serious charge of assault with intent to ravish, whereas the judge would have found him guilty only of aggravated assault. The judge, operating within the full precision of the law, is doubtful that the evidence supports a genuine sexual attack. The jury, offended by the admitted impropriety of the father's handling of the child, has no patience with such a technicality. The judge sums up the matter as follows:

> I would have convicted of aggravated assault instead of assault with intent to ravish because of doubt left in my mind that father intended or attempted any sexual connection. I think it clear that his conduct was criminal. [I-1610]

In a similar case, judge and jury again disagree on charge, the jury finding statutory rape, the judge, only assault with intent to commit rape. This time the daughter is thirteen years old; although there was considerable sexual play, the problem centers on whether there was in fact sexual penetration so as to complete the technical crime. The child so testifies, but the judge is left with a doubt. He states the reason for his decision:

Inasmuch as reasonable doubt should be resolved in favor of the defendant, I would in good conscience hold him guilty of assault with intent to commit rape.

He then adds the reason for the jury's more severe decision:

The crime is so reprehensible that it may have had something to do with the verdict. [I-0049]

In still another child sex offense the jury finds the defendant guilty of attempted sodomy with an eight-year-old boy, whereas the judge would acquit. Perhaps this time there is nothing more involved than an evidential dispute. The judge reports that he had difficulty making up his mind and states:

This is the closest criminal case I have ever tried . . . I have some doubt about his intent to commit sodomy. The jury is justified from the evidence in deciding the way it did.

The judge, however, appends a sentence disclosing the source of the jury's irritation and impatience with the defendant:

There is no doubt in my mind that the defendant was present and impaired the morals of a minor. [I-1209]

It is not difficult to perceive the norm the jury is implicitly following in these cases, that a gross sexual approach to a young child is a sufficient crime in itself and that its gravity need not be graduated according to the completeness of the sexual act.

Another case suggests that the jury response to the offensiveness of what the defendant did may be quite complex. Here the jury finds the defendant guilty of attempted rape of a sixteen-year-old girl where the judge acquits. The case is intriguing because the girl has a poor reputation and was a prior acquaintance of the defendant and was willing to go out with him, thus perfectly fitting the type of female victim whom the jury uncharitably treats as assuming the risks of sexual misbehavior.[2] The decisive offsetting circumstance, however, is that the defendant, as the judge puts it, "left his wife and

[2] The cases are discussed in Chapter 17, pages 249 et seq.

children to go out on an all-night toot." And he adds the telling economic fact that "the wife supported the husband." The upshot is that it is the judge who finds the girl's testimony sufficiently untrustworthy to move him to acquittal, while the jury is so indignant at the impropriety of the defendant's escapade, no matter what the facts as to rape, that it is moved to punish. [II-0926]

In the remaining sex cases the jury's umbrage takes on a racial strain. Thus, in two Mann Act prosecutions in which the judge acquits because of evidential difficulties, he makes clear what bothered the jury:

> It is my opinion that the jury probably did not take time to consider the evidence but merely based its decision on the fact that a colored defendant was on trial for white slavery involving both colored and white prostitutes. [II-0894] [3]

And again:

> This defendant did not take stand, but because of his association with the white victims . . . he may have made a bad impression on the jury. [II-0897]

In these cases the jury's response to the interracial sexuality has caused it to weigh the evidence against the defendant harshly. In the final case in this group, the jury's sense of irritation moves it again to override a legal distinction. A young Negro boy is charged with indecent exposure in a theatre. The undisputed facts are that the manager of the theatre, using a flashlight, discovers him masturbating in the dark. The judge acquits on the grounds that the crime of indecent exposure requires exposure to the public. The jury overrides this distinction, because on these facts it is offended by the boy's conduct, whether or not anyone saw it. The judge tells us:

> The jury could not get the morals of the case out of their minds. They saw only a colored boy masturbating in the theatre with white women and children in the audience. [I-1534]

[3] Compare note 15 in Chapter 26.

In another cluster of cases, the offensive circumstance engendering an equity against the defendant is somewhat unexpected. The defendant has conspicuously failed to come to the aid of the victim, and it is this gross act of neglect which arouses the jury. In a sense the defendant is convicted for not having been a Good Samaritan.

Thus in one case there is a close question of fact as to whether in a dispute over wages the defendant struck the victim, a farm laborer, or the victim fell down the stairs. The judge would resolve the doubt in favor of the defendant and acquit. He discloses however the telltale circumstance that alienated the jury:

> Victim was a pathetic looking figure and doubtless inspired sympathy. He had been taken to his "shack" and left there unattended for 24 hours. [I-1600]

The same sentiment is traceable in a case of an auto accident where defendant's auto knocks down a female pedestrian. The jury finds him guilty of reckless driving, the judge, only of the lesser offense of leaving the scene. The judge explains:

> The evidence was strong that he did leave the scene of the accident. I believe the jury was imbued with the thought that the defendant had little regard for the rights of others and that he was inclined to wholly disregard all laws which in any way interfered with personal activities. [I-0548]

The unusual feature of this case is that the jury is so incensed at the defendant for leaving the scene of the accident that it is not satisfied to find him guilty of the very crime that angers them but must go on to find him guilty of reckless driving as well.

In a brutal assault by a husband on his wife, a subtle disagreement on charge once again reflects the Good Samaritan response. The defendant is charged with beating his wife severely. The jury finds malicious wounding "with his feet"; the judge finds only malicious wounding "with his fists." The offsetting circumstance is that the defendant, after the beating, dragged his wife to a lonely spot and left her. As the judge puts it:

His leaving woman in bushes to die without help. [I-1909]

Here again the jury sentiment might translate into a possible rule of law, one which, like tort law, would hold defendant for not aiding the victim of his violence, making this an aggravated version of the crime.[4]

The theme finds some re-enforcement in a group of cases in which parents are charged with child neglect or non-support. Here again the jury is impatient with a legal refinement. The law limits the crime to *willful* neglect. In a series of three cases the judge acquits each time on the ground that the evidence fails to show that the defendant's conduct was willful, but the jury, offended by the pitiable condition of the children, each time takes a harsher view of the matter.

Thus, in one case the judge describes the parents favorably:

Parents made a good showing of efforts used to care for children, but they both were markedly ignorant.

He is willing to write off the neglect on the ground of ignorance. The jury, however, is moved by the fact that the children were "helpless infants," one of them ten months old and, as the judge notes:

The actual poor condition of the children was very evident. They were malnourished and had skin ulcers. [II-0166]

In a similar case the judge sums up the competing influences:

Defendants were not willfully neglectful but poverty stricken with four minor children. [I-1039]

Another case presents the same picture: minor children not properly cared for and a defendant whose claim of inability to provide support because of the lack of a job falls on deaf ears.

---

[4] The Restatement of Torts formulates the tort rule as follows: "If the actor by his tortious conduct has caused such bodily harm to another as to make him helpless, the actor is under a duty to use reasonable care to prevent any further harm which the actor then realizes or should realize as threatening the other." §322.

The jury sentiment in another group of cases is perhaps best described by the maxim that Caesar's wife should be above suspicion.[5] In each case the defendant, an official, has permitted himself to be placed in a compromising position, and this is enough for the jury, although not for the judge. The point is neatly illustrated by companion cases in which a policeman and a magistrate are charged with perjury before a grand jury investigating gambling. In each case the judge would acquit the defendants. The jury, however, hangs with respect to the policeman but finds the magistrate guilty. The unusual circumstance is that in each trial the prosecution uses precisely the same testimony and witnesses. The jury seems to believe them in one case and disbelieve them in the other. However, the cases illustrate not how erratic jury judgment about credibility can be, but rather a more interesting point, which the judge sums up persuasively. The chief witness against the defendants is a confessed gambler who had turned state's evidence and who undoubtedly had some contact with the magistrate.[6] The judge tells us:

> While I disagree with verdict, and even prosecutor probably disagrees, I would not criticize jury. Perhaps of significance to jury was communication between witness and defendant. Defendant, a magistrate, should order a character of this sort to stay away. [I-1043]

A bribery case is somewhat analogous. The defendant, superintendent of a housing project, is found guilty by the jury

[5] The expression of this sentiment has harsh origins which it may be of interest to relate. Plutarch supplies the background detail in his Life of Caesar. A young man disguised as a woman was caught in the act of spying on a religious ceremony, traditionally for women only, which was being supervised by the dictator's wife. Caesar immediately divorced her. Later, at the trial of the intruder for sacrilege, Caesar, summoned as a witness for the prosecution, said that he did not know whether the event had taken place. When asked on what grounds, then, he had divorced his wife, he made the now famous reply.

[6] "Defendant admitted that he knew [the gambler] and that he visited him (while a judge) to borrow small sums ($1, $2) for medicine."

of attempting to bribe an FHA inspector. It is clear on the record that the defendant offered the inspector an unspecified sum of money. What is not clear is whether it was offered as a bribe or as a gift, and on the basis of this doubt the judge acquits. Once again the jury is overriding a legal refinement and is operating on the premise that it is sufficient that the defendant deliberately approached a government official with an offer of money. [I-1982]

The offending circumstance in the eyes of the jury in the final case of pure prosecution sentiments is perhaps the most subtle. The jury finds the defendant guilty of manslaughter whereas the judge would have acquitted on the grounds of self-defense, accepting the claim of the defendant that he came to the defense of his son who was being attacked. We have seen earlier that the jury has a more generous view of self-defense than the law. But in this case, its normal sympathies' are more than offset by a bizarre circumstance: the fight takes place at a funeral and the homicide weapon was in fact the grave digger's shovel. The judge makes it clear that the jury's sense of decorum was deeply offended:

> The difficulty occurred at a Negro funeral. The deceased was the funeral director. The jury evidently agreed with defendant's defense but felt that the trouble should not have taken place at a funeral. [I-1759]

In the cases dealt with thus far, the jury is moved by what has been called a *pure* pro-prosecution sentiment, whether in the form of hostility toward narcotics, anger at sexual approaches to young children, impatience with child neglect, indignation at defendant's failure to be a Good Samaritan to his own victim, belief that persons in a position of public trust should be like Caesar's wife, and, finally, that self-defense carried to the point of killing is excessive at a funeral.

In the cross-over cases to which we now turn, the sentiment is of a different sort. It is simply the converse of some sentiment we have already met as a source of normal disagreement between judge and jury. In these cases the theory, we repeat, is that the public is *ambivalent* about the values involved and that some fraction of it has a view which is the exact opposite of that held by the majority.[7]

We begin with an extreme case in which the jury can be said to be doubly ambivalent. They find the defendant guilty of bookmaking where the judge would have acquitted. The defendant is tending bar at the time and does nothing more than take money across the counter and deliver it to a bookie at the other end of the bar, a very minor role in the transaction. Further, it appears that the bet is made by a state trooper in civilian clothes and there is strong evidence of entrapment. In convicting the defendant in this case the jury departs from two of its firmly held sentiments: first, hostility toward holding gambling a crime, especially where it is, as here, simply bookmaking away from a track; and, second, hostility toward entrapment. The existence of the case confirms the suggestion, made earlier in the narcotics cases,[8] that some jurors think that entrapment should not be a defense; and it further suggests that some jurors hold stringent views about gambling.

We noted earlier a tendency on the part of the jury to sympathize with the citizen in an altercation with the police.[9] We now confront two arrest cases in which the jury is more sympathetic to the police than is the judge. In one, two policemen in plain clothes attempt to arrest the defendant on the sidewalk, because he was "supposedly staggering." There is some sort of a fracas in which the defendant loses his glasses. The judge characterizes the defendant as "not too intelligent" and adds that: "His sight was poor without glasses." The jury finds the defendant guilty of resisting arrest with force,

---

[7] The move from normal disagreement to cross-overs involves a major change in attitude. Strictly speaking, two steps are necessary, between three ranks of attitude; the middle position is where judge and jury agree to convict. This is why we may speak of ambivalent jury sentiments where we encounter the same sentiment *with a different sign,* in normal and cross-over disagreements.

[8] See above pages 395-396.

[9] Chapter 16, pages 236-239.

which is a felony. The judge finds him guilty only of resisting arrest, and adds that he "did not believe under the circumstances that the defendant should be found guilty of a
felony." [II-0793]

In the second arrest case the range of disagreement between
judge and jury is at a minimum. The defendant is charged
with disorderly conduct, and the judge would acquit. The
jury hangs, with a single juror holding out for guilty. The
precise issue is whether the defendant had conducted himself in
a disorderly manner prior to his arrest, and the judge explains:

> One juror apparently believed that the police are justified in
> making an arrest anytime without any reason. [I-1368]

Another area in which the jury is sometimes ambivalent is
in determining the impact of insanity on criminal responsibility. Thus, a man who kills his common law wife by stabbing
her several times with a butcher knife defends on the grounds
of insanity and has a history of being in and out of mental
hospitals with a diagnosis of schizophrenia. The judge would
accept the defense, but the jury finds murder. One unusual
feature in the report of the case is that it was sent back for a
new trial because of an error in the instructions on insanity.
We have the report on the new trial where once again the
judge would find the defendant not guilty because of insanity, yet the jury finds murder. The judge states:

> There was no dispute that the defendant was legally insane,
> although the state did not expressly admit it.

The judge then characterizes the sources of the jury's hostility
toward the insanity defense:

> Belief that defendant would not be confined as long if sent to
> a mental institution. [II-0545, II-0564] [10]

Another case presents the same factors and the same judge-
jury reaction. The crime involves a wild form of sexual muti-
lation and the judge thinks it clear that the defendant was
legally insane. The jury nevertheless finds the defendant

---

[10] For other evidence as to jury concern about confinement, see discussion in Simon, The American Jury — The Defense of Insanity (1966).

guilty of assault with intent to kill, and the judge again explains the reaction:

> Probably a belief on jury's part that defendant would be more securely confined if sent to penitentiary rather than to an institution for the criminally insane. [II-0563]

These insanity cases mark the most extreme form we have of jury revolt in favor of greater severity.[11] They embody the dilemma the insanity defense poses for the popular mind: the more heinous and violent a crime the more obvious the insanity of the actor, but also the greater the danger he presents to society.[12]

We find a similar ambivalence with respect to intoxication. In three homicide cases the jury is unwilling to recognize intoxication as reducing the degree of criminal responsibility, although the law involved authorizes it. Where a defendant beats his wife so badly that she dies from the injuries, the judge finds as the extenuating circumstance the fact that the defendant and his wife had been in a drunken stupor for weeks. He would, therefore, find only first degree manslaughter, whereas the jury finds second degree murder. He adds as a further comment on this disagreement:

> Under the law a homicide committed while too drunk to entertain the intent to take life is manslaughter for which the maximum punishment is imprisonment for ten years. The jury's verdict was probably a compromise between the extremes; that is, those who wanted to inflict capital punishment and those who wanted to acquit. [II-0281][13]

In a second case where the defendant while drunk stabs and kills the victim with a knife, the judge, disagreeing with the

[11] These are virtually the only cases in which the judge rates the case as clear for acquittal where the jury nevertheless refuses to acquit. The two remaining non-evidence cross-over disagreements are discussed at page 398 (I-1534 — indecent exposure in a darkened theater) and page 401 (I-1982 — bribery of an FHA inspector).

[12] See Simon, note 10 above.

[13] The case illustrates the ready possibility that a sentiment may be represented ambivalently in a single jury. The device of the compromise verdict suggests the possibility of a small minority giving final direction to the verdict. See also Chapter 38.

jury, would hold the charge down to second degree murder, noting as the extenuating circumstances: "None — other than intoxicated." [II-0557]

Finally, there is a complex triangle situation. The defendant was married previously to the wife of the victim; all three became embroiled in a drunken brawl — "the fracas began after taunts" — and the current husband was kicked and stomped to death. And the judge holds the charge down to murder without malice, noting that all three parties had been drinking, and adding "also people of low intelligence and also low morals." [I-1757]

The jury's ambivalence toward intoxication shows up again in a few drunken driving cases. We noted earlier that these prosecutions are often unpopular and that the jury is often more tolerant of drinking than is the law. We now pick up cases in which the judge acquits yet the jury would either convict or hang. In one such case the judge comments:

> I would have given the defendant the benefit of the presumption of innocence in view of the weak evidence of drinking. [I-1388]

And in the second case the judge makes the point explicit:

> I believe the majority was convinced as I was that the people had not proved the case beyond reasonable doubt. The ones who voted guilty were ardent drys. [I-0911]

There is one further vivid illustration of the jury's feelings about liquor. This time the defendant is charged with keeping and maintaining a disorderly house. The facts show that he served beer to friends at 3 o'clock in the morning, but there is no showing that there was any nuisance or disturbance in the neighborhood. The judge, following the precision of the law, would acquit because there was no public disturbance.[14] He explains the jury's disagreement in the following manner:

[14] In this case the jury disregards the legal requirement that there be a *public* disturbance. See Case I-1534, page 398 above, where the jury convicts for private indecent exposure, again overriding the literal but, in these instances, liberal distinctions of law. There are 17 such cases in all; the two cases cited are by far the most vivid.

I believe the jury in view of the evidence to the effect that there was drinking in the defendant's home with other persons present, after midnight . . . arrived at the conclusion that the defendant deserved to be punished simply because he maintained a home that was open for the purpose of congregating, and drinking. I believe the jury ignored the court's instruction that in order to convict a defendant there must be evidence there is a disturbance in the neighborhood. [I-1503]

Another cluster of cases illustrates ambivalence in jury views about inadvertent conduct as criminal. Here again we find the jury departing from a sentiment it was previously seen to espouse. It more than once finds the defendant's inadvertence sufficiently careless to be criminal, although the judge finds it below the legal threshold. The circumstance in these cases that alienates the jury is obvious: harm is done.

In two cases the charge is drunken driving, and in both the judge would acquit. Here the directive circumstance for the jury is that there was an accident and serious harm:

This case involved an accident in which a man was killed. [I-0507]

Small child injured by defendant's vehicle on Fourth of July. [II-0810]

Then, there is a case in which the jury finds negligent homicide and the judge explains his decision: "Lack of wanton and wilfulness the law requires." Again, the decisive fact appears to be that two people were killed in the accident. [II-0098]

A few cases suggest that the jury may be somewhat ambivalent also in its attitude toward self-defense. We saw earlier that the jury, in disagreement with the judge, is often sensitive toward provocation as justifying retaliatory violence. But in the handful of cases to which we now turn, the jury each time appraises the defendant's use of violence more harshly than does the judge. It may even override a legal defense of self-defense. Thus, it convicts of aggravated assault and battery in a case where the judge would acquit on the grounds of self-defense, apparently alienated by the fact that the defendant had stabbed the victim four or five times and had put out his eye. [II-0282] Again, in the domestic triangle situation, in which the jury normally extends a special privilege to the jealous spouse, it may on occasion reverse its response. In one case the defendant in a fit of jealousy kills his wife for having been indiscreet; the judge would have found only manslaughter, the jury convicts of murder. The jury overrides the fact that jealous rage can be a legally mitigating circumstance. The judge perhaps gives us the clue:

> Killed his own wife and mother of his three children. [II-0243]

Two final cases deserve brief mention in the sequence of cross-over sentiments. Although on the facts they are very different, they bear a strong analogy to each other. In one the defendant is charged with armed robbery of a small grocery store. The distinctive circumstance is that the gun he used had no stock and was probably not loaded. The jury finds him guilty of aggravated robbery; the judge, only of robbery without aggravation. The judge notes:

> The defendant did not or could not have fired the rifle had the victim resisted. [II-0038]

Whatever the rule of law here,[15] it is enough for the jury that the defendant creates the impression of being armed.

In the other case, the defendant is accused of having obtained goods from a department store by giving false information at the time she opened a charge account. There is no dispute that she did give false information. There is, however, a problem about satisfying the legal definition for criminal fraud, and the judge acquits because "in view of the obvious and diligent investigation the management made, there is serious doubt that it relied on her statement." [I-1802]

---

[15] It has been held that commission of a robbery with an imitation or unloaded gun is armed robbery within the meaning of the statute. See, e.g., N.Y. Penal Law §1944 and People ex rel. Griffin v. Hunt, 267 N.Y. 597, 196 N.E. 598 (1935); Miss. Penal Code §2367 and Cittadino v. State, 199 Miss. 235, 24 So. 2d 93 (1945).

Here, whatever the rule of law,[16] it is enough for the jury that the defendant deliberately made a false statement.

The two cases with their widely different fact circumstances illustrate once again a recurring theme of the cross-over section: the precision of the law may sometimes work more for the defendant than the jury's free-roving sentiment.

It may be helpful at this point to draw together in summary form the various strands of jury cross-over sentiments we have been tracing. Table 100 provides such a quantitative profile.

TABLE 100

Jury Pro-prosecution Sentiments on the Law

Source	Pure	Ambivalent
Narcotics	3	—
Sex with young children	4	—
Interracial sex	4	—
Gambling	—	1
Drunken driving	—	5
Intoxication	—	3
Disorderly house, drinking	—	1
Philandering husband	1	—
Good Samaritan obligation to victim	3	—
Caesar's wife for public officials	2	—
Unseemly conduct	1	—
Entrapment	—	3
Insanity	—	3
Technical definition of crime	—	17
Inadvertence, where harm results	—	3
Inadvertence, neglect of children	4	—
Excessive self-defense, provocation	—	6
Total	22	42

[16] The common law required, to sustain a conviction for criminal fraud, that the victim's reliance on a misrepresentation had to be reasonable under the circumstances. Modern criminal law protects all victims of deceit, no matter how foolishly they were duped, so long as they in fact relied on a misrepresentation. In cases of misrepresentation, where no reliance can be shown, there may still be prosecution for attempt.

Table 100 not only summarizes the cross-over sentiments on the law, but, equally important, it also, in the ambivalence column, rounds out the impression of the sentiments that cause normal disagreements.[17]

[17] As, for example, Chapter 16 (self-defense), Chapter 17 (contributory negligence of the victim in sex crimes), Chapter 19 (unpopular laws), Chapter 23 (police), Chapter 24 (inadvertence as criminal), and Chapter 25 (insanity and intoxication).

CHAPTER 32

Cross-overs: The Judge's Special Role

The role of the judge in the cross-over case may differ significantly from his role in the normal disagreement. As a matter of law he has no power over jury verdicts which, in his view, are too favorable to the defendant. In the cross-over case, however, the judge may have legal power to intervene.[1] Thus, a novel question arises when the disagreement goes in this direction: what does the judge do about verdicts he feels are too harsh?

Although pursuit of this question is something of a digression, the data offer so unique an opportunity to attempt an answer that we pause here to discuss briefly the occasions in which the judge intervenes.

The question raises the interesting possibility that the defendant in choosing trial by jury may have the best of both possible worlds. If the disagreement is normal, he gets an un-

---

[1] The judge cannot upset a jury acquittal, but on conviction there are several avenues open to him. He may direct an acquittal notwithstanding the verdict, when, as a matter of law, the evidence is insufficient to sustain a conviction. Or he may grant a new trial in the event of newly discovered evidence which probably would have changed the verdict, or because a procedural error or violation has prejudiced the defendant's rights. See American Law Institute, Code of Criminal Procedure §§361-368 (1931). As a last alternative, the judge can moderate the penalty. In most cases this results in probation or a suspended sentence. Perhaps the most extraordinary example of penalty adjustment we have occurs in a conviction for lesbianism. The judge fines the defendant twenty-seven dollars to be paid at the rate of twenty-five cents a week. [I-1205]

touchable acquittal;[2] and, if the judge would have been more lenient, he may still have an appeal to the judge's conscience. Does it work out then that if the defendant elects a jury trial he cannot lose — because he is the beneficiary of whoever would have been more lenient?

Table 101 gives the basic answer.

TABLE 101

Disposition After Jury's Guilty Verdict If Judge Would Have Acquitted or Found on Lesser Charge

| | Judge Would Have — | | |
	Acquitted*	Found Guilty of Lesser Charge	Total
	%	%	%
Sets aside verdict	14	0	10
Gives minimum penalty	38	25	34
Fully respects verdict	48	75	56
Total	100%	100%	100%
Number of cases	63	24	87
Disposition not reported	14	2	16
Total cases	77	26	103

* Excluded are 40 cases where the judge acquits and the jury hangs.

Table 101 makes it evident that the defendant who selects jury trial does not always have the best of it. Reading the total column, we see that some defendants who select jury trial might have been better off to stay with the judge. In 56 per cent of the cases the judge lets stand a verdict he would not have reached himself. His intervention, when it occurs, comes chiefly in the form of reducing the sentence. In only 1 in 10 cases does he set the verdict aside.

Though Table 101 answers the basic question, there re-

[2] In a minority of states the prosecution may appeal an acquittal, on certain statutory conditions, to clarify the law. The major limitation to such a move is the double jeopardy clause in the Fifth Amendment, which has its counterpart in the constitution of almost every state. See Palko v. Connecticut, 302 U.S. 319 (1937). Under present law, where there is concurrent jurisdiction over a single crime between a state and the Federal Government, the defendant may be retried without violation of due process. Bartkus v. Illinois, 359 U.S. 121 (1958).

mains one further line of inquiry which we might follow up briefly. What determines *when* the judge will intervene?

Table 102 shows, as one would hope, that when the crime is a serious one, the judge interposes his own judgment approximately twice as often as when the crime is minor.

TABLE 102

Judge's Intervention by Seriousness of Crime
(*Disagreement on Guilt Only*)

	Serious crimes %	Minor crimes %
Sets aside verdict	19	5
Gives minimum penalty	42	25
Fully respects verdict	39	70
Total	100%	100%
Number of cases	*43*	*20*

We can also relate the judge's response to the basic analysis of the reasons for disagreement. Table 103 gives the results for the three familiar categories: Facts alone, Facts and Values, and Values alone.

TABLE 103

Judge's Intervention by Cause of the Jury's Disagreement

	Facts alone	Facts and Values	Values alone
Sets aside verdict	12	17	50
Gives minimum penalty	24	38	25.
Fully respects verdict	64	45	25
Total	100%	100%	100%
Number of cases	*17*	*42*	*4*

Although the numbers are small, their direction seems clear. The incidence of the judge's restraint declines from 64 to 45 to 25 per cent as we go from pure evidence to pure sentiment.

In the end the institutional arrangement is impressive. It gives the jury autonomy to do equity on behalf of the criminal defendant. Where the jury's freedom leads to "illegally" harsh results, the judge is at hand, ready to erase them.

*C*HAPTERS 33 AND 34 ENABLE us to approach the full universe of disagreement from new angles. Chapter 33 explores how more active participation by the trial judge can effectively reduce the jury's autonomy and thereby the extent of its disagreement with the judge. Chapter 34, in detailing how the judge feels about verdicts with which he disagrees, makes it possible to see the judge as a critic of the jury's performance.

Chapter 35 is in effect somewhat of a digression in that it involves a question of penalty. Although we do not treat with such disagreements elsewhere, in view of the great contemporary interest in the issue of capital punishment we report out the cases in the sample in which either the judge or the jury or both gave the death penalty.

CHAPTER 33

Procedural Controls of the Jury

It is useful to think of the relationship of judge and jury in a criminal trial as a system of checks and balances. Not a little law has been concerned with varying this equilibrium. Jurisdictions vary, for example, on whether the jury should be given formal instructions only on the law; whether instructions should be in writing so they may be taken into the jury room; at what stage the instructions should be given; whether the form of the jury verdict should be changed so as to require answers to a series of specific questions of fact, leaving it to the judge to apply the law and reach a verdict in terms of the jury's response; whether and to what degree the deliberation process can be opened to scrutiny after a jury has reached its verdict; and the degree to which the jury can be disciplined, if it goes astray.[1]

Our data enable us to study one additional dimension of this judge-jury complex: the degree of active guidance by the trial judge in the area of jury fact-finding.

It has often been remarked that a major difference between the jury system in England and in the United States lies in the role of the trial judge. In England he invariably plays a vigorous role during the trial, but especially when he turns the case over to the jury. The summing up by the English judge not only gives the jury general instructions on the relevant law but provides a rounded summary of the evidence with some indica-

[1] For a useful summary of the methods of controlling the jury, see James, Civil Procedure, pp. 240-248 (1965).

tions as to how the judge feels about its credibility.[2] The role of the American trial judge is usually more modest. In the majority of cases he will not do more than instruct the jury on the law. The autonomy of the English jury is thus narrower than that of the American jury. Indeed, some critics of the American jury system have argued that it would be desirable to bring our jury closer to the British model.[3]

We come here to a question about judge-jury disagreement that is different in kind. Up to now we have been concerned with the substance of the jury's disagreement rather than with the procedures that may permit it. We now ask whether these procedures could be varied so as to subject the jury to greater judicial control and hence reduce disagreement.

Once again, the pluralism of American law enables us to re-create an experimental situation and pick up one strand of a general issue. We can compare the operation of several modes of trial within the system. There are essentially three patterns of judicial control to be found:

(a) the judge may instruct the jury on the law only;

(b) in addition, he may summarize the evidence; and

(c) in addition, he may comment on the weight of the evidence and the credibility of witnesses.

In every American jurisdiction the judge instructs the jury

[2] Something of the freedom and power with which the English judge sums up can be garnered from the recapitulation of one of Mr. Justice Devlin's charges, in Bedford, The Best We Can Do (London 1958), an account of the trial of Dr. Adams, pp. 219-250, especially at 249: "I dare say it is the first time you have sat in that jury-box. It is not the first time I have sat in this chair. And not infrequently I have heard a case presented by the prosecution that seemed to me to be manifestly a strong one, and sometimes I have felt it my duty to tell the jury so. I do not think, therefore, that I ought to hesitate to tell you that here the case for the defense seems to be manifestly a strong one."

[3] There are some suggestions in data from other parts of the Jury Project that in spite of legal restrictions, the American judge too, at times, reveals his opinion of at least parts of the case by his demeanor during the trial, and that the majority of jurors are both interested and skillful in reading his reactions. The present chapter deals only with the major, formal controls of the jury.

on the law; whether he can go further and summarize or comment on the evidence varies widely by jurisdiction. Table
104 shows the legal power of the judge, by jurisdictions.[4]

Table 104 can give the formal pattern only and no indication
of how the actual practices are distributed. It is an old experience with legal procedures that optional rules produce a great
diversity of practices. In general the option will be declined
more frequently than it will be used.[5] Tables 105 and 106
show that this holds true for the judge's option to summarize
or comment.[6]

[4] The following data is based on Kurland, The Administration of
Criminal Justice in England: Some Invidious Comparisons (Review of
Devlin, The Criminal Prosecution in England), U. Chi. L. Rev., v. 26,
pp. 193, 203 (1958). See also, Vanderbilt, Minimum Standards of
Judicial Administration, pp. 224-234 (1949). The constitutions of two
of our states, Maryland and Indiana, allow the jury in criminal cases
to be judges "of the facts *and* the law," thus apparently giving the
jury one more degree of freedom to dissent from the judge, whose
instructions on the law are only advisory. But in Indiana the courts
have refused to take the rule literally and have consistently reduced its
scope. As to Maryland, it may be noted that in spite of its constitutional provision, it belongs to the minority of states that allow the
judge to summarize the evidence. Howe, Juries as Judges of Criminal
Law. Harv. L. Rev., v. 52, p. 582 (1939), gives a view of the history of
the doctrine.

The cases in our study do not enable us to make a statement on
whether or not this constitutional provision affects the rate of jury
disagreement, especially since Maryland is atypical also in its inordinately high rate of jury waiver. How complicated the analytical
problem may be is shown in Judge Ulman's discussion of the Baltimore
Criminal Court. Ulman, A Judge Takes a Stand, p. 252 (1933).

[5] Other examples of this judicial inertia are: the rare use the courts
make of the appointment of an impartial expert in addition to the adversary experts; or the ordering of separation of the issue of liability
from that of damages in civil trials. See Zeisel, The New York Expert
Testimony Project: Some Reflections on Legal Experiments, Stan. L.
Rev., v. 8, p. 730 (1956); Zeisel and Callahan, Split Trials and Time
Saving: A Statistical Analysis, Harv. L. Rev., v. 76, p. 1606 (1963).

[6] The data in this and the following tables come from the tabulation
of Q.11 of the Sample I questionnaire and Q.24 of the Sample II questionnaire found in Appendix E.

It is difficult to ascertain fully the actual form of the judge's com-

TABLE 104

The Judge's Right to Summary or Comment

States Allowing Neither Comment nor Summary	States Allowing Summary Only	States Allowing Both Summary and Comment on the Evidence
Arizona	Alabama	California
Arkansas	Delaware	Connecticut
Colorado	Georgia	Michigan
Florida	Iowa	New Hampshire
Idaho	Kansas	New Jersey
Illinois	Maine	New York
Indiana	Maryland	Pennsylvania
Kentucky	Massachusetts	Rhode Island
Louisiana	Minnesota	Utah
Mississippi	Nebraska	Vermont
Missouri	Nevada	Wisconsin
Montana	New Mexico	Federal Courts*
North Dakota	North Carolina	
Oklahoma	Ohio	
Oregon	South Dakota	
South Carolina	Tennessee	
Texas	Wyoming	
Virginia		
Washington		
West Virginia		

* Hawaii and Alaska acceded after our field work was completed; cases from these states are included under Federal Courts.

Table 105 gives the frequency with which the judges, in the seventeen states that allow summary only, make use of this procedure.

It also shows that in only three of the seventeen states (Tennessee, North Carolina, and Maryland) does the judge summarize the evidence in a majority of the trials. For New Mexico, Ohio, and Massachusetts, the frequency drops to 30 per cent, 15 per cent, and 14 per cent respectively; for three other states the percentages range between 4 and 1 per cent, and for the remaining eight states, from which we have a total

ment since it is so largely a matter of practice. But the impression remains that even when the American judge comments on the weight of the evidence, he is not as free as the English judge.

TABLE 105

How Often Judges Summarize the Evidence in
States That Allow Only Summary

	Frequency of Summary (In per cent of all reported trials)	Number of Trial Reports from State	Number of Judges Reporting
Tennessee	94	(51)	2
North Carolina	84	(81)	8
Maryland	50	(28)	6
New Mexico	30	(33)	3
Ohio	15	(108)	28
Massachusetts	14	(14)	2
Minnesota	4	(51)	21
Georgia	3	(33)	6
Kansas	1	(69)	10
Alabama, Delaware, Iowa, Maine, Nebraska, Nevada, South Dakota, Wyoming	—	(265)	57
Average for 17 states*	32%	(733)	143

* The average is computed by applying the above percentages to the number of jury trials in each state as reported in Table 6, rather than to the sample figure in the second column of this table.

of 265 trial reports, there is not a single case in which the evidence was summarized. Except for a handful of states, then, the judges make only spotty use of their option to summarize the evidence.

Table 106 gives the comparable information for the eleven states and the federal court system which allow the judge both to summarize the evidence and to comment on it.

In these jurisdictions the judge shows on the whole a greater propensity to do more than instruct on the law. It would seem that freedom to summarize *and* comment creates a climate which encourages judges to become more active. The range in the use of the procedure is again extreme, going from Pennsylvania where there is comment or summary in 64 + 29 =) 93 per cent of the reported trials to Utah and

TABLE 106

How Often the Judge Summarizes or Summarizes and Comments on the Evidence in Jurisdictions That Allow Both

State	Neither Comments nor Summarizes	Comments or Summarizes and Comments	Summarizes Only	Number of Trial Reports from State	Number of Judges Reporting
	(Per Cent of All Reported Trials)				
Pennsylvania	7	64	29	(226)	22
New Jersey	10	71	19	(401)	29
New York	21	35	44	(57)	9
Wisconsin	25	50	25	(8)	3
Connecticut	31	44	25	(16)	5
Vermont	50	50	0	(8)	3
Michigan	50	18	32	(88)	12
Federal Courts	52	21	27	(347)	71
California	85	14	1	(581)	83
Utah	95	5	—	(20)	5
New Hampshire	100	—	—	(9)	2
Rhode Island		[No cases in sample]			
Average for 12 jurisdictions*	47%	32%	21%	1761	244

* See footnote to Table 105.

New Hampshire where there is virtually never such participation by the trial judge.[7]

Taking all jurisdictions together, it is possible to provide a synopsis of the results of Tables 105 and 106 to show how often the judge will only instruct on the law, or summarize, or comment. Table 107 gives this information.

In the majority of all jury trials, then, the jury receives only instruction on the law, and in only 8 per cent of all trials does

[7] The percentages in Tables 105 and 106 are, of course, subject to sampling errors. Hence, the fact that the limited number of New Hampshire trials in the sample show neither comment nor summary 100 per cent of the time in Table 106 does not exclude the possibility that a larger sample of New Hampshire trials would have revealed some trials which had summary and/or comment.

TABLE 107

Frequency of Summary and Comment
(*All Trials*)

	Per Cent*
Judge —	
Instructs only	74
Summarizes only	18
Summarizes and comments	8
Total	100%

* These percentages are obtained by applying the frequency of usage to the actual frequencies of jury trial as found in Table 6. See note to Table 105.

the judge summarize and comment on the evidence and thus approach the English mode of trial.[8]

Since the procedures are used with such varying frequencies, there is interest in exploring why they are sometimes used and sometimes not. Tables 105 and 106 have given the answer for a good part of the cases. Where the jurisdiction shows a pattern of use either in virtually all trials or in virtually no trials, one may infer that there is something like a *regional judicial custom*.[9]

Table 108 carries this analysis a step further. For judges

[8] It is of interest to note to what the judge's comments apply:

Judge comments on —	Per Cent
weight of the evidence	25
credibility of witnesses	16
both weight and credibility	59
Total	100%
Number of cases	*638*

[9] We have noted earlier another regional custom in legal procedure: the decision to go before a jury or to waive jury trial, seemingly made on a case-by-case basis, was shown to be largely the result of custom. See Table 3, and Chapter 29, note 4. There is evidence that such legal regional customs extend beyond judges and lawyers into the community at large. It was found, for instance, that the citizens in some regions of the country are much more likely than others to file a claim for a given accident. See the discussion of claim consciousness in Zeisel, Kalven, Buchholz, Delay in the Court, Ch. 20 (1959).

TABLE 108

Summary and Comment Patterns Followed by Judges*
(In Per Cent of Judges)

| | Jurisdiction permits — | | |
	Only Summary	Summary and Comment	Total All Judges
Summarize and/or Comment —			
never	78	42	54
always	9	28	21
Total established pattern	87	70	75
Sometimes do; sometimes don't	13	30	25
Total	100%	100%	100%
Number of judges	*105*	*200*	*305*

* Those reporting at least two cases.

who have more than one case, it shows whether they follow the same pattern through all their cases or not.

It is apparent that beyond the fixity of regional customs there are *habits of the individual judge* which may have become equally rigid. Thus only 25 per cent of all judges vary their practice with the individual case; 54 per cent never exercise their option, and the remaining 21 per cent always make use of it.[10] The rigidity is even more apparent in the jurisdictions that allow summary only: here 87 per cent of all judges follow fixed pattern; moreover, in these jurisdictions 78 per cent of the judges never use their option.

There is some interest in exploring, for the minority of judges who vary their procedure from case to case, whether something in the particular case induces them to use the judicial control or not. We begin with the expectation that the judge will use his control power more frequently in serious crimes. Table 109 confirms this.

[10] These figures, however, almost certainly overrepresent somewhat the rigidity of the judicial pattern, because of the small samples of cases we have from some judges.

TABLE 109

Frequency with Which Judge Summarizes and/or
Comments in Serious and Mınor Cases

(For Judges Whose Pattern Varies)

Type of Case		Number of Cases
Serious	70%	*640*
Minor	48%	*314*

We can readily advance further hypotheses: the judge will be more likely to use a control when there is disparity in the quality of counsel; and again, he will be more likely to talk about the evidence when the case is close or is difficult. It turns out that only one of these hypotheses is validated.[11] Table 110 suggests that the judge will be more likely to summarize or comment on the evidence when the case is close.

TABLE 110

Frequency of Judge's Comment in Clear
and Close Cases

(Serious Crimes Only)

Type of Case		Number of Cases
Close	72%	*107*
Clear	61%	*129*

Having discussed at some length the incidence of judicial control, we turn to the key question for our study of judge-jury disagreement: What difference, if any, does judicial control make?

As always, cross-tabulation requires that we hold constant the factors known to be significant for the rate of disagreement: closeness of evidence, sympathy, and record. Here, however, we meet a vexing methodological complication. Since some judges make their use of control dependent on the case, we would be in danger of a circular argument if we included their cases. Only by restricting the comparison to cases from judges who always follow the same pattern, irrespective of the

---

[11] The data reveal no difference in the judge's use of controls where counsel are imbalanced.

particular case, can we be sure that the control was not selected because of the greater likelihood of agreement or disagreement in the particular case.[12] Only by restricting our comparison in this way can we be sure that we are testing the cause and not the effect.[13]

TABLE 111

Effect of Judicial Control on Amount of
Judge-Jury Disagreement in Serious Crimes,
Under a Variety of Conditions

(Per Cent Disagreement on Guilt)*

[Only judges with fixed patterns]

	Evidence is Clear				Evidence is Close			
	Sympathetic Defendant		All Other		Sympathetic Defendant		All Other	
	No Record /Stand	All Other	No Record /Stand	All Other	No Record /Stand	All Other	No Record /Stand	All Other
Judge uses controls: always	—	—	—	1	50	67	50	25
Number of cases	2	1	46	52	10	3	28	16
never	11	26	4	6	32	25	38	28
Number of cases	28	17	106	140	34	18	92	80

* Hung juries are counted as $\frac{1}{2}$ acquittal.

Reading Table 111 vertically, we inquire whether the percentages of disagreement increase, in any of the eight columns,

[12] For another illustration of this methological point, see on the decision whether or not to employ the split trial mechanism, Zeisel and Callahan, Split Trials and Time Saving: A Statistical Analysis, Harv. L. Rev., v. 76, p. 1606, at p. 1614, Table 4 (1963).

[13] This method of analysis yields an approximation at best. The only truly reliable way of determining this issue is through a controlled experiment in a jurisdiction which allows, at the discretion of the judge, both summary and comment on the evidence. In such a jurisdiction a lottery should decide in advance which of the three alternatives should be applied in each particular case. In the end one would have these comparable samples of cases (Summary Only, Summary and Comment, Neither) for which the verdict pattern would reveal the effect of this judicial control. See Rosenberg, The Pre-Trial Conference and Effective Justice (1964); Zeisel, The Law, in Uses of Sociology (Lazarsfeld ed. 1966); Zeisel, Kalven, Buchholz, The Case for the Official Experiment, ch. 21 in Delay in the Court (1959).

as we move downward from control to no control. It is apparent that in none of the columns where the case is close does anything of interest show up. For the clear cases, however, an effect is discernible. Where there is no control, disagreement ranges from 4 to 26 per cent. But where control is used, disagreement never rises above 1 per cent, and, indeed, of the 101 clear cases under judicial control, there is only one in which the jury disagrees on guilt.[14]

The finding appears paradoxical. We would have expected that there would be no point to controls in clear cases, and that if controls were to have any impact, they would have it on the cases where by definition the evidence is part of the jury's problem. This apparently is also the judge's expectation, since he tends to exercise controls more often in close cases.

Upon analysis, however, we read the results as making an important point about the jury's revolt from the law. It has been a basic thesis of this study that the jury by and large responds to the discipline of the evidence, and where it does not, it conceals from itself its own response to sentiment, under the guise of resolving issues of evidential doubt. In only an extreme minority of the cases does the jury, directly in the face of the evidence, follow the lead of a special sentiment. Table 111 reveals that the discipline of the evidence and the discipline of the judge's comments re-enforce each other with the result that, when both are present, they virtually eliminate disagreement. The moral then is that the momentum of the jury's revolt is never enough to carry the jury beyond both the evidence and the judge.

[14] This single case represents a narrow escape from a perfect result. It is a narcotics case in which the jury hangs, eleven jurors voting for conviction. [II-0414]

CHAPTER 34

The Judge as Critic

In his comments on the cases before him, the judge has with some frequency reported not only what the jury did but what he thought of it. He has been moved to comment on the verdicts, sometimes indignantly, sometimes approvingly, and sometimes flatly as though he were grading a paper. We now take a brief look at the judge as critic of the jury's performance in the particular case.

In the judge's comments we often find quiet expressions of approval:

The verdict was about right. [I-0640]

Verdict of jury was correct in my judgment. [I-0779]

Or again, there are statements accepting the inevitability of some disagreement:

It was just a borderline case. [I-0858]

A bad mistake, although I can understand. [I-1055]

More interesting are instances in which the judge, while disagreeing with the verdict, expresses admiration for the jury system and a kind of envy of the jury freedom to reach a decision which he as judge could not reach.

[M]aybe the jury could look past the confession; the court could not. The jury, not knowing the cold technicalities of the law, could conscientiously bring in this verdict. [I-0929]

For the most part, as expected, the judge is more colorful and emphatic when he is criticizing the jury than when he is praising it:

This was an outrageous verdict. There was direct evidence

from a witness who saw defendant set fire to the house plus immediate flight to another state. Heaven knows what the jury had in mind. [I-0181]

I felt the result of this case was a clear miscarriage of justice. [I-0382]

There appeared to be no justification for verdict which jury returned. [I-0538]

In spite of three positive identifications and no defense, except character witnesses, the jury returned a verdict of not guilty. [I-0611]

This jury simply went wrong. [I-0791]

God only knows. [I-0513]

When we prepared the Sample II questionnaire, we made an effort to systematize this type of capsule criticism by including the following question:

Did you feel that the jury's verdict was —
    [Check one]
        ☐ without any merit?
        ☐ a tenable position for a jury?
        ☐ one a *judge* might also come to?
        ☐ quite correct?

Table 112 gives the relevant figures. It provides a unique evaluation of the jury system in criminal cases. The special strength of this criticism is that it depends on case-by-case evaluation, not on general opinions and general impressions.

TABLE 112

Intensity of the Judge's Disagreement
(All Cases)

	Per Cent
Jury verdict was —	
Without merit	9
Tenable for a jury	14
One a judge might also come to	8
Quite correct	69
Total	100%
*Number of cases**	*1152*

* Sample II only; the question remained unanswered in 39 cases.

The striking point is that in only 9 per cent of all cases is the judge critical of the jury's performance.[1] But as always, our interest centers primarily on the disagreement cases. As Table 113 shows, when we look only at the disagreement cases, not 9 per cent but roughly one third fall under the heavy criticism of "without merit" from the judge.

TABLE 113

The Judge's Evaluation of the Verdict
(Disagreements Only)

	Disagreement:			Total
	Hung Jury	On Guilt	On Charge	
	%	%	%	%
Without merit	43	34	8	30
Tenable for a jury	35	45	59	46
One a judge might also come to	22	21	33	24
Total	100%	100%	100%	100%
Number of cases	40	226	64	330

Table 113 also shows that there is variation in the judge's criticism depending on the type of disagreement. Not surprisingly, the criticism is least where the disagreement goes only to charge. It is highest in the case of hung juries, but here the interpretation is difficult because the judge is sometimes simply expressing irritation over the fact that the jury is unable to reach a verdict.[2]

[1] As a general matter one would expect some difference between general impressions on a given question as against a count of concrete experiences. In this instance, however, we find interesting evidence to the contrary. We have adverted earlier to a poll of the nation's judges which the Project conducted. Chapter 1, note 3. On that questionnaire the judge was asked: "In your experience, in approximately what percentage of all [criminal] jury trials did the jury bring in a verdict which in your opinion was: without any merit," etc. The weighted result for the thousand or so judges answering the question "without any merit" was 8.3 per cent.

[2] Thus there are cases where the jury hangs which, though close on the evidence, are still rated as without merit. See Chapter 18, note 44. But sometimes the judge seems actually to approve a hung jury: "Two diametrically opposed personalities; no corroboration possible of

Table 114 traces whether the judge's evaluation varies by the direction of the disagreement.

TABLE 114

The Judge's Evaluation by Direction of Disagreement
(*Close Cases Only*)*

	Disagree: Hung Jury		Disagree on Guilt		Disagree on Charge	
	Jury more lenient	Judge more lenient	Jury more lenient	Judge more lenient	Jury more lenient	Judge more lenient
	%	%	%	%	%	%
Without merit	43	20	20	7	3	—
Other	57	80	80	93	97	100
Total	100%	100%	100%	100%	100%	100%
Number of cases	*23*	*10*	*143*	*28*	*31*	*14*

* Because virtually all cross-over cases have evidentiary problems, the comparison is limited to close cases.

The results are perhaps to be read more as a comment on the judge than on the jury, but the point is unmistakable. The judge is more critical of the jury's performance when the jury has disagreed in the direction of being more lenient. And this is perhaps most impressive in the case of hung juries. We have then the judge's decisive ballot on how well the jury system is performing.

It is more interesting and more relevant to the study to put another question. Since, as we have just seen, the judge is not critical of the jury's performance in roughly two thirds of the cases in which he disagrees with its verdict, the question is just what kinds of jury disagreements does he regard as improper?

It will be recalled that the basic threefold classification of disagreements on Facts alone, on Facts and Values, and on

---

either story; this is the perfect case for a hung jury and I would anticipate no other result whenever this case is adequately tried on both sides." [II-0008]

Values alone provided a frame for the study. Table 115 matches the judge's level of criticism against these three types of disagreements.

TABLE 115

Reasons for Disagreement and Criticism of the Judge
(Normal Disagreements Only)*

	Values alone %	*Facts and Values* %	*Facts alone* %
Without merit	78	23	15
Other	22	77	85
Total	100%	100%	100%
Number of cases	*40*	*90*	*53*

* For the sake of simplicity the further analysis is restricted to normal disagreements on guilt. The hung jury evaluations, as explained in note 2 above, have an element of ambiguity, and there are few disagreements on charge of which the judge entirely disapproves. The cross-overs on guilt are also few in number and are limited to cases with evidentiary problems. See note to Table 114.

The results are most striking. Where the disagreement is over Facts alone, the judge is more sympathetic to the jury and rates only 15 per cent of such verdicts as seriously in error. Where, however, the disagreement is over Values alone, the results are polar opposites, and in 78 per cent of such verdicts he is seriously critical. Finally, in the cases where both Facts and Values are involved, i.e., cases in which what we have called the liberation hypothesis is at work, the judge is just slightly more critical than he is of the cases in the Facts alone category. To restate the figures of Table 115 in terms of the underlying structure of the book, the judge is least critical of the jury's performance when, being a pure finder of facts, it ends up disagreeing with him. He is most critical of its performance when in the teeth of the facts, it gives reign to its own sense of values. And, finally, when the jury is engaged in what is perhaps its most distinctive activity, responding to values in the course of resolving ambiguous questions of fact, the judge is again not seriously critical. The conclusion is that for the judge as well as for the jury, evidentiary ambiguity legitimates the importation of values.

Table 115 has worked so well that it is tempting to let the analysis rest at this point. There is, however, one further refinement to be pursued.[3] One persistent source of jury disagreement has been present in the small cluster of unpopular crimes: gambling, liquor violations, game law violations, and drunken driving. As we have noted, these are the modern cases which are closest to classic instances of jury revolt and nullification.[4] Here the jury is not simply rejecting an inequitable application of an otherwise sound law but is coming close to rejecting the law itself. It is worth asking, therefore, how the judge reacts to this "revolutionary" jury performance. Table 116 gives the relevant data.

TABLE 116

The Judge's Criticism of Verdict by Selected Factors*

	Values alone		Facts and Values		Facts alone	
	Unpopular Crimes	Other	Unpopular Crimes	Other	Unpopular Crimes	Other
	%	%	%	%	%	%
Without merit	93	69	30	21	22	14
Other	7	31	70	79	78	86
Total	100%	100%	100%	100%	100%	100%
Number of cases	14	26	23	67	9	44

* Normal disagreements only. See note to Table 115.

It is apparent that the response we saw in Table 115 is intensified if we add the dimension of unpopular crimes. The judge's serious criticism rises from 69 per cent to 93 per cent, from 21 to 30 per cent, and from 14 to 22 per cent respectively for our three categories.

[3] At one point we explored the possibility that there might be some correlation with deliberation time on the view that the judge would be extremely critical of short deliberations when they resulted in verdicts with which he disagreed. The data offer only slight confirmation. For more on deliberation time, see Chapter 36.

[4] See Chapter 19, Unpopular Crimes.

C H A P T E R   3 5

A Somber Postscript: Decisions on
the Death Penalty

The reversal of civilized opinion on the death penalty during the past century and a half has been truly remarkable.   It is
an example of law in the process of radical change.[1]

As late as 1825 England had no less than 230 capital crimes
on its law books.   By the turn of the century legislative inroads
had reduced the capital list to murder and treason, and, after
an attempt to reduce it still further to certain types of murder,
the English evolution has come to completion and the death
penalty has now been abolished for all crimes.[2]   Although in
England the death penalty, wherever applicable by statute, was
mandatory on the trial process, the English jury played a major
role in its gradual attenuation.   On many occasions the jury
simply refused to convict a clearly guilty defendant in order to

---

[1] The topic has had a vogue in the last decade, yielding a burst of
writing, especially in England.   See, for example Gardiner, Capital
Punishment as a Deterrent and the Alternative (1956); Gowers, A Life
for a Life (1956); Koestler, Reflections on Hanging (1956); O'Donnell,
Should Women Hang? (1956); and. Rolph, Common Sense about
Crime and Punishment (1961).   For a general overview and a complete
bibliography see Bedeau, The Death Penalty in America (1964) and
the forthcoming article on capital punishment by Allen, in the New
Encyclopedia of Social Science.

[2] The Homicide Act of 1957 limited capital punishment to murder
of a police officer or prison guard, in the furtherance of theft by shooting or explosion, and to repeated murder, 5 & 6 Eliz. 2, c. 11, §§5, 6.
In 1965 Parliament abolished even this limited use of capital punishment for a trial period of five years.

avoid the death penalty, and this nullification had its impact on the legislature.[3]

In the United States the development has been different and more complicated, and the role of the jury even more important. While the number of capital crimes has at no point been as high as in England, a similar legislative process has been making inroads into the death sentence, so that today 10 states have abolished it altogether and other states limited it severely.[4]

In addition, the death penalty has ceased to be mandatory. The legislatures have left it to the discretion of the trial process, and it is now predominantly the jury which is called upon to exercise this discretion, even in states where the jury has no voice in other penalties.[5]

The discretion which the jury in the United States is asked to exercise is, it should be emphasized, striking: there is neither rule nor standard to guide it.[6] For this reason comparison of judge and jury decision must here depart from the standard pattern of analysis which discussed disagreement in terms of why the jury differed from the judge. We have viewed the latter as a kind of baseline representing the law, and we have tried to trace the nuances of jury judgment as it deviated from the legal norm of the judge. For the death penalty, however, the judge is not "the law" but merely another decider. In no meaningful sense can it be said that the judge's decision is more representative of the law than is the jury's.

We have in all 111 cases in which either judge or jury found the defendant guilty of a capital crime and hence *could* have

[3] See note 7 in Chapter 21.

[4] Only within the last year two states, Iowa and Oregon joined the abolition group and New York limited capital punishment to the murder of a police officer or prison guard.

[5] For the power of the jury to set the penalty, see Chapter 20, note 1.

[6] In the words of Justice Tobriner of the Supreme Court of California: "[T]he Legislature fixed no standards for the guidance of the jury in determining whether a defendant should suffer the penalty of life imprisonment or death, and to that extent left the function of the jury in a somewhat nebulous state." People v. Terry, 61 Cal. 2d 137, 141, 390 P.2d 381, 384 (1914). California allows for a separate trial on the issue of the death penalty. See below, note 29.

given the death penalty.[7] Table 117 sets forth the pattern of agreement and disagreement.

TABLE 117

Frequency of Death Sentence for Defendants Found Guilty of a Capital Crime

| | Jury Gave — | |
	Prison	Death Penalty
Judge Gave — Prison	68% 76	6% 7
Death Penalty	13% 14	13% 14

Number of cases   111

    The upper lefthand cell represents the approximately two thirds of all cases where both judge and jury withhold the death penalty. In only 13 per cent of all cases (lower righthand cell) do both jury and judge agree on the death penalty. When they disagree, the jury is somewhat more lenient, but the imbalance is modest.[8] Neither jury nor judge imposes the death penalty with any great frequency. The jury does so in only (13 + 6 =) 19 per cent of the cases, the judge somewhat more often, in (13 + 13 =) 26 per cent of the cases.

    [7] These 111 cases are those in which the defendant was convicted of a crime that permitted a finding for the death penalty and in which the judge agreed with the guilty verdict of the jury. They happen to be all murder cases. While in some states there are other capital crimes on the books, e.g., forcible rape and kidnaping, there was no such guilty verdict in the sample, partly because these situations are relatively rare and partly because our southern sample is relatively small.

    [8] It is of interest to see the full extent of the disagreement in the 21 cases where only one decider opts for death:

| | *Extent of Disagreement on the Death Penalty* | |
| | Judge gives death penalty | Jury gives death penalty |
	Jury	*Judge*
Agrees on capital charge but not on death penalty	10	7
Convicts on lesser (non-capital) charge	4	—

This then is an over-all view. We shall look first at the individual cases to learn what we can about what moves the jury and the judge in their respective judgments. Finally, recent studies of executive clemency make it possible to round out the discussion by bringing in a third decider, the chief executive, who is as a rule called upon to make the final decision on this awesome issue. We can thus attempt a rough comparative study across these three institutions.

The cases in which jury and judge agree that the defendant should pay for his crime with his life are marked for the most part by peculiar heinousness. In many, a clear pattern emerges; there is an aspect of almost gratuitous violence. Five involve multiple victims. In one the defendant kills his wife and her brother. [I-1254] In another the defendant exterminates his entire family, although the trial is limited to the murder of his nine-year-old son. [I-0647] In a third domestic murder case the defendant comes upon his separated wife at her mother's home, kills her, and severely stabs the mother as well. [I-0366]

The theme of multiple murder is at times aggravated by the patent defenselessness of the victim. Thus there is a burglary case in which an old man and his wife are beaten to death with a tire iron:

Victim wounded a dozen times with a metal tool. Asleep in his home when aroused. [II-0861]

Another case adds still other alienating factors to the multiple victim theme: special ugliness in the tools of a murder with sexual overtones.

Defendant, a sex deviate, murdered two girls — one aged 8 years, the other 18 years. Both killings were with a screw driver. [II-0017]

Two other cases pick up the sex element; both are murders committed in the course of rape. In one, a strangulation, the judge adds that this was defendant's seventh criminal offense of a violent nature, a fact also known to the jury. He says:

> This was a violent and brutal killing, a heinous crime by a sadistic defendant. [I-1567]

In a burglary case, after the burglary is complete and almost as an afterthought, the defendant rapes and then stabs to death "with a paring knife" a woman who a few moments before had been secure and asleep. [I-0643]

Then there is perhaps the ugliest of these cases, which the judge describes as follows:

> Defendant was charged with the rape and sodomy of a four and a half-year old child who was also his step-child. The penetration of the anal canal resulted in massive hemorrhage which caused shock and ultimately death ensued. [II-0095]

The mark of the beast is perhaps a little less evident in the remaining cases in which judge and jury agree on the death penalty. In one the victim is an elderly truck driver making his last trip prior to retirement. During a stop, his helper in the truck steals his receipts and shoots him while he is asleep, leaving the body in the van on the desert. [II-0085] In a second case the defendant, refused credit by a village merchant, returns with his rifle and shoots the seventy-two-year-old grocer in the back through the window of his office. [II-1126] And in a domestic murder case, where husband and wife have been separated, the judge notes with pungent brevity:

> Husband killed wife. Six pistol shots, 2:30 A.M., at wife's home. [II-0740]

Finally, in a robbery-mugging case, the defendant brutally beats an elderly, crippled man, then drags him to a lonely spot in the woods where he strangles him. [II-0697]

These cases in which judge and jury have agreed on the death penalty give, at first impression, a strong sense of unity. Among cases of premeditated killing they seem to stand out as especially vicious. The trouble is that some aspects of this viciousness verge so much on the clearly pathological that the criterion loses some of its usefulness. Moreover, as we shall see, many of the murder cases in which the judge and jury disagree on the death penalty appear no less heinous than those in which they agree.

We now turn to the cases where jury and judge disagree on the death penalty. The cases of disagreement, as may be recalled from Table 117, exceed the agreements 21 to 14.

The first group of cases involves a measure of mental and emotional instability on the part of the defendant, which falls short, however, of insanity.[9] In the first case, where the violence is atrocious, it is the jury which is lenient.[10] A twenty-two-year-old inmate of an institution for defective delinquents kills an aged guard in an unprovoked and ferocious attack. The judge tells us:

> Defendant had been in one school or institution after another from the age of ten. His father and mother separated when defendant was approximately two years of age. The defendant had been an inmate of this institution for six years prior to the commission of this crime. I believe the jury reached the conclusion that, even though the defendant knew the difference between right and wrong, and even though he was not insane, nevertheless he did not possess a normal mentality and for this reason I believe the jury concluded not to impose the supreme penalty of capital punishment . . . . This conclusion, coupled with the story of the defendant's hardships during his early life, probably led the jury to conclude that despite the enormity of the crime, the defendant should not be required to suffer penalty of death. [1-1493]

A second case presents the same pattern: a crime of violence, an unsuccessful plea of insanity as the leniency-disposing fac-

[9] See above, Chapter 25, especially note 8, on diminished responsibility.

[10] The organization, as noted, here departs from that used throughout the book because often the explanation given by the judge is put in terms of the leniency-disposing factors. Moreover, historically, the problem has developed as one of making exceptions to the death penalty. And, finally, as indicated, we wish to compare the decisions of judge and jury with those of executive clemency, which, of course, are always in terms of reasons for leniency.

tor, and the jury as the lenient decider. This is the judge's description:

> The defendant in this case beat and broke the neck of a young woman then cut her throat and threw her in a lake. He went then to the police, told them what he had done, and asked them to have him executed as soon as possible. His attorneys pleaded insanity. He was examined by the state authorities, and found to be sane. He pleaded insanity through his attorneys on the trial. The insanity plea was submitted to the jury. He did not take the stand, and the jury agreed as to his guilt, but disagreed as to death penalty. I automatically sentenced him to life in the state penitentiary.

The judge notes that he thinks "the defendant feigned insanity" and adds:

> This was a very cruel murder. Defendant said he killed her because he loved her. [II-0492]

In these two cases the suggestion is that the jury is responding to a level of insanity or instability not sufficient to preclude a verdict of first degree murder but sufficient to avoid the death penalty. Two other cases however show how much judgment may waver when the death penalty is the issue.

In a multiple victim case, we are told:

> The defendant stopped at a filling station and because of his conduct was requested to leave. Station owner approached the car owner a second time whereupon the defendant shot him and when his wife ran out defendant shot and killed her.

This time it is the judge who is lenient. He explains:

> I believe the defendant shot the husband [station owner] because he said "You damn niggers get the hell out of here," and killed the wife because his anger toward the husband was not satisfied when he shot him down. [I-0959]

The judge, who, unlike the jury, did not respond to the touch of insanity in the first two cases, does accept this sudden anger as a sufficient reason for withholding the death penalty. And the jury, sensitive to the marginal responsibility in the previous cases, is deaf to the wild anger in this one.

The final case in this cluster deals with a killing committed in the course of an armed robbery. There are two accomplices, but the defendant is the actual killer; once again there is an unsuccessful plea of insanity, and again it is the judge who is lenient. The circumstance which divides judge and jury is set forth by the judge as follows:

> The conduct of defendant and his counsel was such as to antagonize the jury and in the opinion of the court caused the imposition of death penalty rather than life imprisonment. The defendant indulged in repeated outbursts of vile language and finally was handcuffed to seat and his mouth taped. At one point, defendant jumped up and threw a book at jury. Defense lawyer was entirely incompetent although of defendant's own choice — in fact defendant refused any other counsel. Conduct of defendant and his counsel was such to antagonize jury and in the opinion of the court caused the imposition of death penalty rather than life imprisonment. [I-3129] [11]

It is easy to see what alienated the jury here, but we can only surmise what moved the judge to leniency. Possibly, he distrusted the ability of the trial process to render fair judgment on the issue of death where the circumstances have been made so prejudicial to the defendant, albeit by his own conduct and that of incompetent counsel.

Another group of disagreement cases involves, in differing ways, situations of domestic tension. Here the context tends to belie somewhat any deliberate intent to kill. A husband and wife are charged with the murder of their four-year-old daughter, who died "after the administering of a brutal beating." The jury, which is lenient, finds only second degree murder — thus precluding the death penalty, which the judge would have given. Little background is supplied about the case, but there may be a clue in the fact that the husband pleads insanity as a defense. Presumably there was no literal intent to kill the child. The judge finds first degree murder pur-

[11] This case presents an extreme example of two points we have noted earlier. On the disadvantages of obnoxious language, see Chapter 30, page 382; on the alienation of the jury by counsel, see page 392.

suant to the legal rule which holds the actor liable, as if he intended it, for a death that occurs in the course of a felony.[12] In this context the jury will not accept the legal fiction of intent. Further, with respect to the wife, the jury may have been following its special form of chivalry in not imposing the death penalty on a woman;[13] and the husband may accordingly have been the beneficiary of a desire, at least where the death penalty is at issue, to treat partners in crime with an even hand.[14] [II-04791&2]

In another domestic case the defendant kills his estranged wife, whose reputation was "poor so far as marital relations were concerned." There is a record of prior abuse by the defendant of the victim, "a good looking woman." The jury is lenient, and the judge is explicit as to why:

> Eternal triangle if this is extenuating. Perhaps the so-called unwritten law. [II-0418] [15]

In another version, a man jealous of his paramour because she tried, as the judge puts it, to "quit being familiar with him," stabbed her to death — in the daytime on a public street while she was running from him." The jury is lenient. The judge adds the following comment to the explanation suggested by the jealousy theme:

> A Negro killing a Negro, that is, the jury did not attach enough importance to the value of a human life due to race. [I-1726] [16]

[12] The felony murder doctrine provides in general that if a death occurs in the course of the commission of a felony, or certain felonies, the crime is murder in the first degree, even if the intent was not to kill. See Perkins, Criminal Law, pp. 33-36 (1957).

The felony murder rule is the harshest instance of strict liability in our criminal law. See note 3, Chapter 24.

[13] See generally, O'Donnell, Should Women Hang? (1956), and below note 27. See also Chapter 15, note 14.

[14] Preferential treatment is discussed in Chapter 22.

[15] See Chapter 16, pages 234-236, for the discussion of "eternal triangle" cases, and page 232 for the significance of evidence of prior abuse, particularly at note 17.

[16] See Chapter 26, A Note on Crime in a Subculture.

Perhaps one other case is conveniently placed here.. The body of the victim, a woman of poor reputation, is found in the desert. Her boy friend confesses to the killing. On the witness stand he boasts of his criminal reputation. This time it is the judge who is lenient because of the status of the victim. He explains:

> I felt that because the victim was herself an underworld character and was guilty at least of keeping company with a person of defendant's reputation — society because of her wrongful death did not require the supreme penalty of the defendant. [I-1023] [17]

Other disagreement cases pick up a theme touched on in the case of the parents who beat their child to death. In each case there are partners in the crime and the defendant is not the actual killer. The felony murder rule precipitates the disagreement.[18] The jury rebels at imposing the death penalty for the vicarious criminal responsibility of the defendant. One illustration will suffice. Four defendants conspire to rob a seventy-six-year-old woman in a hotel room. In the course of the robbery the victim is gagged and she accidentally strangles. The defendant has been a mere go-between in recruiting accomplices to the crime. Three of the accomplices, the judge reveals, have "been tried, found guilty of first degree murder and given life by the jury." [II-1145] There are two leniency-disposing factors: the defendant did not commit the act of violence and the death penalty had already been withheld for the partners in the crime.

[17] This is an example of judicial response to a sentiment which the jury at times exhibits in a non-death case. Chapter 18, pages 282-284.
[18] We had anticipated that, because of the rigidity of the felony murder rule, the jury's sense of equity would produce a broad area of disagreement. It turned out, however, that disagreement over the rule emerges only at the level of the death penalty. The American Law Institute, Model Penal Code, proposes to limit the felony murder rule to a rebuttable presumption, §201.2(1)(b) Tent. Draft No. 9 (1959). It is worth noting that the first step in the evolution away from the death penalty in New York was to repeal the law that made the death penalty mandatory in cases of felony murder.

A final source of disagreement is somewhat curious. In two instances the judge, when asked for his hypothetical decision "had he tried the case without a jury," refers to what he would have done had the defendant in fact waived a jury trial:[19]

> The killing was wanton but on a plea of guilty or a bench trial, I would have spared his life. [I-3130-1]

> The jury verdict of first degree murder without recommendation of mercy was, in my opinion, justified by the nature of the attempt to escape although I would have imposed a life sentence rather than invoke the death penalty if I had tried the case myself without a jury. [II-0026-1]

The waiver is apparently regarded as a gesture of cooperation warranting withholding the death penalty.

It will be helpful to summarize at this point the reasons which moved jury or judge to withhold the death penalty in cases where one of the two decided for it.[20]

Table 118 imposes, if for a brief moment, a sense of regularity on the discretionary allocation of the death penalty. The leniency categories have a plausible ring. But the brute fact is that each time one of the factors listed was persuasive to one of the deciders, it was unpersuasive to the other. Either the judge or the jury was willing, despite the presence of the leniency-disposing factor, to have the defendant executed.

Having explored in detail the pattern of decision for our two deciders, the judge and the jury, we look now at the record of the third decider, the executive. Although commutations are seldom accompanied by published reasons, we know something about these reasons. In 1949 in the United Kingdom, the Home Office itself submitted an illuminating memorandum to the Royal Commission on Capital Punishment[21] and there is a

[19] See Chapter 2, page 26.

[20] Table 118 attempts to group the reasons by using previously established categories. Admittedly, in several cases the fit is not very good. Some cases, which have not been specifically adverted to in the text to avoid repetition, are included in the table.

[21] Royal Commission on Capital Punishment, Minutes of Evidence, p. 1 (1949).

TABLE 118

Factors Evoking Leniency in Cases Where One Decider Gives Death Sentence

	Number of Cases
Law	
Diminished responsibility	
Abnormal mentality, though not legally "insane"	2
Provocation, anger, jealousy	
Lovers, triangle	4
Neighborhood fight	1
Child-beating	2
Negro is called "nigger"	1
"Worthless victim"	
Underworld characters	1
Negro kills Negro	1
Felony murder	
Others involved did not get death penalty	7
Defendant not the actual killer	4
Procedural	
Trial process distrusted, because defendant's behavior prejudiced trial against him	1
Guilty plea or jury waiver would have mitigated	2
Defendant	
Defendant a female	2
Father cried on stand	1
Counsel	
Incompetent counsel	1
Evidence	
Prosecution witness — contradiction between first and second trial	1
Unexplained	2
Total Cases	21*

* Factors add to more than 21 because of multiple reasons.

fine recent study on the variety of commutation procedures in the United States.[22]

It will be convenient to follow the structure of the American study, noting the analogous English materials.[23] The study

[22] Executive Clemency in Capital Cases, N.Y.U.L. Rev., v. 39, p. 136 (1964).

[23] The appropriate page references are given in the text.

lists thirteen factors or standards that influenced clemency.[24]
The Nature of the Crime. "[A]cts which, because of the status
of the victim and the viciousness of the crime, most offend the
community." "The more heinous the crime, the less chance
for clemency." (p. 159.)
Doubt as to Guilt. The study says this is a less frequent basis
than one might expect, because the executive is often hesitant
to displace the jury as fact-finder. (p. 160.)
Fairness of Trial. "[The question] usually arises in a situation where there has been considerable publicity surrounding
the trial." (p. 162.)
Relative Guilt and Disparity of Sentences. "The principle [in
felony murder trials] that the acts of one shall be the acts of all,
insofar as it fails to recognize relative degrees of culpability,
leaves to the clemency authority the opportunity to inquire
into the defendant's personal responsibility and the directness
of his participation. . . ." (p. 163.)[25]
Geographical Equalization of Sentences. "The acceptance of
this standard is rooted in the belief that the locale of the crime
should not dictate the severity of the sentence." (p. 165.)
Mitigating Circumstances. "The existence or lack of mitigating circumstances accompanying the commission of the crime,
such as duress, provocation, intoxication and self-defense, is of
some importance. . . ." (p. 165.)
Rehabilitation. "Rehabilitation appears to be a standard for
commutation only in cases where the defendant has managed
through court action to remain alive for a number of years after
the original date of execution." (p. 168.)

[24] The following list gives the British counterpart, by citing the corresponding passages from the Report of the Home Office, as given in the
report of the Royal Commission (see note 21 above). *Doubt:* p. 4, §21;
Trial: p. 4, §27; *Guilt:* p. 4, §26; *Mitigation:* p. 4, §§23, 25; *Physical
Condition:* p. 2, §2; *Recommendation:* p. 3, §16; *Politics:* p. 4, §27.

[25] The English formulation refers to cases where two or more persons were involved and "it may be right that the principal should be
executed and the secondary partners reprieved [or where] the principal
has escaped trial, conviction, or execution, [and] it may be expedient
to reprieve the accomplices."

Mental and Physical Condition of the Defendant. "Dissatisfaction with the *M'Naghten* rule and the artificial line between 'legal' and 'medical' insanity has led more than a few clemency authorities to commute a sentence on the basis of medical insanity where the defendant had previously been judged legally sane." (p. 168.)

Dissents and Inferences Drawn from the Courts. "Certain pardon officials have given special consideration to a case where in the appellate court one or more judges dissented. . . . Somewhat similar . . . is a written opinion which, while affirming the death penalty, intimates that the case might be appropriate for the exercise of executive clemency." (pp. 170, 171.)

The Clemency Authorities' Views on Capital Punishment. "[T]he views of a clemency official on the issue of capital punishment will have some influence. . . ." (p. 175.)[26]

The Role of Precedent. "There is generally a discernible continuity of policy in the actions of a governor within his administration and in those of a board within its term of office." (p. 177.)[27]

The comparison of executive discretion with that of the judge and jury is suggestive. There are, of course, several points — rehabilitation, judicial dissent, political pressure, prosecutor recommendation, geographical equalization — which in the nature of things have no parallel in the judge-jury situation. But for other factors the parallelism is worth noting. Thus, heinousness offends both. And provocation, marginal insanity, the rigors of the felony murder rule, and

[26] "Political motives would have doomed a murderer when Sir Herbert Samuels was Secretary but might have operated to save him during the incumbency of Lord Brentford."

[27] The American study offers us two other bases: recommendations of the prosecution and the trial judge (p. 171) and political pressure and publicity (p. 172). The Home Office mentions in addition other possible areas of extenuation, e.g.: suicide pact survivals, p. 4, §20; physical deterioration to such a degree that the execution would not be humane, p. 4, §22; certain instances of felony murder, p. 4, §24; special consideration to females, p. 4, §28; and, finally, youth, p. 4, §29.

procedural fairness are visible leniency factors in both forums. Somewhat surprisingly, doubt as to guilt is not a salient factor in Table 118.[28]

The empirical data about jury, judge, and the executive, however, do little to upset an a priori conviction that the administration of the death penalty today is singularly agonizing. The jurisdictions that retain it follow the same policies. There is agreement that not all of those convicted of first degree murder should be executed, and also it is a dominant policy that the legislature does not specify by a general rule any category of defendants for whom the death penalty and its execution should be mandatory. As a result the law can only leave to discretion the decision as to who is to die. The materials just reviewed show how difficult the exercise of this discretion is, whether by the jury, the judge, or the executive.

Procedural changes are being attempted to improve the administration of the discretionary death penalty. Thus, California and New York now require a separate trial on the issue of death, so as to permit the jury access to the broadest possible evidence about the defendant.[29] The new penal code for Illinois requires explicit agreement of jury and judge for the death penalty.[30] The cases we have reviewed lend considerable support to such a move.[31]

But even these techniques for locating a hard core of capital cases do not put to rest the concern about evenhanded justice. In the end the task is one of deciding who, among those convicted of capital crimes, is to die. Whatever the differences

[28] What the Home Office calls a *scintilla of doubt*, p. 4, §21, may appear substantial in the shadow of the death penalty.

[29] See, Note, The Two-Trial System in Capital Cases, N.Y.U.L. Rev., v. 39, p. 50 (1964). Some judges have suggested that the system may be resulting in an increase in capital cases.

[30] The death penalty may be imposed only if the jury explicitly recommends it; the recommendation is not mandatory on the court. Ill. Rev. Stat. 38, §1-7(c)(1961).

[31] Table 117 shows that of the 35 cases in which one of the two deciders would demand the death penalty, there is a failure to agree 60 per cent of the time.

on which this decision hinges, they remain demeaningly trivial compared to the stakes.[32] The discretionary use of the death penalty requires a decision which no human should be called upon to make.

[32] The point was made years ago with distinctive force by Professor Wechsler: "It is obvious that capital punishment is the most difficult of sanctions to administer with even rough equality. A rigid legislative definition of capital murders has proved unworkable in practice, given the infinite variety of homicides and possible mitigating factors. A discretionary system thus becomes inevitable with equally inevitable differences in judgment depending on the individuals involved and other accidents of time and place. Yet most dramatically when life is at stake, equality is . . . a most important element of justice." Symposium on Capital Punishment, N.Y.L.F., v. 7, pp. 250, 259 (1961). We found a moving personal documentation of this dilemma in a report by the Danish psychiatrist George L. Stürup, now a visiting professor at the University of Chicago Law School. After World War II, Denmark temporarily resumed capital punishment for those found guilty of treason and torture as Nazi-Quislings. It then became Professor Stürup's task to examine these convicted defendants and decide whether or not they were psychotics. His decision was tantamount to sending these defendants before the firing squad or saving them. After describing the agony of making these truly impossible decisions he concludes: "Should the future involve risks of being faced with similar medico-legal questions . . . the author would simply prefer to leave this field of work and dissuade others from exposing themselves to the personal stress involved in these activities." A Problem of Simulation in Modern Legal Psychiatry, Acta Psychiatrica et Neurologica Scandinavia, v. 30, fasc. 1-2, pp. 343, 349 (1955).

*T*HIS CLUSTER OF four chapters brings the study to a close. Chapter 36 deals with the hung jury. In Chapters 37 and 38 we return for some last considerations of methodology. Chapter 37 puts the question: What difference does it make to our results that no two judges and no two juries are alike?

Our exclusive preoccupation thus far has been with disagreement cases. In Chapter 38 we examine what can be said about the cases in which judge and jury completely agree.

Chapter 39 makes some final observations, in the light of the study, about the jury as an institution.

CHAPTER 36

The Hung Jury

The hung jury is, in a way, the jury system's most interesting phenomenon. In one sense it marks a failure of the system, since it necessarily brings a declaration of mistrial in its wake. In another sense, it is a valued assurance of integrity, since it can serve to protect the dissent of a minority. Also, in terms of sheer numbers, the hung jury is an important phenomenon, since more than 5 per cent of all juries, or some 3000 trials per year, end in such a mistrial.[1]

This ambivalence toward the hung jury is mirrored in the law's difficulty in defining the degree of pressure the judge may put on an apparently deadlocked jury. In most courts, the charge in *Allen v. United States*[2] variously dubbed the "dynamite charge," the "third degree instruction," or the "shot gun instruction," designates the permissible line. There the trial judge told the jury:

> . . . that in a large proportion of cases absolute certainty could not be expected; that although the verdict must be the verdict of each individual juror, and not a mere acquiescence in the conclusion of his fellows, yet they should examine the question submitted with candor and with a proper regard and deference to the opinions of each other; that it was their duty to decide the case if they could conscientiously do so; that they should listen, with a disposition to be convinced, to each others argument; that, if much the larger number were for conviction, a dissenting juror should consider whether his doubt was a reasonable one which made no impression upon

[1] See Appendix A, note 3, and Tables 140, 142.
[2] 164 U.S. 492 (1896).

the minds of so many men, equally honest, equally intelligent with himself. If, upon the other hand, the majority was for acquittal, the minority ought to ask themselves whether they might not reasonably doubt the correctness of a judgment which was not concurred in by the majority.

Concern about the *Allen* charge has been mounting on two grounds: that it may give the jury the impression that the judge agrees with the majority position on the jury, and that he is in fact suggesting to the minority that it capitulate without being convinced.[3] Out of this criticism emerged, among

[3] In 1949 the Arizona Supreme Court, rejecting the instruction, said: "This instruction has been before us four times. . . . It now appears that its continued use will result in an endless chain of decisions, each link thereof tempered and forged with varying facts and circumstances and welded with ever-changing personalities of the appellate court. This is not in keeping with sound justice and the preservation of human liberties and security. We are convinced that the evils far outweigh the benefits, and decree that its use shall no longer be tolerated and approved by this court." State v. Thomas, 86 Ariz. 161, 166, 342 P.2d 197, 200 (1959). And in 1962, the United States Court of Appeals for the Fifth Circuit, in Green v. United States, 309 F.2d 852, in a unanimous opinion rejected the Allen charge, citing with approval the dissenting opinion of Judge Brown (a member of the Court in the Green case) in an earlier case, Huffman v. United States, 297 F.2d 754, 759, (5th Cir. 1962): "I think a mistrial from a hung jury is a safeguard to liberty. In many areas it is the sole means by which one or a few may stand out against an overwhelming contemporary public sentiment. Nothing should interfere with its exercise. In the final analysis the Allen charge itself does not make sense. All it may rightfully say is that there is a duty to consider the views of others but that a conscientious person has finally the right and duty to stand by conscience. If it says that and nothing more it is a superfluous lecture in citizenship. If it says more to declare that there is a duty to *decide*, it is legally incorrect as an interference with that rightful independence. The time has come, I think, to forbid this practice. Like the silver platter, this is too dear to keep. The cost in fundamental fairness is too great."

On the other hand, the Allen charge has by no means set the limits of how far a judge may try to go in his efforts to "save" a trial. In Powell v. United States, 297 F.2d 318 (1961), the judge used the following language and was reversed for it: "It is no credit to a juror to stand out in a pure spirit of stubbornness. . . . If you follow the principles of law given you by the Court and if you recall the evidence in this case you ought to be able to agree on a verdict."

others, a standard instruction for the federal courts that is more responsive to the juror's right, if not duty, to hang a jury under certain circumstances:

> If much the greater number of you are for a conviction, each dissenting juror ought to consider whether a doubt in his or her own mind is a reasonable one, since it makes no effective impression upon the minds of so many equally honest, equally conscientious fellow jurors, who bear the same responsibility, serve under the same oath, and have heard the same evidence with, we may assume, the same attention and an equal desire to arrive at the truth. On the other hand, if a majority or even a lesser number of you are for acquittal, other jurors ought seriously to ask themselves again, and most thoughtfully, whether they do not have reason to doubt the correctness of a judgment, which is not concurred in by many of their fellow jurors, and whether they should not distrust the weight and sufficiency of evidence, which fails to convince the minds of several of their fellows to a moral certainty and beyond a reasonable doubt.

The instruction then goes on to say:

> In the performance of this high duty, you are at liberty to disregard all comments of both court and counsel, including of course the remarks I am now making.
> Remember, at all times, that no juror is expected to yield a conscientious conviction he or she may have as to the weight or effect of evidence.[4]

This study has given relatively little attention to the hung jury as a distinctive result of a jury deliberation. It will be recalled that we combined the hung juries with the verdicts on which judge and jury disagreed, counting them as one half of a disagreement, since only some of the jurors, not all of them, were in disagreement with the judge, and since as a practical matter, a hung jury will mean for the accused a higher than average chance of avoiding a conviction. We reduced the sixfold table to a fourfold table, at the same time rounding the numbers off:

[4] Mathes and Devitt, Federal Jury Practice and Instructions, §15.16, pp. 166, 167 (1965).

TABLE 119

Translating Hung Juries into Verdicts*

	Jury A	Jury C	Jury H		Jury A	Jury C
Judge A	13.4	2.2	1.1	Judge A	14	3
Judge C	16.9	62.0	4.4	Judge C	19	64
		Total 100%				Total 100%

* See Tables 11 and 12.

In this chapter we look at the hung jury in its own right to see what we can discover about the circumstances that spawn its emergence. We begin by recalling the reason analysis of hung juries, under which we treated the hung jury as a full disagreement. Table 120 compares the reasons for disagreements on guilt and hung juries.

TABLE 120

Reasons for Full Disagreements and Hung Juries

	Full Disagreements %	Hung Juries %
Sentiments on the law	30	17
Sentiments on the defendant	11	7
Evidence factors	52	71
Facts only the judge knew	3	1
Disparity of counsel	4	4
Total	100%	100%
Number of cases	*634*	*161*

It appears that the reasons for hung juries, except for the understandable increase in evidence reasons and some decrease in sentiments on the law, are basically like those for disagreements on guilt. But this does not take us far; it tells us only that the reasons why some segment of a jury disagrees with the judge are like the reasons why a whole jury does so. Our quest is for reasons why some juries hang and others succeed in reaching unanimity.

We do not propose to solve this complex problem here, but rather to make a first stab at it by offering three kinds of data: on the characteristics of the case that is likely to produce more hung juries, on the time that elapses before the judge declares a mistrial, and, finally, on the constellation of the jury's first ballot vote. The complexity of the problem is indicated by the fact that each of these disparate lines of data makes some contribution to the question of when juries hang.

First, there are some data on the frequency of hung juries by difficulty and closeness of the case.

TABLE 121

Frequency of Hung Jury by Type of Case
(Sample II)

Clear — Easy	2%
Clear — Difficult	5%
Close — Easy	10%
Close — Difficult	10%

As one might expect, the incidence of the hung jury is smallest in clear-easy cases; it is somewhat higher in clear-difficult cases and it reaches 10 per cent for all close cases, whether easy or difficult.[5]

We turn next to the deliberation time. As we have said, we know precious little about the complex reasons that make some juries hang while other succeed, but we know that, whatever these reasons, there is a certain time limit which the judge will observe before he accepts the jury as deadlocked. In a way, the reaching of this time limit by a deadlocked jury becomes an intervening cause for the judge's decision to give up and declare

---

[5] The data in this study do not go into details as to what makes a particular case "difficult" for the jury. But one of the Jury Project's experimental studies suggests that the issue posed by the judge's instructions might at times be one of the causes of such difficulty. It was found that when the defense of insanity is raised, the Durham instruction is more likely to engender hung juries than the M'Naghten instruction. See Chapter 25, note 1. The experiment will be reported out in Simon, The American Jury — The Defense of Insanity, Ch. 4 (1966).

a mistrial. Table 122 gives these time limits for four trial groups of various lengths.

TABLE 122

Deliberation Time of Hung Juries
by Length of Trial

	The Trial Lasted				
Deliberation Time in Hours	One Day or Less	More Than One, Less than three	Three to Five Days	Over One Week	Total
Under 2	50	9	6	—	11
2-4	33	45	9	13	35
5-10	17	44	50	40	42
Over 10	—	2	35	47	12
Total	100%	100%	100%	100%	100%
Number of cases	12	117	34	15	178 *

* The figure differs from Table 120 because unexplained cases are excluded there.

Table 122 indicates that the judge's decision to declare a mistrial because the jury is unable to reach a verdict is not done mechanically after a certain number of hours. In 11 per cent of our hung juries this decision was reached before two hours had elapsed; and in 12 per cent of the hung juries the mistrial was not declared until ten hours had elapsed. The deliberation time allowed varies, of course, with the length of the trial. For instance, 50 per cent of the hung juries in trials that lasted one day or less reached that stage in less than two hours, whereas no jury in cases that lasted longer than a week was declared hung after so short a time; and, conversely, in no trial lasting a day was the jury permitted to deliberate for over ten hours, while in trials lasting a week, 47 per cent of the deliberations lasted this long.

It will be of interest to compare for each trial length the average duration of the successful deliberations with the average length of the hung jury deliberations. The latter set of figures is simply the average time for the four columns in Table 122 above.

TABLE 123

Length of Hung Jury Deliberations
Compared to Deliberations Ending in Verdict

	The Trial Lasted			
Average Deliberation Time in Hours	One Day or Less	More Than One, Less Than Three	Three to Five Days	Over One Week
Hung Juries	2.5	4.9	10.8	10.0
Juries with verdict	.8	1.9	3.7	7.3

Table 123 clearly shows that the average hung jury deliberates longer than the average jury that reaches a verdict, at a ratio of about three to one. In trials that last longer than one week the ratio becomes somewhat smaller.

Finally, we show for the most frequent trial length the incidence of hung juries in relation to the successful juries for various lengths of deliberation.

TABLE 124

Per Cent Hung Juries by Deliberation Time
(For 2001 Trials of 1 to 2 days length)

Per Cent of All Jury Deliberations

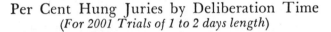

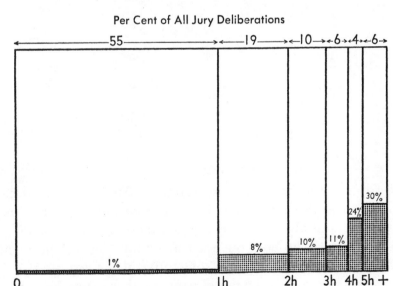

Hours of Deliberation

The percentage of hung juries is minimal when the jury has not deliberated for more than one hour, and only average when it has deliberated two hours. But from then on the probability of a hung jury increases sharply. And once the jury (in such a relatively short trial) has been out five hours or longer, the odds that it will hang are almost 1 in 3.

We may conclude from these figures that the judge allows sufficient time before accepting as final a jury's inability to reach a verdict. His function, therefore, is clearly only a declaratory one, and the causes for the jury's failure must rest in the case and in the jury itself.

We turn now to the third of our lines of analysis and inspect the vote at which the jury is found deadlocked.

TABLE 125

Last Vote of Hung Juries

Votes for Conviction	Per Cent	
11 : 1	24	
10 : 2	10	
9 : 3	10	63% Majority
8 : 4	6	for Guilty
7 : 5	13	
6 : 6	13	
5 : 7	8	
4 : 8	4	
3 : 9	4	24% Minority
2 : 10	8	for Guilty
1 : 11	—	
	100%	
Number of cases	48*	

* Sample II only.

Table 125 suggests two observations. The first concerns the *direction* of the final vote. We note that the jurors holding out for acquittal are hanging the jury more than twice as often as the jurors who hold out for conviction, and so one might easily conclude that there is something in the acquittal position that makes a juror more stubborn than when he is in a minority position with a guilty vote. But this would be a wrong conclusion to draw. We remember that jury verdicts split apart for the juries in general at about the same ratio: two thirds for conviction and one third for acquittal. Hence, the proper conclusion to draw from Table 125 is that the probability that an acquittal minority will hang the jury is about as great as that a guilty minority will hang it.

The second observation suggested by Table 125 goes to the *size* of the vote that eventually blocks unanimity. The question has significance for the possibility of allowing a less than unanimous verdict, as some of our states do.[6] Table 125 permits an estimate of the number of hung juries that could be avoided if the jurors were permitted to bring in a 10:2 or 11:1 verdict. Projecting from our sample, the number of hung juries would be reduced by $(24 + 10 + 8 =)$ 42 per cent.

Table 126 allows one more reading on this problem by comparing the actual percentage of hung juries in jurisdictions that require unanimity with the percentage in those allowing majority verdicts.

TABLE 126

Frequency of Hung Juries in States With and Without Unanimity Requirement

Unanmity Required	Allows Majority Verdicts
5.6%	3.1%
3512*	64*

* Number of trials.

The jurisdictions that allow majority verdicts have $(5.6 - 3.1 =)$ 45 per cent fewer hung juries than those that require unanimity. This result is very close to the 42 per cent measure we derived above for this difference by a different route.

[6] Numerous states allow for a majority verdict in civil cases. For criminal trials, only five states permit a conviction on less than a unanimous verdict; three of these states allow majority verdicts in trials of crimes below the grade of felony or in criminal cases tried in inferior courts: Idaho allows five sixths, Montana, two thirds, and Oklahoma, three fourths. Louisiana provides for a 9:3 verdict in cases involving less than the death penalty. In Oregon, for non-capital crimes, the verdict must have at least ten votes behind it. For details see J. Am. Jud. Soc., v. 33, p. 111 (1949).

We can now round out this inquiry into the hung jury by drawing on findings from another part of the Jury Project. At one point we interviewed jurors in two metropolitan criminal courts on the development of the voting situation from the first ballot to the final one.[7] Table 127 reveals the first ballot

TABLE 127

First Ballot and Frequency of Hung Jury

First Ballot		Jury		Number
for conviction	for acquittal or undecided	reached a verdict	unable to agree	of Cases
11	1			
10	2	100%	0%	78
9	3			
8	4			
7	5			
6	6	85%	15%	52
5	7			
4	8			
3	9			
2	10	93%	7%	22
1	11	100%	0%	3

constellations from which hung juries are likely to develop.

To begin with, Table 127 confirms our earlier conclusion that the likelihood of hung juries is not dependent on the direction of the minority votes: the distribution of hung juries is roughly symmetrical.

But there is a new point that emerges from this table, shedding some light on the popular notion of the "hanging juror." According to this notion, juries hang not so much because of the objective situation of the case, but rather because once in a while an eccentric juror will refuse to play his proper role.

The table shows that juries which begin with an overwhelming majority in either direction are not likely to hang. It requires a massive minority of 4 or 5 jurors at the first vote to develop the likelihood of a hung jury.[8]

[7] See Chapter 38.

[8] Table 127, to be sure, is based on a sufficiently large sample of trials, would be likely to produce some hung juries for the 11:1 or

If one may take the first ballot vote as a measure of the ambiguity of the case, then it follows that the case itself must be the primary cause of a hung jury.

But the substantial minority need exist only at the beginning of the deliberations. During the process it may be whittled away, and we know from Table 125 how small it may be at the end when the judge gives up and declares a mistrial.[9]

Nevertheless, for one or two jurors to hold out to the end, it would appear necessary that they had companionship at the beginning of the deliberations. The juror psychology recalls a famous series of experiments by the psychologist Asch and others which showed that in an ambiguous situation a member of a group will doubt and finally disbelieve his own correct observation if all other members of the group claim that he must have been mistaken. To maintain his original position, not only before others but even before himself, it is necessary for him to have at least one ally.[10]

10:2 first ballots, and probably many more for the 6:6 first ballot, but our general conclusion is not likely to be proven wrong.

[9] It is in this reduced sense that the notion of a hanging juror might still be relevant: the member of a group who holds out although the others have surrendered their positions. The structure of the deliberation process encourages an original expression of dissent, conceivably as a carryover from the adversary character of the trial, but it tends to discourage dissent at the end of the deliberation process.

[10] See Asch, Effects of Group Pressure upon the Modification and Distortion of Judgments, in Swanson, Newcombe, and Hartley, Readings in Social Psychology (1952).

CHAPTER 37

Methodology: No Two Juries
and No Two Judges Are Alike

It may have been noticed that there has been conspicuous quiet throughout the study about the well-known secret that no two juries, and for that matter no two judges, are alike. One implication, however, has been present throughout the discussion. Findings have been presented as probabilistic, true for some juries but not for all.[1] This variation among juries and judges suggests an analytic possibility we are now obligated to consider: can we connect the background characteristics of juries and judges with their decisions?

In the prior discussion of the non-homogeneity of judge and jury we satisfied ourselves that these variations did not affect our findings, and that it was appropriate for the main purpose of the study to speak of comparing *the* judge with *the* jury. At this point, however, we would relax, take cognizance of the actual variation, and speak of judges and juries. What dimension can we add thereby to the analysis?

Connecting individual background characteristics with decisions, attitudes, or opinions has been a major achievement of modern social science research. It can often yield stunning results. We will cite just one example. The classic study of voting,[2] made during the Willkie-Roosevelt campaign of 1940, produced data which provided a basic insight into the structure of the American electorate.

---

[1] See the discussion in Chapter 7 at pages 101-102.
[2] Lazarsfeld, Berelson and Gaudet, The People's Choice (1944).

TABLE 128

Per Cent of Republican Voters by Background *

	Rural		Urban	
	Well-Off	Poor	Well-Off	Poor
Protestant	73%	60%	67%	41%
Catholic	34%	26%	23%	16%

* The data in this table are re-ordered for our purposes. The final data were secured by correspondence with the authors.

In this instance the linking of voting behavior to three background characteristics, religion, economic status, and size of community, captures, in a single table, a basic architecture of American politics.[3] Well-off Protestants living in rural areas show the highest proportion of Republican voters (73 per cent), whereas poor Catholics in urban areas show the smallest (16 per cent); between these extremes the three factors provide clear gradations of the electorate.

The table is impressive in the success with which it answers the question posed: can a correlation be established between background characteristics and decision-making in a national election? We ask the parallel question: can a correlation be established between jury backgrounds and decision-making in criminal trials? Given the necessary limitation of the materials in this study, the answer is a quick "no." [4]

The question however opens onto a prospect so inviting that we pause to illustrate, albeit feebly, the kinds of insights about the jury such analysis could lead to. It is not hard to

[3] At the time of that study, 1940, race was not a political force on an order with the variables employed.

[4] In sum, it would be a task of very great magnitude to establish for each of our probabalistic findings about the jury the exact background correlates which would locate the kinds of juries that do act on a particular sentiment. However, the Jury Project has amassed considerable data on individual juror background and individual juror behavior which is yet to be reported out. A good indication of the nature of this information will be found in Simon, The American Jury — The Defense of Insanity (1966).

put engaging hypotheses. For example, there is reason for thinking that regional variations among juries in criminal cases would reveal differences in jury behavior. The bar has always held firm views about such variations in personal injury cases.[5] And indeed in another part of the Project we found a pattern of regional variation in damage awards. The size of damage awards given by juries for comparable personal injuries was strongly related to the jury's domicile. The larger the community from which the jury came, the larger the award; in addition, juries in the states along the two seacoasts proved to be more generous than juries from the Midwest and the South. City size and region cumulated so that there was a maximum spread between awards from juries from large eastern or western cities and those from small midwestern towns.[6]

The suggestion then is to test whether the breakdown by regions, which worked so well in civil cases, will discriminate for juries in criminal cases. Will there be a commonality between "high award" juries in civil cases and "high leniency" juries in criminal cases?

The hypothesis is full of interest; the difficulty is that we cannot do it justice within the limitations of our data. This difficulty becomes painfully apparent as soon as we attempt to translate the hypothesis into tabular form.

We can readily distribute the cases among the same four major regions of the United States, and within each region, among the same three city sizes, recording in each of these twelve cells the net leniency.[7] This does not, however, take us

---

[5] One result of this is the so-called migratory tort. A suit may be brought at a considerable distance from the original place of harm merely because defendant has wide contacts, allowing the plaintiff to sue in the jurisdiction he deems most favorable to his cause.

[6] The study involved estimates supplied by a sample of insurance adjusters. A description of the method is given in Zeisel, Social Research on the Law: The Ideal and the Practical, in Law and Sociology, p. 124 (Evan ed. 1962). The results are to be published.

[7] We have now completed the analysis of disagreement by directionality, i.e., normal disagreements and cross-overs, and return to jury net leniency, or the difference between the two.

far, because of the risk that the kinds of cases may vary by region. We cannot eliminate this risk because when we attempt to hold our customary factors constant, we run out of cases.

But on the view that we here engage primarily in a methodological exercise, the twelve-cell regional breakdown is offered, for whatever interest it may have, as Table 129.[8]

TABLE 129

Jury Leniency on Guilt by Region and City Size
(Serious Crimes Only)

City Size*	East		South		Midwest		West		Total
Large	14%	415	12%	49	13%	270	10%	313	12%
Medium	7%	121	10%	154	17%	76	15%	144	14%
Small	14%	87	18%	376	21%	191	20%	222	19%
Total	13%		16%		16%		14%		

Total number of cases 2418

* Defined by the size of the metropolitan area of which it is a part.

For another example we pursue a closely related theory about regional variation.[9] The novelty is that this time the

[8] There is another hypothesis which suggests itself and which has some appeal. One might suspect, for example, that juries from the smaller communities tend to yield more to sentiments, as is suggested by the following comment: "This is a mining community and the men in the community will not convict in gambling and drunken driving cases. Women in the community refuse jury duty." [II-0317]   But as the following reveals, the proportion of Values alone disagreements is virtually the same for communities of all sizes.

Community Size and Reasons for Disagreement

	Small	Medium	Large
Values alone	21	22	21
Values and Facts	46	51	40
Facts alone	33	27	39
Total	100%	100%	100%
Number of cases	483	149	330

[9] Not surprisingly, all our examples are based on regional or com-

regional classification is tied to variation in attitudes toward a specific crime, drunken driving, which happens to be sufficiently represented in our sample to permit analysis.   The basic

TABLE 130

Verdict Pattern for Drunken Driving
(455 Cases = 100%)

		Jury	
		Acquits	Convicts
Judge	Acquits	12	3
	Convicts	27	58

Net leniency: (27% − 3%) = 24%

verdict pattern for these cases is as follows.[10]   We can refine the analysis along a geographic dimension by dividing the cases between two groups of states: the states from which we have comments that the community considers the law on drunken driving as too severe,[11] and the states where no such comments were made.[12]   We thereby obtain the following picture:

---

munity variation, since locale is the main variable our questionnaire was designed to isolate.

It might be appropriate to note here that juries differ not only in the people who constitute them but also because jury procedures differ somewhat between jurisdictions.   Not all criminal juries need to be unanimous in order to arrive at a verdict.   The states of Idaho, Montana, and Oklahoma allow majority verdicts in misdemeanor cases, and Louisiana and Oregon allow majority verdicts except for the most serious crimes.

Finally, at one point the amusing possibility arose that the cases might vary by the time of the year in which the trial was held.   Impetus for the view was supplied by a handful of explanations that offer Christmas as a reason, e.g., page 202.   [Case I-2006] The hypothesis that the jury is calendar conscious was not however borne out on analysis.

[10] This table repeats the basic data offered in Table 19.

[11] Question 15 on the Sample II questionnaire.   The community sentiment as detected from Sample II was projected onto the Sample I cases from the same state, and thus Table 131 gives the results for the states for which the sentiment could be determined.

[12] Strictly speaking, the "in accord" jurisdictions are those for which

TABLE 131

Drunken Driving Pattern by Community Sentiments

	Law Too Severe (212 Cases = 100%) Jury			In Accord (173 Cases = 100%) Jury	
	Acquits	Convicts		Acquits	Convicts
Judge Acquits	11	3		10	2
Judge Convicts	33	53		22	66

Net leniency: (33% − 3%) = 30%   (22% − 2%) = 20%

A trend emerges: in both groups of states the judge acquits at about the same rate, 14 per cent in the one, 12 per cent in the other. But jury acquittals are (11 + 33) = 44 per cent in the one, and only (10 + 22) = 32 per cent in the other, producing the resulting difference in net leniency.[13]

One underlying assumption of the book has been that the judge is more disciplined than the jury, by virtue of tradition and his official role, and can therefore be taken as a base line against which to plot jury disagreement. The truth is, of course, that although individual variations will be smaller, no two judges are quite alike. In this sense the non-homogeneity of judges parallels that of juries.

This is not the place for a full analysis of the variance in decisions among judges.[14] We have, however, biographical

---

fewer than 5 per cent of the cases reflected a sentiment adverse to the law.

[13] A further refinement of Table 131 by size of community revealed a slight increase in leniency in smaller communities.

[14] An increasing number of efforts are being made to study differences in adjudication by judges operating under the same rules of law. It is not altogether surprising that these are largely studies of sentencing in the trial courts and of constitutional adjudication in the United States Supreme Court. Since sentencing standards are avowedly a matter of the judge's discretion, one should expect the judge's personal view to be a key factor; and since constitutional principles

are so generous, there is a similar though more limited invitation to discretion.

The pioneering study in the field of sentencing was Gaudet, Individual Differences in the Sentencing Tendencies of Judges, Archives of Psych., v. 32, pp. 5 and *passim* (1938). Later studies confirmed Gaudet's findings with the possible exception of Green, Judicial Attitudes in Sentencing (London 1961), but Green's interpretation of the data is controversial. For a general view, see the fine bibliography on Disparity of Sentencing, prepared by the Institute of Judicial Administration (1954). In some way, one of the most arresting investigations of judicial decision-making is one of the earliest ones: Everson's study of the New York City Magistrate Court during the year 1915. Of the 13 judges who there passed on more than five hundred defendants, one judge, for example, discharged 73 per cent of the defendants charged before him with intoxication, while one of his colleagues discharged only 1 per cent. J. Crim. Law & Criminology, v. 1, p. 90 (1919).

The author of the pioneering study of the Supreme Court adjudication was Pritchett, who in Divisions of Opinion Among Justices of the U.S. Supreme Court, Am. Pol. Sci. Rev., v. 35, p. 890 (1941), started a whole field of inquiry.

From this beginning an ever more detailed line of studies developed, making use of a variety of sophisticated mathematical techniques, foremost among which is scale analysis. This is a device which permits one to test the hypothesis that in certain types of cases the members of a court will vote consistently in a rank order fashion. The order indicates that if one judge votes in favor of the issue and his neighbor to the right in the rank order votes against it, then all the judges to the left of the judge who voted in favor will also vote in favor; and all the judges to the right of the judge who voted against will also vote against. And this voting pattern will remain more or less constant for the class of cases for which this rank order was established. This type of analysis raises a number of problems, but fewer than lawyers like to think. One is the meaning and relevance of the class of cases to which the analysis is applied; another is the significance of exceptions, which invariably occur; and, finally, the nature of the relationship between the judge's position in the rank order and the reasons he gave for his vote in the opinion he either wrote or joined in. We might note in passing the analogy between such a rank order and our fourfold table. In a way, we rank jury and judge, and what we call cross-overs are the exceptions to the rank order.

Efforts to go beyond establishing the existence of constant differences in adjudication patterns, that is the search for reasons that link personal and background characteristics of the judges to their decision pattern, have on the whole not succeeded. Compare, however, Ulmer's amazing findings on the relationship between party affiliation and propensity

attitude data on some of the judges in the sample which offer a few suggestive lines for analysis.[15]   Because the trial judge is an individual, it is easier to differentiate profiles among judges than it is among juries.

For example, there is a widely held view that judges who were prosecutors before coming to the bench will be more severe toward the defendant than judges recruited from the defense side.   Table 132 shows the distribution of the judges for whom we have this information, with respect to their background.

TABLE 132

Background of Trial Judge

	Per Cent
Had been —	
prosecutor (but not defense counsel)	22
defense counsel (but not prosecutor)	14
neither or both	64
Total	100%
Number of judges	*325*

It is perhaps a happy circumstance that the large majority of judges appear to be neutralized by having neither background or both.

The hypothesis can be tested in a preliminary way by comparing the acquittal rates for judges with the three types of background.   The prediction is that the former prosecutor will show the lowest acquittal rate; the former defense counsel, the highest.   Table 133 confirms that expectation.

---

to decide in favor of claimants under workman's compensation: The Political Party Variable in the Michigan Supreme Court, J. Pub. L., v. 11, p. 352 (1962).   Schubert, himself a major contributor to the field, has compiled a useful reader which contains most all of the relevant studies: Judicial Behavior (1964).

[15] We did not solicit biographical information from the judges in our basic sample directly.   These data come from a separate poll of judicial opinion, to which 325 of the judges who cooperated in the jury study responded.   For other references to this survey see Chapter 1, note 3, Chapter 4, note 3, and Chapter 34, note 1.

TABLE 133

The Judge's Background and Acquittal Rate

	Per Cent of Defendants Acquitted by These Judges	Number of Cases
Former prosecutor	13%	482
Neither or both	16%	1396
Former defense counsel	22%	449
The Jury	33%	2327

Since there is no reason for suspecting that the cases assigned to these three groups of judges will vary with the background of the judge, Table 133 offers good prima facie evidence that background to some extent does affect the judge's decision.

As a final turn of the data, we pursue the relationship between verdict pattern and *views* the judge holds about the jury. From a battery of questions put to the judge,[16] three have been selected to build a scale on which to rank attitudes. Each of these questions allows the judge to express a negative attitude toward the jury. Hence we can classify the judges into four groups: those who have registered a negative reaction on all three opportunities, or in two, or in only one, or in none. The hypothesis is that the more objections the judge has to the jury in the opinion poll, the more frequently will he be in disagreement with it.[17] Table 134 tests this hypothesis.

---

[16] The judge opinion poll asked sixty questions in all.

[17] The specific questions are as follows:

Which of these statements best fits your over-all attitude toward the jury system?

In Criminal Trials: (Check one)

On balance, the jury system is thoroughly satisfactory ...... ☐

The jury system has serious disadvantages which could be corrected and should be corrected if the system is to remain useful .... ☐

The disadvantages of the jury system outweigh its advantages so much that its use should be sharply curtailed ...... ☐

Constitutional difficulties aside, would you favor eliminating the right to jury trial in some kinds of cases where it is now available?

TABLE 134

Judge's Attitudes Toward Juries and Frequency of Disagreement

Reservations Toward Jury:	Per Cent of Cases in Which Judge Disagrees with the Jury	Number of	
		Cases	Judges
None	25%	1141	166
One	26%	433	71
Two	27%	423	49
Three	32%	330	39

There is only the most modest correlation between attitude and verdict pattern. In any event it would not be clear which of the two is the cause and which the effect.

We rest at this point in the hope that the analysis has been carried far enough to indicate two things: how a new dimension of insight would be added if one were to exploit fully the fact that no two judges and no two juries are alike. And how monumental that enterprise would be.

In Criminal Trials:
    ☐ No; favor no further elimination of jury.
    ☐ Yes; the jury should be eliminated in the following types of criminal cases:
Why?
Among the case where jury trial is now available, are there any kinds which you, as a judge, would personally prefer to have tried before you without a jury?

Criminal Cases:
    ☐ No; prefer a jury trial wherever available.
    ☐ Yes; prefer jury-waiver in the following kinds of criminal cases:
Why?

CHAPTER 38

Methodology:
Have We Studied the Wrong Thing?

We have now presented our full answer to the two questions we set ourselves in this study: how much do jury and judge disagree, and what are the explanations for their disagreement? It might be the better part of valor at this point to leave well enough alone and bring the study to conclusion. It is difficult, however, not to face up to one final challenge. Have we not been working in just one corner of the world of the jury and ignoring a substantial part of the total phenomenon? Have we not, that is, let the real quarry, the nature of jury decision-making, escape?

The challenge takes two forms, both of which appear at first blush disturbing. By scrupulously confining attention to that one third of all cases in which jury and judge disagree, we have virtually ignored that other two thirds of the jury's activity, namely, the cases in which they agree. Furthermore, the methodology of this study has cut us off from what would appear to be the humanly most interesting and colorful aspect of the whole jury enterprise, the deliberation process. Since the jury deliberates privately, the question of what the jurors do in the secrecy of the jury room has been a topic of endless anecdote, curiosity, and fascination. And it has been thought by many that if one could only get into the jury room and hear the jurors talking, one would have the key to all the secrets of juror psychology.

We shall, in this chapter, make some efforts to discuss these two points. On the first, the agreement process, we can add a significant commentary simply by spelling out some implications of what we have already done. On the second point, we can, at this stage of our reporting of the Jury Project data, offer little more than educated guesses as to the true significance of the deliberation process for the decisions of the jury.

We begin with the discussion of the agreement cases. In a sense, a theory as to what causes judge-jury agreement has been implicit throughout the book. It is nothing more complicated than that agreement is caused by the absence of whatever causes disagreement. When a factor was said to be a cause of disagreement, the implication was that, but for the presence of this factor, jury and judge would have agreed. It may be well at this point to repeat a few lines from our earlier statement [1] of the basic sources of disagreement:

> . . . the theory is that all disagreement between judge and jury arises because of disparity of counsel, facts that only the judge knew, jury sentiments about the defendant, jury sentiments about the law, and evidentiary factors, operating alone or in combination with each other; and as a corollary, that the judge is less likely to be influenced by these factors than is the jury. There is some gain in emphasis if we invert the statement: unless at least one of these factors is present in a case, the jury and the judge will not disagree.

What is involved is more than a tautology. In an important sense, only deviation or disagreement is accessible to explanation. Indeed, it was a chief methodological strategy of the study to recognize that it would be well nigh impossible to attempt to explain the jury's verdict in agreement cases directly.

An analogy may help to illumine the point. Assume that two students independently solved a lengthy problem in a mathematics test. If they both arrived at the same result, to explain why they did so would involve nothing less than duplicating the entire course of calculation. But suppose they

[1] Chapter 8, pages 108-109.

came to different results. The explanation of why they did so would immediately become more focused.

For example, A might have misread a certain figure, or B, at some point, might have added where he should have subtracted. In brief, and this is the point of the strategy, the explanation for a difference in outcome can be very concise and yet satisfying, because it bypasses all the manifold reasons that account for the full decisional process.[2]

However helpful the analogy, it is misleading in one important respect. We cannot with assurance assume that when jury and judge reach the same result they, like our mathematics students, necessarily went through the same pattern of calculation. There is some reason to think that the jury, even when it agrees with the judge, may follow a process that is more intuitive and less explicitly rational.[3]

Happily, the explanations of disagreement suggest some specific insights into the sources of agreement; they suggest a typology of agreement cases, which is more complicated than we might have imagined from the statement that the jury will agree with the judge when there is no specific stimulus to disagree with him.

The typology emerges from what is no more than a recapitulation of points already made. First, as the discussion has just indicated, there must be a certain number of bland cases, that is, cases which contain no stimuli or disturbing factors to which the jury is sensitive.

Again, there are cases in which a disturbing factor is pres-

[2] See Chapter 7, The Logic of Explanation. The need for rendering complex causal structures amenable to research, by specifying the point of focus, is particularly great in the social sciences. To study, for instance, the causes of crime, a job that will fascinate forever reformers and politicians, can only make the social scientist weary. To study the question at all, one must turn it around and ask it in terms of specific experimental measures designed to reduce criminality, for instance, through reducing recidivism by some penal or correctional device.

[3] We know this to be especially true in civil trials, where the jury is called upon to make the difficult determination of the size of the damages to be awarded. See Kalven, The Jury, the Law and the Personal Injury Damage Award, Ohio State Law J., v. 19, p. 158 (1958).

ent but in which its power is insufficient to generate disagreement. It will be remembered, for example, that neither a superior defense counsel nor a sympathetic defendant — although they offer an important cause of disagreement — is strong enough to produce disagreement every time it is present in a case. Indeed, imbalance of counsel served to produce disagreement in only one of every nine cases in which there was imbalance; and the sympathetic defendant factor produced a disagreement in only one out of every five cases in which it was present. Thus the agreements will include a not insubstantial number of cases in which judge and jury agree despite the presence of a disturbing factor.

The third and perhaps most complicated instance of agreement is one in which a disturbing factor is present but is offset by a counter-factor. On this view the jury agreement is really the result of stimuli which tug in opposite directions.[4]

It is possible to trace empirically this last notion that some agreements are the result of an offsetting process. The hypothesis, stated precisely, is that a factor which has the power to cause normal disagreements will also have the power to cause a reduction in cross-overs; and, conversely, that a factor which has the power to cause cross-overs should also have a depressive impact on normal disagreements.

The data on the imbalance of counsel will serve as a suitable testing material. In the discussion of the role of the lawyer in causing normal disagreements, it will be remem-

---

[4] At times such opposing stimuli lead to the so-called compromise verdict, where two sharply opposed factions arrive through bargaining at a logically indefensible middle point.

In a case from the sample where the defendant is charged with the statutory rape of a girl of low morals, the jury splits into two factions, one which would acquit because "you can't corrupt the corrupted," and another which apparently recognizes that equity but refuses to let the defendant go because he made the girl pregnant. The result is a compromise on the lesser charge of contributing to the delinquency of a minor. But, as the judge points out, this is a legally impossible finding, since the girl's poor reputation is a complete defense against that charge. See Chapter 18 at note 43. The compromise verdict must often be the practical alternative to a hung jury.

bered that we compared the cases with superior defense counsel with all other cases. And, conversely, in tracing the impact of counsel in causing cross-overs, we compared cases having a superior prosecutor with all other cases. That simple dichotomy sufficed there, but now the comparison can be made more sensitive. Each time the judge would have convicted or acquitted there are *three* possibilities with respect to counsel: superior defense, balanced counsel, and superior prosecution. Table 135 presents this total picture, and in so doing supplies the last word on the impact of the lawyer on the criminal jury trial.

Table 135 consists of two parts: the upper part represents the 17 per cent of all cases in which the judge would have acquitted; the lower part, the 83 per cent in which he would have convicted. Each of these parts is divided into three vertical columns. The broad middle column represents the cases with balanced counsel; the column on the left, the cases with superior defense; the column on the right, those with superior prosecution. And in each of these $(2 \times 3 =)$ 6 subgroups, the white area represents the amount of judge-jury agreement.

Looking first at the lower part of the table, the cases where the judge convicts, we observe three levels of jury agreement. The baseline is provided by the cases where counsel are balanced. There, where counsel is not a factor, the level of agreement is 65 per cent. If defense counsel is superior, the agreement drops to 50 per cent, which is simply to say once again that superior defense counsel may be a cause of normal disagreements. In the present context, however, our interest focuses on the third column, the cases in which the prosecution is superior. Here the agreement rises to 71 per cent, which is to say that superior prosecution is a factor in causing agreement; it operates by offsetting to some degree factors in the case that would cause the jury to disagree.

The upper half of the table presents the mirror image of the same point, this time with respect to cases in which the

TABLE 135

The Over-all Role of Defense Counsel and Prosecutor

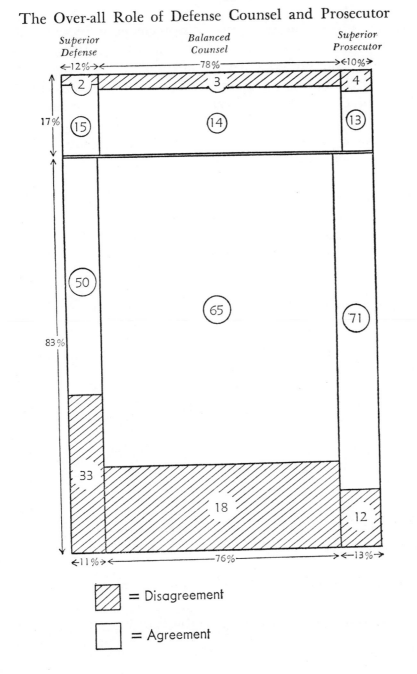

judge would have acquitted and in which disagreement takes the form of the cross-over.

This theory that judge-jury disagreement is in part the result of offsetting factors can be taken one step further empirically. We can add to the impact of counsel, traced in Table 135, the impact of the individual defendant, which, like counsel, has three dimensions: sympathetic, average, and unattractive. If we mark factors favorable to the defendant with a plus sign and factors unfavorable to him with a minus sign, we obtain the following nine-cell matrix.

DEFENDANT

		Sympathetic (+)	Average	Unattractive (−)
C O U N S E L	Defense Superior (+)	+ +	+	+ − Offset
	Equal	+	Bland cases	−
	Prosecution Superior (−)	− + Offset	−	− −

+ Favors defendant
− Favors prosecution

Defined by the various combinations of plus and minus signs, the cases form six categories. Table 136 adds to the picture by giving the proportion of cases that fall into each of these categories.

Under this definition the bland cases constitute half of all cases, with the remainder distributed about evenly on both sides.[5]

Where the judge acquits, we would predict that the cases

[5] Table 136 necessarily overstates the proportion of bland cases and understates all others, since it does not include the cases in which a jury sentiment on the law is present. These sentiments cannot be included because we do not know when they are present in the agreement cases.

TABLE 136

Distribution of Cases by Balance of Factors

Type of Case	Symbol*	Per Cent
Favoring defense —		
strongly	(+ +)	3
somewhat	(+)	19
Bland cases	( )	50
Offset cases	(+ −)	4
Favoring prosecution —		
somewhat	(−)	21
strongly	(− −)	3
Total		100%
Number of cases		*1191*

* From the matrix above.

with factors favoring the defendant would have the highest agreement rate; the cases with factors favoring the prosecution, the lowest agreement rate. The large group of bland cases, which have no factors favoring either side, and the offset cases, which have factors favoring both sides, we predict will fall somewhere between these two extremes. The prediction is just the converse in cases where the judge convicts, but once again we expect the bland cases and the offset cases to fall somewhere in the middle. Table 137 gives the actual agreement rates for the various categories.

The hypothesis turns out to be fully corroborated. Not

TABLE 137

Judge-Jury Agreement by Balance of Factors

Type of Case*	Per Cent Jury Agreement Where —	
	Judge Convicts	Judge Acquits
Favors prosecutor —		
strongly	92	25
somewhat	85	63
Bland cases	76	87
Offset cases	77	88
Favors defense —		
somewhat	59	91
strongly	45	94

* See Table 136.

surprisingly, in the end, agreement and disagreement turn
out to be little more than opposite sides of a coin, so that
the explanation for the one is necessarily also the explanation
for the other.   In theory we should be able to describe in advance a category of cases so lacking in disturbing factors that
we could predict that judge and jury would almost invariably
agree.   But Table 137 marks the final point to which we can
prudently push the data.[6]

We turn now to the second half of the challenge, our neglect of the deliberation process.   Can we really know what
the sources of jury decision-making are unless we know what
goes on in the jury room?   Can we offer compelling explanations of why jury and judge disagree, or for that matter, agree,
without knowing what transpired during the deliberation
process?

We have, as we said, a considerable amount of information
about jury deliberation, partly from detailed post-trial interviews with jurors,[7] and partly from complete records of the
deliberations of juries that took part in our experimental
trials.[8]   At the moment we can do little more than suggest a

[6] The main reason that prevents us from doing this is our lack of
knowledge of the full incidence of the law sentiments; see note 5
above.

[7] Professor Dale Broeder, for the better part of a year, accompanied
a federal district judge on his circuit and interviewed in great detail
almost every juror who participated in the judge's trials.   Some of his
work is now published: The Negro in Court [1965] Duke L.J., p. 19;
Plaintiff's Family Status as Affecting Juror Behavior, J. Pub. Law, v. 14,
p. 131 (1965); Voir Dire Examination, So. Cal. L. Rev., v. 38, p. 503
(1965); Previous Jury Trial Service Affecting Juror Behavior [1965],
Ins. L.J., p. 138.

[8] These experiments were conducted to test the effect of various
procedural and substantive law changes on the outcome of jury trials.
The deliberation from which we reproduce excerpts is from a series
of experiments that form the foundation of Simon, The American Jury
— The Defense of Insanity (1966), and is published in full therein.   See
also Strodtbeck, Social Process, The Law and Jury Functioning, in Law
and Sociology (Evan ed. 1962).   The deliberations of such mock juries
are surprisingly lifelike.

bridge between the present study and that of the deliberation process proper and outline some of the interesting questions that remain to be confronted. Unfortunately, at the moment we can stir more questions than we can put to rest.

We begin by quoting a typical page or two from the opening of one of the experimental deliberations. The jury is deliberating in a prosecution for incest where the defense is insanity; it has been instructed under the Durham rule.[9] The discussion begins with the election of the foreman. This then is a sample of how the jury sounds.[10]

> As long as you're sitting in the head chair, you may as well take it.
>
> Well, I have never served before on a jury, and they tell me you have. You know a little more about the procedures, supposing you sit up here.
>
> I don't believe it's really necessary to know anything about it really, it's merely a discussion to find out whether . . .
>
> No, you're just supposed to run the discussion. See to it that no two people talk at the same time.
>
> Well.
>
> Well, what would be the opinion of the guilt or innocence of the defendant?
>
> Well, I think you should invite an open discussion.
>
> Why don't you . . .
>
> I'm too tired to get up.
>
> Oh, you can stay right where you are.
>
> Go on, you act as foreman.

[9] The defendant is an officer of the fire department who has over a long period of time had repeated sexual intercourse with his two minor daughters. The case is distinguished by the contrast between this pathological streak and his otherwise unexceptionable behavior at home and at work. For the Durham rule, see Chapter 25, note 1.

[10] The following discussion involves several jurors, men and women. But since our present purpose is to provide a glimpse of the over-all deliberation, and involves nothing so precise as individual content analysis, the specific jurors speaking are left undesignated.

With the election out of the way one of the jurors loses no time in providing the jury with his opinion of the case:

Well, let's talk it over. See what, what's been bothering me, those two doctors . . .

The defendant is a sex pervert; but he knew what he was doing. He knew that it was wrong but he did it to satisfy his own desire. Even the psychiatrists could not come right out and say that an oversexed man is insane.

I'll tell you he may have been emotionally disturbed until he committed that, but when he committed that, he really was insane.

The very fact that he was cautious enough to use a preventative indicates that he might not have been off . . . but, he also was crafty enough and sly enough not to want anybody to know. Or, to have any repercussions as far as that is concerned. Now most insane people are a little on the sly secretive side . . .

They are.

But, I think he was sane enough to not want any scandal. Now whether that would be from his own viewpoint or for his daughter's sake we can't tell. But, he couldn't have been thinking very much of his daughter on that score, so it had to be solely on his own, which is selfishness. To some extent selfishness and slyness run in insanity cases, I think, where they are always very crafty and want to outwit somebody else, their associates, or somebody they are connected with. But on the other hand, the very fact that he carried on his job, had friends and still was ashamed to make any effort to seek outside help, what would you call that?

The defendant was only insane on a certain subject. He spoke about it as if it was nothing. That shows he was insane. He didn't understand what it was all about.

But remember how long he has been doing this. He started on the younger daughter when she was twelve.

The mother was more insane than he was. It is just like murdering her daughter. Even if she were half crazy, she would still fight for her child.

For the next few minutes the discussion drifts off in several directions. Some jurors ask about the son's role in the family. Others consider the relationship between organic disorders and mental illness. A few continue to discuss the mother. Finally, one juror addresses the group as a whole:

He is insane. He is absolutely insane, without question. A normal person would not do anything like that. He was insane and I think this man should be committed.

Well, let's see what the two psychiatrists said about degrees of insanity. All they kept harping on was "emotionally disturbed." See, there is a fine point. How about the judge's instructions? Is there anything in there . . .

I was just trying to read it over and find it.

I don't see where the judge said how to determine the degree of insanity. That's what we have to find out.

The foreman then reads the first few pages of the instructions, up to the part about differentiating between lay and expert witnesses, when one of the jurors interrupts:

All right now, the prosecution's doctor did not observe the defendant.

Oh, that one, that's right.

He made absolutely no personal observations of the defendant.

No, all he was asked was, "Is a sex pervert insane?" And he said "no."

Okay. Go ahead.

See. Now these two other fellows didn't say that a sex pervert was insane. They didn't say that.

He was a psychotic.

Yes, but what does that mean? In our language. Crazy?

Psycho, that means he's got a neurosis, that at certain times he's crazy and at certain times he can think straight.

Most of us would be in the nuthouse if that there were the case.

Well, this is an emotional disturbance. This is a mental disorder of the brain.

Well, I think the man, even in going over what he did, he knew what he did, but I think in his mind, I think he thought he was right.

That's right.

And so it goes. The initial impact of this deliberation, judging from our experience, is fairly standard. There is at first, in William James' phrase about the baby, the sense of buzzing, booming, confusion. After a while, we become accustomed to the quick, fluid movement of jury discussion and realize that the talk moves in small bursts of coherence, shifting from topic to topic with remarkable flexibility. It touches an issue, leaves it, and returns again. Even casual inspection makes it evident that this is interesting and arresting human behavior. It is not a formal debate; nor, although it is mercurial and difficult to pick up, is it just excited talk.

The precise question then is what would we learn about jury decision-making from a patient, systematic analysis of the deliberation process, assuming we had somehow solved the problem of obtaining access to the jury deliberations in the 3576 cases that constitute this survey.

To begin with, we suspect that the jurors' talk may often be not very revealing. If the theory of this book is correct, the real cause of a juror's decision will be in many instances a factor he himself is only dimly aware of and perhaps unable to articulate. A cornerstone for the theory of this study has been what we call the liberation hypothesis: that is, the yielding to sentiment in the guise of evaluating factual doubt. There is little reason to believe that most jurors would be conscious of doing this, and, therefore, if we look only at what they say in the deliberation room, we are likely to conclude that the problem is simply one of handling evidential doubt.

But even when the juror is aware of his motives, he may not wish to disclose them. He may choose to argue his point more in terms of proper legal considerations than in terms of the extra-legal ones he privately finds persuasive. Finally, we know that some jurors either cannot or prefer not to talk much and rather limit their participation to voting. We are thus disposed to assert that the analysis of jury deliberation would add little to a theory of why the jury disagrees with the judge.[11]

We can come at the matter from still another angle. We know from other parts of our study something about the relationship between the first ballot vote and the final vote. Materials from a pilot study made some years ago will serve to illustrate for present purposes. From post-trial interviews in actual jury cases we were able to reconstruct the first ballot votes for 225 trials.[12] Table 138 gives the breakdown.

TABLE 138

The Jury's First Ballot

Number of Guilty Votes*	Per Cent of Trials
0 (unanimous)	12
1–5	18
6	4
7–11	47
12 (unanimous)	19
Total	100%
Number of trials	225

* Not all the remaining votes were "not guilty," some were "undecided."

[11] Under a somewhat different view of the role of the deliberation process, at one point the Jury Project, with consent of the trial judge and of the attorneys, recorded the actual deliberation of the jury in five civil cases. See Hearing Before the Subcommittee to Investigate the Internal Security Act of the Senate Committee on the Judiciary, 84th Cong., 1st Session (1955); and see preface.

[12] These interviews were conducted, with the approval of the presiding judge, in the criminal courts in Chicago and Brooklyn. The final outcome of these 225 deliberations is, interestingly enough, very similar to the outcome of the 3576 cases of this study:

	This Study %	225 Separate Cases %
Guilty	63	62
Not guilty	32	33
Hung	5	5
	100%	100%

By showing that in only 12 per cent of the cases the jury is initially unanimous for acquittal and in only 19 per cent initially unanimous for conviction, the table provides an important clue to the nature of the deliberation process. Since in the end the jury in all cases reaches a unanimous verdict,[13] the deliberation is almost by definition a process of reaching consensus from positions of initial disagreement.

Table 139 shows the relationship between first ballot votes and final verdicts and thereby highlights the function of the deliberation process.

TABLE 139

First Ballot and Final Verdict

	Number of Guilty Votes on First Ballot				
	0	1–5	6	7–11	12
Final Verdict	%	%	%	%	%
Not Guilty	100	91	50	5	—
Hung	—	7	—	9	—
Guilty	—	2	50	86	100
Total	100%	100%	100%	100%	100%
Number of cases	26	41	10	105	43

If we look first at the third column, we see that where the jury is split 6-6 the final verdict falls half the time (it so happens, exactly half the time) in one direction and half in the other. However, in the instances where there is an initial majority either for conviction or for acquittal, the jury in roughly nine out of ten cases decides in the direction of the initial majority. Only with extreme infrequency does the minority succeed in persuading the majority to change its mind during the deliberation. But this is only to say that *with very few exceptions the first ballot decides the outcome of the verdict.* And if this is true, then *the real decision is often made before the deliberation begins.*[14]

[13] To be exact, as note 12 shows, in 95 per cent of all cases; in 5 per cent the jury hangs.

[14] The first ballot may relate at still another point with the final verdict: there is a question whether a connection exists between the jury's first ballot and the likelihood that its final verdict will differ

The upshot is a radical hunch about the function of the deliberation process. Perhaps it does not so much decide the case as bring about the consensus, the outcome of which has been made highly likely by the distribution of first ballot votes. The deliberation process might well be likened to what the developer does for an exposed film: it brings out the picture, but the outcome is pre-determined. On this view the deliberation process offers fascinating data on human behavior and should reward systematic study. The topic, however, is not so much how juries decide cases but how small groups produce consensus.[15] From what we have been able to perceive thus far, the process is an interesting combination of rational persuasion, sheer social pressure, and the psychological mechanism by which individual perceptions undergo change when exposed to group discussion.

The theory of this book as to why judge and jury agree and disagree might be rephrased as a theory of predicting first ballot votes. The factors we have designated as sources of disagreement decide the first ballot votes. The social process of the jury deliberation then carries these first ballot votes to the final verdict.

---

from that of the judge. Unfortunately in only a very small number of cases do we have all three elements, the jury's and the judge's verdict, and the jury's first ballot.

	First Ballot Vote			
	Jury Unanimous	*Majority of 11 or 10*	*Majority of 9 or 8*	*Majority of 7 or less*
Judge–Jury —	%	%	%	%
Agree	100	100	50	33
Disagree	—	—	50	67
	100%	100%	100%	100%
Number of cases	*3*	*6*	*4*	*3*

There is a suggestion that the more evenly the jury is split on the first ballot, the more likely is the final verdict to be in disagreement with that of the judge.

[15] A determination of the extent to which the fact of an initial majority in and of itself decides the outcome of a case would, of course, require an elaborate research undertaking. The data from the 225 trials here are therefore to be read as suggestive only.

We must not push the point too far. In roughly one case in ten, the minority eventually succeeds in reversing an initial majority, and these may be cases of special importance. It is likely that when this happens the arguments used by the minority will more often reflect the true reasons for the decision.

It is in these special and limited senses then that, on our view, the jury deliberation process has a role in producing agreement or disagreement between judge and jury.

We have taken these speculations about the role of the jury as far as we can within the confines of the present study. There remains, however, a jurisprudential postscript worth adding. This discussion of the relevance of studying the jury's deliberation has a curious resonance to a controversy of an earlier day over judicial decision-making. Then the point centered on the relevance of judicial opinions to the understanding of the judicial process. The point has been put in various ways by various students, but perhaps best in Professor Herman Oliphant's presidential address in 1927 before the Annual Meeting of the American Association of Law Schools.

Under the title *A Return to Stare Decisis*,[16] his address urged that we begin to build a science of law by exploring "non-vocal judicial behavior." In a famous passage, Oliphant had this to say:

> There is a constant factor in the cases which is susceptible of sound and satisfying study. The predictable element in it all is what the courts have done in response to stimuli of the facts of the concrete cases before them. Note not the judges' opinions, but which way they decide cases, will be the dominant subject-matter of any truly scientific study of law.[17]

Our study of the jury, to adapt Oliphant's phrase, emphasizes the non-vocal behavior of juries. At least with respect to

[16] Published in Am. L. Sch. Rev., v. 6, p. 215 (1927). Quotes are at pp. 225 and 228.

[17] Although the address is mainly remembered for this emphasis, on a re-reading it proves to be a complex analysis that is considerably removed from what has the appearance of radical behaviorism.

the decisions of juries, we are inclined to think that this early view is correct.   We are less certain that the point is totally well taken with respect to the judicial process.

In any event, the tracing of connections between this study of jury behavior and various theories of judicial behavior, however tempting, will have to await another day.

CHAPTER 39

A Last Word

There are so many difficulties in providing a systematic chapter of conclusions for a study of this sort that we have decided not to attempt it. The architecture of the book is, we hope, sufficiently and accessibly explicit to make tedious and unnecessary a summary of specific points and findings. We have completed what we set out to do, to pass before the reader the total business of the contemporary American jury in criminal cases and to permit him to be a spectator at close range of its decisions. The companion report on the jury in civil cases is to follow. It will be time enough, if then, to confront the larger significances of our lengthy inquiry into the jury.

In this brief epilogue we aspire to nothing more than a few final reflections on the venture and its results.

As to method, just two comments. It has been characteristic of the study both carefully to count cases as units and to experience them intimately as individual instances. We trust we have shown that quantification of behavior can be powerful and sustained and at the same time blend in partnership with qualitative emphasis. Indeed, we would argue that this partnership is needed for successful study of social institutions. We see no war here between two cultures.

And it is a special advantage of empirical studies of legal institutions that the law supplies a pre-existing framework of significance and expectation to which the quantitative dimension can be added; it permits, that is, measurement with meaning.

At the technical level, it is appropriate to emphasize once

more the wide use of the technique of reason assessment in individual cases, the method which provided the key to much of the study. And it is noteworthy that on several occasions we were able to confront the results of the reason assessment with the corresponding cross-tabulations, thus corroborating the one method by the other.

As to matters of substance, it is hard not to bring to mind here particular ideas or reactions of the jury that struck us as especially flavorsome, as though we were sketching the profile of a colorful personality we had come to know. We note especially its perception that Providence may have punished the defendant enough, its sympathy for the sexual difficulties of the cripple, its recognition of intoxication only when it appears to have altered the character of the defendant, its feeling that young men old enough to fight for their country are old enough to drink in it, its sense of humor, and its new concept of petty robbery. But to go down this road would involve us in simply restating a substantial portion of the text and so we come at the matter in a more general way.

In the large, the mind of the jury in criminal cases might perhaps be said to exhibit four dominant traits. First, there is the niceness of its calculus of equities; it will treat provocation as justifying defensive moves by the victim but only to the extent of the one-punch battery; it may even treat injury to the victim as punishment for the actor, but only where the relationship is close and the conduct is inadvertent. Second, there is the jury's broad tendency to see little difference between tort and crime and thus to see the victim rather than the state as the other party to the case, with the consequence that the public controversy is appraised largely as though it were a private quarrel. Third, there is a comparably broad tendency to merge at several points considerations of penalty with those of guilt. Finally, and this is a point on which we will say more in a moment, there is a quality of formal symmetry about the jury's responses. In what we have called the simple rape cases the jury seems to say, whatever kind of offense the defendant had committed, it just was not rape; conversely, in the cases of sexual approach to children, it says that whatever the defendant did, even though far short of rape, it was some kind of offense. Thus while the jury is often moved to leniency by adding a distinction the law does not make, it is at times moved to be more severe than the judge because it wishes to override a distinction the law does make.

It is true, of course, that our study has its provincial aspects. It is the study of only one decision-making institution in a particular country and at a particular time. Nevertheless, it has been possible at various points to generalize about how the American jury performs today, and these generalizations constitute a kind of theory of the jury. Since these points have been scattered throughout the text, there may be some value in collecting them here.

Although a substantial part of the jury's work is the finding of facts, this, as has long been suspected, is not its total function in the real world. As a fact-finder it is not in any interesting way different from the judge, although it will not always reach the same conclusion. When only pure fact-finding is involved the jury tends to give more weight than the judge to the norm that there should be no conviction without proof beyond a reasonable doubt. And there is every indication that the jury follows the evidence and understands the case.

The more interesting and controversial aspects of the jury's performance emerge in cases in which it does more than find facts; where, depending on how one looks at it, the jury can be said to do equity, to legislate interstitially, to implement its own norms, or to exhibit bias.

All this is fairly familiar. The distinctive bite of this study resides in the following supplementary propositions about the jury as legislator.

First, we can estimate with some precision how frequently the jury engages in more than fact-finding. It will be recalled that about three quarters of the time it agrees with the judge; and that most, but not all of the time it agrees with him, it is not importing values of its own into the case. But roughly two thirds of the disagreements with the judge are marked by some jury response to values.

Second, the jury imports its values into the law not so much by open revolt in the teeth of the law and the facts, although in a minority of cases it does do this, as by what we termed the liberation hypothesis. The jury, in the guise of resolving doubts about the issues of fact, gives reign to its sense of values. It will not often be doing this consciously; as the equities of the case press, the jury may, as one judge put it, "hunt for doubts." Its war with the law is thus both modest and subtle. The upshot is that when the jury reaches a different conclusion from the judge on the same evidence, it does so not because it is a sloppy or inaccurate finder of facts, but because it gives recognition to values which fall outside the official rules.

Third, we suspect there is little or no intrinsic directionality in the jury's response. It is not fundamentally defendant-prone, rather it is non-rule minded; it will move where the equities are. And where the equities are at any given time will depend on both the state of the law and the climate of public opinion.

Fourth, the extent to which the jury will disagree with the judge will depend on the selection of cases that come before the jury. Since, under current waiver rules and practice, the defendant in effect has the final say on whether there is to be a jury trial or a bench trial, the cases coming before the jury will be skewed and include a disproportionate number in which there are factors that appeal to the jury. The selection will be affected also by pleas of guilty and, to a lesser degree, by decisions of the prosecutor not to prosecute, and even in some instances by decisions of the police not to arrest. Thus the commonplace impression that the criminal jury is defendant-prone may be largely an artifact of the dynamics by which the cases are sorted out for jury trial.

Fifth, we have said, the jury's reaction will in part depend on the lay of public sentiment on any given point. The extensive agreement between judge and jury indicates that there is in our society at this time widespread consensus on the values embodied in the law. As a result, a jury drawn at random from the public, does not often have representatives of a dissenting view.

On some points there is sufficient dissent so that the random drawing will at times place on the jury representatives of a view contrary to the existing law. Indeed on some matters the public will even be ambivalent, with factions that deviate from the law in opposite directions.

Thus, it makes a good deal of difference in this decision-making who the personnel are. The consequence of the fact that no two juries are alike is that statements about trends in jury decision-making are probabilistic at best. We cannot assert that all juries will always feel that a man who has suffered personal disasters since committing the crime has been punished enough. We can only say that this idea is prevalent enough so that it has some chance of moving the jury away from the judge in any given instance in which it is present.

Sixth, the explanation of how a disagreement is generated requires one more fundamental point. The thesis is that to a substantial degree the jury verdict is determined by the posture of the vote at the start of the deliberation process and not by the impact of this process as rational persuasion. The jury tends to decide in the end whichever way the initial majority lies. The result is that a sentiment need be spread only so widely among the public as to produce enough representatives on the jury to yield the initial majority. On this view the study can be thought of as a study of the sentiments that will lead to initial majorities.

Seventh, and as a corollary, the deliberation process although rich in human interest and color appears not to be at the heart of jury decision-making. Rather, deliberation is the route by which small group pressures produce consensus out of the initial majority.

More than once in the course of the book we have had occasion to note parallels with the concerns of the legal realists who so shook up American jurisprudence in the twenties and thirties. They emphasized the translation of rules of law into patterns of official behavior and took a skeptical view of the public reasons offered by courts for their decisions. Their quest was for a law in action as contrasted to a law on the books, and for latent or hidden reasons. A fair description of our study is that it is an effort to trace the law in action, to see how juries, the final arbiters of so much criminal law, really decide cases.

What emerges perhaps as something of a surprise is that this reality has so legal a texture. When the jury deviates from the official rules and writes its own law, the categories of thought are familiar. For the largest part the hidden reasons of the jury are reasons which can stand public scrutiny; not infrequently the jury's rule turns out to be the law in another jurisdiction. The realist emphasis seemed often to lend itself to a kind of inside dopester jurisprudence in which the real reasons for decisions would be very different from the surface reasons, and probably rather nasty. Insofar as this study can be said to be a venture in realism, it suggests that the ideas embodied in the formal rules and doctrines of law are close to the policies that actually motivate decision-makers in the real world.

As we attempt to step back and gain some distance from the detail of the study, it may be useful to put two quite general and interrelated questions: Why do judge and jury ever disagree, and why do they not disagree more often?

Judge and jury have experienced the same case and received the same rules of law to apply to it; why do these two deciders ever disagree? We seek for the moment an explanation more general than that offered throughout the book in terms of specific factors of evidence, sentiment, and defendant. Why do they not react the same way to the stimuli? Why does the judge not move over to the jury view, or the jury stay with the judge?

The answer must turn on the intrinsic differences between the two institutions. The judge very often perceives the stimulus that moves the jury, but does not yield to it. Indeed it is interesting how often the judge describes with sensitivity a factor which he then excludes from his own considerations. Somehow the combination of official role, tradition, discipline, and repeated experience with the task make of the judge one kind of decider. The perennial amateur, layman jury cannot be so quickly domesticated to official role and tradition; it remains accessible to stimuli which the judge will exclude.

The better question is the second. Since the jury does at times recognize and use its de facto freedom, why does it not deviate from the judge more often? Why is it not more of a wildcat operation? In many ways our single most basic finding is that the jury, despite its autonomy, spins so close to the legal baseline.

The study does not answer directly, but it does lay the ground for three plausible suggestions. As just noted, the official law has done pretty well in adjusting to the equities, and there is therefore no great gap between the official values and the popular. Again, the group nature of the jury decision will moderate and brake eccentric views. Lastly, the jury is not simply a corner gang picked from the street; it has been invested with a public task, brought under the influence of a judge, and put to work in solemn surroundings. Perhaps one reason why the jury exercises its very real power so sparingly is because it is officially told it has none.

The jury thus represents a uniquely subtle distribution of official power, an unusual arrangement of checks and balances. It represents also an impressive way of building discretion, equity, and flexibility into a legal system. Not the least of the advantages is that the jury, relieved of the burdens of creating precedent, can bend the law without breaking it.

For the very last word it is appropriate to return to the tradition of controversy over the jury system. Can we now at long last answer whether the jury is a worthy institution or whether it would be more sensible to have all cases tried to judges alone? As foreshadowed in Chapter 1, we cannot answer, and there is no embarrassment that so lengthy and systematic a study does not end more conclusively for this issue.

Our purpose was not to evaluate but only to find out as

carefully as we could how the jury actually performs. And in the detailed inventory we have provided of its behavior, assuredly both friends and critics will find new ammunition for their case.

Whether the jury is a desirable institution depends in no small measure on what we think about the judge. We have given a candid and rounded picture of the jury, but we treated the judge as abstract, a baseline representing the law. We know, of course, that on the side of the judge too, discretion, freedom, and sentiment will be at work, and that the judge too is human. Until an equally full and candid story of the judge is available, we have only half the knowledge needed.

And there is another point which goes to the time limitations of our study. We have noted that at this moment in history the jury's quarrel with the law is a slight one. But there have been times when the difference was larger and such times may come again.

But no additional facts can decide the policy issue; they can only make it more precise. In the end, evaluation must turn on one's jurisprudence, on how, given the limitations of human foresight, experience, and character one hopes to achieve the ideal of the rule of law. Whether or not one comes to admire the jury system as much as we have, it must rank as a daring effort in human arrangement to work out a solution to the tensions between law and equity and anarchy.

How Many Criminal Jury Trials in the United States?

We discovered in the course of the study that nobody had ever counted the number of jury trials that take place in the United States. Of the forty-eight states[1] only a handful provide a complete count of their criminal jury trials.

In most cases, therefore, the Jury Project had to collect the relevant statistics, or make estimates, or have estimates made by experts for their respective jurisdictions. The jury trial total for the United States cannot therefore be expected to be more accurate than its components. Nevertheless, the estimate we make here is to be taken seriously; it is the best that could be secured by competent investigators through a search that extended over an entire year.

That it took such an extraordinary effort to produce even this rough statistic on an institution as important as the American jury is a commentary on the sad state of judicial statistics generally.

Table 140 gives the number of estimated jury trials for the year 1955, the year which lies fairly in the center of the period over which our field work extended.

Although we do have for a few jurisdictions, as pointed out, an exact count of the number of jury trials, for the overwhelming majority of jurisdictions we have only projections from either partial data or data from a different year. Therefore, we have rounded off all figures to the nearest ten, including the handful we know to be correct to their last digit, to avoid the impression of a greater exactitude than we can claim.

[1] At the time of our field work the courts of Alaska and Hawaii were still part of the federal system.

TABLE 140

The Number of Criminal Jury Trials in the United States
(1955)

Census Region and State	Number of Trials	Trials per 100,000 Population
New England	**3020**	**30**
Maine	210	22
New Hampshire	50	8
Vermont	120	30
Massachusetts	2490	51
Rhode Island	80	10
Connecticut	70	3
Middle Atlantic	**6340**	**20**
New York	2710	17
New Jersey	850	16
Pennsylvania	2780	25
East North Central	**3060**	**9**
Ohio	550	6
Indiana	650	15
Illinois	640	7
Michigan	1010	14
Wisconsin	210	6
West North Central	**2540**	**17**
Minnesota	100	3
Iowa	290	11
Missouri	1090	26
North Dakota	40	7
South Dakota	60	9
Nebraska	250	19
Kansas	710	35
South Atlantic	**15,840**	**67**
Delaware	30	8
Maryland	440	16
District of Columbia	450	59
Virginia	1940	53
West Virginia	1070	55
North Carolina	3950	92
South Carolina	580	26
Georgia	5300	144
Florida	2080	66
East South Central	**9770**	**83**
Kentucky	1160	51

Census Region and State	Number of Trials	Trials per 100,000 Population
Tennessee	3180	93
Alabama	4270	135
Mississippi	1160	53
West South Central	**4640**	31
Arkansas	250	14
Louisiana	390	13
Oklahoma	290	13
Texas	3710	43
Mountain	**2410**	40
Montana	50	8
Idaho	170	27
Utah	420	55
Wyoming	170	54
Colorado	1020	66
New Mexico	170	21
Arizona	360	35
Nevada	50	21
Pacific	**5760**	33
Washington	300	12
Oregon	520	31
California	4940	38
Federal District Courts	**2290**	
Grand Total	**55,670**	34

The first surprise Table 140 offers is the enormous range in the frequency of jury trials between states. One expects, of course, the smaller states to have fewer jury trials; North Dakota had only 40 jury trials during the year, Nevada only 50, as against 5300 jury trials in Georgia and 4270 in Alabama. But the variation is almost equally great if we correct for the size of the state and compute the frequency of jury trials on a per capita basis. By this standard Connecticut and Minnesota rank lowest: 3 jury trials per 100,000 population, as against 144 jury trials in Georgia or 135 in Alabama. Generally the Southeast shows the highest per 100,000 population ratios: 83 for the East South Central region and 67 for the South Atlantic.

Broadly speaking, three factors determine the relative frequency of jury trials: the amount of crime, the range of crimes for which the law allows jury trial, and the degree to which regional custom restricts or engenders jury waiver. In all three respects some of the southern states rank highest, and some of the northern states lowest.

Sources

Alabama
> Special survey by the authors of all Circuit Courts.

Arizona
> Third Report of the Administrative Director of the Supreme Court (1964).

Arkansas
> Legislative Council Research Report No. 84 (1958).

California
> Crime in California (1955) (superior courts); 15th Biennial Report Judicial Council (1954) (municipal courts); estimate by state official (justice courts).

Colorado
> Special survey by the authors of selected district, county, and justice courts.

Connecticut
> Fourteenth Report (1954).

Delaware
> Special survey by the authors of all courts.

District of Columbia
> U.S. Administrative Office of the U.S. Courts (1955).

Federal
> U.S. Administrative Office of the U.S. Courts (1955).

Florida
> Fifth Annual Report, Judicial Council (1959); population projection for counties not reported.

Georgia
> Estimate by state official (1963) and a limited survey by the authors for purposes of corroboration.

Idaho
> Estimate by state official (1963) corroborated by U.S. Dept. of Commerce, Judicial Criminal Statistics (1945).

Illinois
> Report of the Supreme Court of Illinois (1963) provides data on circuit courts. Other courts, estimates by various state and county officials.

Indiana
> Special survey by the authors of all prosecuting attorneys.

Iowa
> Unofficial report to the authors from a state official for the years 1958-1962.

Kansas
> Kansas Judicial Council Bulletin (1955) reporting *all* trials (bench

and jury); per cent jury trials derived from U.S. Dept. of Commerce, Judicial Criminal Statistics (1941-1945).

Kentucky

Circuit Courts Information Bulletin No. 16 (1957) reporting *all* trials (bench and jury); per cent jury trials estimated by a state official. Justice court estimate based on the number of justices hearing criminal cases as reported in Bulletin No. 16.

Louisiana

Special survey by the authors of all parish courts.

Maine

Unofficial report to the authors by a state official (1962).

Maryland

Second Annual Report of the Administrative Office of the Courts (1957).

Massachusetts

Thirty-first Judicial Council Report (1956) for *all* trials (bench and jury); per cent jury trials estimated by three state officials.

Michigan

Supreme Court Annual Report (1957).

Minnesota

Estimate by state official (1963) corroborated by U.S. Dept. of Commerce, Judicial Criminal Statistics (1945).

Mississippi

Special survey of all district attorneys and a limited survey by the authors of the county courts.

Missouri

Judicial Conference — Consolidated Report on Criminal Cases (1956) reporting *all* trials (bench and jury); per cent jury trials based on an estimate by judges. Magistrate and municipal courts estimates from special survey by the authors.

Montana

Special survey by the authors of district clerks, requesting estimates of jury trials in all courts.

Nebraska

Special survey by the authors of district clerks, requesting estimates of jury trials in all courts.

Nevada

Special survey by the authors of all courts.

New Hampshire

Sixth Report of the Judicial Council (1955).

New Jersey

1954-1955 Report of the Administrative Director of the Courts (superior courts); per cent jury trial for reported total trials in county courts is estimated.

New Mexico

Unofficial report to the authors from a state official for 1961-1963.

New York

Unofficial estimate by a state official for 1961-1962, corroborated in part by the U.S. Dept. of Commerce, Judicial Criminal Statistics (1945).

North Carolina

Unofficial report to the authors from a state official for 1956.

North Dakota

Report of the Judicial Council for the State (six-month period, 1964).

Ohio

Thirteenth Report of the Judicial Council (1957) gives the number of jury acquittals. The authors assumed this to represent one third of all jury trials.

Oklahoma

Judicial Council Report (1962) (bench and jury); per cent jury trials derived from a poll of judges.

Oregon

Unofficial report to the authors from a state official.

Pennsylvania

We combine U.S. Dept. of Commerce, Judicial Criminal Statistics (1945), and an unofficial report to the authors by a state official (1962).

Rhode Island

Special survey by the authors of all courts.

South Carolina

Special survey by the authors of selected courts, only Charleston courts reporting.

South Dakota

Unofficial report to the authors from a state official (1963).

Tennessee

Unofficial report to the authors from a state official (1963) citing the total number of criminal trials (1956-1957), with estimate of the per cent tried to juries.

Texas

Unofficial estimate of a state official (1963).

Utah

Special survey by the authors of the city and district courts.

Vermont

Report of the Judicial Council (1953 and 1955). The 1955 report notes that the jury trials are about the same as those listed in the 1953 report, except for an increase in traffic cases in municipal court, the size of which is estimated by the authors.

Virginia

Unofficial report to the authors from a state official for 1954 and 1962.

Washington

Unofficial report to the authors from a state official for 1958 and 1962.

West Virginia

Sixth Annual Report (1947) supplies the total number of jury trials in justice courts. For circuit courts the number of total trials only (bench and jury) is reported; the per cent jury trials is derived from a poll of judges.

Wisconsin

Unofficial report to the authors from a state official (1962).

Wyoming

Special survey by the authors of selected district and justice courts.

Table 141 presents a summary of these 50 sources and thereby gives numerical expression to the deplorable state of the official statistics.

TABLE 141

Sources for the Count of Jury Trials

Published official statistics	9
Incomplete official statistics* supplemented by our own survey** or estimate	13
Estimate by local official	14
Our own survey	14
Total number of jurisdictions	50

* The shortcomings of an incomplete count are nicely illustrated by the story of the man who was to make sure that a deposit box of dollar bills contained exactly one thousand notes. After a long time of counting, he finally came to "nine hundred ninety-one, nine hundred ninety-two," and then exclaimed with satisfaction, "It's been all right up to here; it must be right for the rest," whereupon he stopped counting.

** By collecting the data from a sample of individual courts in the jurisdiction and projecting from that sample.

Normally, even the few jurisdictions that count their jury trials do not count the jury trials that, for one reason or another, do not go to verdict. A number of causes may account for the abortive endings: the judge may dismiss the case; he may direct an acquittal; the jury may hang, or the judge may declare a mistrial because an essential rule of procedure has been violated; or finally, the defendant may, during the course of the trial, change his plea to guilty.

The number of commenced but unfinished jury trials is an important although, as it turns out, largely unrecorded dimension of our jury system. From an administrative point of view these trials too consume substantial court time and jurors and court facilities.

Our efforts to obtain some statistics of these incomplete trials found meager reward: we received data from only four jurisdictions; they are summarized in Table 142. The table gives for all four jurisdictions the total number of jury trials that do not go to verdict, and for three jurisdictions a more detailed breakdown for each type of disposition. The frequencies are presented as percentages of the number of jury trials that go to verdict. Thus, the first figure 7 indicates that in New York City there are 7 hung juries for every 100 jury trials that go to verdict, and so forth.

TABLE 142

Jury Trials Commenced But Not Completed
(In Per Cent of Cases Tried to Verdict (= 100%))

	New York City	Los Angeles	New Jersey	North Dakota
Hung juries	7	15		—
Other mistrials	6	2		—
Case dismissed	4	3	no	15
Directed acquittal	8	—	details	—
Defendant changed plea to guilty	36	2		21
Total	61%	22%	30%	36%
Number of cases	*1003 **	*133 ***	*1204 **	*53 **

* Court year 1963-1964
** May, June, 1956

Incomplete as these figures are, they seem to allow one rough projection: for every 100 jury trials that go to verdict, there are probably one third again as many that commence but do not end in a verdict.[2] Since we estimate the number of jury trials going to

[2] The comparable figure for jury trials in civil cases, if one may generalize from a careful count of cases in the Manhattan Supreme Court, is for every 3 that do go to a verdict, there are 2 trials that do not. See Table 33 in Zeisel, Kalven, and Buchholz, Delay in the Court (1959).

verdict to be about 60,000, probably another 20,000 trials or so begin but end without a verdict.[3]

[3] There could be seen, perhaps, in Table 142, a suggestion that our sample underestimates the number of hung juries by giving it as somewhat below 6 per cent of all trials that go to verdict. Conceivably, some judges might have failed to report some hung juries, since technically they are mistrials. If so, we would have expected that this notion would have gained currency particularly among the judges who sent us only one or two trial reports. But the appropriate tabulation dispels that suspicion.

	From Judges Reporting Varying Numbers of Trials				
Proportion of hung juries	1	2-5	6-10	11-25	over 25
	6%	6%	6%	6%	4%

We are inclined, therefore, to trust our sample figures with regard to the frequency of hung juries.

A P P E N D I X   B

Jury Requests

Although this study had by its nature no direct access to the deliberation process, it has yielded some unusual data about the 3576 deliberations of our juries: we know how long each lasted,[1] we know how often the jury was unable to reach a decision,[2] and we know how often the jurors interrupted their deliberations to come back with a request to the judge.

We take up here the data, reported in Chapter 11, on the frequency with which juries come back to the court with a question.

TABLE 143

Frequency of Jury Requests by Difficulty of Case

		Number of Cases
Easy, clear	13%	618
Easy, close	19%	406
Difficult (clear or close)	28%	167
Total all cases	17%	1191

    * This table is based only on Sample II, which allows classification by difficulty of case.

Given the jury's basic inexperience with trials, it is perhaps surprising how infrequently it elects to come back to the judge for help. On the average, it has a question in about 1 out of every 6 deliberations. And even if the case is "difficult," it comes back in only about 1 out of every 3 or 4 cases. Table 144 shows the *type* of request which the jury makes.

[1] Data on deliberation time are found in Chapter 11 at pages 155-157, and in Chapter 36 on the hung jury.

[2] Chapter 36.

TABLE 144

Type of Jury Requests
(Samples I and II)

	Per Cent	
Law		
Nature of charge	21	
Details of law	30	
Form of verdict	1	
	—	
		52
Evidence		28
Sentence		9
Procedures in jury room		8
Miscellaneous		3
Total		100%
Number of requests		*584*

More than half of all requests concern questions on the law. A few examples will suggest the diversity of questions that bother the jury:

Jury requested further instructions as to the law governing assault with intent to commit manslaughter. [I-4120]

On the legal definition of assault and battery. [I-0035]

The law governing circumstantial evidence. [I-0559]

Reasonable doubt. [I-0541]

They wanted to know if the law stated any minimum amount in quantity [of marijuana] before conviction could be had for possession. They were told it did not. [I-0791]

Another third of the requests concern questions of evidence.

Wanted to hear more testimony. [II-1077]

Asked for dictionary. [I-0747]

Desired to know what previous felony the defendant had been convicted of. [I-0404]

Wanted to know [in a larceny case] why prosecution witnesses didn't tell how police got the wallet. [II-1068]

In our legal system not every question the jury asks is a good one. And there may, of course, be practical problems about securing the presence of counsel at the time the request is to be dealt with. Table 145 shows how often the judge answers the particular request.

TABLE 145

How Often the Request Is Answered

	Per Cent Answered in Each Category
Law	
Nature of charge	99
Details of law	90
Form of verdict	100
Evidence	90
Sentence	58 *
Procedure in jury room	89
Miscellaneous	75
Total all requests	85

* Questions concerning the sentence may be proper if in that case the jury has some say in it, be it because it is a capital case or because in that particular jurisdiction the jury sets the sentences in all cases. The average of 58 per cent granted requests splits as follows: in cases where the jury was to decide the sentence, 62 per cent; in cases where the jury was *not* to decide the sentence, 38 per cent.

Table 145 suggests an interesting point about jury administration. In normal practice the jury is not encouraged to come back. Since in most instances, the judge will answer a request if the jury happens to make one, might it not be good policy for the judge, when he finishes instructing the jury, to invite it to return to him if questions arise in the course of deliberations about the charge, the instructions, the verdict form, recorded testimony, or jury room procedure?

It would now seem an intriguing question whether the handling of the jury's request has any traceable effect on its verdicts, that is, on the frequency of its disagreement with the judge or, possibly, on the frequency with which it hangs. The data permit no inferences on this point, because there are so few cases in which the judge refuses to answer the jury's question. But as Table 146 shows, the very fact of the jury's coming back has some predictive power.

TABLE 146

Request and Verdict Pattern

	Jury Has Request				Jury Has No Request		
	Acquits	Convicts	Hangs		Acquits	Convicts	Hangs
Judge Acquits	9	2	3		14	2	1
Convicts	16	60	10		17	63	3

(100% = 584 cases)	(100% = 2992 cases)
Total disagreement: (16 + 2 =) **18%**	(17 + 2 =) **19%**
Total hung juries: (3 + 10 =) **13%**	(1 + 3 =) **4%**

While the percentages of disagreement on the verdict hardly differ between the two groups, the chances of a hung jury do vary: it is about three times as great in cases where the jury comes back.[3]

[3] The jury request is of course not the cause of the hung jury; rather both the request and the hung jury are caused by the closeness and difficulty of the case. For the relationship between difficulty and frequency of requests, see Table 47 and Table 143; for the relationship as to closeness, difficulty, and hung juries, see Table 121.

Note on Comparative Empirical Studies: England, Denmark, Austria

Since the participation of lay judges is, as we pointed out in Chapter 1,[1] almost universal in criminal procedure, there is special point in looking for data from other countries. The harvest is limited. We obtained a summarizing opinion from the Lord Chief Justice of England; we discovered a Danish study; and perhaps most significant, we were able to stimulate a large-scale study of the role of lay judges in the courts of Austria.

England

Upon our suggestion that it would be of great interest to compare the findings from this study with data on English juries, Lord Chief Justice Parker of Waddington was kind enough to send us the following communication:

> Since your visit to this country I have had the opportunity of consulting all the senior Queen's Bench Judges. As I told you none of us has kept any figures, and accordingly such information as I have obtained is largely a matter of impression. I can I think fairly summarise it as follows: —
> (1) Cases of "ordinary crime" in which the Jury reaches a verdict which the Judge sitting alone would not have arrived at.
>   (a) The cases in which the Judge would have acquitted where the Jury have convicted are very rare.
>   Such cases as have been specifically referred to comprise sexual cases where the Jury have approached the matter in a common sense way whereas the Judge would have

[1] Note 1.

been more influenced by legalistic considerations such as the absence of corroboration.

(b) Cases in which the Judge would have convicted where the Jury have acquitted range from 3% to 10%.

These include cases when a Jury convicts of a minor offence rather than the grave offence, e.g. convicts of unlawful wounding and not wounding with intent to do grievous bodily harm.

(2) Cases in which the Judge has been unable to say after consideration that the Jury may have been right, i.e. where the verdict is perverse, are very rare. The answers received describe them as "none", "negligible", "very rare" or "hardly ever".

Those cases that are specifically mentioned include cases where a verdict has clearly been influenced by danger of the death penalty being imposed, in which case the verdict would be one of manslaughter, or where the Jury felt that the complainant and the prisoner were morally both to blame.

I mentioned at the beginning that these views concern "ordinary crime". I said that because nearly all the Judges have excluded from their consideration cases of causing death by dangerous driving of motor vehicles.

To translate Lord Parker's letter into the fourfold table used throughout this study, we apply his data to trial statistics published for England and Wales:[2]

TABLE 147

Estimated Verdict Pattern of English Criminal Juries

	Jury Acquits	Jury Convicts	Total
Judge Acquits	17	1 *	18
Judge Convicts	7 *	76	82
Total	24	76	100%
Number of cases			8740

* Approximations based on Lord Parker's estimates.

[2] Home Office statistics, Table III, pp . 34-35 (1952), give jury acquittals as 2083 and convictions as 19,971. The latter figure includes guilty

To set up a precise comparison with the American data, it is necessary to adjust also for the fact that English juries deal only with serious offenses.[3] The verdict pattern of American juries for serious crimes then is as follows.

Verdict Pattern of American Juries for Serious Crimes

	Jury		
	Acquits	Convicts	Total
Judge Acquits	13	3	16
Convicts	17	67	84
Total	30	70	100%
Number of cases			*2418*

There seems to be no doubt then that English juries dissent less frequently from the judge than do their American counterparts. Whether this is due to a greater conformity of sentiment or to the greater control of the English judge over the trial process would be a most interesting topic for future investigation.

Denmark

In many civil law countries mixed tribunals — usually consisting of two learned and two lay judges — provide the major forum for the participation of lay personnel in the criminal trial. The lay and learned judges constitute a single bench, which decides jointly on guilt as well as penalty.[4]

Theoretically, the power of the lay judges in these tribunals is great, because their number is usually equal to or greater than that of the learned judges. Since a majority is necessary for a convic-

---

pleas, which Lord Devlin estimated at "roughly two thirds." Trial by Jury, p. 176n. (1953). Here we estimate jury convictions at 6657.

[3] For a more precise discussion of the ambit of the English jury see Chapter 2, note 5.

[4] The major exceptions are the courts of lowest jurisdiction over which one single lay judge presides. Foremost examples are the English magistrates and the People's Judges in the Soviet Union.

tion, the lay judges can force an acquittal against the learned judges. Actually, very little is known about their influence. Most countries veil these bench deliberations with the utmost secrecy.

But in 1944 a Danish judge, F. Lucas, who for several years had presided over a mixed tribunal of three learned and three lay judges, published data that offer a basis for comparison with the findings from this study.[5] Judge Lucas kept an account of a sample of cases coming before his court and recorded the division of votes between the learned judges and their lay colleagues. The court is not a trial court of first instance, but an appellate court for all criminal offenses other than major felonies tried before a jury. The court, however, hears evidence de novo when relevant to the appeal. The following tables are our summaries of his account.

On the question of guilt the tribunal's record was as follows.

TABLE 149

Agreement and Dissent Between the 3 Lay and the 3 Learned Judges on the Issue of Guilt

		Per Cent
All six judges unanimous*		85
Split Vote		15
One lay judge for acquittal	4	
Two lay judges for acquittal	—	
Three lay judges for acquittal	2	
Three lay judges and one learned judge for acquittal	2	
One lay judge for lesser included offense	2	
Vote is split but details not indicated	5	
Total		100%
Number of cases		*123*

* Judge Lucas does not report whether on conviction or on acquittal.

Thus in only 15 per cent of all cases was the verdict not unanimous. Whenever it was split, if we disregard the 5 per cent of cases that were not identified, the lay judges were the ones to favor more leniency.

In only 4 per cent of all trials did the lay judges overrule the majority among the learned judges and thereby determine the ver-

[5] F. Lucas [J.], Erfaringer af Betragininger Vedrrende Laegdommere, Ugeskrift for Retsvaesen Kbenhavn, Vol. 78 (1944); Afdeling B., pp. 1-24. Professor Johannes Andonaes of the University of Oslo brought the paper to our attention, and Inga Davis kindly translated it for us.

dict: that is in the 2 per cent of the cases in which the three lay judges voted for acquittal (a majority of votes is required for conviction) and in the 2 per cent of the cases in which the three lay judges helped a minority learned judge to a majority.

In the deliberations on the sentence which Judge Lucas recorded, the vote went as follows.

TABLE 150
Deliberations on Sentence

	Per Cent
Unanimous	81
Split vote	19
Total	100%
Number of cases	*268*

Approximately half of the split decisions turned on the granting of probation, the other half simply on the severity of the sentence. Table 151 shows the split between lay and learned judges on the question of probation.

TABLE 151
Split Votes on Probation

	Lay Judges %	Learned Judges %
For probation	67	21
Against probation	33	79
Total	100%	100%
Number of individual votes	*75 **	*75 **

* Three judges in 25 cases.

Table 152 shows the split vote on sentencing.

TABLE 152
Split Votes on Sentencing

	Lay Judges %	Learned Judges %
For more lenient penalty	58	40
For more severe penalty	42	60
Total	100%	100%
Number of individual votes	*78 **	*78 **

* Three judges in 26 cases.

Again, on the average, the lay judges were more favorable to the defendant.

As to the type of situation in which the lay judges disagreed with the learned judges, the report is less precise, but it does give a few interesting hints. It must be difficult for the learned judge in a divided court to believe that the lay judges could be right. Judge Lucas, therefore, comments in terms of "questions that proved particularly difficult for the lay judges." He gives these examples: evaluation of child evidence in sex cases; judging evidence concerning estimates of time and distance (lay judges, he thinks, require more accuracy from the prosecution witnesses than one may reasonably expect); judging the good faith of a receiver of stolen goods (where the experienced judge knows how carefully the outward decorum is preserved in such transactions); and overestimating the significance of minor contradictions in testimony. Finally, in 15 drunken driving cases before the court, the judge reports disagreement in 5 cases, a disagreement rate of 33 per cent in contrast to an average of 15 per cent for all crimes.

Judge Lucas's over-all conclusion is that in his experience the lay judges have made no significant contribution to his court. He admits that this does not preclude the possibility of such a contribution in the trial courts of first instance. Comparable statistics would be interesting indeed, because there one learned judge is flanked by two lay judges.

Judge Lucas also has a few reflections on jury trial, remarking that it is only there that one will find "deviations from objective fact-finding." The reason, he thinks, is because in the jury trial the role of the learned judge is limited to presiding over the trial and he has no part in the deliberation. In the mixed tribunal, the learned judge is offered a chance for discussion, and, as Judge Lucas puts it, for a "clearing-up of misunderstandings."

Austria

The Institute for Advanced Studies in Vienna, in co-operation with the judiciary and under the sponsorship of the Ministry of Justice, has just embarked on an empirical study of the role of lay judges in the Austrian courts. That role takes a variety of forms.

The criminal courts have eight-man juries for murder and a few other major felonies. Most of the felonies remaining are tried before a *Schöffensenat* consisting of two learned judges, one of whom presides, and two lay judges.

The labor courts have lay judges both on the trial and the appeals levels. Here the lay judges, however, are not simply chosen from the general citizenry but are representatives of the respective organizations of employers and employees. They are as a rule officers of their particular organizations, hence by no means lay judges in the sense of the *Schöffen* in the criminal courts. These judges are deliberately chosen for their partisan origin. To learn the extent to which they maintain this partisan view on the bench and merely balance their influence, or rather lose it and become objective judges, is one of the objects of the Austrian study.

The commercial courts, finally, offer still another variant. Here the trial judge is flanked by two lay judges, respected businessmen, made permanent *commercial counselors* on the general theory that their knowledge of business customs and usages will aid the court in arriving at the proper decision.

The design of the Austrian investigation follows closely the design of the American jury study; the presiding judge is to be asked to report on contrasting positions between the lay and learned judges, and the reason that accounted for the difference. The Austrian project should round out our knowledge and bring us a major step closer to a general theory of the role of lay judges in the judicial process.

Prior Studies of Judge-Jury
Disagreement

We were not the first to record the frequency with which judge and jury agree on a verdict. Several judges, who themselves presided over jury trials, kept notes and some of them published some interesting statistics, with parallels to our findings.

The first of these data came in 1925 from Judge Philip J. Mc-Cook, of the Supreme Court of New York, who published two detailed reports on jury trials over which he had presided in ten civil trial terms.[1] His data are here transposed into the form of our basic fourfold table.

TABLE 153

Verdict Pattern in Civil Cases
(McCook, J.)

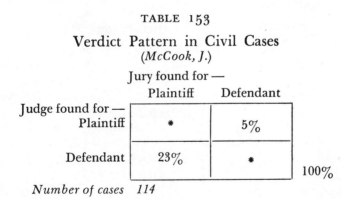

Jury found for —

	Plaintiff	Defendant	
Judge found for — Plaintiff	*	5%	
Defendant	23%	*	100%

Number of cases   114

* The distribution of the 72 per cent agreement cases was not given.

Although Judge McCook does not reveal which way the verdict went in the agreement cases, he tells us that in 32 of the cases in

[1] See The Jury, N.Y.L.J., v. 74, p. 1 (1925), and Judge, Jury and Justice: Two Years of Trial Term, N.Y.L.J., v. 78, p. 1 (1928).

which he agreed with the jury on liability, he differed with respect to the award. Interestingly enough, in two thirds of these disagreements he would have given more than the jury. It is of special interest that Judge McCook also provided a qualitative rating of the jury's performance. He asked himself: "Were the verdicts of my jury fair and just?" and answered as follows.

TABLE 154

Was the Jury Verdict Fair and Just?
(McCook, J.)

	Per Cent
Yes	72
Doubtful	10
No	18
Total	100%

In the 72 per cent agreement cases he had no difficulty in giving a positive answer. In more than one third of the disagreement cases he was in doubt whether the verdict was fair; but in about two thirds of the disagreements, his answer was clearly negative.[2]

In 1949, Judge Richard Hartshorne of the Court of Common Pleas in Newark, New Jersey, reported that he had kept notes over

TABLE 155

Judge-Jury Verdict Pattern
(Hartshorne, J.)

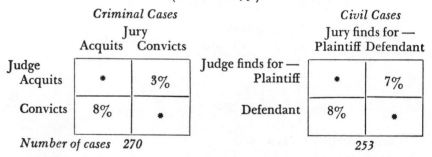

	Criminal Cases			Civil Cases	
	Jury			Jury finds for —	
	Acquits	Convicts	Judge finds for —	Plaintiff	Defendant
Judge Acquits	*	3%	Plaintiff	*	7%
Convicts	8%	*	Defendant	8%	*
Number of cases	270			253	

* Judge Hartshorne reports 89 per cent agreement in criminal cases and 85 per cent in civil cases. He too does not say how often he and the jury agreed on acquittal or on conviction, or on a verdict for the plaintiff or the defendant.

[2] This is translatable into our intensity of disagreement scale and quite similar to our findings. See Table 112.

a period of years on 270 criminal and 253 civil jury verdicts.[3]   His findings, transformed into our fourfold tables, tend to corroborate the difference in disagreement patterns between civil and criminal cases we had noted in Chapter 5.

Judge Joseph N. Ulman, of the Supreme Bench of Baltimore, in his book *A Judge Takes the Stand* (1931), also has much to say about juries.   But the remark that interests us particularly is that ". . . by actual count [civil] jury verdicts are practically identical with the verdicts I should reach in over seventy-five per cent of the cases I hear." (p. 22).

Similarly, Judge Gustavus Loevinger, who sat on the District court of Ramsay County, Minnesota, from 1931 until 1955, kept a "record of his own agreement or disagreement verdicts over a period of more than ten of those years.   His results were in substantial agreement with those of the Chicago experiment." [4]

Finally, in 1952, Judge Emory A. Niles, also of the Supreme Bench of Baltimore City, reported on his effort to determine "how far [the juries'] decision differ from mine."   He found — again, the statistics pertain only to civil cases — himself in agreement with the liablity finding of the jury in 83 per cent of all verdicts.[5]

[3] Jury Verdicts: A Study of Their Characteristics and Trends, A.B.A.J., v. 35, p. 113 (1949).
[4] Lee Loevinger reports on this in Jurimetrics: The Methodology of Legal Inquiry, Law & Contemp. Problems, v. 28, p. 32, n.79 (1963).
[5] American Oxonian, v. 39, p. 173 (1952).

APPENDIX E

The Questionnaires

Questionnaire for Sample I

Research Project
The University of Chicago Law School

Questionnaire for
CRIMINAL JURY CASES

Date.............................195........

Name of judge..Court...

City...............................State...............................

Name of case..Docket No..........................
(If more than one defendant was tried, please use
additional questionnaires as required)

★

1. *a*) With what crime(s) was defendant charged?
   No. 1: ....
   No. 2: ....
   No. 3: ....

   b) Was the jury also instructed on any lesser included offense(s)?
   No. 1: ....
   No. 2: ....

2. Briefly, what was this case about and what were the main issues before the jury?

   ....

   ....

   ....

3. Before return of the jury verdict, please indicate how you would have decided the case had you tried it without a jury:

   a) Principal charge(s):
   No. 1 ☐ Guilty ☐ Not guilty
   No. 2 ☐ Guilty ☐ Not guilty
   No. 3 ☐ Guilty ☐ Not guilty

   b) Lesser included offense(s):
   No. 1 ☐ Guilty ☐ Not guilty
   No. 2 ☐ Guilty ☐ Not guilty

4. What verdict did the jury render?

   a) Principal charge(s):
   No. 1 ☐ Guilty ☐ Not guilty
   No. 2 ☐ Guilty ☐ Not guilty
   No. 3 ☐ Guilty ☐ Not guilty

   b) Lesser included offense(s):
   No. 1 ☐ Guilty ☐ Not guilty
   No. 2 ☐ Guilty ☐ Not guilty

   c) If the jury was hung, how was it split?
   ....Guilty ....Not guilty

5. *If less than unanimous verdicts are permitted in your court,* please indicate how many jurors agreed to the verdict rendered.

   ....jurors

6. *Answer this question (6a and 6b) only if the jury determined the penalty.*

   a) What was the jury's decision?
   - ☐ Capital punishment
   - ☐ Imprisonment for.............yrs.; ....mos.
   - ☐ Fine of $.........................

   b) What penalty would you have imposed had you tried the case without a jury?
   - ☐ Capital punishment
   - ☐ Imprisonment for.............yrs.; ....mos.
     Suspended? ☐ Yes ☐ No
   - ☐ Indeterminate sentence of from.............to.............years
     Suspended? ☐ Yes ☐ No
   - ☐ Fine of $.........................
     Suspended? ☐ Yes ☐ No
   - ☐ Probation for.............yrs.; ....mos.

7. In the event of a significant difference between the judgment you would have rendered and the jury's verdict, please indicate why you think the jury's verdict was different.

   Was it because of:

   a) *The composition of the jury?*

   b) *Crucial events during the trial?*

   c) *Personalities in the case* (defendant, witnesses, attorneys)?

d) Peculiarities of the case?

e) Other reasons?

8. Did the defendant take the stand? ☐ Yes ☐ **No**

9. Did the defendant have a criminal record?
  ☐ No
  ☐ Yes, but the jury *did not learn* of it
  ☐ Yes, and the jury *did learn* of it

10. Defendant's

  a) Age
    ☐ Below 21
    ☐ 21-30
    ☐ 31-55
    ☐ Over 55

  b) Sex
    ☐ Male
    ☐ Female

  c) Race
    ☐ Colored
    ☐ White

11. In your instructions to the jury:
  a) Did you summarize the evidence? ☐ Yes ☐ No
  b) Did you comment on the weight of the evidence? ☐ Yes ☐ No
  c) Did you comment on the credibility of any of the witnesses?
    ☐ Yes ☐ No

12. Did the jury receive written instructions which were taken into the jury room? ☐ Yes ☐ No

13. *a)* Did the jury during its deliberations request any further assistance from the court? ☐ Yes ☐ No
  b) If "Yes," on what subject?..
  ....

14. *a)* Did the jury at any time indicate to the court an inability to reach agreement? ☐ Yes ☐ No
  b) If the division of the jury was revealed, how was it divided?
    ☐ 11-1   ☐ 9-3   ☐ 7-5
    ☐ 10-2   ☐ 8-4   ☐ 6-6

529

15. Was the maximum penalty the court could impose mentioned before the jury? ☐ Yes ☐ No

16. *a*) Length of trial:............day(s); ....hrs.

    b) Length of jury deliberations: ....hrs.

    c) What time was the jury sent out? ............A.M. ................P.M.

17. Was the defendant's attorney an experienced trial lawyer? ☐ Yes ☐ No

18. Was the prosecuting attorney an experienced trial lawyer? ☐ Yes ☐ No

19. How many of the jurors on this case had served on other cases within the past year?
    Approximately............jurors   ☐ Don't know

20. What was the subsequent disposition of the case?
    ☐ Judgment of not guilty
    ☐ Capital punishment
    ☐ Imprisonment for term of ....yrs.; ....mos.
       Suspended? ☐ Yes ☐ No
    ☐ Indeterminate sentence of from............to............years
       Suspended? ☐ Yes ☐ No
    ☐ Fine of $........................
       Suspended? ☐ Yes ☐ No
    Probation for ....yrs.; ....mos.

SPACE FOR FURTHER COMMENTS:

The University of Chicago Law School

QUESTIONNAIRE FOR CRIMINAL JURY CASES

Trial began.............................195........

Name of judge...Court..

City..State..

Name of case..

(If several defendants, please use *separate questionnaire for each*.)

```
╔══════════════════════════════════╗
║     DESCRIPTION OF THE CASE       ║
╚══════════════════════════════════╝
```

1(*a*). With what crime(s) was defendant charged? (List in order of severity; specify degree and other qualification: *e.g., aggravated* assault, *statutory* rape, etc.)

No. 1: ....

No. 2: ....

No. 3: ....

(*b*). Was the jury also instructed on any lesser included offenses?

No. 1: ....

No. 2: ....

2. Please give a description of the case:

```
╔══════════════════════════════════╗
║           THE VERDICT            ║
╚══════════════════════════════════╝
```

3. How would you have decided the case had you tried it without a jury? (Fill in if possible, before jury returns.)

Principal Charge (s)

No. 1	6/1 ☐ Guilty	2 ☐ Not Guilty	
No. 2	3 ☐ Guilty	4 ☐ Not Guilty	
No. 3	5 ☐ Guilty	6 ☐ Not Guilty	

Lesser Included Offense (s)

No. 1	7 ☐ Guilty	8 ☐ Not Guilty	
No. 2	9 ☐ Guilty	0 ☐ Not Guilty	

4. What was the jury's verdict?

Principal Charge(s)

No. 1	7/1 ☐ Guilty	2 ☐ Not Guilty	
No. 2	3 ☐ Guilty	4 ☐ Not Guilty	
No. 3	5 ☐ Guilty	6 ☐ Not Guilty	

Lesser Included Offense(s)

No 1	7 ☐ Guilty	8 ☐ Not Guilty	
No. 2	9 ☐ Guilty	0 ☐ Not Guilty	

8/ ☐ Hung Jury: The split was (*fill in*):

........jurors for acquittal   ☐ Split not

........jurors for conviction   known

5. Did you feel that the jury's verdict was (*Check one*)

9/1 ☐ without any merit?

2 ☐ a tenable position for a jury to take, though *not for a judge?*

3 ☐ one a *judge* might also come to?

4 ☐ quite correct?

531

6. What was the major defense(s)?
   (*Check all that apply*)

   10/1 ☐ Mistaken identity, alibi
      2 ☐ Lack of intent
      3 ☐ Consent
      4 ☐ Self-defense
      5 ☐ Insanity
      6 ☐ Coercion, entrapment
      7 ☐ State's evidence unlawfully obtained
      8 ☐ Simply: prosecution lacks proof, general denial
      9 ☐ If other, please state ....
   ....
   ....

7. The evidence for the <u>prosecution</u> consisted of
   (*Check all that apply*)

   11/1 ☐ complainant as witness
      2 ☐ accomplice turning state's evidence
      3 ☐ police
      4 ☐ expert witness.............................
          (*specify, e.g., physician*)
   ....
      5 ☐ confession
      6 ☐ friends or relatives of complainant
      7 ☐ disinterested eye witnesses
      8 ☐ fingerprints, etc.
      9 ☐ If other, please state:...................
   ....
   ....

8. The evidence for the <u>defense</u> consisted of
   (*Check all that apply*)

   12/1 ☐ defendant himself
      2 ☐ family or friends
      3 ☐ independent eyewitnesses
      4 ☐ expert witness............................
          (*specify, e.g., physician*)
   ....
      5 ☐ character witnesses
      6 ☐ If other, please state:...................
   ....
   ....

9. About how many witnesses were there?
   (*Please fill in number*)

   13/ ....for the prosecution
   14/ ....for the defense

10. Did any witnesses involve themselves in contradictions at any point? (Check for <u>both</u> sides.)

    prosecution witnesses   defense witnesses
    (*check one*)   (*check one*)

    15/1 ☐ major contradictions ☐ 16/1
       2 ☐ ....only minor........ ☐ 2
       3 ☐ .... none .... ☐ 3

11. Compared to the average criminal case, was the evidence as a whole

    17/1 ☐ easy to comprehend?
       2 ☐ somewhat difficult?
       3 ☐ very difficult to comprehend?

12. From the factual evidence in the case was the defendant's guilt or innocence

    18/1 ☐ very clear?
       2 ☐ a close question whether or not he was guilty beyond a reasonable doubt?

13(a). Were there circumstances in this case which made the crime <u>particularly</u> atrocious?

    19/1 ☐ Not out of the ordinary
       2 ☐ Somewhat so
       3 ☐ Very much so

    (b). What were they?................................
    ....
    ....
    ....

14(a). Were there extenuating circumstances in <u>this</u> case?

    20/1 ☐ No such circumstances
       2 ☐ Somewhat
       3 ☐ Decidedly so

    (b). What were they?................................
    ....
    ....
    ....

15. What is the community's sense of justice with respect to this type of crime?

    21/1 ☐ In complete accord with the letter of the law
       2 ☐ Regards the law as *too severe*
       3 ☐ Regards the law as *not severe enough*
       4 ☐ Don't know

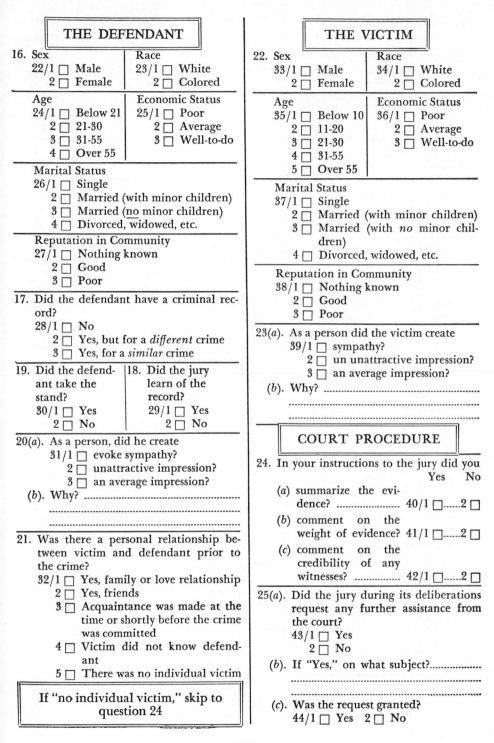

THE DEFENDANT

16. Sex

22/1 ☐ Male	Race
2 ☐ Female	23/1 ☐ White
	2 ☐ Colored

Age
24/1 ☐ Below 21
2 ☐ 21-30
3 ☐ 31-55
4 ☐ Over 55

Economic Status
25/1 ☐ Poor
2 ☐ Average
3 ☐ Well-to-do

Marital Status
26/1 ☐ Single
2 ☐ Married (with minor children)
3 ☐ Married (<u>no</u> minor children)
4 ☐ Divorced, widowed, etc.

Reputation in Community
27/1 ☐ Nothing known
2 ☐ Good
3 ☐ Poor

17. Did the defendant have a criminal record?
28/1 ☐ No
2 ☐ Yes, but for a *different* crime
3 ☐ Yes, for a *similar* crime

19. Did the defendant take the stand?
30/1 ☐ Yes
2 ☐ No

18. Did the jury learn of the record?
29/1 ☐ Yes
2 ☐ No

20(a). As a person, did he create
31/1 ☐ evoke sympathy?
2 ☐ unattractive impression?
3 ☐ an average impression?
(b). Why? ....

21. Was there a personal relationship between victim and defendant prior to the crime?
32/1 ☐ Yes, family or love relationship
2 ☐ Yes, friends
3 ☐ Acquaintance was made at the time or shortly before the crime was committed
4 ☐ Victim did not know defendant
5 ☐ There was no individual victim

If "no individual victim," skip to question 24

THE VICTIM

22. Sex

33/1 ☐ Male	Race
2 ☐ Female	34/1 ☐ White
	2 ☐ Colored

Age
35/1 ☐ Below 10
2 ☐ 11-20
3 ☐ 21-30
4 ☐ 31-55
5 ☐ Over 55

Economic Status
36/1 ☐ Poor
2 ☐ Average
3 ☐ Well-to-do

Marital Status
37/1 ☐ Single
2 ☐ Married (with minor children)
3 ☐ Married (with *no* minor children)
4 ☐ Divorced, widowed, etc.

Reputation in Community
38/1 ☐ Nothing known
2 ☐ Good
3 ☐ Poor

23(a). As a person did the victim create
39/1 ☐ sympathy?
2 ☐ un unattractive impression?
3 ☐ an average impression?
(b). Why? ....

COURT PROCEDURE

24. In your instructions to the jury did you

	Yes	No
(a) summarize the evidence?	40/1 ☐	2 ☐
(b) comment on the weight of evidence?	41/1 ☐	2 ☐
(c) comment on the credibility of any witnesses?	42/1 ☐	2 ☐

25(a). Did the jury during its deliberations request any further assistance from the court?
43/1 ☐ Yes
2 ☐ No
(b). If "Yes," on what subject?....................
(c). Was the request granted?
44/1 ☐ Yes 2 ☐ No

533

26(a). Length of trial:........ 45/ ....day(s)
46/ ....hours

(b). Length of jury
deliberations: .... 47/ ....hours

---

27. Was the case tried equally well on both sides?

48/1 ☐ Yes
2 ☐ No, prosecutor was better
3 ☐ No, defense lawyer was better

---

28. Did the prosecution press the case

49/1 ☐ very hard?
2 ☐ with normal firmness?
3 ☐ with implied leniency?

29(a). What sentence did the defendant receive?

50/1 ☐ None, was acquitted
2 ☐ Capital punishment
3 ☐ Imprisonment:
Fixed term: for..................yrs.
..................mos.
Indeterminate: from.............
yrs. to ....yrs.
4 ☐ Fine $........................

(b). Check if:

51/1 ☐ Penalty suspended
2 ☐ Defendant put on probation
3 ☐ Neither

---

30. Who set the penalty (or could have)?
52/1 ☐ The jury
2 ☐ The judge

31(a). What penalty would you have set (if you had tried the case or if the jury set the penalty)?

53/1 ☐ None, would have acquitted
2 ☐ Capital punishment
3 ☐ Imprisonment:
Fixed term: for..........yrs.........
mos.
Indeterminate: from.............
yrs. to ....yrs.
4 ☐ Fine $........................

(b). Would you have

54/1 ☐ suspended sentence?
2 ☐ put defendant on probation?
3 ☐ Neither

---

32. Would the penalty you imposed (or would have imposed—see Question 31a) have been

55/1 ☐ close to or at the statutory *maximum?*
2 ☐ close to or at the statutory *minimum?*
3 ☐ in between, about average?

---

33. Final disposition of case:

56/1 ☐ Judgment of not guilty
2 ☐ Above noted sentence imposed
3 ☐ New trial granted
4 ☐ Other ....
(specify)
....

---

34. If you disagreed with the jury, what in your opinion was the main reason for the jury's verdict?.......................................
....
....
....
....
....
....
....
....
....
....
....

---

35. SPACE FOR FURTHER COMMENTS:
....
....
....
....
....
....
....
....
....
....
....
....
....
....

534

LIST OF TABLES

CHAPTER 8

CHAPTER 9

CHAPTER 10

CHAPTER 11

CHAPTER 12

CHAPTER 13

CHAPTER 14

CHAPTER 15

CHAPTER 16

CHAPTER 17

CHAPTER 18

CHAPTER 33

CHAPTER 34

CHAPTER 35

CHAPTER 36

P R O J E C T   B I B L I O G R A P H Y

The following, it is hoped, is a fairly complete listing of publications made by colleagues on the Jury Project over the past years. Something of the longevity of the Project, and perhaps its productivity as well, can be gathered by a quick review of the years over which these writings have appeared; publication has been continuous and spans well over a decade.

Although we have on hand a number of papers which we plan to publish, the list includes only a few articles unpublished as of now, and these are definitely scheduled for publication. Some have been published more than once, as reprints in behavioral science texts. It is a point of interest that distribution is about equal between the law reviews and social science journals. There have also been two doctoral dissertations in sociology based on jury study data.

Each of the listed publications has stemmed either directly from the over-all study materials, or indirectly, through the author's experience with them. In some instances connection with the Jury Project may not be evident from a given title, particularly in the case of the few book reviews which have been included. But all are in the family.

In addition to the sixty-odd articles below, we list two other books of the Jury Project: Zeisel, Kalven and Buchholz, Delay in the Court (1959), and Simon, The American Jury — The Defense of Insanity (1966).

B

BLUM and KALVEN, "The Art of Opinion Research: A Lawyer's Appraisal of an Emerging Science." *University of Chicago Law Review*, v. 24, p. 1 (1956).

BROEDER, "The Functions of the Jury: Facts or Fictions?" *University of Chicago Law Review*, v. 21, p. 386 (1954).

——— "The Jury Project," *South Dakota Bar Journal*, v. 26, p. 133 (1957).

—— "The University of Chicago Jury Project." *Nebraska Law Review*, v. 38, p. 744 (1958).

—— "Jury." *Encyclopaedia Britannica*, v. 13, p. 205 (1963).

—— "The Negro in Court." [1965] *Duke Law Journal*, p. 19.

—— "Plaintiff's Family Status as Affecting Jury Behavior: Some Tentative Insights." *Journal of Public Law*, v. 14, p. 131 (1965).

—— "Previous Jury Trial Service Affecting Juror Behavior." [1965] *Insurance Law Journal*, p. 138.

—— "Voir Dire Examination: An Empirical Study." *Southern California Law Review*, v. 38, p. 503 (1965).

—— "The Impact of the Vicinage Requirement: An Empirical Look." *Nebraska Law Review*, v. 45, p. 99 (1966).

—— "The Importance of the Scapegoat in Jury Trial Cases: Some Preliminary Reflections." *Duquesne Law Review*, v. 4, p. — (1966).

—— "Occupational Expertise and Bias as Affecting Juror Behavior: A Preliminary Look." *New York University Law Review*, v. 41 p. — (1966).

—— The Pro and Con of Interjecting Plaintiff Insurance Companies in Jury Trial Cases: An Isolated Jury Project Case Study (to be published).

H

HAWKINS, "Interaction and Coalition Realignments in Consensus Seeking Groups: A Study of Experimental Jury Deliberations." University of Chicago Ph.D. thesis, Sociology (1960).

J

JAMES (SIMON), "Jurors' Reactions to Definitions of Legal Insanity." University of Chicago Ph.D. thesis, Sociology (1957).

—— "Jury's Assessment of Criminal Responsibility." *Journal of Social Problems*, v. 8, p. 58 (1959).

—— "Status and Competence of Jurors." *American Journal of Sociology*, v. 64, p. 563 (1959).

—— "Jurors' Evaluation of Expert Psychiatric Testimony," in "Law and the Mentally Ill: A Symposium." *Ohio State Law Journal*, v. 21, p. 75, (1960) (to be reprinted in a reader on Law and Psychiatry (Katz and Goldstein eds.)).

—— "Mental Patients as Jurors." *Human Organization*, v. 22, p. 276 (1963).

—— "Prisoners on the Jury." *Human Organization*, v. 23, p. 334 (1964).

—— "Trial by Jury: A Critical Assessment." *Applied Sociology* (Miller and Gouldner eds. 1965).

—— *The American Jury — The Defense of Insanity* (1966).

—— Attitudes Toward Mental Illness and Assessments of Criminal Responsibility (to be published).

———— Juror's Perceptions of a Defendant Charged with Incest as Measured by the Semantic Differential (to be published).

K

KALVEN, "Report on the Jury Project of the University of Chicago Law School, Conference on the Aims and Methods of Legal Research." University of Michigan Law School (1955).

———— "Report on the Jury Project." *University of Chicago Magazine,* p. 1 (1956).

———— "The Jury in Auto Cases: Invitation to Research." *Virginia Law Weekly,* v. 8, No. 22 (1956).

———— "A Report on the Jury Project of the University of Chicago Law School." *Insurance Counsel Journal,* v. 24, p. 368 (1957).

———— "The Jury, the Law and the Personal Injury Damage Award." *Ohio State Law Journal,* v. 19, p. 158 (1958).

———— "Some Comments on the Law and Behavioral Science Project at the University of Pennsylvania." *Journal of Legal Education,* v. 11, p. 94 (1958).

———— "The Bar, the Court and the Delay." *Annals of the American Academy of Political and Social Science,* v. 328, p. 37 (1960).

———— "The Jury and the Principles of the Law of Damages." University of Chicago Law School, Dedication Papers (1960).

———— Review of Cohen, Robson and Bates, "Parental Authority: The Community and the Law." *Rutgers Law Review,* v. 14, p. 843 (1960).

———— Review of Elliott, "Improving Our Courts: Collected Essays on Judicial Administration." *American Political Science Review,* v. 55, p. 169 (1961).

———— "A General Analysis of and Introduction to the Problem of Court Congestion and Delay." *ABA Section of Insurance, Negligence and Compensation Law,* p. 322 (1963).

———— "The Dignity of the Civil Jury." *Virginia Law Review,* v. 50, p. 1055 (1964).

———— and SCHWARTZ, "Administration of the Law of Torts: The 1961 Summer Research Training Institute on Interrelations of Law and Other Social Institutions." *Journal of Legal Education,* v. 14, p. 513 (1962).

———— and TYLER, "The Palo Alto Conference on Law and Behavioral Science." *Journal of Legal Education,* v. 9, p. 366 (1956).

———— and WOOD, "Research in the Field of Torts." *Social Science Research Council,* v. 14, p. 42 (1960).

M

MELTZER, "A Projected Study of the Jury as a Working Institution." *Annals of the American Academy of Political and Social Science,* v. 287, p. 97 (1953).

S

SIMON. *See* JAMES (SIMON).

STRODTBECK, "Social Process, the Law, and Jury Functioning." *Law and Sociology,* p. 144 (Evan ed. 1962).

—— and HOOK, "The Social Dimensions of a Twelve Man Jury Table." *Sociometry,* v. 24, p. 397 (1961).

—— and JAMES (SIMON), "An Attempted Replication of a Jury Experiment by Use of Radio and Newspaper." *Public Opinion Quarterly,* v. 21, p. 313 (1957).

——, —— and HAWKINS, "Social Status in Jury Deliberations." *American Sociology Review,* v. 22, p. 713 (1957), reprinted in *Readings in Social Psychology* (Macoby et al. eds. 1958) and in *Sociology in Perspective* (Lipsett and Smelner eds. 1961).

—— and MANN, "Sex Role Differentiation in Jury Deliberations." *Sociometry,* v. 19, p. 715 (1956).

Z

ZEISEL, "The Significance of Insignificant Differences." *Public Opinion Quarterly,* v. 19, p. 319 (1955).

—— "The New York Expert Testimony Project: Some Reflections on Legal Experiments." *Stanford Law Review,* v. 8, p. 730 (1956).

—— "Sociology of Law, 1945-1955." *Sociology in the United States of America,* p. 1 (UNESCO 1956).

—— "The Jury and the Court Delay." *Annals of the American Academy of Political and Social Science,* v. 328, p. 46 (1960).

—— "The Uniqueness of Survey Evidence." *Cornell Law Quarterly,* v. 45, p. 322 (1960).

—— "Delay by the Parties and Delay by the Courts." *Journal of Legal Education,* v. 15, p. 27 (1962).

—— Review of Hunting and Neuwirth, "Who Sues in New York City?" *New York Law Journal* (June, 1962).

—— "Social Research on the Law: The Ideal and the Practical." *Law and Sociology,* p. 124 (Evan ed. 1962).

—— "The Pre-History of Legal Sociology," Review of Sawer, ed., *Studies in the Sociology of Law. University of Toronto Law Journal,* v. 15, p. 493 (1963).

—— Review of Joiner, *Civil Justice and Jury. Annals of the American Academy of Political and Social Science,* v. 348, p. 196 (1963).

—— "Splitting Liability and Damage Issue Saves 20 Per Cent of the Court's Time." *ABA Section of Insurance, Negligence and Compensation Law,* p. 328 (1963).

—— "What Determines the Amount of Argument Per Juror?" *American Sociology Review,* v. 28, p. 279 (1963).

—— Review of Brown, *Explanation in Social Science. American Journal of Sociology,* v. 59, p. 427 (1964).

——— "Facts for the Law Maker: Three Recent Studies," Review of LA FAVE, *Arrest: The Decision to Take a Suspect into Custody;* CONARD ET AL., *Automobile Accident Costs and Payments: Studies in the Economics of Injury Reparation;* ROSENBERG, *The Pretrial Conference and Effective Justice. University of Chicago Law Review,* v. 33, p. 166 (1965).

——— "The Law, Gambling and Empirical Research," Review of Tec, *Gambling in Sweden. Stanford Law Review,* v. 17, p. 990 (1965).

——— "Die Rolle der Geschworenen in den U.S.A." *Oesterreichische Juristen Zeitung,* v. 21, p. 121 (1966).

——— and CALLAHAN, "Split Trials and Time-Saving: A Statistical Analysis." *Harvard Law Review,* v. 76, p. 1606 (1963).

——— and CRAMTON, Review of Schubert, *Quantitative Analysis of Judicial Behavior. University of Chicago Law Review,* v. 28, p. 182 (1960).

——— and KALVEN, "Law, Science and Humanism." *The Humanist Frame,* p. 329 (Huxley ed. 1961).

———, ——— and BUCHHOLZ, "Is the Trial Bar a Cause of Delay?" *Journal of American Judicature Society,* v. 43, p. 17 (1959).

———, ——— and ——— *Delay in the Court* (1959).

———, ——— and ——— "Delay in the Court: A Summary View." *Record of New York City Bar Association,* v. 15, p. 104 (1960).

INDEX

A

Accomplice testimony
  as cause of disagreement, 174-177
  for defense, frequency of, 137, 142, 143
  for prosecution, frequency of, 137, 142, 143
Age. *See* Defendant
Aggravated rape. *See* Rape
Agreement of judge and jury
  analysis of, 474-482
  as evidence that the jury understands, 152
  blandness as cause of, 476, 480
  borderline cases, 52-53
  frequency of, 56-57, 481, 495-496
  offset as cause of, 477-481
  theory of, 51, 109, 475-476
Allen charge, 453-455
Ambivalence of jury, 237n, 293n, 312n, 343n, 395, 402-410. *See also* Non-homogeneity
Arrest. *See also* Facts only the judge knew; Police practices improper
  excessive force by police, 236-238, 320
  police discretion in making, 14n, 342n
Asch, social psychological experiments of, 463n
Assault and battery. *See also* Self-defense

evidence items in, 141-143
one-punch calculus, 228-229, 265
verdict pattern for, 69
Assumption of risk, 242-257, 397. *See also* Contributory fault of victim; Tort and crime
Attempt, 266-267. *See also De minimis*
Attractive defendant. *See* Defendant; Sympathy
Austria, 13n, 222n, 254n, 258n, 269n, 324n, 334n, 368n, 519-520. *See also* Comparative law

B

Ballot. *See* First ballot; Hung jury
Bench trial, 17-18. *See also* Waiver of jury
Blackstone, comments of, on the jury, 7. *See also* Jury, criticism of
Blood test, 124-125, 165-166. *See also* Facts only the judge knew
Burden of proof, 136n, 145

C

Caesar's wife, 401-402. *See also* Pro-prosecution sentiments
Capital punishment
  agreement on, 437-439